Religions in Global Society

Saying the word 'religion' in today's world evokes a bewildering and often contradictory variety of images and attitudes. From the Dalai Lama to Falun Gong, from mosque to temple, 'religion' covers a multitude of practices, worldviews, and cosmologies.

Peter Beyer, a distinguished sociologist of religion, offers a way of understanding religion in a contemporary global society, by analyzing it as a dimension of the historical process of globalization. *Religions in Global Society* introduces theories of globalization, and shows how they can be applied to world religions. Through this exploration, Beyer reveals the nature of the contested category of 'religion': what it means, what it includes and what it implies in the world today. Written with exceptional clarity, and illustrated with lively and diverse examples ranging from Islam and Hinduism to African Traditional Religion and New Age spirituality, this is a fascinating overview of how religion has developed in a globalized society. It will be ideal reading for students taking courses on sociology of religion, religion and globalization, and religion and modernity.

Peter Beyer is Professor of Religious Studies at the University of Ottawa, Canada. He is the author of *Religion and Globalization* (1994) and the editor of *Religion in the Process of Globalization* (2001).

Religions in Global Society

Peter Beyer

Routledge
Taylor & Francis Group

LONDON AND NEW YORK

First published 2006
by Routledge
2 Park Square, Milton Park, Abingdon Oxon OX14 4RN

Simultaneously published in the USA and Canada
by Routledge
270 Madison Avenue, New York, NY 10016

Routledge is an imprint of the Taylor & Francis Group, an informa business

Typeset in Sabon and Gill Sans by
Taylor & Francis Books
Printed and bound in Great Britain by
Antony Rowe Ltd, Chippenham, Wiltshire

British Library Cataloguing in Publication Data
A catalogue record for this book is available from the British Library

Library of Congress Cataloging in Publication Data
A catalog record for this book has been requested

ISBN10 0–415–39318–3 ISBN13 9–780–415–39318–8 (hbk)
ISBN10 0–415–39319–1 ISBN13 9–780–415–39319–5 (pbk)

To my mother, Irene Beyer
and
in loving memory of my father,
Konrad Beyer

Contents

Acknowledgements

The first idea for this book came as I was writing the conclusion to the 1994 volume, *Religion and Globalization*. At that point I realized that only very restricted aspects of that overall topic had actually been dealt with there and that a subsequent volume would have to go beyond the question of religion's continuing importance in global society to consider what, sociologically speaking, religion in global society actually was. In the twelve years since that realization a great many people have helped me in researching and writing my attempt to respond, and in more ways than I can recount or acknowledge. Here I would like to thank some of those whose role was more direct. These include John Simpson, Detlef Pollack, Roland Robertson, Frank Lechner, Meredith McGuire, José Casanova, Jim Spickard, Michael Wilkinson, Radhika Sekar, Rubina Ramji, Jiwu Wang, Qiang Li, Shandip Saha, Kyuhoon Cho, Ulrich Berner, Irena Borowik, Jim Beckford and Bill Garrett. Some of these have been my mentors, some my students, some my colleagues; but all of them have been the source of ideas, corrections, inspiration, and a great deal more.

A special thanks goes to many of my other former students, especially those from my graduate and senior seminars. More than they realized, they gave me the opportunity to hear myself think about the numerous issues involved. My thanks also to my colleagues in the Department of Classics and Religious Studies at the University of Ottawa for providing me with a stimulating academic home these past eleven years. Of course, none of the above is in any way responsible for what use I have made of their inspiration and suggestions in this book. Almost all the material in this book is entirely new or reworked from previous publications and conference papers. Finally, I want to express my deepest gratitude to Sheila and Bridget. I have a rich life outside the academic setting; for the most part that is the two of you.

Introduction
Religion as concept and social reality in global society

Observing religion

Saying the word 'religion' in today's world is likely to evoke a bewildering and often contradictory variety of images and attitudes. A great many of us will see everyday religious ritual such as Muslims at prayer or Hindus doing *puja*. Religious leaders like the Dalai Lama and the Pope may come to mind; or buildings such as synagogues, temples and churches. Under this heading will also fall diverse phenomena ranging from Pentecostal speaking in tongues and shamanistic trance to erudite theological discourse and formal decisions in religious law. People frequently associate religion with moral codes or with foundational worldviews and cosmologies. We may use the term to refer to anything in life that is taken very seriously or to the most basic self-evidences that inform our approach to the world. Yet woven into the diversity are sometimes sharply differing opinions as to what belongs in the category and what does not. In English, as in most other major languages around the world, a number of distinctions serve to make this kind of discrimination possible. Is Falun Gong religion or is it a 'cult'? Is New Age channelling religion or 'spirituality'? Are household shrines to ancestors religion or 'culture'? Is astrology religion or 'superstition'? Is healing that invokes the gods religion or 'magic'? These frequently invidious contrasts point to others, seemingly more internal to the religious domain. Beside more neutral distinctions like sacred/profane, transcendent/ immanent, this-worldly/other-worldly, lie the more judgemental differences such as between orthodoxy and heresy, faith and apostasy, or piety and sacrilege. Here would also fall questions of distinctions between religions. Is, for example, Baha'i an offshoot of Islam or is it a separate religion? Are Unitarian-Universalists Christians? What about Mormons or Unification- ists? Moreover, beside different ways of delimiting what counts as religion and how to distinguish one religion from another are divergent evaluations of the domain as such. Positive judgements of religion as the necessary foundation of human existence exist alongside dismissive attitudes that label it as, for example, benighted illusion, imperialist imposition, or remnant of an earlier stage of human evolution. For many it is a natural and self-evident dimension of the world we inhabit; for others it is at best an irrelevance. Finally, this diversity of manifestation, attitude and orientation can be found in virtually every region of the world.

The heterogeneity of religion, the contested nature of the category as to what it means, what it includes and what it implies in the contemporary context, calls for ways of observing religion that focus explicitly and precisely on the peculiarity of the notion in that setting. That sort of observation, a theoretical account of religion in today's global society, is the central focus of this book. My aim is to offer a way of understanding the variety and the contradiction, of comprehending religion as form and function, as mainspring of power, conflict and cohesion, as social resource and social problem; but only in contemporary global society. To date, scholarly work that has focused on religion as a whole has tended to construct theories that seek to encompass religion – however defined more precisely – in all times and places. Such a 'universal' theory of religion is not my purpose here. Instead, mine is a descriptive and historical task, not one of universal typology let alone sociological law and prediction. Although I work with a host of generalized sociological concepts, I claim validity for them only as reflective of a particular historical situation, the globalizing society of the present and recent centuries. My effort does not pretend to be a theory of religion for all times and societies. To be sure, nothing stops it from being applied to these other situations, but it is not for them that the theory is constructed.

The chapters that follow are then an exercise in sociological theory, a set of reflective observations that seeks to account for the data, for what seems to be happening in our world. In this light, its main object is not to report original research data with which one could test current theories. Accordingly, my sources of information are for the most part the reported research of others, secondary literature which treats one or several of the regions, manifestations, attitudes and orientations which are relevant for understanding religion in global society. It is also important to state at the outset how I conceive the purpose and limits of sociological theory. Somewhat in contrast to many contemporary sociologists such as Jonathan Turner (1986), Rodney Stark (Stark and Bainbridge 1987) and Randall Collins (1975), I would suggest that social-scientific theory can only to a very limited extent be about generating testable and universal propositions, ideally erecting a deductive edifice of such premises in which testing one part has automatic implications for all the rest. Deduction of this sort depends on being able to establish precise and unique relations among the different concepts and variables, and thus among the propositions. In the absence of a mathematical language and fungible quantities that they can express (*pace* economics), such relations in social realities are difficult to discern beyond a very limited range. What may look like deductive relations among concepts and propositions will more likely be inductive relations in disguise (Beyer 1998c). In addition, the particular historical circumstances which the social sciences seek to understand are insufficiently uniform to allow the kind of generalization that is key to the predictive power of laws in the natural sciences. Such sociological laws as are possible, therefore, become not so much inaccurate as useless, unless respecified for a particular social context. And that particularization robs them of their predictive power. My position with regard to social-scientific theory is therefore fundamentally Weberian (Weber 1968): general laws in sociology, while perhaps important heuristic tools, by themselves have no explanatory, let alone predictive, power because they must always be applied to particular historical situations which contextualize them beyond the capacity of the sociologist to maintain other things equal. Sociological principles always operate in an environment of *ceteris imparibus*. From this perspective, the test of a social-scientific theory is in its descriptive explanatory power, in the range of data for which it can account. Rather than a matter of being able to predict 'what will happen if . . . ', sociological theory in this book is one of 'what can we see if . . . ?'

A core theoretical notion informs the entire discussion which follows. It is, in a nutshell, that much can be gained from observing religion in contemporary global society as one of several differentiated function systems. The idea of function system I draw and adapt from the work of Niklas Luhmann (1984, 1997). I reserve extensive explanation of the concept for Chapter 1 and as it applies to religion for Chapter 2. At this point, it is important to emphasize that this is at root a historical observation and a circumscribed one. Function systems, including the function system for religion, are historical and very peculiar social constructions. They are not common to all societies and need not have developed at all; but they did and the emergence of contemporary global society in the form that it has taken is a consequence. What is more, to say that religion has taken the form of a function system in this context is only to claim that the dominant social meanings of religion derive from the fact that it has become the principal name of that system. The variable and contested understandings that we have of the word 'religion' and its various cognates (sometimes neologisms) in other languages are all significantly conditioned by the historical emergence of a particular social structure, an institutional domain, which is the religious system of global society. Yet that system by no means includes everything conceivably religious; it is in fact highly selective and to an extent arbitrary in what it includes or excludes, as are all function systems. Nonetheless, the development of this religious system has brought about a new model of religion, one that does not so much subsume difference as allow and encourage it in new and peculiar ways. There exists a global religious system but certainly not a single global religion. On the contrary, our social world is populated with an increasing number of mutually identified religions, very much in the plural. And there is much of religious importance that hovers at the margins and even outside of these religions. As with globalization and global society itself, the homogeneity implied by the notion of a global religious system is actually the reverse side of religious heterogeneity, both in conception and in form. The hypothesis of the development of a religious function system and the limitations to what that means are absolutely central to my argument.

Conceptualizing religion

Max Weber is well known for having refused to define religion and yet having written very extensively and effectively on it. At the beginning of his chapters on religion in *Economy and Society*, he wrote: 'To define "religion", to say what it *is*, is not possible at the start of a presentation such as this. Definition can be attempted, if at all, only at the conclusion of the study' (Weber 1978: 399). To a degree, Weber's position applies to the present study[1] in that the conception of religion is a main outcome of analysis and not something defined at the beginning. Only in light of the overall presentation will it become clear what religion may mean; and the argument will in any case not lead to a clear and univocal definition of religion.[2] Nonetheless, both as a way of beginning and for the sake of giving the reader some introductory orientation as to its overall direction, it seems wise to say a few words about definition of religion already here in the introduction.

Corresponding to the variety of phenomena that the idea evokes, academic disciplines concerned with the study of religion have produced substantial yet inconclusive discussion as to the best conception of religion (Clarke and Byrne 1993; Lawson and McCauley 1990: 12–31; O'Toole 1984: 10–51; Paden 1992). In the sociology of religion, that debate has most often centred on the difference between substantive and functional notions (McGuire 2002: 8–14). Substantive definitions, seeking to delimit what religion *is*, generally focus on some transcendent or supraempirical aspect as the central defining moment. Functional definitions try to circumscribe the field by saying what religion *does*, what social or psychological purposes it serves, and thereby avoid central reference to transcendence. In this volume, I opt very much for a substantive orientation, but not because I wish to argue that it is somehow inherently more appropriate to the phenomenon. It is rather that the function system for religion that I analyze has for historical reasons constructed itself more in a substantive way and it is this that gives substantive definitions their current cogency, even self-evidence. Yet functional approaches are in this light not inadequate. Their validity stems from the selectivity of the function system, namely that it does not encompass all social processes that have something religious – however conceived – about them. Functional orientations respond to that feature. Their salience is an indirect reflection of the limiting character of the religious system. In this light, a main reason that debates between defenders of one approach or the other are inconclusive is that they do not take sufficiently into account the conditioning social context in which their observations take place. The function system for religion skews such debate. As long as the search is for a universally applicable definition or conception – for the single *best* orientation – the existence and operation of the religious system will make substantive definitions seem highly appropriate; yet that system's historicity and selectivity will at the same time justify resort to functional conceptions in order to address all that, both today and historically, seems to be left out or inadequately included.

A further aspect of the relation between conceiving religion and function systems becomes clearer if we look at another persistent and inconclusive debate, this time within the discipline of religious studies. Here arguments have centred on whether one has to adopt the perspective of a religious 'insider' in order to understand religion properly; and on whether observation in this discipline is not often entirely dominated by theological agendas as opposed to religiously neutral or scientific ones (McCutcheon 1999; Penner 1989; Segal 1992; Smith 1991). Although these controversies are quite complex, translated into the analytic terms that I present here they are also a reflection of the construction of two differentiated function systems, the religious and the scientific. As I shall discuss below, each of these systems has its own ways of dealing with and understanding the world. These are not reducible to one another, resulting in the futility of arguments which insist that either scientific or religious (theological) standards should take precedence. Positions that privilege 'insider' observation, maintaining that only such perspectives can truly appreciate what religion is all about, are in effect mounting a defence of religion as a distinct and differentiated domain. By contrast, orientations that, for instance, assert the superiority of 'naturalistic' observation (McCutcheon 1997) are declaring the autonomy of scientific perspectives, especially from religious tutelage but also from other, notably political, interests.

Translating problems in conceiving religion into the question of which systemic interests are at play not only helps one to understand why these controversies are so inconclusive, it also allows a view to a further dimension of the issue. As will become clear in the chapters that follow, the historical construction and differentiation of a function system for religion is but one moment in a broader development that has seen the emergence of several other such systems, the already mentioned scientific system, but also ones for capitalist economy, sovereign political states, academic education, positive law, mass media, medicalized health, art and sport. Observation of religion is possible from each of these systemic perspectives;

and in the cases of states, education, and law especially, has important effects on the religious system and correspondingly on what we count as religion. These perspectives are neither 'theological' nor 'scientific'; they are also not 'folk' or 'popular' conceptions. A more accurate label for them would be 'official'[3] in so far as they are conceptions made manifest in the legal decisions, the state constitutions, the political policies and the educational curricula of different countries around the world. Far from being inauthentic or unimportant, I will argue that they have a significant effect on how both theological (religious) and scholarly (scientific) observers understand religion, and thus on how contemporary society constitutes this social domain (Beyer 2003a).

Contesting religion

Disagreements about how to define religion exemplify the broadly contested nature of this social category in today's world. Arguments among scholars and theologians about the correct understanding of what the term means are only part of that picture, however. These would be, well, 'academic' if religion did not also have a, broadly speaking, political component, if it were not also thoroughly implicated in the creation, distribution and application of social power. Such contestations occur along several lines roughly following the conceptual disagreements just discussed. They concern the range of religious power, the question of what one can claim in the name of religion. They centre on what and who belongs to religion and to which religion. And they pertain to the relations with local or global 'others'. These dimensions are all related in the sense that each involves disputed social boundaries; and each of them reflects the particular way that the religious function system has been constructed, either by rejecting that construction, modifying it or seeking to take advantage of it.

To appreciate how the range of religion becomes a contested issue, one can begin with a common example. It is not at all unusual to hear a pious Muslim declare that 'Islam is not just a religion, it is a way of life'. Representatives of most other religions can be found to have made similar statements for their religions, so this orientation is not peculiar to Islam. Such declarations assert that religious precepts and perspectives should not be limited to a circumscribed domain deemed strictly religious. Islam, in this case, is said to go beyond matters of ritual and personal piety to encompass all other areas of life. That, of course, implies that someone or something seeks to deny this claim; that being considered only a religion means limitation of Islam, for instance to matters of individual, private or other-worldly concern. Contesting the range of religion in this way can also appear with different emphases and valuations of the idea of religion. Thus, for instance, school curricula in Taiwan include teaching about religions, but exclude Confucianism from that category because, so argue Taiwanese educational officials, while the former represent the worldviews of, in effect, sectarian subgroups of society, the latter is a foundational philosophy and ethical system which forms the basis of the greater common good (Meyer 1987). Similarly, when deliberately constructing State Shinto during the late nineteenth and early twentieth century, Japanese elites declared and enforced it as a matter of general patriotic duty, not as religion to which one could adhere or not (Hardacre 1989). The idea of religion in all these cases implies a restrictive differentiation, and this is precisely what the actors in each case seek to avoid. The contestation is directed against what they perceive as, not an illusion or simply an erroneous nomenclature, but an actual social reality: religions exist, they are saying, but 'ours' (Islam, Confucianism, Shinto) is not one of them or more than one of them because that would diminish it.

Related to the contentious issue of the range of religious relevance is that of belonging. The example of contemporary India is instructive in this regard. There religion (or *dharma*) is more often than not viewed as expansive and inclusive, yet ambiguously plural. The problematic side of this plurality is clear in that public discourse reserves the word 'communalism' for what in China and Japan is suspected about religions in general, namely a tendency towards narrow and excluding sectarianism. The current Hindu nationalist movement seeks to cut across this sort of classification with a kind of 'State-Shinto-ization' of Hindu identity, but the result is a serious increase in contestation and conflict around religious identity more broadly. An intriguing feature of this strategy is that its attempt to deny the differentiation of religious and national identity also leads to their practical re-differentiation, especially through recognition that 'Hinduness' (*Hindutva*) can accommodate different religions (notably Sikhism, Jainism, and Buddhism), the corresponding lack of explicit religious content in what Hinduness means, and the organizational creation of a separate arm of the movement that has a more explicit Hindu religious identity, namely the Vishva Hindu Parishad (VHP) or World Hindu Organization. In addition, a critical moment in this religio-national movement is that those who do not belong, the 'others', are defined in explicitly religious terms, namely as above all Muslims and Christians. In conjunction with the cases mentioned in the previous paragraph, these Hindu and Muslim examples show how religion can serve as pivotal resource in today's world for mutual, sometimes antagonistic, group identification. A social modality that for many observers envisages and purports to ground the social whole becomes by that token a prime way of establishing difference in a global society that increasingly pushes us all into a single social unit. Yet key for my purposes in this book is that such 'nationalization' or 'communalization' of religion is both probable and problematic. Much as contestation about the range of religious relevance seems to imply contextual factors that conspire to delimit such import, so religion as a category and social reality also appears to be partially but importantly incongruent with attempts to restrict it to a general designation of social belonging. Hinduism is both more and less than what Hindus are; the same for Islam and Muslims. To be sure, precisely what we mean by 'religion' in all this is not immediately clear; but that is, after all, the underlying theme and core purpose of the present study.

One could easily multiply these examples of contestation on the basis of religion, and many more illustrations inform the chapters that follow. What almost all of them have in common, however, is the consistent implication of two distinctions that together largely define the lines of dispute. One of these is the difference between religion and non-religion, which is to say how the religious field is delimited and thus created. The other is the contrast between one religion and another, in particular the question of whether something is or is not *a* religion; not just if it is religion, but more centrally if it is 'one of the religions'. Instances of the latter sort of conflict abound. To the issue of Falun Gong mentioned at the outset, one could add the status of Scientology in Germany as contrasted with the United States, the treatment of indigenous religious cultures as religion (*agama*) or culture (*adat*) in Indonesia, the position of African Traditional Religion (ATR) in South Africa, or the situation of Baha'is in Iran. In each case, contestation is over whether these are one of the religions and, if so, which one. The religion/non-religion distinction appears clearly in the examples considered above, but also in other guises such as the question of whether New Age orientations or North American Aboriginal 'religious ways' are religion, spirituality or something else. As I will discuss especially in Chapter 6 and as I briefly indicated above, spirituality is one of those terms which marks off the peculiarity of modern religion. Designating a variety of activity or orientation as spirituality is a way of seeking exemption from certain of the characteristics of what has come to be regarded as religion, but not others. It is a way, as it were, to 'look like a duck and quack like a duck', but avoid identification as a duck.

Overall the frequent contesting of religion and in the name of religion indicates an arena that can be quite important, but one that is also problematic in various ways. That combination of power and vagueness in religion, its incontrovertible reality along with its seemingly elusive ambiguity are two of the constant *leitmotifs* in the analyses that follow. The argument for a global religious function system very much includes the contestation and the ambiguity. More pointedly, it is a way of accounting for them.

Communicating religion

As an exercise in sociological theory, this study treats religion almost exclusively as a social phenomenon. Psychological and religious realities especially are, like the physical and the biological, important only in so far as they condition the social or become thematized in it. What happens in the consciousnesses of individuals or in the worlds of gods, spirits and other supraempirical planes is of concern to the extent that they impinge upon or contextualize the social, but not beyond that. Claiming the relative independence of the social in this way, however, means that one has to be able to say explicitly what distinguishes it from the psychological or the theological. Historically, neither the discipline of sociology as concerns the psyche or consciousness, nor that of religious studies as concerns the spiritual/ultimate/divine has been very consistent in making such distinctions clear. Here I want to do precisely that because my aim is to analyze the historical construction of religion specifically as a contemporary social reality, and not primarily as the 'expression' of aggregate individual experience/belief or the human response to divine initiative or ultimate reality. Putting the emphases on these latter aspects tends to shift the questioning away from how the social operates in its own terms in favour of the relation between the psychological and the social or the theological and the social. Important as these may be from other perspectives, locating the observation of religion too much at these junctures obscures the ways that social processes also follow their own logic; and above all how these are highly contingent, which is to say more changing than the psychological structures of human beings or purportedly transcendent or ultimately grounding planes. Focusing on the independence of the social allows one to see the specificity and the change more directly. It can thereby become clear, for instance, that individuals can believe and even practise, but that that by itself is not sufficient to constitute religion socially; and religion can persist as a social reality without everyone or even the majority of people believing or practising. Thus, to give but a couple of examples, Chinese or Japanese people may believe in the reality of spirits and gods and may even perform activities in relation to those beliefs, but that is not sufficient to constitute such belief and activity as religion. Similarly, but in reverse, a great many Western Europeans may not believe in a God or even engage in religious practice very often, but the Christian religion can nonetheless remain an important social reality in countries like Sweden or France. It is not that individual belief and practice are unimportant for the constitution of religion. Usually they are essential. But they are not already by themselves religion; they do not already operate socially as religion. At a minimum, they also have to be observed as religion.

Attempts conceptually to isolate the specifically social are not uncommon in the sociological and anthropological literatures. Ideas such as collective representations, social action, interaction and culture have been among the possibilities. They do well in pointing out how the social is more than the fact of people living in groups, more than the sum of consciousnesses, but instead a product of what these conscious humans do.

For my purposes, I avail myself of a conceptualization that maximizes the emergent and independent quality of the social vis-à-vis these humans, not least because, as I shall argue, an important feature of modern global social structure, namely its high degree of impersonality, resonates with such a strategy. This is Niklas Luhmann's idea that the social consists in communications, operations that are to be identified not simply as the 'expressions' (or externalizations) of consciousness, as the transmission of information from one human being to another, as the activity or action of human beings, nor as the products of human endeavour or 'labour'. Instead, communications from a Luhmannian perspective are a synthesis of three selections, namely information, imparting (*Mitteilung*) and understanding, and these somewhat in abstraction from who or what does the selection of the information, the imparting of the information, or the understanding of the information thus imparted (Luhmann 1984, 1997). The details of this theory of the social and of communication need not detain us here because the purpose in introducing it is to prepare the way for observing religion in a particular way, namely as something quintessentially social, which here means as communication (Beyer 2001; Tyrell 2002; Tyrell *et al.* 1998).

From this Luhmannian point of departure, to observe religion as a social phenomenon is to observe it as communication, but this is not another way of defining religion. It is only to say that, to the degree that religion is a social phenomenon, it will construct itself as communication and not as something else like experience or consciousness, let alone mystical insight. We have not defined religion in claiming that it is a variety of communication; we have merely set the parameters of observation in which the conceptualization of religion will take place. These parameters religion will share with all other social phenomena. Some of the more important include the following: first, the elements of religion are events that impart information, and only in that context are things like 'experience', 'tradition', 'sacrality', 'supernatural presence', 'devotion', 'enlightenment' and 'transformation' produced and reproduced, structured and given social meaning. The religious communication generates the *social* reality of both human piety and divine nature. The extent to which the reverse also applies is not relevant so long as the communication happens. Second, and flowing from the first, religion, like all communication, is self-referential or recursive: the only thing that gives religious communication meaning is previous and subsequent religious communication or communication about religion. Social meaning is context, and that context can only be provided by other or more communication. Third, what counts as specifically religious communication will depend on its thematization as something called religion, usually in implicit or explicit contrast to communication that is not religion. That thematization has to happen in communication, whether religious or not. Therefore, if religious communication or communication about religion ceases, so will, socially speaking, religion. To suggest otherwise is precisely to engage in such structuring and thematization. Treating religion as communication disallows any essentialist understanding of religion as a social reality, because that essence of religion has first to be generated as essence in communication. Among the many consequences of this position is, of course, that my observing religion in this way is itself part of the construction of religion, but only if my communication (namely, this writing) is understood and thematized in subsequent communication.

Focusing on the close relation between 'religion' and 'thematizing as religion' is fairly important for the argument of this book because it allows one to trace key social changes through an analysis of historical shifts in the semantic meanings of words; or at least to begin the discussion there. Accordingly, as I shall detail in Chapter 2, when Europeans of the early modern centuries began to use the word 'religion' to refer to a distinct and systematic unit which manifested itself only as a plurality of 'religions', that signalled not an insignificant localized usage and especially not a distortion of a purportedly 'original meaning'. Instead, it indicated a change in how these Europeans understood religion and how they structured religion in their communication and hence in their social institutions. Similarly, when South Asians in the nineteenth century began to use the Sanskrit word *dharma* (and its vernacular variations) also to mean something like what the Europeans who then ruled the region meant with 'religion', that marked not just a translation of a foreign word but also a shift in how many South Asians began to see their own cultural traditions and therefore how they began to reformulate and restructure these as 'religions'. A comparable observation applies, for instance, to the changed ways that older words like *zongjiao*, *shukyo* and *agama* came to be used in countries like China, Japan and Indonesia: semantic shifts as aspects of the (re)structuring of a peculiarly modern religious domain. Of note in all these examples are both the changes and the continuities. Older words come to have changed meanings. We are not dealing so much with the pure invention of social realities that were not there before – although that is also the case to some extent – as we are with the partial dissolution of received patterns of communication and their recombination with new elements to create a new form that bears a strong resemblance to old ones. From this combination of continuity and discontinuity derives the understandable twin observation that the 'religions' were already always there at the same time as they are modern inventions. Recognizing that the social is communication, and that all communication exhibits this combination of old and new thereby obviates the question of which is more 'authentic', which is more appropriate for describing social realities in a particular place and time. Instead, one asks as to which communicative patterns prevail and how these patterns developed out of what happened before.

This way of understanding what, socially speaking, constitutes religion also leaves ample room for considering the contested aspects of the construction of this modern religion and for the involvement of these contests in the relative distribution of social power and influence. It permits an appreciation of how religion can at one and the same time be constructed as a domain *sui generis* (McCutcheon 1997) and yet thoroughly implicated in other social processes, including the economic and the political.

The basic feature of communication by which it is at the same time in continuity and in discontinuity with previous and subsequent communication is also a way of saying that communication, and thus sociality more generally, is always self-referential and recursive: in constructing itself it refers to itself and only to itself (Leach 1976). This recursiveness, in turn, points to the possibility of self-referential systems of such social communication of which society as a whole is merely the most encompassing. What is of interest in the current context, however, is not just this encompassing system of communication – which I shall argue in the next chapter is a globally extended society – but the smaller subunits or subsystems within this larger one. Even though, ultimately, all communication that constitutes a society can be said to refer to all other communication, in reality the range of communication that is relevant in any given instance or situation is far more limited. It is by establishing such limits that subsystems generate themselves. Social subsystems are therefore structures of boundary creation and boundary maintenance, but not in the sense of strictly delimited parts, like the pieces of a pie. Instead, social subsystems are ways of continuously regenerating certain kinds of boundaries of meaning. Their purpose varies. They may serve to create concentrations of particular sorts of social power or knowledge; they may exist to render communication more manageable by limiting the variety of themes and meanings that structure their elements; they may allow different and even contradictory sets of communicative rules to operate, thereby creating possibilities for 'dissent' or 'deviance' with respect to the larger social environment. Systems are in this respect conceptual parallels to the idea of 'social groups', except that they consist of communications rather than people. It is the communications which humans help to generate that refer to one another and thus constitute the system; the humans, strictly speaking, are just tools or instruments like the instruments of an orchestra. They are essential so that music can be made; the system is like the music, and specifically the making of the music.

Continuing this metaphor, my purpose in this book is to explore the extent to which religion has been 'composed' and is being 'performed' as a particular kind of social system in modern and by now global society. Like a complex symphony, this system has been generated in certain ways and not others: it is not everything that religion could be or has been. It remains now in this introduction to outline how I will carry out and present this analysis.

Presenting religion

As is evident from the foregoing, central to the analysis I offer here is the theoretical framework in which I set my arguments. This owes a great deal to the work of Niklas Luhmann, especially as concerns core concepts like social system, function system and communication. In Chapters 1 and 2, I go into much greater detail about the first two ideas since my view of the development of global society over the last centuries and the emergence of modern forms of religion owes much to these notions. Luhmann's work is, however, by far not the only important influence and source for the theoretical structure presented in those chapters; nor is my use of Luhmann's concepts anything more than Luhmannian, meaning that my adaptation of them probably differs in various substantial ways from what Luhmann himself may have done. Thus, just to take a couple of examples, in his own voluminous work, Luhmann actually pays relatively little attention to globalization as such, and even less to the question of the globalization of religion as either a category or a system. Inevitably, anyone who, like myself, applies his conceptual tools in those directions will have to interpret them in corresponding ways, often with the aid of other theoretical material. Luhmann, for instance, included a fairly lengthy analysis of religion in his multi-volume work on social structure and semantics (Luhmann 1989a), a series that had as one of its main foci how changes in the meaning and use of words reflect broader social transformations in the historical emergence of modern society. Yet an analysis of the notion of religion as such is not undertaken there. In filling this gap, I have therefore relied on the original research of others into the history of this idea and supplied my own interpretation of how this development worked both in Western countries/languages and in other parts of the world. Indeed, a key purpose of Chapters 3 to 5, on two of the Abrahamic religions, Hinduism and East Asian religions respectively, is to concretize this extension of the Luhmannian point of departure which itself is the main subject of Chapter 2. Moreover, and as a second example of critical adaptation, in analyzing individual function systems, Luhmann stayed quite close to the idea that these are structured around core dichotomies or binary codes which inform elaborate programmes that set the rules as to how the codes are to be applied. In order to account for what I see as a primary feature of religion in today's world, namely the division into a variable set of religions (especially so-called 'world religions'), I have found it necessary to deviate somewhat from this theoretical strategy when it comes to observing a global religious system. First, rather than starting with a single binary code, which for Luhmann is immanence/transcendence, I start with the historical (re)formation of the most solidly institutionalized of these religions and with corresponding semantic transformations, thereby leaving the question of the 'singularity' of the religious system either more open or more vague, depending on one's perspective. Second, although I address the question of the binary code for religion, I argue for a different code than does Luhmann; and I stop short of asserting that this code is univocal. In both cases, however, I would argue that my adaptations and extensions are in tune with the logic of Luhmann's theorizing.

Observing religion as a specifically global religious system implies more than mere global extension of a particular way of forming and doing religion. A very pivotal part of the argument is that this religious system, along with various other systems, is an important socio-structural component of what is by now a world society. The historical emergence of the religious system is an aspect of the historical development of global society. It is only a slight exaggeration to say that the globalization of society over the past few centuries is incomprehensible unless one includes what has happened to religion during this time. Religious constructions and transformations are by far not the only such vital factor, but they are one. Given this close relation between religious and societal transformation, Chapter 1 is dedicated to a discussion of the globalization of society. It begins with a look at the recent appearance and usage of the term, primarily in social scientific discourse, but also as a politically charged popular term. I argue, with Roland Robertson (Robertson 1992), that a significant feature of the globalization of society is the rising thematization in communication of society as global. The recent prominence of the term 'globalization' thus appears as a semantic correlate of that development. Yet the idea, like religion, is also highly contested, both in scholarly and popular discourse. Reflective of that aspect, the chapter then looks at certain consistent features of theories of globalization, notably their frequently dialogical character, their tendency to precipitate around the difference between global and local or between universal and particular. The argument is, again with Robertson but also in this case with Wallerstein (Wallerstein 1979), that we are dealing here with a very basic feature of global society, one that manifests itself also through religion. On those foundations, the chapter offers an analysis of the role of function systems in the construction of world society. These, I contend, are structurally fundamental; without their historical emergence, society today would unlikely be as truly global as it is. Close attention to what these function systems are and how they emerged is important not only for the sake of understanding globalization, but also religion in globalization.

The religious system has its unique features and its own combination of features that are also found in one or more of the other globalizing function systems. These are the focus of Chapter 2. They relate, first of all, to the construction of the religious system, not as a singular and richly articulated system like the global capitalist economy, but as one that constitutes itself through a series of mutually identified religions. These religions, I argue, are not so much variations on a common model of what a religion looks like – although such modelling has also occurred – as they are diverse expressions of a single idea that they together help constitute. Like nations or cultures, religions represent powerful and socially consequential abstractions which manifest themselves in particular, identifiable forms such as religious organizations or religious movements. A second topic of discussion is the relative power of the religious system in comparison with others, notably economy, polity and science. Much sociological ink has been spilled over this question, above all in debates about secularization and privatization. Here I treat it in three ways: as a question of the internal structures of the religious system, notably under the heading of religious orthodoxification and religious authority; as a question of the relation of religions to one another; and as one of the relation of this system to the others, which is to say as a matter of the secularization of these other systems. Finally, both the issues of religious structure and religious power bear a close relation to that of form. The communication that constitutes any system, including the religious system, gravitates around or tends to become concentrated in various particular forms which are instrumental in rendering the system visible and above all in controlling the structure of the communication that counts as religion. Historically, in the sociology of religion these forms have been discussed under the heading of types of religious organization, especially through the church/sect distinction and its elaborations. For understanding the forms characteristic of the global religious system, that typology is more or less inadequate. The discussion in Chapter 2 about modern religious forms begins with this classic difference, but then proceeds to dismantle it. It focuses on forms other than religious organizations, even though these are of capital importance for the religious system as they are for all other function systems. These others include primarily religious movements and religious networks. Beyond these, however, I analyze the degree to which religion as a system is given form through other, non-religious systems, especially other function systems like the state, law, education and mass media. These latter cannot substitute for organizations, movements and networks; they are supplementary. But what I shall call the ambiguity of the global religious system makes them nonetheless very important.

Chapters 3 to 6 are essentially elaborations and illustrations of the theoretical assertions of the first two. The overall argument is primarily historical; the emergence of global society and the religious system of global society happened in the way they did, to some degree for discernible reasons. They did not have to happen, however. They represent neither universal pattern, necessary development nor prognosis for the future. The story of the different religions, for instance Christianity, Islam or

Hinduism, is therefore a combination of common pattern and unique chronicle. In keeping with the role of social-scientific theory outlined above, a proper understanding of each religion has to include both analysis of the universal pattern and of the particular local and historical formations in each case. The construction and reconstruction of a world religion called Christianity displays the common pattern – some would say it has determined it – but it is also unique in what, where and how it came about. The modern historical transformation of Islam in certain respects follows the path of Christianity and other religions; many critical aspects of this story are, however, peculiar to Islam. Islam portrays the common pattern with its own characteristically modern emphases. Similar statements apply to all the other religions and the 'non-religions', here referring to those instances, especially the case of Confucianism and Chinese religious complexes, in which the historical process did not result in the social construction of one of the religions, and this not accidentally but quite deliberately with reference to the (other) religions. Each of Chapters 3 to 6 therefore illustrates the common pattern but also relates important aspects of a unique narrative. I say aspects, because those things discussed in each case are of necessity quite selective; a thorough treatment of each case would take volumes and a level of expertise with each case which I neither have nor claim.

Since the so-called 'world religions' are those that are most globalized both in terms of their presence and their institutionalization as religions around the world, they are the subject of Chapters 3, 4 and 5. The division of these chapters is, however, not strictly according to religions. Not even all the most universally recognized world religions receive extended treatment; notably Judaism is left out and Buddhism considered only very partially. Instead, each is devoted to cases that illustrate a major direction in the formation of the global religious system. Accordingly, Chapter 3 treats primarily Christianity and Islam. Together they illustrate the reconstruction of already historically well-differentiated and mutually identifying religious traditions as modern religions or subsystems of the global religious system. These, along with Buddhism and Judaism, were in most respects 'always already there', so the main issue is one of reformation and reconstruction, rather than more historically original invention and imagination. The fourth chapter, on Hinduism, focuses on just this latter possibility, namely a religion that did not have a clear and singular identity as such before the modern era. There were certainly myriad cultural goods and communicative practices which were, from the modern perspective, religious; but these had never been imagined and socio-structurally formed as a single, self-identified and recursively constituted religion. Even today, the construction of Hinduism is still incomplete, contested and somewhat elusive. Chapter 5 elaborates on yet a third possibility, and that is the failure to re-imagine local religio-cultural complexes as one or more religions. This is the case of East Asia more generally, and China in particular. The East Asian example is, however, far from a simple case of failure or rejection. Aside from the refusal to imagine Confucianism as a religion, this region has nonetheless contributed to the overall construction of the global religious system. Several of the major efforts to fashion modern Buddhism as one of the religions have their origin and home there. The partial reconstruction of Shinto as religion, state ideology and non-religion demonstrates some important possibilities. And the degree of institutionalization of religions in other systems is perhaps clearer in this part of the world than anywhere else. Finally, if the chapter on East Asia introduces certain important ambiguities in the formation of the religious system, the last chapter on new religions and de-institutionalized or 'penumbral' religion addresses several other significant aspects of religion construction and deconstruction. These include questions of how new religions form and come to be accepted or rejected as 'one of the religions', the central issue of religious contestation and control of the religious category, and the rise and regional prevalence of 'religioid' forms. These, on the one hand, get their visibility, as it were, in the shadow of the religious system. Yet, on the other hand, they seem to challenge the very existence of the religious system, pointing to the distinct possibility of the future disappearance or dissipation of that system. In combination, then, the illustrative chapters serve to put meat on the argument, but also to challenge and contextualize it, thereby showing what directions future research in this entire area might take.

Notes

1   Although that is not the case for what Weber writes a couple of lines thereafter: 'the external courses of religious behavior are so diverse that an understanding of this behavior can only be achieved from the viewpoint of the subjective experience, ideas, and purposes of the individuals concerned' (Weber 1978: 399). Although certainly individual ideas and purposes are important and must be included in any explanation, I will treat them more as enabling conditions for the possibility of religion in global society, not as its root determinant.

2   In this respect, I depart from the strategy I adopted in *Religion and Globalization* (Beyer 1994: 9f.) because that approach did not take sufficiently into account the degree to which the definition I offered was dependent on the systems-theoretical analysis that followed.

3   The implicit contrast here between 'official' and 'nonofficial' religion is reminiscent of the same distinction made by Meredith McGuire (2002: 97–148). The two conceptualizations are, however, different in that mine applies strictly to contemporary society that exhibits a dominance of the function systems I am discussing. McGuire's notion has broader applicability and therefore a correspondingly different rationale.

Chapter 1

Globalization and global society

Globalization: the emergence of a neologism

At the beginning of the twenty-first century, globalization stands as a highly familiar and highly charged term. In popular and mass media usage, as well as in much of the burgeoning scholarly literature on the subject, it has primarily an economic reference, signalling the observation that most regions and peoples of the world are now increasingly tied together through the operations of global capitalist markets, transnational business firms and their cultural by-products in the form of mass consumer goods, mass media and the like. The evaluation of this process varies about as much as it could, ranging from those who consider globalization as both inevitable and good for the world and humanity, all the way to those who condemn it as unjust and destructive of lives, cultures and the natural environment. What is perhaps rather strange in this currently raging debate is that the term 'globalization' is relatively new, whereas most of the developments that it describes have been the subject of analysis and controversy for a significantly longer period. Transnational capitalism is at least several centuries old, and its observation as such begins already in the nineteenth century, especially with Marx. Even the ecological component dates back to at latest the 1960s, two decades before this term became popular. And indeed, it was only in the mid- to late 1980s that globalization became part of our vocabulary (Levitt 1983; Robertson and Chirico 1985; Robertson and Lechner 1985), and only in the 1990s that it attained its current stature. The reasons for coining a new word for old processes are instructive.

Even a cursory look at older literature on the developments that globalization describes shows that we are dealing with a successor term. Specifically, globalization, while not simply a synonym for capitalism and modernization, in effect largely replaces them in popular and scholarly discourse (Roberts and Hite 2000). It is important to understand why this has happened. As concerns capitalism, the reasons can be read from the timing of the switch: 'globalization' as a word becomes popular at exactly the same time as the Soviet empire disintegrates and the state socialist alternative that it represented effectively disappears. As Eastern Europe and the former Soviet republics switched to market economies and as Mao's vilified 'capitalist roaders' carried the day in China, one did not have to be overly perceptive to conclude that international capitalism had become truly global capitalism. Globalization, especially in its dominant popular and media usages, is capitalism, but now without the concrete and institutionalized socialist alternative. The relation between globalization and modernization is somewhat more complicated. It includes the capitalism-to-globalization shift, but also points to a basic reassessment of all that has gone before. In a sense, changing to the idea of globalization is a way of saying that modernization is now no longer regional but rather unavoidably global. What seems to require a different term, however, is that it has become increasingly difficult to conceive modernity as singular: there are evidently multiple modernities, various ways of changing social structures and fundamental orientations to the world (Eisenstadt 2001; Featherstone *et al.* 1995). A similar understanding is captured in the notion that we now live in a postmodern world, one in which metanarratives of how we all got here and where we are all going are no longer convincing. In light of such pluralization of modernity, globalization suggests itself as the new singular, as the new term for the universal historical process in which we are all implicated.

If we then consider that, at a minimum, globalization indicates an awareness of this singularity, then tracing that recognition historically is one way of further understanding how the idea has replaced modernity in this capacity. Following the analyses of Roland Robertson (1992: 15–24) and Martin Albrow (1990), by the mid-nineteenth century, European thinkers such as Saint-Simon, Marx, Comte and Spencer had already taken critical steps in this direction. They felt that the processes of modernization evident in their own society were universal, which meant that they were destined to incorporate all the peoples of the world. Although they accepted the age-old distinction between the 'civilized' and the 'barbarian', they transformed this social (and geographic) difference into a temporal and temporary one: those who *still* lived under barbaric conditions were destined to become civilized. This spread of modernity was not simply a matter of imperial conquest with the civilized powerful ruling over the barbaric subaltern. In their progressive and utopian visions, barbarism itself was to be eradicated with the spread of universal civilization to encompass the entire world. The spatial limits of this Western sociality were temporary. Nor were these intellectual elites alone in their thinking. The colonialist visions of European soldiers, administrators, explorers and merchants frequently incorporated this universalizing component. And Christian missionaries, beginning already with the Spanish conquests of the sixteenth century and the Catholic missions of the seventeenth century, envisioned a universal conversion of the heathen quite analogous to what the more sociological thinkers had in mind (Mignolo 1998).

Indeed, this Christian parallel points to the possibility of seeing the fore-runners to globalization even earlier and also outside the European sphere. At least after the eighth century CE, Islam became in fact as well as in principle just such a universalizing vision; and one could even make a similar argument for Buddhist and Hellenistic impulses of several centuries before that. Quite aside from showing just how far back one could extend the history of the historical developments to which globalization now refers, these precursors also raise the question of what specifically has been different about the current phase. Above all, one has to ask why the universalizing visions of nineteenth-century European men like Comte and Marx, and not those of the Greeks, the Buddhists or the Muslims, actually eventuated in the global society of the present. As with the passage from modernization to globalization as key terms, the differences between the developments initiated by the modern Europeans and those of other people in other times and places are as important as the similarities.

Looking at the views of thinkers like Marx, Comte and Spencer simply as European or Western is, in fact, somewhat misleading. For mixed into their universalism was usually (Marx is an exception) a concomitant particularism in the form of nationalism or at least nationally oriented perspectives. Certainly by the nineteenth century, and to a significant degree before, most Europeans tended to see their universal visions through national eyes, whether British, French, Russian, Dutch, Spanish, Portuguese, Danish, German, Italian, Swedish or Belgian. The universal in these visions also expressed itself in terms of the particular. That is vital for understanding the eventual inadequacy of modernization as an umbrella notion and the corresponding switch to globalization. Indeed, by the end of the nineteenth century, the national particularism among Europeans became rather dominant over the globalizing universalism. This development was instrumental, for instance, in bringing about World War I in the early twentieth century, an event that demonstrated just how particular and non-universal the Europeans were or had become. Moreover, in the scientific domain, we see an analogous manifestation in the eventual orientation of the new universalist discipline of sociology. There the idea took root – and is still quite strong – that the core word 'society' applied more or less self-evidently to national states; that the world consisted not of one society or even a small number of regional ones, but rather of a large number of societies that were more or less coterminous with these states of extremely variable sizes. The question of modernization, which is to say the 'spread' of the universalism, had to be asked in the first instance with reference to those states, at most in terms of clusters of these states, and not, or only in utopian fashion, with respect to the global geographic or social whole. The fact that, already by the latter half of the nineteenth century, various clearly non-European 'national' elites in countries such as Japan, China and India were actively adopting this vision of 'national societies' only contributed to the logic of the development. Yet during the same period, we see a dramatic increase in the sort of economic, political and generally communicative ties that we now regularly point to when talking about a compressed global world. This was the period of the steamship, the railroad, the telegraph, of the beginnings of telephone and radio communication, of significant global migrations, as well as of sharply increased global trade and finance; not to mention that the 1914–18 European war was called and to a real extent was in fact a world war (MacMillan 2003). Modernization, as an idea with nationally particular orientation, could not encompass this aspect. Not surprisingly, then, this period also marks the beginnings of another new discipline, that of international relations, the very title of which reflects the particularistic basic unit of analysis. The global, in effect, appeared as a matter of *relations* among more localized forms, as derivative, not as constitutive of them (Albrow 1990; Robertson 1992: 18–24; Stichweh 1996).

The post-World War II era marked the beginning of the end of this particularistic ascendancy, but not simply in favour of a universalistic global vision. Instead, what we have witnessed is an intensification of both faces with the corresponding realization that previous conceptualizations must at the very least be enhanced. World War II was itself more truly global than all previous wars; and yet represented a clash and thus the violent relations between incommensurate particularisms with universal pretensions. The post-war era then continued this sort of confrontation in a different guise: rather than nationalist fascisms versus nationalist liberalisms, each represented through several nation-states, there emerged the Cold War division between communism and liberal democracy in the form of two superpower states and their respectively allied states. These particularistic socio-political units, moreover, were at the same time multiplying as numerous independence movements succeeded in erecting new sovereign states upon the structures of the European colonial empires. Under these circumstances, what appeared most evident was not one world, but rather, in the prevalent jargon of the time, three: the First, the Second and the Third Worlds. Each of these seemed evidently to be composed of states or 'national societies'. In terms of modernization, the first two denoted capitalist and socialist versions of this universalist idea(l), whereas the last incarnated the 'not yet' modernized, the underdeveloped but also develop*ing* world. Under the idea of 'development' the older universalizing impulse of spreading modernity, 'civilizing the barbarian' and even 'converting the heathen' (cf. Mignolo 1998) received a new incarnation.

Several occurrences conspired to make this vision less convincing after the 1960s and thus make room for the rising notion of globalization; not, as I say, as a replacement for the universalist notion of modernity, but rather as an enhancement and to some degree as a counterpoint that allowed the particularity of modernization to come to the fore. As a concept, globalization would account much better for the relative differences in how the supposedly universal modern project manifested itself from one place to another. More critically, it put into much sharper profile the extent to which the relations among 'societies' were not merely derivative, but just as much constitutive of them. To better appreciate the 'societies', they also had to be treated as subunits of an encompassing unit of analysis, whether that was to be called a 'system' or also a 'society'.

A catalogue of the post-1960 events and developments that encouraged the semantic shift to the idea of globalization can be quite long (see Beyer 2002). My selections from the possibilities are somewhat arbitrary and are meant only to illustrate the difficulty of maintaining the national society as the basic unit of understanding. One could begin with pre-1960s events such as the already mentioned *world* wars, the fact that the Cold War divisions effectively included the entire globe, the proliferation of international governmental and non-governmental organizations in the immediate post-war era, or the advent of television and regularly scheduled air service around the world. It is, however, the intensification and multiplication of such phenomena in the period after 1960 that have been the real triggers. The 1969 moon landing with its indelible image of the globe floating in space might be a place to start as a symbolic event. Of greater real effect were probably other developments. These include the first wave of worldwide environmentalism; nuclear proliferation and the corresponding peace/ban-the-bomb movements; the already mentioned extension of sovereign statehood status to virtually all inhabited parts of the world; the definitive accession of the first non-Western country, Japan, to 'First World' status; and changes in the immigration laws of various Western countries that enlarged the prime sources of migrants to include the entire globe. The rapid intensification of numerous other communicative processes could be added, such as the explosion of tertiary education; the continued increase in the number and complexity of international non-governmental organizations; much greater density of telecommunication, travel and tourism; and, related to this, the computerization of business, government, education, science and media. During the 1980s and 1990s, when globalization took on its current popularized meaning, key trigger events could include, for instance, Black Monday in October 1987, the recognition of the East Asian Tiger economies, the resurgence of a now sustained environmental activism and concern in the wake of the Chernobyl nuclear disaster, the AIDS pandemic, the 1991 Gulf war, the advent of the Internet, and, of course, the fall of the Soviet empire with its seeming victory of capitalism. The catalogue could be increased almost at will. Of key importance in the present context is what social-scientific theories have made of this, which is to say how globalization has come to be understood.

Theorizing globalization: the global and the local

Accepting that a concept like globalization is necessary does not by itself already say what the new term means. Globalization intends to capture vital aspects of contemporary social reality which notions like capitalism and modernization do not address satisfactorily; but what exactly are those aspects? Theories of globalization in fact vary a great deal. A quick survey of the relevant literature, however, reveals the clear dominance of one particular perspective, which sees globalization as in essence the worldwide extension and intensified operation of the capitalist economy. This orientation owes a great deal to and can even be said to have its origins in the world-system theory of Immanuel Wallerstein, whose publications beginning in the early 1970s are among the first to theorize the entire globe as a single social whole (Wallerstein 1974–80, 1979). World-system theory shows a decidedly Marxian influence, not least in the priority it gives to economy *as* society and in its use of class divisions as a basic organizing principle. The Marxian flavour of this relatively early globalization theory is perhaps not surprising given that Marx was himself one of a very few classical nineteenth-century social thinkers who did not display a noticeably national orientation; and, indeed, like Wallerstein, treated the modern nation-state as a phenomenon derivative of supposedly more fundamental economic processes. Correspondingly, many of the contributions to the literature that adopt the globalization-as-capitalism approach are highly critical, seeing globalization as an ideology of the global capitalist class which is having devastating effects on the majority subaltern populations of the world. Philip McMichael's formulation is typical: globalization is 'a set of institutional and ideological relations constructed by powerful social forces (e.g., managers of international agencies, states and firms, academic ideologues)' (McMichael 2000: 275). There are, of course, formulations of this position that see globalization as generally positive (e.g. Levitt 1983). What all these approaches have in common is that globalization for them amounts to the intensification of the global reach of capitalism and its concomitant universalizing project of modernization. Yet, dominant as this perspective is, it does not go unchallenged by other views. It is, in fact, rather seriously lacking if it proposes to be a theory of the global social whole. Such economistic theories of globalization, if stretched to that point, are forced to explain everything that has been happening in the contemporary world as an expression of global capitalist modernization, as resistance to it, or as irrelevant. The result is that significant globalizing domains of social life are underanalyzed, ignored or accounted to the residual categories of irrelevance or resistance. That applies especially to the main subject of this book, religion.

A further group of influential approaches to globalization that goes some way to addressing the one-dimensionality focuses on the worldwide system of political states. Consonant with international relations perspectives, these see states as prime actors in the global system, but further focus on how states actually constitute themselves with reference to this system (Defarges 2002; Luard 1990; McGrew and Lewis 1992). One particularly well-developed version of this direction, represented by John W. Meyer and his collaborators (Meyer *et al.* 1997; Thomas *et al.* 1987), even refers to this system explicitly as a 'world polity', paralleling the Wallersteinian 'world economy'. Political orientations of this sort address the problem of one-dimensionality by adding and emphasizing an inherently plural global unit of analysis, the state. They thus introduce heterogeneity, not as victim or attempted negation of globalization, but as constitutive of it.

In their emphasis on more than one dimension and on the constitutive role of heterogeneity, politically oriented theories of globalization are examples of a wider group of theories that see it principally in terms of a dialogical and mutually constructive relation between the universal and the particular, or, as it is expressed more frequently, between the global and the local (Beyer 1998a). The global, in these perspectives, is not simply an imposition, as it were from the top down; it is at the same time the product of the reconstruction of the local. In addition, the local is not merely what was or is there in the absence of the global; it is a consequence of how the global constitutes itself. My somewhat paradoxical formulation signals what is different in these cases. It hearkens back to the discussion in the previous section on the historical simultaneity of nationally particular and globally universal visions. And in as much as the world-system model of Wallerstein and his school represents the first explicitly global version of globalization as capitalism, so has the work of Roland Robertson (see Robertson 1992; Robertson and Chirico 1985; Robertson and Lechner 1985) pioneered this dialogical orientation.

Robertson's way of expressing this core idea is to say that globalization is at the same time the universalization of the particular and the particularization of the universal. Translating somewhat, one can express the basic idea like this: globalization has consisted and consists in the simultaneous and sequential operation of three logical moments. There is (1) the spread of various particular social forms across the globe, which constitutes their universalization. Those forms were at one point in their development the particular products of a certain region or a certain subgroup, albeit frequently already with reference to matters outside that region or subgroup (see moment 3). These universalized forms, however, do not simply spread as such, but (2) become particularized to various other local situations. That particularization of the universal repeats the universal, but also transforms it, thus relativizing the original. Such transformation, in turn, can become the particular subject of (3) another universalization, which in turn becomes reparticularized in other contexts and other times. And so on. The global expresses itself only as local, and the local expresses itself in global terms.

Several aspects of this basic model should be underlined. First, it very much includes unequal power relations and conflict. Sometimes universalization involves imposition, with the possibility of resistance. That resistance, however, may also be an active form of appropriation; or the form of resistance itself may become a particularization subject to universalization or spread elsewhere. Even anti-globalization movements have become rapidly global, as such and in localized and transformed versions. In this sense, they further globalization in its most obvious sense of the increased communicative or social connection of the whole world; and in the awareness of that world. Moreover, the idea that particular resistance to certain universalizations can itself become the subject of further universalizations points to another dimension of the overall process. Although the most obvious universalizations may be the particular products and impositions of the most powerful regions, groups or actors on the rest, the sources of universalizing particulars and the direction of their 'flow' need not be and are not in fact uniformly of that sort. There are also 'reverse flows' (from seemingly subaltern to dominant) and 'cross flows' (not involving the dominant) which make their own real contribution to the development of a more global social world.

These features are not difficult to illustrate. The development of a globalizing capitalist economy in Europe already produced a resistant form there, namely socialism which turned out itself to be a capitalist variant. Rather than receiving its most typical concrete form in the dominant capitalist countries, however, the eventually most concretely elaborated versions of socialism arose elsewhere, in Russia and then in East Asia, principally the Maoist variant. In the latter half of the twentieth century, these then spread in particularized forms to virtually every corner of the world before collapsing in the 1990s. On a rather different front, when after the sixteenth century European powers brought large numbers of Africans as slaves to their New World colonies, they thereby also contributed significantly to the globalization of African cultural forms which, in the re-particularized or localized versions of the Americas, have been having significant influences on, for example, twentieth-century globalized art and religion. Jazz, Reggae and Pentecostalism, to mention only three of the most obvious, are by no means simply African; but they are to an important degree the product of displaced, transmuted and transformed forms of African origin. It is to this sort of process that another observer of globalization, Jan Nederveen Pieterse (Nederveen Pieterse 1995), applies the term 'hybridization', by which he means both the creation of social forms (e.g. African culture) and their ongoing transformative combination (e.g. Pentecostalism) with other similarly generated forms (e.g. Wesleyan Methodism, Holiness movements). The notion that what hybridizes constitutes itself in the same process as the hybridization points to another critical aspect of this dialogical view of globalization, one already encountered in the brief consideration of political theories of globalization.

Very much implied in Robertson's model of globalization is what he calls simultaneous homogenization and heterogenization (Robertson 1995). As society globalizes, the people of the world come to have more in common in how they organize their social lives; but part of that commonality, part of that homogenization, is common ways of establishing, identifying and asserting heterogeneity. Ways of 'doing difference' themselves are the subject of globalization. Some of the most important social forms and categories that have been globalizing over at least the last two centuries are those that allow people to establish for themselves and for almost everyone else how they are different in an increasingly integrated world. The globalized forms and categories include above all the individual, gender, nation, people, class, culture, race, civilization, ethnie, tradition and – of vital importance in the present context – religion. A more recently arising such category may be sexual orientation. In spite of their diversity, what all these terms have in common is that they name a particularity that both their carriers and outsiders deem to *exclude* universalization. As a mark of this limitation, they connote 'natural' identities, ones that for supposedly historical or biological reasons are beyond technical human disposition: we effectively have no choice in these matters. Nonetheless, contemporary observation also often recognizes the degree to which these supposedly natural categories of difference are themselves the product of historical 'invention' or construction. Invention here does not mean creation from nothing, but rather the dissolution of received ideas and forms out of their previous contexts and their recombination in new ways with sometimes new characteristics to yield a new particular identity suitable for the current globalized circumstance. Thus, to take and expand the African example just raised, cultural complexes that we now recognize as African have existed for quite some time; and have their own (perhaps only dimly known in many cases) history of transformation. What we have invented is the idea of 'Africanness', a cultural and racial singularity that unites otherwise disparate peoples and ways of life; and that gains a good part of its meaning from what it is not: white, European, Asian, Arab, and so on. This Africanness not only identifies those people and those sociocultural features that are deemed to belong, it is also a category of contestation, an identity in terms of which one can appear on the integrated world stage and make claims to recognition, resources, influence and power. It is thereby also a category of particularization, one with which one can appropriate and to some degree reconstruct global forms such as state, economy, religion or art in a particular, in this case African, image. None of this, of course, excludes variation and contestation over what is African, or even whether the idea is valid. Similar analyses are possible of all the other categories of difference, from the French nation and the female sex to East Asian civilization and Hindu religion. The question in each of these cases is not primarily whether such a thing exists or predates the contemporary era. It is, rather, what contemporary global and local forms do these notions represent and how do they operate in today's global society? The idea is central for understanding the reconstruction of the religious as religions and thereby as a religious function system in today's society.

The fact that these categories of heterogeneity also have a history points to further dimensions of this dialogical globalization thesis, ones that restrict the sorts of claim that can be made for it. These concern the contemporary social extent of globalization and the degree to which the development is in certain respects not unprecedented.

Globalization names an encompassing development, but not a totalizing one. By this I mean not that the effects of globalization are superficial, touching only the surface of most social lives, but rather that it is socially incomplete. The thesis does claim that social lives all around the world are significantly affected by the simultaneously globalizing and localizing processes under discussion; that the level of global integration of social worlds has increased to the point that we must speak about a single global society. The degree of that effect, however, varies; and throughout the world, large numbers of people still live much or most of their lives outside globalized social forms like the monied economy, the active regulation of the state, the infiltration of mass media or the organizations/movements of world religions. And many others live only partially in some of these, but by no means all. Nonetheless, perhaps one of the most solid witnesses to the power and extent of globalization is that, with few exceptions, the people who are least incorporated do not so much lead alternative social lives in different social systems as live lives at the margins of the dominant systems, more excluded from global/local society than included elsewhere. In that light, a mark of the extent and fundamentally 'imperialistic' nature of this globalization process, its impetus to occupy all the social space available, is that life entirely outside its forms is not only increasingly impossible, but most of those inside (and possibly outside) them also view such life as unacceptably marginal and, indeed, as inhuman. That includes many of those who are otherwise quite critical of the entire phenomenon. Much of the opposition to globalization, however conceived, in fact criticizes the process as much for its lack of success as for its deleterious effects (see e.g. Hines 2000). This is another symptom of how anti-globalization can and does further globalization.

If the incompleteness of globalization is one aspect that tempers the claims that can be made for it, another is the sense in which what the word describes is not, historically speaking, unprecedented. To some degree, this is the case for economistic views of globalization: economic 'world systems', united neither politically nor through cultural continuity, have existed before the fifteenth century (see Abu-Lughod 1989). It also holds for those perspectives that stress the dialogical relation between local and global or universal and particular. As I indicated briefly at the beginning of this chapter, the Hellenistic world of the centuries immediately before the Common Era and the world of Islam between the tenth and seventeenth century, to name only two, also exhibited that combination. Names typically given to these world systems, for example Hellenism and Islamdom, denote the universal dimension, parallel to the word 'globalization' today. The particularizations, the way that Hellenistic and Islamic culture became appropriated or localized in different places, also went by various names, perhaps those of particular regions, political empires or peoples (cf. Smith 1986, for examples 'from below'). That much is similar and justifies those observers who stress either the degree to which globalization is not that new or who locate the beginnings of the process as far back as the fifth to sixth centuries BCE, at the time of Plato, Kong-zi and Gautama Buddha. The latter perspective is especially useful for appreciating the degree to which contemporary and modern globalization is very much in historical continuity with what went before, and not just the West. Globalization does not represent a radical departure so much as discontinuity within a context of continuity, like all historical change. That said, the peculiarities of this latest development are just as important.

While the most obvious differences between current globalization and older examples may seem to be their global extent, contemporary theories of globalization stress not that extent so much as the reasons for it. One of these in much of the literature is a higher degree of interdependent multi-dimensionality. Thus, for instance, various summarizations of globalization perspectives divide their presentation according to different dimensions of globalization, at a minimum the economic, political and cultural. They thereby also stress the interdependence of these dimensions.[1] Robertson, for example, adopts a broadly cultural perspective with its stress on images and awareness of globality. He also includes economic, political and individual dimensions. Yet key to the entire model are the relations of the dimensions, what Robertson analyzes as their mutual relativization. Anthony Giddens, by comparison, includes the for him highly interdependent dimensions of self, economy, states, militaries, means of communication and social movements (Giddens 1990, 1991). However one decides which aspects are the most important, the upshot of all this literature is that contemporary globalization, as it were, stands on many legs, but that these are highly interdependent: globalizing forms have shown a combination of independent development and highly interdependent operation. When we look at most previous, more regionally restricted world systems, such as the politically based empires of Rome and the Middle East or such cultural world systems as medieval Islam, ancient Hellenism and the caste-based system during much of pre-Mughal India, it is the highly interdependent multi-dimensionality that is less evident. Pre-modern political empires relied heavily for their continuation on the efficacy of bureaucratic and military means attached to the rulers at their cores. Economic ties either followed different limits, or they were a direct creature of political, bureaucratic and military influence. Economic world systems such as that described by Abu-Lughod (1989) were precisely that: economic. There was little to no political integration and other communicative links were occasional and haphazard. And religio-cultural systems like medieval India or the Islamic world at its height were unified only or certainly primarily on exactly those bases. The other dimensions of those systems, while not absent, were far less constitutive of them.

The uniqueness of contemporary globalization should not, however, blind us to the ways that it shares characteristics with previous world systems of lesser geographical reach. Nor should its peculiarities obscure the degree to which we are dealing with a process of uncertain historical duration, one in continuity with what went before. While very little of the literature on globalization treats it as a phenomenon only as old as the word used to describe it, there is much disagreement over when (and even where) precisely we should locate its origins. For the purposes of this study, I will locate those origins in Western Europe in the early modern period, roughly beginning in the late fifteenth century. The justification for this decision as concerns religion will become evident in the following chapters.

Narrating contemporary globalization as history

The postmodern turn in contemporary sensibilities declares an end to grand narratives, exposing these as selective and historical constructions which, to say the least, could have been done differently. An approach to social reality that sees this as an articulated complex of meaningful communications, however, will regard all knowledge in society as narrative, as selective relations of invented categories. To observe globalization in the form of a historical narrative, therefore, is to claim that the story is true at the same time that it is contingent, to be judged by its consequences as a way of understanding and not as some sort of final word that excludes all others. Accordingly, locating the beginning of contemporary globalization in early modern Europe need not ignore the many antecedent developments before this time and in other places. The modern course of globalization would simply not be comprehensible without the previous existence of the Roman empire in the ancient Mediterranean world, medieval Chinese civilization, the trading system that incorporated West Africa and the Middle East with the substantial role of Islamic culture, the succession of empires in South Asia, and a great deal else. The story of globalization is not written on a clean slate nor in an entirely new language. As story, it must have a beginning; as social process it cannot. And just as a fairy tale assumes the lords, the princesses, the ogres and the donkeys it tells about, so does a narrative of globalization presuppose a complex world whose transformation it seeks to describe.

Western Europe in the late Middle Ages was not the most powerful society in the world of that time. Compared with Islamic civilization from northern Africa to the Indian subcontinent or with China of the Ming dynasty, it was a technological, economic, artistic and military backwater. Even its own elites saw it as a pale reflection of the Greek and Roman civilizations that had preceded it in the region. Yet between the late fifteenth and the twentieth centuries, the irregular northwestern peninsula of the Asian landmass came to see itself as a continent, becoming the centre and carrier of such powerful technological, economic, artistic, military and even religious forces – precisely those dimensions along which it had hitherto been unremarkable – so as to spread its influence to every part of the world, without exception. One part of a narrative of contemporary globalization has to deal with this development, with what we can call the modernization and imperial expansion of Europe. As already noted, this cannot be the whole story; modernization and globalization are related, but far from identical. Understanding European modernization is nonetheless critical.

I begin with a brief survey of standard ways this story has been told, at least until quite recently and in some cases still. One of these begins with the voyages of European exploration, with Vasco da Gama, John Cabot, Christopher Columbus and many more. Symbolic as they perhaps are, they point to several critical aspects. First, European transformation included from the beginning of the story the expansion of influence beyond Europe. Second, budding European political powers were from early on in competition with one another; Europe was not the centre of an expanding empire and these were voyages of exploration, not (at least in initial intent) conquest. Third, the European explorers did indeed represent different political powers, but their primary aim was to find alternate trade routes that bypassed the Muslim-controlled direct routes; they began as a way of participating in a long-standing world trading system, not as the initiation of a new one. Fourth, therefore, these early efforts do not in themselves already show that they are symptoms of a radical historical transformation. Their symbolic status depends on narrative hindsight. The explorers are not the only standard place to begin, however. And the fact that the overall narrative consists in a number of sub-narratives is itself an important aspect of the tale.

Another standard beginning tells of intellectual transformation. It is the story of Copernicus and Galileo, of Descartes and Francis Bacon, of a long series of modern thinkers and scientific pioneers. What these men do is signal a break in thinking, above all away from the tutelage of traditional and religious worldviews. Their new foundation rests in the individual and in empirical observation, far less in received and socially established authority. With the explorers, they share the symbolism of a positively valued discontinuity, of 'discovery'. Knowledge is not a heritage to be passed on so much as it is something to be created and continually increased. The story of the modern philosophers and scientists thereby also indicates a change in temporal orientation. From the authority and standards of the past, we pass to the normativity of the future as the possibility of 'progress'. Through this aspect, we see the purpose of the narrative: it is an open-ended account of how we are now on a path to a purportedly better and better future. Hence, the way the story is told and the reasons for telling the tale are themselves part of the story. Like all good mythic tales, modern histories are stories of the past that mark out the future and thereby structure the present.

A related, third sub-narrative is the story of religion. I shall have much more to say about this segment in Chapter 3. The protagonists in this case are the Protestant Reformers, above all Luther and Calvin. Analogous to the explorers and the modern thinkers, a standard version shows these also as engaging in a radical questioning, as throwing off the dead and corrupt hand of benighted authority and reclaiming religion as an affair between the individual and God. The Reformers become the champions of freedom of conscience in the way that the philosophers promote freedom of thought. Discovery, enlightenment and freedom are the battle-cries everywhere. The narrative asserts their inevitable progress.

A fourth sub-narrative, again very much related to the previous three but also with its own independent plot, documents the progress of democracy. Here eighteenth-century thinkers like Voltaire, Rousseau and Locke represent the intellectual call to which historical events like the American and French revolutions respond. The nineteenth century is then the period during which nations and peoples progressively shake off the yoke of autocratic and aristocratic domination in favour of the ever greater participation of an ever greater number in political process. Slavery is abolished, nations are united, monarchs lose their remaining power, and, at the beginning of the twentieth century, women receive the right to vote, while nations are confirmed in their right to self-determination. Then, after an unfortunate hiatus of fascism and, in a dominant Western version of the tale, communism, we return to the onward march as new nations arise around the world, throwing off the bondage of colonialism, and, towards the very end of the century, totalitarian and racist regimes fall and dictatorial autocrats are overthrown, from the former Soviet Union to South Africa, from South Korea and the Philippines to Eastern Europe and Latin America. The story has variations, as do all the sub-narratives. In a related version, it is socialism that is the inevitable carrier of the impulse to freedom and democracy. The servitude of feudalism gives way to the exploitation of capitalism, but the workers of the world will unite and throw off this final burden as well. Taking all the variants into consideration, if the previous sub-narratives are those of enlightenment and progress, this one also represents that of progressive inclusion, of the increasing empowerment of individuals and groups.

Finally, we have what to many may seem to be the dominant sub-narrative, that of economy. This is the tale of industrialization or capitalism. Its Marxian version is not only critical of the entire history, but also claims to be a narrative of the whole, not a sub-narrative. We may have here an important reason that economistic globalization theories have caught on so much more quickly than dialogical ones, which largely have to undo the idea of a single modernization story. Globalization as capitalism makes for a single and familiar account that can nonetheless address the felt insufficiency of overly positive modernization perspectives such as the other sub-narratives represent. The non-Marxian variant also carries its totalizing claims, often virtually equating modernization with industrialization. Modern nations are those that are industrialized.

My purpose in adumbrating these versions of the modernization narrative is, of course, not simply to repeat them, let alone champion them. It is rather to highlight certain peculiarities that can help us understand the bases of European imperial success. The upshot of all these sub-narratives is that (European) modernization has been a set of interrelated and yet also independent developments. That combination is also a large part of what allowed the Europeans to be so successful.

Sociological theory has taken up this sort of explanation of modernization since the classics, especially Weber and Durkheim. Indeed, sociological literature has been one of the prime carriers of most of the sub-narratives just outlined. In the twentieth century, probably the clearest formulation is that of Talcott Parsons: modernization consists in, among other things, the acceleration in the development of a set of 'evolutionary universals'. Immediately from this label the universalization aspect of modernization is clear. For Parsons, these universals include value generalization, inclusion, differentiation and adaptive upgrading.[2] All four are relevant in the present context and appear in the sub-narratives, especially the last three. The narrative of democracy is a story of inclusion. The fact of various sub-narratives is symptomatic of differentiation, and the notions of progress and enlightenment point to adaptive upgrading. One critical aspect of this theoretical vision is that the four factors are interdependent, which means especially that differentiation and adaptive upgrading are linked. Differentiation refers to the development of relatively independent institutional domains, each of which focuses on a particular function or purpose. Adaptive upgrading points to the increased power and efficacy that this sort of differentiation permits and entails. Thus, to take but two examples, differentiation of specialized economic institutions like modern

capitalist firms and monetary systems allows these institutions to concen-
trate on the production of wealth as capital and to do this in more
powerful and efficient ways. Differentiation of state political institutions
brings in its wake more powerful and far-reaching modes of public administration and regulation along with more effective ways of reaching and
enforcing collectively binding decisions. A strictly related aspect of this
process is that it is open-ended: the whole system is geared towards ever
increasing upgrading, which is to say towards the fundamental value of
progress. Each of the institutional spheres orients itself towards the ever
greater production of its typical specialization, whether that be capital/
money, political power, knowledge, influence or commitment.

Parsons' theoretical efforts envisioned 'national societies' primarily and
conceptualized the spread of these modernizing processes in terms of the
modernization of these 'societies'. It was not a theory of a global society
that could be conceived to be modern or modernizing as a whole. Its logic,
however, indicates a way of understanding European success. As the
carriers of differentiated and adaptively upgraded institutional spheres, as
the promoters of a universalizing and inclusive value orientation that was
utopian, progressive and future-directed, the Europeans were possessed of
the means and the ends for a very different kind of imperial expansion and
conquest. Their means were powerful and ever more powerful. They eventually had better guns than anyone else; but they also kept on producing
ever better guns. To stand up to them, other civilizational centres couldn't
just produce European guns; they also had to adopt something like their
restless attitude. Accordingly, unlike other imperial expansions of the past,
European expansion did not remain and was not even founded for the
most part on the sort of superficial suzerainty that imposed a thin extrac-
tive ruling-class veneer over societies that at the local level were pretty
much left alone so long as the tribute kept flowing (see Gellner 1983: esp.
8ff.). On the contrary, what the modernizing Europeans carried and in
many areas tried to impose was far more corrosive than that: it implied the
fundamental re-ordering of the local, its re-creation in terms of these globalizing models.

Although thus furnishing a way to understand key aspects of European
hegemony and providing a clear and comprehensive theory of modernization, Parsons' theory also shows in its very structure the limitations of the
modernization hypothesis and therefore the need for the sort of reformulation that the notion of globalization embodies. What is particularly
limiting is the way his theory is tailored to the national society as the
fundamental unit of analysis. This feature is especially evident in the A–G–
I–L structure of his theory which sees society as operating in terms of four
constitutive functions, one of which is necessarily a normatively conceived
integration (the I-subsystem). The differentiated institutional domains are
deemed each to focus on one of these functions. The theory therefore

cannot say with any clarity what becomes of these systems and their corre-sponding institutions outside a social unit such as the nation-state that can be conceived as normatively integrated. A global social system obviously lacks that kind of coherence. With Parsons we cannot move to that system as the basic unit of analysis, which is precisely what the idea of globaliza-tion requires. Yet his analysis of the power of the most typical modern institutional spheres remains useful. For this reason, I want to move away from Parsons' way of conceiving those spheres and the processes that produce them to adopt a more flexible theoretical orientation, one that can preserve the sense of the modernization narratives but render them less dependent on a territorial unit of analysis in general and on the European experience in particular. This orientation I draw largely from the work of one of Parsons' erstwhile students, Niklas Luhmann. It is to his analyses of function systems and of world society that I now turn.

Narrating globalization: a Luhmannian approach

In the introduction, I discussed the Luhmannian idea that society consists of communications as its basic elements. They form a system by referring to each other, by constituting themselves with reference to other communi-cations. My writing here is an example: it refers in complex ways to other communication, both past (e.g. my own writing, that of others in English and other languages, and so forth) and future. It has its meaning only through such reference. Moreover, following a Luhmannian model, it is not complete unless it is understood (whether correctly or not). People are necessary for this, but as text, it also has a life of its own: it is communica-tion not consciousness.

From this rudimentary starting point, two implications are critical for my main themes of globalization and religion. These concern the range of communications and the division of communications, the extent of the system that is society and the subunits of that society. One leads to the observation of a global society; the other to subsystems of that society, including function systems.

If society consists of communications, then the extent of a society corre-sponds to how far those communications are accessible, to the range of places and people where and with whom information imparted can be and is understood. If, for instance, this book finds its way to Montreal, Melbourne, Murmansk, Mumbai, Mombassa and Montevideo; and it is read and understood there; then that suggests that the society of which it is a component reaches to all those centres. Considering the amount of communication in today's world that has this sort of reach, it becomes easy to understand how, from a Luhmannian perspective, most of us today live in a global society. The passage to global observation is comparatively straightforward. We do not have to think alike; we do not have to share the same set of values and norms; we simply have to be participating in the same web of imparted and understood communication, something that includes the possibility that we might be trying to kill each other. Whatever else the destruction of the World Trade Center in New York did, it certainly made a statement! Indeed, this horrific example shows how, on this communicative model, society is not a matter of solidarity or consensus, of similarity at some basic level like worldview or sense of belonging. It is only about the interconnectedness of communication.

Aside from revealing the contemporary world system rather straightfor-wardly as a society, the focus on the social as communication also opens up and largely defuses the question of when the globalization of society began. On this view, it started already when communication of any sort extended its reach over larger and larger areas. The development of writing in different regions is of central importance in this respect. World systems of various sorts before the modern era qualify to a degree. Clearly important varieties of communication had a very broad geographical range, even though these social networks were not worldwide and the types and amount of communication were far more limited than is the case now. The early modern period was similar both in the regions it did not reach, and in the intensity of communicative connections. What separates this example from others dating back to centuries before the Common Era is only that we know with hindsight that it eventuated in the current, clearly much more intensely globalized situation; both in terms of effec-tively and constantly reaching almost all corners of the world and in the sheer amount of communication that knows no frontiers. What the Luhmannian point of departure then does is to shift the question in from 'When did globalization begin?' to 'What have been the specific differences that, historically speaking, made this most recent world system different, leading for the first time to a truly global society?' This question leads to the other critical implication of the communicative starting point, namely how society divides its communication.

Beyond quite simple social situations, the complexity of the possible sources of communication, of the meanings in which communications are embedded, and of the possibilities for what are to be the subjects of communication becomes so high that ways of simplifying communicative situations are needed. One effective way of doing this is to divide commu-nicative processes into relatively clear social subunits so that possible sources, meanings and themes are more manageable in each case. Historically, sociology has tended to conceive this type of solution according to groups or subunits of social actors; and that is indeed one very common way of accomplishing the divisions: limit the participants in communication to certain categories of people who are the carriers of more restricted meanings and orientations. Durkheim and Marx have given us classic formulations in their analyses of the division of labour in society. Insightful and influential as these theories have been, their strength is also their main limitation. By identifying social divisions primarily as divisions of people into groups, they block the ability to see this strategy as only one possibility among several. Society is thus composed of individual persons who are further subdivided into groups like clans, families, villages, professions, classes, nations; or, in more updated fashion, genders, cultures and the like. The insufficiency of thus making social categories so heavily dependent on physical human bodies is that people in most societies through their communication also cross-cut such divisions. Here we find the main impetus for the development of role theory in sociology: people play different roles, sometimes predominantly one role, and it is these roles that are subdivided to constitute important social divisions. In situations where one role seems to determine all the other ones that a person might occupy, social convention and sociological observation can treat that person as if they were that role. One is a proletarian, a woman, an adult or a Samurai. All else follows. This historically very prevalent strategy, however, should not blind us to the possibility of making social divisions on a rather different basis. Going a step further to conceive the basic social unit, not as roles, which are still too much attached to persons, but as communications allows a maximum of flexibility in this regard. Such a step further is critical in the present context. To understand the globalization of contemporary society, how it constitutes itself and why it came about when no other world system has had this result, we have to be able to see how what binds into the same society is actually quite 'impersonal', very much abstracted from individual persons and individual bodies, even though it also assumes these and avails itself of them in communication. Put somewhat differently, the globalization of society has been dependent on the development of social divisions which largely abstract from persons and from solidary groupings of persons. Those solidary groupings, in turn, far from disappearing, instead take on a different importance in the overall social structure that is contemporary global society. I treat them in more detail later in this chapter.

A Luhmannian approach to social subdivisions thus begins with communications. These, and not in a direct sense people, generate the subdivisions of a society in the form of social systems. In his own work, Luhmann clearly analyzed only three types of such social system, namely interactions, organizations and societal systems. Society as such is only the most encompassing version of the last type. In the following chapters, I add a fourth type, social movements, to the other three.[3] I discuss interactions, organizations, and social movements below and in Chapter 2, which centres on the religious system of global society. Here it is societal systems that are primarily at issue. These are the social subdivisions, like clans and classes, that have the greatest effect on the range of societal communication. Depending on which kind of societal subsystem has primacy in any given situation, the society in question will tend to be more restrictive or more expansive in the geographical and social reach of its communication.

Although his analyses varied across his career, Luhmann isolated at most four types of societal subsystem differentiation: segmentary, core/periphery, stratified and functional. These are not logically exhaustive but comparing them allows one to understand the difference of the modern context which exhibits a dominance of functional differentiation.

Segmentary differentiation divides the social processes of a society into subunits that are in principle interchangeable, one subsystem not depending on any of the others. So-called tribal societies are good examples, divided into residential or kinship groups, each of which could continue to exist if one of the others disappeared. The subunits, whether tribes, clans, villages, bands or similar divisions, have important relations with others, perhaps in the form of exogamous kinship relations, seasonal festivals, trading relationships, occasional alliances for specific purposes, or war. The limits of such societies lie in the dominance of this form of differentiation. The level of functional specialization and of stratification is low, reflecting a relatively equal distribution of social power and therefore the comparative absence of conditions for adaptive upgrading, the increase in specialized types of communication. These are oral societies in which communication generally happens in face-to-face situations that depend on the physical presence of the people involved. Their exact boundaries may be somewhat vague since the communication can over a longer period range quite far; but most communication will be local and therefore for all intents and purposes so will the societies.

By contrast, societies that have exhibited a dominance of stratified or core/periphery differentiation structure themselves on an asymmetric principle, with communicative resources and specialized types of communication being concentrated in certain subsystems rather than others. The cores are usually cities and their surrounding areas. Here is where wealth and power are concentrated, where artistic production and specialized knowledge are centred. The peripheries are less notable in all these regards, but they are absolutely necessary for the core to be able to function; the peripheries are those locations from which resources for the core are extracted, whether in the form of food, materials or people. The communication that happens in the core is in most senses different from that which happens in the peripheries, which are themselves more segmentarily differentiated (cf. Gellner 1983). Indeed, people from the peripheries generally do not even have the communicative competence to participate in core life, often speaking different languages and living by different customs. Corresponding to the greater concentration of communicative resources, core subsystems usually developed writing, which was itself a functionally specialized craft. In general, the technological sophistication of these cores was much higher than either segmentary societies or their own peripheries. Core/periphery divisions have therefore been typical of many empires of the past, for example in China, the Middle East or the Americas. Their effective range is more or less identical with the range of core communication which, however, is much greater precisely because of the specialization both in terms of type and mode of transmission. Yet because such communication has to be core communication – that is, identifiable as coming from the core – its range is nonetheless limited; no empire or even world system of the past has managed either to occupy more than a quite delimited portion of the world or to maintain especially vast areas under its control for long periods of time. Above all, core communication is itself subject to segmenting: what were provincial outposts can set themselves up as alternative cores as long as they are effectively out of range of their former metropolis. Thus Alexander's empire did not much outlast him; and the vast Muslim empire of the eighth century quickly became divided thereafter. In both cases, however, what they left behind was a kind of world system which can be considered a single society given the intensity of communication that passed from one end to the other. Core/periphery differentiation can and has produced very far-ranging and often very stable societal systems.

Societies dominated by stratified subsystem formation are in many ways quite similar to core-periphery societies, especially since the latter often included important stratification, not only between core and periphery but, more importantly, within the core. What distinguishes this type is that the subsystems exist more or less in the same place, but establish their boundaries through the artifice of the stratum. What matters is not so much where communication occurs or where it originates, but rather to whom – to which stratum – communication is attributed. Stratified systems such as have existed in South Asia, in pre-modern Europe or in Polynesia feature the concentration of communicative power and resources within the upper strata. They also typically exhibit strong prohibitions or a least limitations on communication among strata, especially since in this case difference of place or mode of communication cannot by themselves ensure the difference among the subsystems. The extent of stratified societies, like the somewhat similar core/periphery ones, is contingent on the range of upper strata communication. Yet because they do not depend as much on separations of place to help define their subsystems, these societies can also be quite small in terms of both population and geographical area. The highly stratified societies of pre-modern Polynesia are good examples of small-scale stratified societies; medieval Europe with its extensive network of noble families covering much of that subcontinent exemplifies a rather larger version. The reference to families is, moreover, quite important because it points to the fact that segmentary differentiation – here into different families – far from disappearing in contexts where core/periphery or stratified differentiation dominate, continues to remain critical but is now used to help structure the dominant form, rather than being the dominant form. Typically in such societies, people 'belong' to a core, a periphery or a stratum by virtue of their belonging to a particular segmentary unit such as a family.

This brief presentation of some of the main features of other forms of dominant societal differentiation sets the stage for considering the difference that functional differentiation makes. All societies have availed themselves to some extent of the possibility of functional specialization, but almost always in the form of divisions of labour where functional specialization expresses or is otherwise a way of helping to structure other, dominant forms of differentiation. Thus divisions of labour in tribal societies usually follow lines of gender, kinship or residence, thereby reinforcing the structuring of communication along kinship or residential lines. Functional specialization in core/periphery societies follows the pattern of this dominant form in that functional specialists reside in core areas and help to lend those areas their prestige. In stratified societies economic, political, intellectual and other specialized roles are assigned a particular stratum, as is evidenced in the complex South Asian caste or jati system with all its variations. Historically, however, only recently has there arisen a society in which functional specialization has become the principle for forming the dominant subsystems as opposed to simply helping to structure these. This is modern and now global society.

Medieval European society in the fourteenth century was a dominantly stratified society, divided essentially according to the distinction between noble and common. At that time, however, and gradually over the succeeding centuries, this was in the process of changing. The rise of the absolutist states, the emergence of a capitalist economy, the growth of science, the development of educational and medical institutions, the emergence of positive law, but also the increasing differentiation of religion in the form of the churches are the main hallmarks of a gradual shift in the dominant way of regrouping communication according to the function or purpose of that communication, less and less according to the larger social identity of the persons engaged in the communication. The multiple subnarratives of modernization discussed above are symptomatic of this shift. They include the superseding of older forms of dominant differentiation, namely stratification, and the putting in their place of a different view of what is of primary importance: no longer the 'glory' of certain strata, but discovery, enlightenment, freedom, (national) fraternity, equality and, for religious carriers, conversion. What is at issue is a reorientation of the primary differentiation of European society towards instrumental, functional priorities. The semantic or ideological correlates of this transformation put people, especially in the form of increasingly differentiated and lionized individuals, at once in the foreground and in the background. They are conceived as autonomous from the developing systems, but the individuals nonetheless distinguish themselves, gain their individuality, mostly in terms of one or a very few of the systems, the progress of which (parallel to the glory of the upper strata or the core) is most fundamentally at issue. This autonomous yet dependent status then throws up the peculiar and persistent question of the relation between individual and society, of Simmel's famous question of how social order can be possible (Simmel 1971). It is this relative abstraction from concrete people, this de-personalization of the more and more dominant functional subunits of society, that, along with adaptive upgrading, allowed these systems to become the carriers of a very different kind of expansion and globalization.

Two characteristics of these systems are of central importance in this regard. First, as in core/periphery and stratified differentiation, the subsystems are asymmetrically structured, meaning that they are both unlike each other and yet profoundly dependent on each other. Just as nobilities are quite different from peasantries and yet are interdependent, so are capitalist economy, political state system, scientific system and so forth quite different from one another and yet each assumes the operation of the others in its social environment. Historically, these systems emerged in tandem, each providing some of the conditions for the possibility of the development of the others (cf. e.g. Huff 2003). The order among the function systems is not, however, hierarchical in any clear sense, even if especially economistic visions of modern society have tried to see them that way. Capitalist economy requires for its functioning political and legal regulation in its environment, technological applications of scientific knowledge, schools for credentialled personnel, and other systems; but these latter are not thereby simply superstructural reflections of that economy. They operate on the basis of their own logic and structure, and are similarly dependent on the rest for their development and proper functioning. This inequality without hierarchical relation has yielded, among other results, that historical feature of Western expansion by which several 'carriers' seem to be operating in tandem and cooperation, yet also somewhat independently of one another. Above all, this expansion has not depended on political conquest for its effect, even though political/military instances have also been quite important. In addition, it has not simply been a capitalist economic expansion, although no narrative can ignore that dimension. Nor, obviously, can we characterize it straightforwardly as a religious expansion, as the spread of scientific knowledge, of mass media, academic schooling or medicalized health. It has been all of these in complex relation and also more than these.

Connected to this relation of independence and interdependence of different functional modalities is another critical factor, what Parsonian theory flags with the idea of adaptive upgrading. Constitutive of these function systems has been what one might call the intensification of their systemic recursiveness, their tendency to refer only to themselves for the rationale of continuing their own communication. This feature is a hallmark of the dominance of functional differentiation in that society. Thus, the primary purpose of capitalist economic communication, which is to say capitalist production and consumption, capitalist selling and buying, is to produce more and more of the same. The purpose of capital accumulation, economically speaking, is capital accumulation.[4] All else is judged in those terms. Similarly, the purpose of scientific communication, which is to say research and theorizing, is to set the agenda or conditions for further research. One pursues knowledge for the sake of knowledge. Similar statements can be made about the rationales or 'autologics' of the other systems: legal decisions become precedents for more legal decisions; the creation of art is for the sake of the art itself; education is good for everyone and everyone ought to receive a seemingly increasing amount of schooling; and so on. In their own spheres, these systems aim for the constant reproduction and increase of their characteristic communication. And that applies also to religion, as I will show in the next chapter.

Considered by themselves, no one of these function systems could have led to the globalized result in which we now live. It is their combination and interdependence as much as their independent concentration on the reproduction of their characteristic instrumentalities that has had this result. Together they seek the constant improvement and expansion of the means that they express. This restlessness has described itself as different tasks. Initially, to its European bearers, it was to civilize the barbarian and convert the heathen. In the twentieth century, that language changed to one of development. Today we still speak regularly in terms of a world divided into the developed and the developing or underdeveloped. And if we look at the typical measures of such development, we will find precisely the main criteria of many of these systems: wealth, education, health, knowledge production, penetration of mass media, artistic production, effective power of the state, rule of law and prowess in sport. Religion, as we shall see, lies somewhat in a different direction to all these; that is another theme of the next chapter.

I do not wish to claim that these function systems offer a complete way of describing contemporary global society. Far from it. Two other major aspects are the subject of attention later on in this chapter. These are the role and nature of other social systems, notably organizations and social movements; and the dialogic question of different particularisms, notably individual and group identities or exclusivities. Moreover, in suggesting that these function systems are major socio-structural features that have led to and now help constitute global society, I do not thereby suggest that this is all somehow positive and unproblematic. The description of these socio-historical developments does not amount to their endorsement, but seeks only to contribute towards their scientific understanding. That said, a more detailed consideration of the general structure of these function systems is still necessary, followed by brief outlines of several examples as a preparation for considering the possibility of a religious version in the next chapter.

Analyzing modernization in terms of a shift to the dominance of functional differentiation of societal systems, and globalization at least in part in terms of the global expansion of those systems, begs the question of what precisely these systems are supposed to be. Another way to phrase the issue is to ask, 'why systems?' and 'what are function systems?' One can respecify the first question by comparing the technical idea of social systems with more general notions of social domains or institutional spheres, and the second question by comparing the Luhmannian notion of social systems which I use here with the similar concept in Parsonian theory.

For many purposes it is probably sufficient to describe things like capitalist economy or nation-state or science as something like institutional domains, and to think of differentiation as the establishment of a number of such domains or social spheres, perhaps represented by their dominant power roles (for example entrepreneur, political leader, scientist, missionary/priest, athlete) or typical institutional expressions (for example state, courts, university, hospital, business firm, church). That language, however, becomes far too imprecise for understanding exactly what constitutes these domains, how they have been constructed and why they persist; and for understanding the relations among them. For instance, why does the capitalist economy persist and even strengthen? Why does a social arrangement where money has value because and only as long as people think it has value not simply collapse in light of its evident arbitrariness and even absurdity? Then again, seeing as governments acquire and spend substantial amounts of money, given that they invest and generate goods and services, does that make them simply part of the capitalist economy? When business firms train their new employees, is that education? If so, what is the difference, if any, between that and what happens in schools? And so on for other institutional domains and the relations among them. If these institutional domains are to be something other than metaphorical images, then scientifically we have to be able to say more precisely what they are and how they operate. The idea of system addresses this issue.

As concerns the preference for the Luhmannian over the Parsonian version of this concept, the reasons are partly what I have already discussed, namely that the four-function model of Parsons is too based on regional social units such as the modern nation-state. This situation does not correspond to global society. Another important reason is that the Parsonian A–G–I–L scheme tries to be too encompassing: all of social reality has to fit into one of these systems or into a subsystem of one of these systems. This is especially the case for the Integration (I) and Latent

Pattern Maintenance (L) systems. The result is that too much has to be forced into these categories and therefore they only make sense at a quite high level of abstraction. The result is again a theory that does not mesh well enough with observable empirical and global social realities.

A Luhmannian notion of social systems adopts a rather different strategy. Here the core operative question is not how social order is possible, how the social 'parts' together form a social 'whole', but rather how sociality reproduces itself, how communication constitutes itself and perpetuates itself. This is another way of asking what assures the success of communication, its establishment as the basis for further communication. In many social situations, and prevailingly in past societies exhibiting one of the other forms of dominant societal differentiation, that success is assured through the perceived reliability of the persons communicating, for instance through belonging to the same village, clan or stratum. It is a matter of the communicative competence of the person who is the source of the communication. Functional systems operate in a similar manner, except that they de-personalize the question of source, translating it more completely into one of the form that the communication takes as opposed to the ascribed form of the person communicating.

Paradigmatic illustrations of the difference can be taken from the economic and political systems. We recognize ownership of an item through purchase, not through the status of the person claiming ownership. If I have enough money, I can buy the item; who I am aside from my role as consumer is not that important. Also, government decisions are binding because the office taking them followed the correct political procedure, not because of the persons occupying government positions. In fact, we can and often do perceive the persons as buffoons or as morally questionable. That may undermine their ability to continue holding office, but not the legitimacy of the office itself (Weber 1978).

As differentiated ways of structuring communication, function systems from a Luhmannian perspective are therefore not ways of simply dividing all the communication that occurs in society into so many parts, the sum of which comprises the whole. Taken together, the function systems do not include all the communication that occurs in society, even though they may have an effect on all such communication. Instead they constitute specific ways of assuring the success of communication in situations where this might otherwise be unlikely. They are differentiated, but differentiated 'out of' the larger society as communicative complexes organized around specific ways of translating what happens in the wider social world. They are less analogous to groups of people than they are to languages, systematized ways of speaking which are not the entire world but can give expression to the entire world.

Luhmann's most typical way of discussing the core structures of these function systems, and one that I adopt here, is to speak in terms of central, binary codes and the attendant and complex programmes which put those codes into operation. Through the codes and programmes, the communicative elements of these systems are generated with reference to one another. The system constitutes itself through its own reflexivity. The binary code is in a key sense what the system is about, its central and unifying point of reference which allows it to distinguish itself from its social environment and therefore from other systems. The two poles of the code are not, however, the same as the distinction between the system and its environment. Instead they consist of a positive pole, which names the system's central concern, and a negative pole which is simply the other side of the positive pole. Thus, to take three examples, economy operates around the binary distinction between owning (Marx's private property) and not-owning; law centres on the difference between legal and illegal; and science functions in terms of true and false. Given that each of these distinctions could be understood in diverse ways, the programmes operationalize the codes to constitute the system; in a real sense they determine what the system is. Accordingly, when speaking of these systems, it is of critical importance to qualify them, for instance, not simply as economy, but as capitalist economy, positive law, empirical science, academic education, medicalized health, and so forth. The qualifier refers in each case to the programmatic aspect. For much the same reason, even outside the Luhmannian framework, it is common to refer to 'modern' versions of all these domains, including, of course, modern religion.

The codes and the programmes thus lend the systems their characteristic identities; but like all social systems, the actual elements of these systems are communications. The codes and programmes compose those elements into a system; they are the instructions of the system somewhat analogous to the way DNA provides the programmes of cells and, through them, bodies. As communications, however, these elements also help constitute the larger society, can be woven into other social systems, and therefore can 'belong' to more than one social system. Accordingly, it would be misleading to try to understand the boundaries of these systems (or any social system for that matter) by distinguishing strictly between elements that are part of the system and those that are not. Instead the system establishes its boundaries through the operation of its code and programmes; it is the meaningful reach of this operating that bounds the system. Indeed, the question of what are the boundaries of a system is something with which the programmes concern themselves, not something somehow naturally given with the inherent characteristics of the elements. That also includes questions of the boundaries of other systems. Thus, to take but one example, as I shall argue in the next chapter, rituals are quite central elements of the religious system. Yet what makes a ritual a *religious* ritual is its role in the religious programme to which it gives expression, not something inherent in the nature of rituals. The upshot of this consideration is that, in terms of boundaries, these systems do not occupy social space; they are not so many pieces of a social pie. Rather, again like languages, they operate within a wider social arena, and their extent is coterminous with the range of their influence, which can be strong and determinative all the way to weak and indirect. This aspect is very important for understanding how a religious system might constitute itself in global society.

A further general characteristic of these function systems, which they also share with any social system, is the possibility of 'internal' differentiation. The reasons for such differentiation are the same as for society as a whole: to make the reflexivity of communication more manageable, so that not everything will be relevant in all circumstances. The types of system that come into consideration are also the same as for the larger society, namely interactions, organizations, social movements and societal systems; and within the latter the different forms of differentiation, namely segmentary, core/periphery, stratified and functional. Thus, to flag some examples, the capitalist economy relies heavily on organizations like business firms and stock exchanges; it still carries significant stratified differentiation in the form of classes (owners/managers vs employees/workers). Schooling still depends significantly on interactions among teachers and students. States often have clear functional differentiation between legislative, executive and judicial functions, between government and civil service. Science structures itself functionally along the lines of academic disciplines. And both the global political system and the global religious system avail themselves of segmentary differentiation between, respectively, states and religions. As this last example indicates, the question of internal differentiation of function systems is particularly salient when one considers the religious system.

The further outlining of the abstract characteristics of function systems can give way to a brief look at several of the concrete and historically developed such systems. My purpose in presenting these is not to be exhaustive.[5] Although not offering a good description of any of them, the exercise will provide important background for the discussion of the global religious system in the next chapter. A central part of the argument is, after all, that religion in today's global society informs one of the function systems among others; that this 'one *among* others' constitutes much of the discontinuity between religion of today and religion (however conceived) of the past and in other societies.

In light of the dominance of economistic understandings of globalization, I begin with the global capitalist system. As noted, its defining binary code centres on the question of ownership. Its programme translates the world into the terms of owning or not-owning. The core elements of the system, buying/selling, communicate the generation or transfer of ownership. That is fundamental economic information. For this purpose, it must look upon everything in the world as something that can be owned: it commodifies. Things become commodities by being subject to ownership and this status is conferred by exchange on the basis of prices: a commodity has to have a price so that it can be subject to ownership. The price of a commodity is again the result of economic operations, namely whatever the 'market' will bear. Market is not a subsystem of the economic system so much as the economic system's term for its own environment. It is a notion that reflects the self-reference of that system: it sees everything in its own peculiar terms. To be recognized economically, everything has to have economic value, even its own symbols, especially money. Money also has a price and can be owned even though it is the power medium through which core economic communication takes place. For the system to persist, this economic communication must persist, which means that the entire system is geared towards perpetuation and increase of this sort of communication. The creation of capital is this perpetuation and increase. Capital is merely the net surplus communicative potential which, if it is not to disappear, has to be incorporated in more economic communication, which is to say invested. Money or capital not spent or invested loses its economic value. Once created it must be spent; in spending more is created. And so on and so on.

Like all the function systems, the economic one relies heavily on organizations to carry out its various supporting operations, especially production, which is to say the generation and selling of commodities. Principal among these are business firms of various types, from the 'mom-and-pop' store and the street vendor to the transnational corporation. Organizations are also very important in various economic control functions, especially banks, international financial organizations, stock markets, and the like. But be it noted that these organizations are for the most part just specialized sorts of producers, pointing again to the reflexivity of the system. The question of internal differentiation beyond organizations is more ambiguous. From one perspective, the economic system avails itself of stratified internal differentiation, especially in the form of classes. If we follow Wallerstein, the global economic system is also differentiated along core/periphery lines.

In the global political system, we find analogous features but also rather different ways of constructing a function system. Perhaps the most notable feature of this system is its internal differentiation. Using the artifice of territory, the global political system clearly divides itself segmentarily into a limited set of sovereign (i.e. politically legitimate) states which together formally cover the entire globe. The singularity of the system expresses itself in part through the fact that the boundaries between these states are precise and frequently 'arbitrary', which is to say justified primarily in political terms. On the basis of this segmented differentiation, the political system operates somewhat variably within each of these formally equal states. Here the operative code centres on government, being in power or out of it, being in government or in opposition. Both poles of the binary code are politically defined, naming political status and not something outside the political system. The name of the game, as it were, is getting, using, and keeping political power, the political equivalent of money and capital in the economic system. The programmes of the political subsystems that are the states vary, but are also consistent in many ways. Even 'revolutionary', anti-global states have political structures quite similar to those that are not, whether in the form of bureaucracies, political parties (even if there is only one), elections (even if for show), armed forces, diplomatic corps, and quite a number of others. Their goals are also similar, namely governing and overseeing their populations, usually regarded as a collectivity like a nation whose interests and 'common good' they further and protect (see Meyer *et al.* 1997). But the way that these goals are pursued is always in the light of getting and maintaining, preferably increasing, political power. States that are weak are precisely those which, for whatever reasons, cannot or do not exhibit the common features and pursue the common goals. The relations among states also follow patterns and are themselves increasingly formalized and bureaucratized, which is to say subject to the same political structuring that typically exists within states. The core elements or most typical communications of the political system are political decisions, including but not restricted to voting. These are treated as collectively binding in and only in the territory of the particular state. It is these decisions or regulations, whether in the form of elections, legislation, executive orders or policy directives, that reproduce the system. In as much as the complex arrangements of the economic system that produce and sell commodities are all geared towards exchange transactions on the basis of monetary price, so do the analogous structures of the political states serve to make possible these regulations, including regulations about regulations. The decisions generate more decisions; there is always something to legislate about, to decide about, to regulate. An effective government is one that communicates a lot of effective decisions. If it does not, other political decisions (e.g. elections and, at a limit, coups d'état) may oust that government. Thus, if left to its own devices, the political system also tends towards the constant increase of its most typical communication. Governments are designed to regulate everything. Beside the commodification of everything, we also witness what seems like the regulation of everything. Thus are these systems intrusive; it is a key aspect of their global spread.

The global science system further illustrates these various features, in particular the way that these function systems translate the world into their own highly specialized, highly technicized and therefore also rather peculiar forms. The operative binary code here is true/false, but what counts as true and false in the science system is not determined by more overarching criteria beyond scientific endeavour, but only by the programmatic requirements of the science system itself. Scientific method, itself the subject of research and theory, refers to the way that scientific communication distinguishes between true and false statements. All such statements, which is to say data, in the final analysis have to be judged in terms of whether or not they conform to that method. The positivist dictum that all statements have to be falsifiable is simply a way of saying that they should be susceptible of being translated into the scientific programme, that one should be able to apply the methods to them. If that is not possible, they cannot become the stuff of scientific communication. It is not that they are false, it is rather that science cannot say whether they are true or false. A paradigmatic example is the statement that God exists. Since no empirical method exists or has been devised which can test – apply the method to – this idea one way or another, it is simply irrelevant to the scientific system.

As in the other systems, organizations play a key role in the science system, especially research institutes, universities, research laboratories, learned societies and other associations. Much as economic production tends to occur in economically specialized organizations, and political regulations tend to flow from state organizations, so does scientific research flow from these scientifically specialized organizations. Moreover, as already mentioned, the science system uses functional internal differentiation, dividing its communication especially according to discipline. So strong is this particular subsystemic form that even social movements within science that try to be cross-disciplinary (e.g. religious studies), multi-disciplinary (e.g. communication) or anti-disciplinary (e.g. cultural studies) end up taking on the character of disciplines. No nefarious plotting need be hypothesized; there is simply too much scientific communication being produced for it not to be divided. The 'renaissance man' is scarcely possible any more; scientific experts are all – usually quite narrow – specialists.

One could do similar analysis for other systems. There is the legal system, which operates on the basis of the binary code legal/illegal. Its characteristic communications are legal judgements. It operates in terms of cases brought to it about which it makes a judgement in terms of whether what the plaintiffs and defendants have done is legal or illegal. The reflexivity of the system consists in that only this question is at issue, not, for instance, whether something is good or bad. It completes this self-reference by applying legal judgements to the law itself. Beside the segmentary differentiation according to states, the system further divides itself functionally, for instance in distinguishing courts and police. The latter function to 'enforce the law', which is to say, help generate cases for the courts. There is the academic education system, which is not as heavily 'nationalized' as legal subsystems but still usually tied to the operation of individual states. Here again, the reflexivity of the system is evident. The educated/uneducated code of the education system translates the idea of being educated into the programmatic criterion of being schooled or credentialled. What the school system is about is highly interconnected programmes of instruction, evaluation and diplomas, not some less technical, more general idea of education. What we learn in life does not count as educated within the terms of this system; receiving instruction and earning the right credentials does. Correspondingly, the health system technicizes its code of ill/healthy (one notes which of these is the 'positive' pole) through programmatic elaborations of disease (diagnosis) and treatment. The former consist of signs and symptoms which cluster together to constitute medical conditions or diseases for which treatments must then be devised and applied. In as much as instruction and grading are the core elements or communication of the academic education system, so are diagnosis and treatment the core elemental communications of the medicalized health system. Outside these terms, there is nothing medical to be done. Health is the absence of disease; death marks the boundary beyond which illness and health are irrelevant.

Other function systems include that for mass media, which is centred on the communication of information or 'news'; sport, whose programmes and subsystems (individual sports) cluster around the binary code of victory/loss (often translated into quantifiable measures); and art (and entertainment), focusing on elemental performances valued according to whether they are good or poor. Each one of these represents another technicized or programmed and recursive system of specialized communication. By now they are all globalized, although in varying degrees of penetration, varying levels of intensity. They are by no means all that there is to globalization, as I discuss in the next section. But they are by and large the main means through which power and influence in global society are generated and apportioned. Not to participate in or benefit from the typical communications of these systems is tantamount to being excluded and marginalized in global society. And, to be sure, large numbers of people and significant regions of the world's surface are thus excluded and marginalized.

Types of social system: interaction, organization and social movement

The brief discussion of the function systems raises many connected questions. One of the more important of these concerns what sort of communication falls outside these systems or at least is only indirectly or marginally included in them. Even a cursory glance at any of our social worlds reveals a fair amount of this. Myriad conversations and day-to-day interactions, letters, telephone calls, e-mail and other forms of understood informing often have little to do with buying, worshipping, performing, learning, recovering, knowing, judging, informing or regulating in such a way as to reproduce these systems. To be sure, it may be difficult to think of social operations that have nothing whatsoever to do with them, except of course among the excluded and marginalized of our world. But if we keep in mind that each of these systems consists substantially of certain recognizable types of core communication, then it becomes apparent that a not insignificant portion of social performances are only tangentially involved. Obvious examples are conversations about the weather, about the flowers and birds I saw on my walk through the park, or the letter from Cousin George telling me about the antics of his dog. The systems are there in the background: I might decide to take a course on meteorology, buy a book to identify those birds and flowers; and Cousin George may be concerned about animal-control by-laws or visit the veterinarian to have his dog repaired. Yet taken by themselves, these illustrative communications do not reproduce the systems; subsequent, previous or other communications might. Moreover, much of what people do is not as such communication. Planting tomatoes in my garden or sitting in my room and thinking are not by themselves communication, although they could become themes or otherwise be incorporated in communication.

Beside communication outside the function systems is another, already adumbrated question, namely that of other types of social system. The just-mentioned interactions are prime examples, as are organizations and social movements. I shall not dwell on the first of these in the present context except to point out that interactions are a type of social system beside the others and not somehow the building blocks of social life more generally. Much social process takes place within interactions. Yet a great deal takes place outside such contexts. Whether we are speaking of direct face-to-face interactions or mediated ones like those that take place over telephones and other electronic devices, these simply do not encompass more than an important portion of communications in contemporary society. To take some examples, scientific communication occurs largely through publications in various forms and not just in formal and informal conversations among scientists; economic transactions occur as often by machine as 'over the counter'; most artists communicate their art without direct interaction with their audience; governments now as in the past communicate with their subjects more often in mediated fashion than face to face; and the pious recitation of sacred text along with much religious ritual takes place away from other people. Non-oral media of communication, especially writing and electronic means, of course play a key role in these possibilities. Thus the difference among types of social system is not merely one of scale, for instance from micro to macro.

If interactions have been a rather universal form of social system in all societies, the same cannot be said for organizations. Although these are by no means unique to modern or global society, their importance, number and differentiation as distinct social systems has increased enormously. The reasons for this proliferation and greater prominence are fairly clear. Following Luhmann's conception of organizations, these are a type of social system that constitutes itself by distinguishing between members and non-members. The rules, and thus roles, that distinguish between the two establish a relatively clear social boundary by which one can identify what communication is part of the system. The expectations for members are different than those for non-members, thereby lending a clear structure to the communication of the system. Like other types of system, organizations allow different rules to prevail for specific purposes without having to claim the entire person, although totalizing organizations, like totalizing societal systems (e.g. strata, kinship groups) are possible and exist. Yet unlike interactions which are too restricted in their range and complexity, and unlike function systems which structure themselves each in unique ways, organizations can be wide ranging, very complex, and be adapted to a virtually infinite variety of purposes. Within organizations, one can do very different things and do things very differently, and this expressly in the context of the same society. They can, therefore, serve to institutionalize important boundaries, but also to cross-cut others.

In the context of modern and contemporary global society, organizations have an essential role in virtually every one of the dominant function systems. Ranging from business firms and hospitals to sports clubs and state bureaucracies, organizations are instrumental in the way that function systems structure themselves and carry out their typical and programmatic communication. Modern function systems would be pretty well impossible without them. If interactions are essential to all types of social system, organizations are essential to two very prevalent modern and global types, function systems and, as I discuss shortly, social movements. Again, these other types are not simply 'macro' versions of organizations: the latter help reproduce these systems; but there is much communication that reproduces these systems that is not or not just organizational communication, governed by the rules of membership in them. If most economic production is organized, much consumption is not; and therefore the core communication of the economic system, purchase or ownership transfer more often than not involves both organizational and non-organizational communication. In some function systems such as the education system, the complementary or 'consumer' roles are also for the most part organizational roles; and in such systems core communication, for instance classroom instruction or the examination, is more completely organizational communication. In other systems such as the art/entertainment system and, as we shall see, the religious system, even the primary/professional or 'producer' roles are frequently not organizational roles; and in these systems less of their core communication, for example artistic performance or religious ritual, is organizational. In all cases, however, organizational communication plays a central part in lending the system definition, in concretizing and identifying it.

The significance of organizations in global society is not limited to their role in the function systems. Just because they permit heterogeneous concentrations of communications in what from other respects is a homogenizing web, namely society, they can serve to focus social resources and social process so as not only to help to define the function systems, but also to subvert or otherwise cross their boundaries. Organizations as diverse as gardening clubs, international aid agencies and revolutionary cells can cut across other systemic boundaries, largely ignore these or seek to undermine them. To the degree that the function systems together can be regarded as the forces of homogenization in the historical process of globalization, organizations present a prime systemic resource for counteracting that homogenization, for expressing different orientations than the function systems represent and even opposing these. It is because of this potential for 'subverting' dominant lines of societal subsystem differentiation that organizations have tended to be problematic in other types of society; that the carriers of dominant power have sought to co-opt or destroy such forms. Today in modern and global society they are often controversial and oppositional as well. Yet they also proliferate, perhaps mostly as expressions of the dominant function systems; but also significantly as the crystallization of different purposes or simply as ways of expressing difference. I return to this issue of 'doing' difference shortly.

In comparison with organizations, a fourth type of social system, the social movement, is both similar and different from societal function systems and organizations. Like the function systems, social movements are much more structured around the particular issues and particular elements that inform them and far less on the basis of a distinction between members and non-members (Ahlemeyer 1995). Moreover, organizations are also instrumental in lending social movements form, just as they are for function systems. Yet like organizations and unlike function systems, social movements are adaptable to almost any purpose, are relatively easily generated, and can come and go individually without the society being changed in any fundamental way. While social movement organizations do in large measure express and stand for particular social movements – for instance, Greenpeace for the environmental movement – the most basic element of a social movement, what constitutes its recursiveness, is the particular communicative event that displays the movement's 'mobilization' (cf. Klandermans *et al.* 1988; Zald and McCarthy 1987). The current anti-globalization movement, for example, amorphous and complex as it is in many respects, produces and reproduces itself in protest communications like demonstrations, marches, protests and a great deal of Internet communication. These communications are not always or even usually organizational communication, and there may be a great deal of controversy as to which of these is actually 'of the movement'. Amorphousness, rather than casting the specificity of such movements into doubt, is one of their more important characteristics. They exist through mobilizing communication of this sort and cease to exist as movements when this no longer happens. In an important sense, social movements are the socio-structural equivalent of Weber's charismatic authority, inherently evanescent and subject to routinization. Social movements can arise quickly and disappear quickly. Their constitutive concerns can also be transposed almost entirely into the communication of other forms. Feminist and ecological agendas can become the stuff of political regulation, educational curricula, legal judgements and economic production. In one sense, such transposition marks the 'success' of social movements; in another it signals their decline or the need to find new issues around which to mobilize. 'Cooptation' for social movements, especially those centred on protest, points to this ambiguity of success.

Social movements do not have to be movements of protest, but they often are. As Alberto Melucci (Melucci 1985) has pointed out, social movements centre on issues, on themes of communication, that do not appear to be dealt with elsewhere. They crystallize matters that other systems do not and even cannot address because of the way these other systems are structured. Thus social movements frequently have first to make their issues real issues. They have to mobilize so that what they address will come to be thematized as a problem requiring a solution, primarily within the social movement, but also critically in other social systems, notably in contemporary society in the dominant function systems. Correspondingly, social movements can and do occur in the context of these function systems and as an aspect of their functioning, not just as voices crying in the wilderness outside them. Social movements, like organizations and interactions, can arise as a way for the function systems to function. Educational movements like that for 'student-centred learning' in the 1960s and 1970s or 'back to basics' in the 1980s and 1990s do not just challenge the educational system; they also reproduce it. Similarly, political reform movements do not have to be 'extra-parliamentary'. They can be as internal to the political system as the rise of a reform movement that seeks to become a political party, or a movement to replace a particular political leader with another. Social movement communication, namely mobilization communication, can also be core function system communication, just as organizational and interactional communication can fill this double role.

Difference and inclusion in global society

As I noted in the above discussion of common narratives of modernization, the tale is often told in terms of certain key ideas or values, above all enlightenment, progress, equality, freedom and solidarity. These are common to all the sub-narratives, and this irrespective of whether the version we are considering is critical or laudatory, whether, for instance, we call them 'bourgeois rights' or 'self-evident truths'. In the Luhmannian frame that I am using here, these refer to an overall and multi-dimensional increase in communicative power – for instance, knowledge, wealth, legal rights, surveillance and health – and the expectation that at least in moderately equitable fashion all people should have access to it. This latter, both in Parsonian and Luhmannian terms, points to the question of inclusion. Somewhat paradoxically, a key dimension of modernization and now globalization has been the assertion of the 'rights' of individuals to inclusion in consonance with the increasing power of distinctly 'impersonal' societal systems. Inclusion in this society amounts to access to the power of these systems, but the systems do not operate in terms of people 'belonging'. In fact, the systems operate and must operate asymmetrically as concerns the distribution of their power. Famously, capitalism depends on inequalities of wealth. Government is the concentration of political decision-making power. Educational credentials reflect differential ability and success. Art must be exceptional. Access to health care, even ideally, depends to a large degree on being ill. And so forth. One important result of this structural feature is that the question of the status or place of persons in this society is of great importance – as reflected in the high degree of individuation the systems generate – but can only partially be answered in terms of incorporation in the dominant systems. Access to their power is part of the answer; those without such access are rather radically excluded. Yet access by itself does not settle the issue because individuation and its valorization dictate a further value-added quality, something about this profiled individual that expresses the individuation, the 'other than' systemic roles. It is in this slot that the highly contested, perpetual and exceedingly varied question of *identity* finds its fertile ground. Because, however, it serves to distinguish the person from systemic roles, that identity must express itself as difference. We come thus to that dialogic aspect of globalization that so many theories emphasize, what here I shall call the Robertsonian dimension of global society.

Robertson's model of globalization, as noted above, places emphasis on two interrelated dimensions. There is the particularization of universalism in conjunction with the universalization of particularism; there is also the emphasis on the relations between or the mutual relativization of four fields, namely the individual, the national society, the system of national societies, and humanity (Robertson and Chirico 1985). The question just posed, that of difference and identity, is clearly central to his entire theory. Although the only function system more or less explicitly contained in this model is the state under the heading of national society, combining Robertson's theory with the Luhmannian frame I am mostly using is relatively unproblematic and has the important advantage of adding valuable conceptual resources for a better understanding of how identity and difference play themselves out in global society. More specifically, Robertson's perspective focuses more clearly than does Luhmann on the fact that the question of identity as inclusion manifests itself both individually and collectively. For Robertson, identity and particularization involve both individuals and groups; and therefore difference is also an individual and group affair. Amalgamating the Robertsonian and Luhmannian points of departure, however, requires that one find the theoretical place where identity questions and the function systems mesh. For this purpose, one can look at semantic and socio-structural manifestations of the problem of inclusion in the form, respectively, of the evolution of human rights discourse and the question of regional appropriation of the function systems or, what amounts to the same and adopting a Wallersteinian formulation, regional incorporation into the world system.

Following the perceptive analysis of James Spickard (2002), human rights discourse over the past century has evolved three related subvariants or generations. Together they offer a good representative look at how the questions of identity/difference, function system access and inclusion have manifested themselves in the semantics of contemporary global society. The first generation rights are those that define the difference or freedom of the individual vis-à-vis society more broadly, and societal systems in particular. These include the so-called 'bourgeois rights' like freedom of speech, of religion, of thought, or from discrimination on the basis of ascribed differences like gender or race. These all define the relation of the individual to (national) society and provide the bases for the independence of individual identities from societal systems. Of note is the naming and therefore recognition of criteria that are critical for identities, but deemed beyond the concern of societal systems. Access to the latter, these rights state, should not be affected by these criteria. If systems use these criteria to determine access to them, that is illegitimate discrimination. First generation rights do not, however, thereby speak directly to the question of the inclusion of individuals in the power of those systems. Second generation rights do. These 'socialist rights' seek to guarantee each individual a certain minimum of access to the power of the function systems. They speak above all of the right to economic resources, the right to education, and the right to health care. Human rights are violated, in other words, if people are excluded from systemic power. The third and most recent generation of rights moves the concerns of the first and second generation to the level of collectivities. These are group cultural rights, not only the right to self-determination, but also the right of cultures or collective identities to the same protection from discrimination and exclusion as the individuals that supposedly carry them. Thus, for example, Aboriginal peoples, tribal peoples and national minorities around the world have the right to preserve their cultures and ways of life, to determine and maintain their identities, without thereby being excluded from systemic access. These collective differences or exclusivities are to have the same value and status as individual ones.

Embedded within the three generations of human rights discourse is of course a fair amount of tension, which is to say different ways of interpreting what human rights imply and which of the many potentially contradictory rights should take precedence. Neo-liberals may claim that the first generation rights by themselves will lead to the other two. Socialists may insist on the priority and defining character of the second generation. Representatives of various cultural minorities and regionally dominant cultures may insist that the first two generations are meaningless without the third, and that insisting on the priority of the first or the second amounts to cultural imperialism and therefore a violation of human rights. Without in the least trying to resolve these questions, they point directly to both the ambiguity of inclusion in contemporary global society and the constitutive tension between particular and universal in that society. In Luhmannian terms, the dominance of the function systems does not mean that globalization amounts to the universal homogenization of society across the globe according to the criteria of these systems, only that these systems condition the ways that people do difference in that society. This brings us to the structural illustration of the same circumstance, namely to the question of the regional and particular appropriation of universalizing social systems, especially the function systems.

Given that in critical respects the dominant function systems began their current development in European society of the early modern period, a question that poses itself with respect to them is whether their spread is in fact not tantamount to the Europeanization or Westernization of the rest of the world. A dialogical perspective on globalization such as I am representing here insists that it is at best misleading to imagine the process in this way; that the inadequacy of the concept of modernization for understanding the emergence of global society lies precisely in its tendency to conflate that development with what has happened in so-called Western societies. Rather than a simple diffusion of structural forms from one part of the world to the rest, globalization refers to the analogous transformation of society in Western and other regions of the world. More specifically, the function systems did not develop first in the West and then spread elsewhere. Their global spread is an integral part of their development; and this not just as Western imperialism, colonialism or imposition, although that also is an important part of the picture. Looking at globalization not simply as the spread of the function systems but also as their development permits a shift in perspective, from globalization as only the universalization of particular social forms to include now also the reverse, namely the particularization of this universalizing. This latter aspect is just as constitutive of globalization as the former. That, in turn, means that incorporation into the global system takes place through both modalities, not just the first. Globalization carries itself out in the 'dialogue', not just as a 'soliloquy'. Pursuing this metaphor, we can say that globalization occurs in terms of multiple voices, different voices, and not just univocally. Inclusion of regions therefore means the appropriation by those regions of the instrumentalities of the global function systems while at the same time doing so in a locally particular way. That localization or particularization is a critical aspect of the universalization or globalization, not just a reaction to it. Thus, for example, as Wallerstein has amply demonstrated, the global economy develops as it incorporates more regions and that incorporation is critical to what it becomes, to its functioning. The global political system emerges with the emergence of states, not simply by the spread of states or the establishment of relations among pre-existing local states. And, as I show in the next chapter, the development of the global religious system is identical with the emergence, construction and imagination of a plurality of mutually identifying religions, not as the mere imposition of a supposedly 'Christian' model on the rest of the world. Imperialism or universalization is in all cases part of the picture; but in no case is it more than a part.

Globalization and means of communication

My theoretical framework for understanding globalization and the development of contemporary global society puts great emphasis on the function systems, their differentiation, their increasingly pervasive operation and thereby their spread to virtually all regions of the physical globe. Function systems do not by themselves account for globalization, they do not simply explain it; but without them, the extent and density of the current global system would not have occurred. In thus stressing these systems of communication, however, it may seem that a rather obvious aspect of this range and intensity is being ignored, namely the actual means by which we communicate in such expanded capacity. Trains, planes, ships and automobiles; books, newspapers, magazines and letters; radio, television, telephone and the Internet are clearly some of the more obvious and visible signs of a globalized social world. They are the means of transmission, the grid that allows events in one part of the world to become immediately known and relevant in others. They are not the communication, but without them global communication would be far more difficult. Their relation to function and other social systems, and to dialogic processes of the global and the local have to be clarified.

In earlier sections of this chapter, I stressed the dynamism, the 'restlessness' of the function systems, their tendency to orient their operations towards the increase of their particular instrumentalities and type of communication. One important outcome of this dominant orientation is ever more enhanced and powerful means of communication to carry this specialized communication. Of course, once developed, these enhanced means are available for non-specialized communication of all sorts, for building social networks, for driving social movements, for long-distance interaction. It is the operation of the specialized function systems, however, that leads to this development. Scientific research yields new technologies; capitalist enterprise produces them and uses them to enhance production/ consumption; governments regulate and ordain their development under such headings as 'infrastructure'; mass media, health, sport, education and religious systems take significant advantage of them. This synergy among the function systems is a key condition for their arising. In earlier days, ships, writing and especially printing were of the greatest significance. Soldiers, administrators, adventurers, merchants, explorers and mission-aries transported themselves and what they had to say via these means. Between roughly the fourteenth and twentieth centuries, but especially beginning in the nineteenth century, the type and sophistication of these means began to increase rapidly. Not only did ships become larger, more numerous and more powerful, print technologies became more efficient, land transport received its first great boost in centuries in the form of the railway, and electronic media in the sequentially developed forms of tele-graph, telephone and radio accomplished an unprecedented compression of communicative time and space wherever they penetrated. In the latter part of the twentieth century that acceleration continued, yielding air travel, television, satellite and computer communication that at times increases its communicative carrying capacity more rapidly than the communication available to it.

Although to a certain extent the form of these technological means of communication has an effect on the actual communication that they help enable – the medium is to some degree the message – for the most part they are neutral: they have the potential to carry an infinite variety of communication, whether that of the function systems, organizations, social movements or interactions. That relative neutrality along with the ever increasing capacity encourages increased communication as elements of all these systems. It provides conditions for the function systems to become ever more powerful, for social movements to emerge and expand, for orga-nizations to complexify and multiply, for social networks of all kinds to proliferate. The reverse side of this obverse face, however, is a greater possibility for the selectivity of communication, for the construction of particular, different and hence selective ways of communicating, albeit always conditioned by the formidable power of especially the major func-tion systems. The high development of means of communication makes it easier, and not harder, to be selective about that communication, for instance to construct and reinforce worldviews that are perhaps different from the majority or dominant ones. As the attacks of 11 September 2001 graphically illustrated, your neighbour may live in a different communicative universe than you do: the perpetrators of these atrocities did not have to come from anywhere; the means of communication allowed them to be here already, whether physically they happened to be in the United States or halfway around the world. The Internet, air travel and cellular satellite telephones do not just favour the operations of transnational corporations and state surveillance. They also allow the anti-systemic, the alternative, the oppositional and the local a greater communicative space. Another way of putting this result is to say that enhanced means of communication sharpen the capacity for particularization *and* for universalization. Social forms can be differently appropriated; different social forms have better possibilities for wider and global distribution. Not just the unavoidably visible, the powerful and the dominant forms are thereby encouraged, so are the relatively invisible, seemingly insignificant and otherwise marginal ones. This face of global means of communication is of the first importance for understanding what has been happening in the domain of religion, perhaps the one function system (art is another possibility) that proliferates even when the power centres of the world are paying little attention.

The question of the effect and role of means of communication has many facets. One of the most important for the subject of religion is that of the physical migration of people, especially transnational migration. If we consider migration, as opposed to, for instance, travel and tourism, to be the relatively permanent transfer of people from one place to another, then its most significant effect in the present context is that it undermines the ability of place or space to act as a 'natural symbol' (Douglas 1970) for social difference. People, considered now as loci of communication, carry their communicative orientations and habits, their particularity, with them, but to a different social context. Migration is thereby a way of universalizing various particulars, but also of particularizing universals as migrants generate adaptations of what they carry with them, transfer these adaptations back to the place of origin and elsewhere, and thus contribute to the transformation or at least pluralization of the original form. In many cases, the migratory situation also generates new forms. In addition, the effect of such migration on social forms in the 'receiving' country or region should not be underestimated. Thus, to take an example, South Asian migrants to Canada are, among other things, carriers of certain religious forms which they may or may not identify as Hinduism. Their new situation in Canada, however, encourages precisely such an imagining of 'their religion' as Hinduism and adaptation of that form so that it becomes not simply a transplanted copy of what prevailed in India, but a different sort of Hinduism which they can then perhaps carry back to India or elsewhere as an authentic version of that religion. Moreover, the religions of Canada, by now having these authentic forms of Hinduism as a more regular part of their immediate social environment, themselves may be under pressure to transform.

I have taken a religious example as illustration because that is the main subject of this book, but the importance of migration is not limited to this system. Migration, as a consequence of the operation of systems and the proliferation of means of global communication, has similar effects in other domains. It helps to pluralize and universalize particularities, particularize universals in different ways, and generate new and different universals. In general, like so much else in global society, it complexifies localization and globalization at the same time.

Summary and conclusion

The purpose of this chapter has been to set the stage for the succeeding analyses in two principal ways. First, it has presented a discussion of globalization, as concept (neologism), as theory and as narration. The sections dealing with these matters provide background and context for considering the subject of religion in globalization. For, to repeat what I wrote in the introduction, this book is not about religion as such, whatever that may mean. It is about religion as a concept and as a social reality in specifically modern and now global society. And for that to make sense, we must first have a clear notion of what we mean by globalization and global society. Accordingly, and given the multiplicity of theoretical approaches to the idea, the different portions of the chapter outline several salient aspects of the theory of globalization and global society that inform the present work. This is an adapted Luhmannian approach which focuses on the critical form and importance of function systems in the emergence and structure of global society, and on communication as the constitutive element of any society. Religion, in the following chapters, is treated as such a communicative function system and the defence of that observation is the main point of the entire book. Yet the Luhmannian conceptualization is not by itself adequate to this purpose, and therefore concluding segments of the chapter added the dialogic component to the understanding of globalization and global society, a component that is far more Robertsonian, but also owes a fair deal to other theorists.

On the basis of this groundwork, I now move in the next chapter to a kind of repeat of this first chapter, but this time with an explicit focus on religion as an expression and constituent dimension of globalization. If the present chapter has been about globalization, the next is about globalization in a religious mode.

Notes

1 See Axford 1995, Bamyeh 1993, Spybey 1996 and Waters 1995 for examples of such summary presentations. Economistic and political models have already been mentioned above. Under cultural emphases, one might place the work of Featherstone (1995), Hannerz (1996) and Appadurai (1996).

2 See Parsons 1966, 1971. These volumes might be considered as hinge texts, beginning to bridge the passage from modernization to globalization. They should, in fact, form part of the early literature on globalization along with, for instance, Luhmann 1971, Moore 1966, Nettl and Robertson 1968.

3 See Ahlemeyer 1995, Luhmann 1997: 847ff. Whether these are a 'true' fourth type or only a variation on the last type need not detain us here.

4 This is exactly the sense of Weber's argument in *The Protestant Ethic and the Spirit of Capitalism*. See especially the discussion of Benjamin Franklin's 'philosophy of avarice' (Weber 1992 [1930]: 16ff.).

5 For exhaustive treatments, it is probably best to consult Luhmann's own extensive works, especially the series of volumes that appeared between 1988 and 2002 on the different function systems. See Luhmann 1989b, 1990, 1993, 1995, 2000a, 2000b, 2002.

Chapter 2

The religious system of global society

Differentiating religion

As noted in the introduction, controversy within the social sciences and religious studies as to what religion is and how it is to be observed are as old as the disciplines concerned with these questions. For various reasons neither substance nor approach has been the subject of any discernible agreement. My contention is that, in large measure, the background to this inconclusiveness has been the historical development of the peculiar function system for religion that is at issue here. A brief look at certain aspects of these controversies demonstrates this relation quite readily.

In 1962, Wilfred Cantwell Smith first published what John Hick has called 'a modern classic of religious studies' (Smith 1991: v). The book does not define religion. Rather, *The Meaning and End of Religion* argues against the scholarly use of the terms 'religion' and 'religions', claiming that the *reification* they imply makes them 'confusing, unnecessary, and distorting' (Smith 1991: 50). Smith is quite unequivocal: 'Neither religion in general nor any one of the religions . . . is in itself an intelligible entity, a valid object of inquiry or of concern either for the scholar or for the man of faith' (Smith 1991: 12). Somewhat less extreme, twenty years later, Jonathan Z. Smith, a religious studies scholar of comparable stature, expressed similar doubts, claiming that 'religion is solely the creation of the scholar's study' and 'has no independent existence apart from the academy' (Smith 1982: xi). During the 1990s, various scholars have added a further dimension to this style of critique. Writers such as Talal Asad (1993), Timothy Fitzgerald (1990, 1997), David Chidester (1996) and Russell McCutcheon (1997), to name only a few, also argue that the concept of religion is (recently) constructed and often distorting. Most of these observers, however, add that the ideas of religion and religions have ideological and political implications, that they have arisen and played important roles in the context of Western imperial expansion, serving as tools of colonial projection and control. The critiques target not only the colonial administrators, missionaries and elites who have supposedly availed themselves of these ideological devices, but also the scholars of religion, including anthropologists and historians of religion. The latter are deemed to have collaborated, wittingly or not, in an overall project of conceptual and symbolic imposition (see especially Chidester 1996: 141; Fitzgerald 1997: 108).

As noted, such critiques and debates within scientific disciplines concerned with religion are not new. Durkheim (1965: 37–117) defended his definition of religion against the misconceptions of others; and Weber refused to define religion (1978: 399). Ever since, the anthropology and sociology of religion, as well as religious studies, have been periodically blessed (or plagued) with ongoing discussions about definitions and conceptualizations of religion (see, as representative examples, Lawson and McCauley 1990; O'Toole 1984; Paden 1992; Penner 1989; Segal 1992). Where certain of the more recent authors go significantly further is in their contention that the concept of religion is too problematic to be of much use at all; that its meaning is essentially bound up with political ends; or that at the very least its salience is to be limited to that of an ideal type.

Upon close inspection, what becomes relatively clear from all these critiques is that the problem these scholars see is mostly with the assumption that religion is a differentiable and independent something – W.C. Smith's reification, McCutcheon speaks of religion *sui generis* – which is independent of the consciousnesses of its human carriers or of wider social structures and processes and can therefore be defined or studied in its own right. Without the claim to social differentiation, their critiques lose much of their force and indeed their target. One has to ask, however, whether the long-standing tendency among scholars and non-scholars alike to treat religion precisely as both differentiable and differentiated can really be attributed so simply to 'error' and ideological 'false consciousness' on the part of its perpetrators. In comparison, one does not hear, for instance, that the ideological dimensions of capitalism reduce that idea to a figment of the scholar's imagination. The critiques claim that religion *is* not a differentiated domain; but on closer inspection, they come much closer to saying that it *should* not be one, or simply that it is not everywhere and has not always been one. The analysis that I am presenting here offers a way through these controversies by accepting their cogency in one respect but denying it in another: differentiated religion is a relatively recent 'invention' and is thoroughly implicated in the historical developments that have brought about today's global society, 'warts and all'. Yet it is not by that token unreal, illusory or only an artefact of the scholar's analysis. Scientifically speaking, there is indeed 'data' for religion in this differentiated sense.[1] Problems arise only when one does not take sufficient account of the historicity and therefore the peculiarity of this construction, when one assumes an a-historical 'essence' for something that owes much of its visibility to these relatively recent socio-structural developments. In order to understand how these critiques are both well taken and insufficient, however, one needs conceptual tools that can distinguish explicitly between the wide variety of analytic meanings of religion which can be applied to a whole range of particular societies and historical periods, and religion as a socially consequential and differentiated domain which operates largely – but not entirely – independently of the scholar's observation. The idea of a modern function system serves this purpose, not only because it allows the observation of religion as such a historically differentiated social reality, but also because it permits one to include in the observation of this religion a variety of observers – each with their own 'agenda' – namely those that observe from the religious system itself (e.g. theologians), from the science system (e.g. social scientists, religious studies scholars), or from other systems like the political (e.g. colonial administrators), the educational (e.g. curriculum planners), the mass media (e.g. reporters) and the legal (e.g. judges).

Preliminary to the elaboration of this idea of a religious function system, I note that this system is not identical with differentiated religious communication as such. Societies that exhibit some form of differentiated religious activity have existed throughout history and around the world. What has been especially common is the separation of particular times, places, social roles and social activities that focus specifically on what today we call religion. Many are the social-scientific and other definitions of religion that take these widespread phenomena as their point of departure. One thinks particularly of Durkheim's use of the sacred/profane distinction in this regard. For Durkheim religion was whatever centred around 'sacred things – things set apart and forbidden' (Durkheim 1965: 62). The cogency of his definition lies in the fact that many societies feature a clear distinction between sacred and profane in their systems of communication. The problem with it is that it can easily be challenged by referring to other societies where that difference is anywhere from unclear to totally absent, but which nevertheless exhibit the sort of ritual and other performative practices that today we commonly associate with religion. The ambiguity can become clearer if we note that such debate centres on religion as a functional category, one that concerns a particular variety of human activity that exhibits certain forms and purposes. Religion refers to a particular sort of communication. It is that which functions to, for example, 'serve the gods', 'deal with ultimate questions' or 'invoke a sacred reality'. The principle of distinction is function. In social contexts where such functional distinctions are not primary, however, they can and do recede in importance and clarity in favour of other sorts of difference. Thus, taking examples from Mary Douglas' work (Douglas 1966, 1975), in ancient Israelite society the functional sacred/profane (or purity/pollution) distinction was very important because it was instrumental in expressing the more dominant difference between Israelites as a group and outsiders. In Pygmy society (see Douglas 1970: 33f.), by contrast, where such group differences are still important but drawn much more fluidly, the same functional difference is almost invisible. Because it does not serve to express and reinforce the primary sort of differentiation, the functional difference is far less evident. The situation in contemporary society is more similar to the Israelite example than the Pygmy one, but it is also very different because modern and now global society uses function as its *principal* mode of primary subsystem differentiation. To the extent that religion has become the subject of one such system, it attains a very high level of clarity precisely as religion. The sacred/profane distinction is now pressed into service to express the primary form of social differentiation and thus defines itself in those terms; and, as it happens, only secondarily in terms of group differences. Where before functional distinctions supported and were subordinated to segmentary, core/periphery, or stratified distinctions, now it is the reverse. The latter support the former.

As in the case of globalization in the last chapter, the focused and detailed presentation of this idea of a religious function system proceeds first historically, and then theoretically and empirically; historically because this is an argument for a social form that arose, somewhat 'accidentally', during a particular time in history, and is therefore not a general aspect of all or even most societies; theoretically and empirically because the observation of this function system requires an adjustment in the way scientific disciplines have hitherto thought about religion. It can no longer be a nomothetic and analytic concept alone; the way the category operates in non-scientific social reality always also has to be worked into the equation.

The historical differentiation of religion and religions

As with the general history of modernization and globalization, this story begins, again somewhat arbitrarily for the sake of having a starting point, in European society of the late Middle Ages. Socio-structurally, that society showed a clear dominance of stratified differentiation, especially between noble and common strata. Yet, at least with hindsight, we can see that it also had a number of antecedents for the eventual shift to a primacy of functional orientations. One of these was without doubt the rather preponderant role and position of the Roman Christian church.

In the context of the later Roman Empire, the Christian church had already from the early centuries CE developed a relatively high degree of organization, most notably in its episcopal structure and in its organized monasticism. These forms not only gave it a relatively differentiated profile, they also survived the fall of Rome in the fifth century, and became over the centuries the only overarching such structure in the western and central portions of Europe; no political empire emerged to successfully claim the same territory. In fact, by the twelfth century the church had become at least as influential and powerful as any contemporaneous, admittedly comparatively weak, political overlord. At its high point, this functionally differentiated and yet multi-functional institution could depose kings. It was a time when the church could initiate the mass mobilization of crusades, when state bureaucracies, such as existed, were largely staffed by clerics, and when the institutions and wealth of the church multiplied. The power and independence of the Roman church is in fact the basis of the idea that somehow the centuries of the high Middle Ages in Europe were an 'age of faith' (Durant 1935). It is unlikely that the amount of religious communication (or, what is the same, the 'religiosity' of the people) was greater than it has been in other times and places; but the overall social influence of organized clerics may well have been unprecedented.

Nonetheless, the church was not the same thing as a political empire. It did not primarily exercise that kind of power. In this regard, although Western Europe of that time was not at all unusual among non-modern societies in also exhibiting strong functionally oriented institutions, it was historically unique in that the institution of the church was not rivalled by an equally or more powerful political institution in the form of an effective imperial structure. The situation contrasts with other societies such as the more or less contemporary Muslim civilization of western Asia and northern Africa, or the Chinese empire of the Song, Yuan and Ming dynasties. In these the clerical castes had neither the institutional independence nor the power of the European churchmen. As it turns out, the independent and influential but not politically dominant church helped create a social context in which not only religious but also other functional subsystems could and did develop. This is a way of saying that, while far from the only important factor, this incipient medieval European religious system proved instrumental for the societal shift to a dominance of functional differentiation. In this regard one thinks particularly of the transmission of Greco-Roman intellectual and legal traditions in the monasteries, the cathedral schools, and then the universities (cf. Pirenne 1957; Southern 1970; Wolff 1968). These provided critical material with which embryonic scientific and legal systems could begin to form. The church during this time embarked on an unprecedented development of canon law which acted as a foil and model for the secular law of budding states (see Berman 1983; Southern 1995). A rivalry emerged between two functional institutions, one of which, the state, was at first much less developed and more consistently expressive of the dominant stratified structures. It was therefore not so much that the church acted as a midwife for these other systems to be born as it was a case of a functionally oriented institution seeking to maintain and enhance its position; and thereby providing conditions for weaker institutions to adopt *analogous but not contradictory* strategies (cf. Huff 2003).

A further contribution of the church was the promotion of individuated consciousnesses through an increasingly elaborate confessional procedure that itself was reflective of burgeoning ecclesiastical religious communication. Encouraging the awareness of sin raised the importance of the church's solution to the problem; but for that sin to be more purely the province of the church's interventions it had to be relatively disembedded from the interests of the stratified structures, and hence more individualized (cf. Délumeau 1983; Luhmann 1989a). The church was by no means independent of the dominant differentiation according to social strata; but its interests dictated that it be comparatively so, thus clearing the way for the further development of other, in this case functional, criteria. Indicative of this circumstance are the official promulgation of clerical celibacy in the eleventh century, thus distancing the church from the family structures that informed the dominant strata; and, on a rather different note, that the church and state represented 'two swords', both 'perfect' societies – possessing all that was needed to fulfil their respective functions – working in conjunction yet distinct from one another.

Further evidence of a changing situation in Europe is to be found in the outcome of the late medieval debate about the relation of faith and reason. From the perspective of clerical thinkers like Anselm and Thomas Aquinas, that relation was clear: faith and reason were different, but the first way of knowing was more certain, prior, and the foundation for the second. Thus did the church take priority over the world just as from a political perspective the popes should take precedence over kings. To that extent, the European debates were quite like parallel ones among Jewish and Muslim thinkers at roughly the same time and before. The difference in the European situation was in the later result: rather than a re-synthesis, as happened for instance in the Islamic world with figures such as al-Ghazali, among the Europeans faith and reason ended up going relatively separate ways, reason crystallizing and specializing eventually in modern science and faith becoming the special and purified property of a much more clearly differentiated religious system.

It is in terms of such purification or different construction of a specifically religious domain that we must see the Protestant Reformation and the subsequent Counter- or Catholic Reformation. These accomplished another critical step towards not the further independence of religious institutions, but rather a different kind of independence, one that was also characterized by a fundamental interdependence. Even a cursory look at what the Reformers criticized and what they proposed in its place shows that what was at issue was the independence of religious concerns from other, worldly concerns: but this very much as an aspect of overall, 'secular' society and not in this-worldly or other-worldly separation from it. Religion was to follow its own differentiated criteria not segmentarily or just organizationally, but functionally. It was to be differentiated within society and in contradistinction to secular preoccupations, but not separate from them. This may sound contradictory, but Luther's insistence on 'justification by faith alone' and his idea of the sanctity of the 'calling' state the matter as clearly as one could wish. Not social performances of a non-religious sort should determine one's salvific state and prospects – and especially not the ability to *buy* salvation in the form of indulgences, masses, and so forth – but only criteria that remained recursively within the programmatic core of religion, namely the Bible and faith. Yet this distinctiveness was to occur within 'normal' social life which itself was sanctified without being sacralized. Everyday social life, including political and economic life, was the religiously sanctioned life, but precisely neutral in terms of religious efficacy. There were not two 'societies', but only one that embodied interrelated yet independent concerns. Referring to Luhmann's suggestion for the basic religious code, one can say that the Reformers (and this includes the Catholic Reformers as well, especially as embodied in organized groups like the Jesuits) sought to augment the immanence and transcendence of religious concerns at the same time.

The high medieval Catholic church, while exhibiting independence, was also multi-functional and thus appeared to the Protestant Reformers as a functionally (religiously) tainted institution. Under the circumstances, they therefore had to proceed anti-institutionally and anti-organizationally, seeking some more acceptable and religiously justified replacement, such as was exemplified in the temporary experiments of Calvin's Geneva and the utopian communities of some of the radicals. In fact, de-institutionalization and dis-organization were not the result. Precisely the opposite happened, including the more complex organization of religion, both Catholic and Protestant, in subsequent centuries. This result is not at all surprising. The purified religion was not meant to flee the world. It therefore required real social bases, concrete forms that could express its independence and assure the reproduction of religious communication as religion. Following the Luhmannian model I am using here, under the circumstances of the sixteenth century as today, three of the primary options were organizations, social movements (the Reformation itself being the prime example) and concretization through other emerging systems, notably the political in the form of the increasingly powerful states. In the next chapter and below, I shall discuss all these in greater detail. At this point, I focus on the role of the states.

As I have argued, the Reformations were at root religious reform movements. Both the Protestant and Catholic Reformers wanted to purify Christian religion and thereby strengthen it. One result, unwished for on all sides, was a long-lasting and seemingly permanent institutional split in the Christian fold, namely the different post-Reformation Christian churches. That particular outcome, however, may not have ensued had it not been for the power of the Roman church combined with the rise of a plurality of political states in Europe. Many of the latter seized the opportunity afforded them by the Protestant Reformers to cast off the influence of the church in Rome or to bring the church under their greater control within the territory that they controlled. They thereby solidified their own power and the incipient religious divisions in the same stroke. The Westphalian formula of 1648 was but the confirmation of this strategy. It sought to institutionalize the coordination of political identity with religious identity in Western Europe, thereby confirming the plurality of both in the process. In the wake and as part of this development, many states, especially Protestant ones, created national churches, in the sense of politically and legally established religious institutions, but also, after the end of the eighteenth century, in the sense of the religious dimension of national identity. For the idea developed that states were not so much the creatures of sovereigns as they were the carriers of nations: that the existence of a nation justified and even required a distinct and sovereign state (cf., for example, Kedourie 1960: 9–19). These nations were in many cases deemed to be inherently Protestant or Catholic, for instance Anglican in England, Lutheran in Sweden or Catholic in Spain. Nation and religion were of a piece. Moreover, in Eastern Europe, which did not experience a parallel to the violent post-Reformation period in the West, the logic also established itself in the nineteenth century in the form of national Orthodox churches, in many ways more clearly divided along national lines than in the West (see e.g. Roudometof 2001).

To be sure, the institutional division of the Christian church and the incorporation of the resulting churches into the projects of state and nation building did not result either in the blending of religion into this political and cultural domain nor in the disappearance of the idea of Christian unity, which is to say the idea of a single, albeit internally divided, Christian religion. We are not faced here with the de-differentiation of religion nor the absolute prioritization of political and cultural criteria of difference over religious ones. Religion in fact maintained and enhanced its status as a distinct and differentiated sphere of activity or communication. What the admittedly partial 'nationalization' of religion does show, however, is that the political system during and in the aftermath of the Reformation period was growing in strength and in terms of its characteristic as a system of sovereign (nation-) states. It also indicates one of the ways in which the path of differentiation as *one of* the function systems has been an ambiguous one for religion, one in which a certain reliance on the resources of other function systems, here the political, was at certain points instrumental. I shall have occasion to return frequently to such ambiguities in the course of my arguments.

The political dimensions of the Reformation also underscore what is of the first importance in this portion of the narrative, namely that we are not dealing simply with the rise of a religious system in the form of the church.

This is much more than just the story of religious reform movements. The Roman church's rise to the sort of unprecedented prominence that it had in the late European Middle Ages and the post-Reformation churches' greater organization were actually part of a more complex process in which several functionally oriented domains were developing, and in which for equally complex reasons the hitherto dominant stratified structures could not or at least did not stop the process or harness it to their own interests. Thus, the rise of the churches becomes at a certain point concomitant with the rise of several, increasingly powerful political states, with the rise of relatively independent legal systems within those states, with the emergence of a capitalist economic system, and with the assertion of a more and more independent intellectual tradition that claimed empirical knowledge as the only legitimate source (cf. Huff 2003). These happened together and, as it were, fed off one another. It is difficult to claim that one of them – for instance the states, the church or the urban based capitalism – was somehow causal of the rest or more fundamental than the rest. The religious institution itself was therefore neither the guiding force nor simply a passive bystander, let alone victim, of this historical development. Religious developments were one aspect of a multi-dimensional transformation that was at its socio-structural core a shift to a dominance of function systems as the most determinative societal systems of that society. Not surprisingly, it is in this context, and above all somewhat later, when several of these systems were more firmly established, that we see the emergence of a new way of understanding religion, a semantic correlate of this process of institutional and structural differentiation according to function.

As a word, 'religion' or *religio* has a long pedigree in European languages. Its history begins centuries and even millennia before the early modern and modern periods that are my focus here. Even a cursory familiarity with the literature, however, immediately shows that what this word meant over this long period varied quite a bit (see especially Despland 1979; Feil 1986, 1992, 1997). It would be a mistake to assume that the meaning of the word in recent times is essentially the same as it was several hundred years ago, just as it would be absurd to suggest that the European social reality of what we today call religion, its institutional expressions, had not changed since the time of Plato and Aristotle. In fact, beginning roughly around the sixteenth and especially into the seventeenth century the prevailing understanding of the term in this part of the world underwent a gradual but very significant shift that corresponds to the structural developments just discussed.

Adapting Peter Harrison's analysis (Harrison 1990: 5–60), we can begin a closer inspection with representative figures in the fifteenth century, that is before the Reformation, and proceed through to the beginning of the eighteenth to show important shifts in meaning along two axes, that between religion and non-religion and that between one religion and another. Harrison cites two figures, Nicholas of Cusa and Marsilio Ficino as representative of what one might call an early 'upgrading' of the concept of religion from a technical term, referring to monastic life,[2] to one that is more systemic in the sense of designating a distinct realm of endeavour. The starting point for this part of the narrative is therefore roughly the same as for the portion just discussed. Accordingly, the concern of both was to understand how religion was one, and this not against but in light of the diversity of religious practices in the world that they knew. Indicative of this *singularity* of religion is the title of Ficino's work, *De Christiana Religione*, which does not mean that only Christian religion is religion, but rather that 'Christian' is a way of talking about the essential aim and ideals of all religious practice. The aim here is to find singularity, not simply pursue the much older project of Christian exclusivity. In Harrison's words, with these figures, '"religion" became for the first time [among European Christians] a generic something which allowed a variety of historical expressions' (1990: 14).

Although the fifteenth century was not a time of religious harmony and peace in Europe, its conflicts paled in comparison with what was to come. Ironically, but also indicatively as already noted, the Reformation brought highly conflictual *splits* into the Western European Christian domain, making the unity of religion that Ficino sought that much harder to conceive and even to hope for. That, however, did not lead to a reversal in the 'reification' of religion as a distinct realm, but rather precisely to its intensification in the idea that the singular 'religion' inherently manifests itself in a plurality of 'religions'. Despland expresses well the relation between the singularity and the plurality when he speaks of a shift from 'religion' as a singular domain to 'a religion' as a systemic entity (in his rendering, 'reified'). Looking at the French example, he writes:

> L'usage français [after 1560] s'établit d'utiliser le mot avec l'article indéfini: *une* religion. C'est nouveau ... C'est fort significatif aussi: l'idée de religion est en voie de réification ... Des lors, avoir de la religion signifie, pour la grande majorité des esprits européens, avoir une religion.
>
> (Despland 1979: 228)

The existence of 'a' religion, of course, only makes sense if there is more than one of them. And indeed, by the end of that century we already see this additional pluralistic component consolidating. According to Harrison, in England the idea of a plurality of religions appears with Hooker's *Laws of Ecclesiastical Politie* (1593) and comes into common usage in the first part of the seventeenth century with Brerewood's *Enquiries Touching the Diversity of Languages and Religions through the Chief Parts of the World* (Harrison 1990: 39).

This semantic change had its roots and its rationale in the historical social changes that European society was undergoing at this time. Despland makes it clear that a critical part of the 'reification' and pluralization was the splits that came in the wake of the Reformation (1979: 227ff.). Yet this important event by itself does not explain why a religious controversy should have such weighty semantic correlates. Even the addition of the just-discussed political dimension, significant as it was, does not account entirely for the pluralization of the idea of religion. If the Christian religion was no longer a source of societal unity, its divisions into Catholic, Protestant and Orthodox versions did not amount to there being three religions. Europeans still only considered it as one religion, unfortunately divided. At least two other factors have to be included in the picture. One concerns the re-visioning of religious differences that had existed in Europe and even helped define Europe. The other, undoubtedly more critical, is reflected in Brerewood's title, namely the growing importance of the 'chief parts of the world.'

Although, as Harrison points out, fifteenth-century thinkers like Ficino could still subsume all religion under the title of 'Christian', there were in fact non-Christian complexes which, as the pluralized notion developed, became the first 'other' religions. These were the religions of the Jews and the Muslims on the one hand, and the religious expression of all others, including the illustrious forebears of the Europeans, the Greeks and Romans who were generally called Pagans. Together, Jews, Muslims and Pagans provided a way of understanding religious difference in contrast to the conflicting varieties of Christianity. Jews had had a periodically troubled existence in European society for centuries, but they were practically and theologically clearly visible religious others. Europe in an important sense virtually defined itself over against Islam, being the territory where Islam's expansion was eventually stopped. This thereby presented a further evident other religion. And the difference of Paganism was a critical part of Christian mythology and a solidly incorporated aspect of European intellectual memory. In the conflictual and divided religious context of fifteenth- to seventeenth-century Europe, these religious others thus provided an almost self-evident foil for the initial understandings of religion as a distinct domain and above all for religions as the necessarily plural manifestations of that domain. This use of these 'religious others' for the imagination of 'other religions' and for the delineation of Christianity in comparison is evident in the works of various European writers of this extended period. That includes those, such as Jean Bodin in the sixteenth century and Herbert of Cherbury in the seventeenth, who sought in vain to recapture religious unity (Feil 1992: 149–61, 1997: 189–206; Preuss 1996), whether inside or outside 'the religions'; and the far more numerous authors and polemicists, such as Isaac Barrow and Humphrey Prideaux in the early eighteenth century, who wished to defend and define Christianity or criticize the entire domain of religion. Indeed, one finds the systemic names for all four religions more or less for the first time in the context of controversial literature of this nature: Christianity as a label appears already in the polemics of the sixteenth century (Despland 1979: 391); Judaism, Mahometanism [sic] and Paganism, as labels for these religions, arrive more or less beginning in the first half of the seventeenth and then especially in the eighteenth century (see Feil 2001: 206–8; Haussig 1999; Pailin 1984; Smith 1991: 60).

The fifteenth and sixteenth centuries were not just times of religious and political ferment in European society. They also marked the beginning of centuries-long expansion along several fronts. Columbus and the Portuguese explorers were in search of trade routes; their sponsors were the same political powers that played such a critical role in the religious outcome of the Reformation period. A few of these states, notably Spain, Portugal, France, England and others somewhat later, established overseas colonies in the 'New World' and sought outposts in various other territories. Products of the Catholic Reformation, in particular the Jesuits, were at the forefront of missionary efforts in regions as distant as East Asia and the Americas. Aside from seeking trade, empire and souls, however, the Europeans also carried with them their ideas, many of which were in the process of transformation, challenge and revision. These included their developing notions of religion and religions. It was in terms of those ideas that they tried to understand, influence and often conquer the peoples and civilizations that they encountered. As concerns religion, the question for them became twofold: did a particular people 'have' religion, and if so, 'which' religion or religions did they have? They could not and of course did not simply ask the people they encountered, 'What is your religion?' The question in that form would have been more or less incomprehensible in Europe a couple of centuries before, let alone in places as different as the Americas, East Asia, South Asia and Africa of the sixteenth to nineteenth centuries. Instead, they looked for what they understood to be religion and religions, sometimes found them, often did not, and in most cases considered what they thus 'discovered' to be inferior to the reconstructing Christian religion that they themselves carried. In a few cases, some of the more elite and influential European observers discovered (or, what amounts to the same, imagined) religions that in one fashion or another they considered to be quite worthy, if not usually equal to their own. Two or three of these ideas have since become globally recognized 'world religions', notably Hinduism and Buddhism (Almond 1988; Frykenberg 1989; Kopf 1969; Marshall 1970). In most other cases, however, their judgement was decidedly negative, labelling what we might today call indigenous religious traditions as at best superstition, often as the absence of religion. This was especially the case with the religions of small-scale, orally based societies such as those of North America and

Africa (Axtell 2001; Chidester 1996; Grant 1984; Peterson 2002). The net result, however, was the reinforcement of the notion that religion expressed itself not as a single quality that admitted of a certain variety in its outward forms (like virtue!), but through a plurality of separate and mutually distinguishable religions.

The more detailed discussion of the discovery or denial, as the case may be, of other religions by European observers informs all the remaining chapters. It was one important factor in the construction or reconstruction of several of today's globally recognized religions. At this point, what I wish to underline is not so much that construction or non-construction, but rather the role that these European imaginings played in the solidification of what was at that time a gradually forming European way of conceiving, understanding and institutionalizing religion. Whether Europeans like the later Jesuits in China (see Jensen 1997) or British orientalists in India (Frykenberg 1989) were 'mistaken' in their imagining of a religion of Confucius or of a Vedic religion later called Hinduism is not the issue at the moment. What is significant is that the European experience of encounter with a wide variety of civilizations and cultures played an integral part in the historical emergence of this peculiar idea of religion as a distinct and systemic domain of endeavour that manifested itself in a plurality of also systemic subunits called religions, one of which was Christianity. It was not that the Europeans possessed an under-standing of religion, say an inherently Christian understanding, as part of their indigenous cultural heritage, which they then proceeded to project or impose on everyone that they encountered. It is rather that the confluence of intra-European developments with the global expansion of European influence provided the conditions for this re-imagining of the religious. Evidence of that order of occurrence can also be found in the fact that the modern names for most of the religions did not appear in the European literature until this process was well under way, as noted above, for the 'old' religions of Christianity, Judaism, Islam and Paganism effectively not until the sixteenth/seventeenth centuries, and for the newly discovered religions like Hinduism, Buddhism and Daoism not until the nineteenth century. In the language of Robertson's dialogical approach to globalization, the new idea of religion and the religions particularized in the process of its own universalization. Like many globalized forms, the concept – and also the system – is as much a product of globalization as it is a contributor to it.

Developments in European society and then among Europeans as they expanded globally constitute only one dimension of the formation of a global function system for religion. To be sure, it is an important one, but by itself at best only half the picture. In keeping with a dialogical under-standing of globalization, the narrative presentation of how the system has come about has to expand to include the role played by non-Europeans and non-Western regions of the world. In principle, as with the European segment, there are two portions to this: the historical developments in various regions and societies before the expansion of European influence after 1500 and to some degree thereafter; and the response of these non-European areas to that often invasive presence, which is to say the way that these appropriated, particularized or in different degrees sought to reject the universals that the Europeans represented or imposed. The former I include in the discussions of the relevant remaining chapters. There I also present a much more detailed analysis of the various cases of particularization. For the moment, I limit myself to a brief consideration of some of the general features of the non-European appropriations and rejections of the developing idea and structures of religion and the religions. These responses have been just as constitutive of the global religious system and the category of religion as the originally European contributions. Without them, the nature of this system would be very different. Indeed, without them there would be no such system.

Non-European responses have varied along a continuum between positive appropriation and negative rejection. In most cases, as one might expect, developments have been an ambiguous mix of the two, but that could be said for the Europeans as well. A few examples can serve to illustrate. In South Asia, various indigenous elites have collaborated in the construction and imagination of a systematic and singular entity called Hinduism or the Hindu religion. As in all instances of particularization, we are not dealing with the invention of this religion, as it were, out of nothing. Nor did these South Asians simply adopt what the European observers discovered. Instead the outcome has been to reconfigure and reinterpret selected religio-cultural traditions and practices, with some innovative additions, as a religion. This Hinduism is today still very much contested and is also still largely a creature of the elite and urban segments of Indian society and the Indian diaspora. Yet for millions of people around the world, the singular Hindu religion is an unquestionable reality of which they consider themselves a part. The more precise characteristics of this religion are, as for every other religion, matters of variation and not infrequent dispute. There is disagreement about what is to be included under the Hindu banner, which is another way of saying that Hindu orthodoxy, authenticity and authority are contentious issues as they are in every contemporary religion. Moreover, the relation between 'Hindu religion' and 'Hindu nation', as among various Europeans, is also a subject of contestation. In general the Hindu case illustrates well the ambiguous relation between 'religion' and 'culture' (here: nation). As I noted above when discussing the consequences of the Reformation, the differentiation of religion as a distinct function system has been neither straightforward nor conflict free. That ambiguity has repeated itself in South Asia where it manifests itself in disputes over Indian 'secularism' and the frequently invidious distinction between religion (*dharma* and its variants in Indian languages) and 'communalism'.[3] Far from such problematic aspects of the construction of Hinduism pointing to the rejection of the category of religion or serving as an illustration of its inappropriateness when applied to Indian society and history, they actually are better seen as evidence of just how typically, if variably, the religious system manifests itself on the subcontinent.

A case of appropriation that includes much clearer rejection of the modern notion of religion is to be found in East Asia, in particular in Japan and China. Here the narrative of response begins towards the middle of the nineteenth century as Japan begins to 'open up' to the rest of the world. In order to translate the word 'religion' in the treaties they signed with the Americans, the Japanese used a technical Buddhist term, *shukyo*. Later in the century that term came to be generally accepted in its new meaning (Hardacre 1989). That much looks like straightforward appropriation. Parallel to these moves, however, the Japanese also pursued the promulgation of what from one perspective was 'one of the religions', but in more important respects was not, namely *Shinto*. This became the word for an imagined religion, but also for a national political ideology and system of ritual practices which was deemed to be 'not a religion' but rather a matter of patriotism and loyalty to the nation. In appropriating the idea of religion, these modernizing Japanese elites recognized that critical ambiguity in the European image of religion, namely the equivocal relation between 'religion' as a differentiable category of social communication and 'religion' as a category of 'cultural' identity and thus of difference vis-à-vis others in global society. They sought to clarify this ambiguity and indeed to take political advantage of it. The Japanese thereby did much more than respond to the Western notion of religion: they developed it while appropriating it.

The situation in China has been similar but also significantly different. As in many other respects, Chinese elites sought to imitate Japanese success but did so only superficially. Aside from adopting the Chinese equivalent to the Japanese *shukyo*, namely *zongjiao*, to denote the modern sense of religion, the Chinese course has gone in different directions. Around the turn of the century, one movement sought to re-imagine the traditions associated with Confucius as the national and officially established religion. This effort to create *Kongjiao* (Jensen 1997) failed more or less completely, largely because most Chinese elites opposed it. The net result has been that what among Western scholars and observers has been called Confucianism has not been reconstructed and imagined as one of the religions. Indeed, the 'national' category of difference that won the day in China of the twentieth century was socialism or Maoism, which was not considered to be religion. Nonetheless, in spite of these clear rejections, the Chinese like the Japanese have appropriated the category of religion. In fact, as I detail in Chapter 5, the understanding of this socially operative notion in both countries is very close to what it is in virtually all other regions of global society. What differs is the valuation of religion: in China as in Japan religion is more frequently regarded as narrow sectarianism than it is in Western regions. There is also a difference in which religions count as 'one of the religions'.

In the context of these ambiguous and rejecting dimensions of East Asian appropriation of religion, one of the more intriguing aspects has been the comparatively unproblematic and almost taken-for-granted acceptance of Buddhism as religion and as a religion. The East Asian region has been witness to a number of Buddhist reform movements which have sought to reconstruct Buddhism as a typically modern religion. Above all, however, few if any of the elites that rejected the reconstruction of indigenous religio-cultural traditions as religion have had any trouble recognizing Buddhism as both.

Islam and Judaism have presented similar cases of relatively easily reconstructed religions. Given that, during the early modern and modern centuries, the latter had its dominant heartland in the same Europe that spawned the emerging conception in the first place, Judaism's conformity may not be that surprising. Certainly in no other case do we see quite the same parallel degree of organization and even denominationalization. And the relation of Judaism to the state and national identity in Israel shows strong resemblances to comparable situations in a few European countries. The same cannot be said for Islam, however. As W.C. Smith demonstrates (1991), Islam had in its own history already undergone a fair amount of 'reification' before the modern era, which is to say that its carriers developed a clear notion of both its internal singularity or self-identifying reflexivity and its corresponding difference from other religions. Islam, therefore, unlike Hinduism, did not have to be invented in that sense. The response or appropriation that has happened in Muslim regions of the world with respect to Islam has therefore been of a different order when compared to the South and East Asian cases just outlined. What we have witnessed since the nineteenth century has in fact been an intensification of the reification. This has taken the form of a series of movements towards a truly global orthodoxification of Islam (cf. Voll 1982, 1999). In consequence, Islamic developments have influenced the global systemic model of what a religion is perhaps as much as have the Christian ones discussed above. The reconstruction of Islam has affected the notion of what is possible and 'legitimate' for a religion to claim and therefore the status of the global function system for religion. As I make clear in Chapter 3, this restructuring of Islam has been very much an aspect of the response and appropriation which has taken place in Muslim regions of the world. It is a prime example of how particularization changes universals and then universalizes those particulars.

The examples I have outlined to this point are all cases of the (re)construction of what are often called 'world religions'. And, indeed, in all these instances greater global spread has been an important aspect of the reconstruction. This is so even for those religions that present themselves as 'non-proselytizing' or 'non-conversionist' such as Judaism and Hinduism. Moreover, nationalization of religions has not precluded such globalization; the latter has just as often been a key contributor to the former. In many regions of the world, however, this sort of re-imagining of more local religio-cultural traditions as religions has not occurred as straightforwardly. Sometimes, as in China, such failure reflects express refusal on the part of those who would be the carriers of such a religion. This has thus far been the case, for instance, with a number of North American Aboriginal groups. More often, however, other factors have been at play. Symptomatic of such cases is the absence in official, popular or even scholarly language of names for these 'non-religions'. Instead, when we do speak of them, we tend to use the name of the region or of the cultural group which is ostensibly their carrier. A common way of designating them is to call them indigenous religions or indigenous religious traditions. Thus we have such general monikers as 'North American Aboriginal', 'African Traditional', 'Indonesian folk', or a variation on 'the religion of . . . '. They are the subject of more focused attention in the context of Chapter 6. Here they serve to underscore just how partial, arbitrary, and haphazard the historical process of modern religion formation has been.

Upon closer inspection, however, the case of indigenous religions may not be as clear-cut as a simple failure of the religion construction process to occur. In quite a number of instances, in fact, it has occurred, except that it has taken on somewhat different guises. Two of these are when 'indigenous' religions are reconstructed as 'new' religions, and when they are reconstructed as 'syncretic' variations on one of the 'world' religions. The former category would include, for example, twentieth-century African religions of the New World such as Vodoun, Santería and Candomblé. The latter, syncretic category, encompasses many more examples. Here would fall twentieth-century African Indigenous churches (AICs) like the South African Zion Christian church and the Aladura churches, reconstructions of 'tribal culture' in Indonesia as versions of Hinduism, and Rastafarianism in the Atlantic world. The line between 'new' religion and reconstructed 'old' religion is, of course, quite blurry in these cases, as is the extent to which these have actually been reconstructed as 'one of the religions'. These, however, are questions that one could pose of all the religions, not just these. They point to ambiguous aspects of the construction of the religious system as such, not just to these cases.

With these last examples, the question of appropriation and response shades over into the larger question of the possibility and reality of entirely 'new' religions as part of the global religious system. That, as well as the indigenous examples, is a major focus of Chapter 6, as is the sort of religiosity that hovers at the edges of religion under such headings as individual bricolage and spirituality. Overall, all these cases outside the realm of the more clearly recognizable and recognized world religions raise with greater clarity the central question of what precisely constitutes the 'systemicity' of this global religious system. The narrative of the category of religion and of the reconstruction and imagination of religions, after all, does not make it at all clear how these developments are to be understood as the construction of a single and singular system. In the next section, I turn expressly to this question using the Luhmannian frame that I outlined in the last chapter. As will become evident, the singularity of the religious system is indeed an important question, one not susceptible to a straightforward or easy answer. In the final analysis, the singularity of the religious system rests on the combined singularities of the different religions in conjunction with the relation of the religious to the other function systems.

The systemicity of the global function system for religion

The previous section could use the strategy of historical narrative to look at both semantic and socio-structural formations which are important for understanding the emergence of a global religious system. Such a story is useful for introductory purposes, but it is less effective for the next step of observing the singularity or systemicity of this system. On what basis can one claim that all these events amount to the social construction of a system and what advantage is there to observing religion as a system? How does this system operate today empirically? Answers to these questions have to maintain a sensitivity for the historicity, for the contingency of this re-imagining of religion. We have to keep in mind that what we are describing is not some transhistorical universal called religion, but a very particular, very selective and in many senses quite arbitrary development. What follows then is the application of a number of theoretical concepts to this historical and contemporary data. It is a way of seeing them which profiles the degree of singularity of modern religion under the idea of system.

If there is a global religious system, then the first order of business is to discern what this system is about, what identifies it in social practice. This would usually be the point at which to insert a discussion about definition. Yet both in the introduction and at the beginning of this chapter, I suggested that one of the reasons that current controversies surrounding the definition of the category of religion are so persistent is that they do not clearly acknowledge the conditioning effect of operatively differentiated religion in their social environment. The Luhmannian frame that I am using here allows one to do just that: focus on differentiation as the logically prior issue and then move to the concept of religion only on that basis. From this Luhmannian point of departure, the first question to ask is not about what defines religion but rather about the basic code of religion, what particular way religion interprets or selectively processes the world and thereby differentiates itself. Moreover, implicit in that question is a comparison with how other systems do that ordering. Identifying the systemically religious depends to some degree on how the non-religious identifies itself.

The search can begin with several possibilities. Durkheim, Eliade and many others focused on the difference between sacred and profane; Luhmann suggests the dichotomy of transcendent and immanent; and very often one hears that religion is about the spiritual as distinguished from the material. Various definitions of religion avail themselves of these as well as others like supra-empirical vs empirical, ultimate vs non-ultimate, absolute vs conditioned, cosmic vs nomic, infinite vs finite, and so forth. Each of these seeks to mark a domain that is the typical concern of religion, thereby defining or delimiting it. In the form that I have stated them, however, none of them goes far enough for the present purposes because they only mark a boundary between the ostensibly religious and non-religious without also indicating how that boundary comes to be established and maintained through recursive, self-referential communications. A closer inspection of how the scholars using them elaborate on these dichotomies usually gives some indication in this regard. Durkheim, for instance, further explains that things are rendered sacred by being set apart and forbidden; and his lengthy volume on the elementary forms of the religious life goes into great detail about how he understood Australian Aboriginal religion to accomplish this separation (Durkheim 1965). Analogously, Eliade translates the question of the sacred into one of, in his terms, hierophanies; Berger explains how a sacred cosmos is established in the process of world construction; and Geertz details how the symbols of ` which he speaks formulate conceptions of a general order of existence and establish a particular reality (Berger 1967; Eliade 1963; Geertz 1966). Although these thereby all present possibilities for observing religion today, they are also designed far too transhistorically to be directly useful for the question at hand. In fact, following the critiques of various scholars, for example, Talal Asad's detailed analysis of Geertz's definition (Asad 1993: 27ff.), this universalizing aim is precisely what is problematic in these efforts. They indicate how religion might construct itself; but in seeking to be so encompassing, they risk projecting too much on to other societies and, critical for my purposes here, missing precisely what is peculiar about religion in our own. The search for the code of a contemporary religious system can therefore use these definitional efforts as a beginning reference, but not really as a guide. To find that code, if it exists, requires a different strategy, one with an empirical focus on the contemporary situation and its historical antecedents.

In the narrative presentation of the last section, I noted several late medieval and Reformation concerns about the distinctiveness of the Christian church with respect to 'the world' and about the purity of religion. The medieval church, for instance, sought to distinguish itself as a *societas perfectas* beside the state and civil society, to assert the difference and superiority of faith to reason, and to increase awareness of sin along with the church's methods, notably the sacraments, for dealing with it (Délumeau 1983; Gössman 1971). The Reformers underscored their conviction that religious goals, namely salvation, were to be attained or determined uniquely by religious means such as faith and the providence of God. What religion was about was thus precisely those factors: salvation, sin, faith, sacraments, providence and other such *religious* determinants. The conditions or prospects of salvation were to be determined by other religious categories like sin, faith or sacraments; not by 'worldly' categories like 'principalities and powers' or 'works'. Providence foresaw sin which pointed to the possibilities of damnation or salvation, which in turn were settled on the basis of faith, sacraments or providence again. The religious determinants were to refer ultimately only to themselves. Given that my purpose in discussing those matters was to show how religion was at that time in the process of becoming increasingly differentiated, it is these semantic items, along with the communications in which they occur, that are likely to be pointing to the code that is recursively operating here. That code, however, cannot be another name for the religious domain; it has to be a binary set with a positive and a negative pole. The code does not express the difference between the system and its environment, between religion and non-religion. Instead it ensures the self-referential or recursive quality of religious communication. It is that recursiveness which enacts the boundary between system and environment. The code therefore has to have two poles which are complementary, thereby totalizing, and *both* religious classifications. Only then can religious communication refer only to itself because even the contradiction of positive religious signification can again receive religious signification. All else has no religious meaning and may not even be visible to the system. Accordingly, looking at what Christian elites of that late medieval, Reformation and post-Reformation time were arguing about, what mattered to them, it becomes fairly clear that the main issues centred around the difference between salvation and damnation. More exactly, the central arguments were about the sort of communication (or, if one wishes, social action) that was productive of salvation and the sort that indicated damnation. The code over which they sought control was something close to blessed/damned, not in any direct sense sacred/profane, spiritual/material, ultimate/relative or similar distinction. Salvation and damnation are both sacred, both spiritual and both ultimate (eternal) states. They are not directly about the other side of those dichotomies. Through this code, all human action had the potential of being sacralized, of being translated into religious terms analogous to the way the economic distinction between owning and not-owning allows anything to be translated into economic terms, which is to say commodified. Moreover, the code operated recursively: the purpose of religion conceived in this way was itself. Salvation and damnation contained their own purpose; they were *ad maiorem gloriam Dei*.

At this point, at least two problems with the argument may seem to be evident. First, although Christians of these centuries were certainly concerned about salvation, that is not at all a new development and is in one form or another as old as the Christian tradition itself. How, then, can it be construed as a version of the code for a *new* global religious system? Second, even if this is what concerned Christians and thus defined the Christian religion during that period, it pertains only to Christianity and cannot be understood as the code for a new *global* religious system. With respect to the first objection, it is not my claim that this system constituted the invention of something radically new. We are dealing at least as much with the re-ordering, literally the re-formation, of received cultural resources as we are with innovation. Luther, Calvin and the Jesuits helped to intensify the importance of various received features which were instrumental in asserting the independent power of religion. They did not advocate an entirely new way of doing religion. Indeed, the early organization, dogmatization, orthodoxification and thus to some degree differentiation of Christian institutions already during the time of the Roman Empire undoubtedly provided critical antecedents for these late medieval and early modern re-formations to take place. In addition, observers of the last few centuries have stressed precisely those aspects of early Christianity that make sense of subsequent developments. The 'histories' of Christianity and the church are correspondingly selective; they stress those features which contributed to the eventual differentiation and thereby have contributed to that process. As regards the second problem, the developments I have just described were only one aspect both in the differentiation of Christianity as a religion among religions and in the formation of a global system for religion. As with all the function systems, the formation and the globalization of Christianity and of the religious system cannot be understood separately; they are of a piece. The search for a religious code perhaps can begin with Reformation Christianity, but it cannot end there.

Just as the question of religious code is best addressed to Christianity as it is already in the process of reformation as a religion among religions, so must we proceed in similar fashion with the other religions. I take the examples of Islam, Buddhism and Hinduism. In each case, one can observe an analogous combination of continuity and discontinuity; reconstruction as religion re-imagines, it does not create out of nothing.

At first glance, Islam may seem to operate much as Christian religion has: they are both 'Abrahamic' in their core belief structures and traditions. And, indeed, salvation/damnation in the context of afterlife and eschatology are important determinants in both traditions. To a significant extent, therefore, the code blessed/damned has operated to structure Islam just as it has Christianity. If one focuses on many of the Islamic reform movements of especially the nineteenth and twentieth centuries, however, a somewhat altered picture emerges. Taking more extreme figures like Mawlana Mawdudi, Sayyid Qutb and Ayatollah Khomeini as representative examples that show the trend with particular clarity, what we see is a partial (but only partial) backgrounding of questions of salvation and damnation and a corresponding valorization of the legalistic aspects of Islamic tradition in the form of Shari'a and its central operating code *halal/ haram*, or permitted and forbidden. Here again, we have a recursively religious dichotomy that allows the transformation or incorporation of everything and anything that happens in the world into specific and selective religious terms. It is around this, formally speaking, secondary code and far less clearly around salvation/damnation or any other possibility that at least a certain portion of the modern and worldwide orthodoxification of Islam has taken place. And the contemporary so-called resurgence of Islam largely centres on this code, thereby contributing significantly to the (further) differentiation of Islam as a distinct religion and thus to the clearer differentiation of religion as a societal system.

The (re)formation of Buddhism over the last century to century and a half shows a similar combination of continuity and discontinuity as just pointed out for Christianity and Islam. A variety of movements have contributed to this reform, for example those associated with Angarika Dharmapala in Sri Lanka, with Tai Hsu in China, the Japanese Soka Gakkai, and Fo Guang Shan in Taiwan. Some of these, such as that of Tai Hsu, have been based in Buddhist monasticism, the Buddhist institution that has undoubtedly been the greatest source of continuity and singularity of the Buddhist tradition and therefore a key factor in the relatively straightforward re-imagining of Buddhism as one of the religions. The monastic code has centred around the distinction between *nirvana* and *samsara*, all actions being capable of translation into terms of whether they contribute to enlightenment and the attainment of *nirvana*, or increase the burden of karma and ignorance and thus bind further into *samsara*. The programmatic practices and regimes associated with monastic Buddhism have, however, not generally been the same as those informing lay Buddhist movements and practice, and one could suggest that a secondary code of merit/demerit also operates in the case of the latter. Nonetheless, the overall aim and order of things is much the same: actions either contribute to eventual enlightenment, hinder such progress, or are religiously irrelevant. There is a clear code operating which ultimately refers only to itself. The purpose or value of enlightenment or the attainment of *nirvana*, the aim of meritorious action such as chanting, feeding monks, building temples or reciting sutras is in the final analysis only itself. It may be evaluated as bliss, but this is simply a way of indicating its intrinsic and ultimate value. It is for its own sake.

The Hindu case presents a rather different trajectory, above all because imagining the singularity of a religion called Hinduism has not been aided either by a long history of such understandings as in Islam and Christianity, or by a dominant and continuous institution like the Christian churches or the Buddhist monasteries. Nonetheless, among that sizeable group of adherents for whom Hinduism is or has become an incontrovertible reality, a reasonably uniform understanding of the religion has emerged. This centres on a more or less neo-Vedantic image which stresses the centrality of the Vedas, the multiplicity of paths to the ultimate religious goal, and the reality of many gods and goddesses, above all Vishnu, Shiva and Devi along with their specific manifestations such as Krishna, Rama, Nataraja, Kali and Durga. Quite a number of movements have contributed to this result, not the least of which are the Ramakrishna movement, the various Sampradaya movements, Sanatana Dharma movements, the Arya Samaj, the Swaminarayan movement and even the Vishva Hindu Parishad. In spite of the diversity that is itself part of the imagined singularity, this Hinduism nonetheless exhibits a central code, one that is quite close to the Buddhist code. What Hinduism is about is *moksha* (seen as anything from union with Brahman to blissful existence in the presence of the one deity), a notion similar to *nirvana* and whose binary opposite is the same, namely *samsara*. Although programmatically – that is, as concerns the programme of the religion – Hinduism is quite different from Buddhism, the two religions share a similar root binary code, much as the three Abrahamic religions of Judaism, Christianity and Islam share versions of the salvation/damnation code. In either case, all actions can be religiously incorporated according to whether they contribute to the ultimate goal of enlightenment or bliss, or further block that road. That said, most Hindus, like most Buddhists, do not expect or even seek the attainment of the ultimate religious goal in their lifetime, and a great deal of Hindu religious communication is structured more by secondary codes such as auspicious/inauspicious, pure/impure or dharmic/adharmic than it is immediately through moksha/samsara. To the degree that contemporary Hinduism converges as a single religion, however, the secondary codes refer programmatically to the primary one.

These brief considerations of what code or codes operate in different religions could continue for other religions such as Judaism or Sikhism.

Examination of the above four, however, already indicates a pattern and therefore at least a certain uniformity in this question. The specific codes and certainly the detailed programmes are quite different from religion to religion; but there is also a recognizable continuity in the structure and purpose of all these codes. Since there is no global religion any more than there is a global state or (thus far) even a single global currency, that consistency has to be abstracted from the concrete religions. There are no central and unifying agencies defining and guaranteeing it; nor is there currently a 'unity of all religions' movement strong enough to institutionalize it. Thus, on these empirical and inductive grounds, one defensible suggestion for the name of the code of religion is in that light the difference between *blessed* and *cursed*,[4] even though these particular words may still sound too 'Abrahamic', perhaps. This or something close to it, I suggest, subsumes the structural intent of all the codes thus far examined and others, including redeemed/unredeemed, enlightened/ignorant, immortal/mortal, harmonious/disharmonious, merit/demerit, pure/impure, auspicious/inauspicious, clean/unclean, and so forth. Luhmann's suggestion of transcendent/immanent, much like the sacred/profane distinction championed by Eliade and Durkheim, while designating reasonably accurately the same commonality, seems to underdetermine the negative religious pole too much and thus misses a good portion of what more fundamentally structures actual religious communications in today's world, namely the avoidance of or struggle against religiously determined evil (as opposed to just the moral pole, 'bad'). More critically, perhaps, it is too close to the this-worldly/other-worldly distinction which is more germane to some religions or subsections of religions than others. In subsequent chapters, therefore, I will try to show how the blessed/cursed code, in spite of seeming perhaps too linguistically particular, applies to all important social formations that operate practically as religion in our contemporary world. For the moment, however, further clarification can proceed through consideration of three further issues regarding religious codes. The first concerns the relation of the religious code to the codes of other function systems. The second touches on code problems: that is, when codes lose their clarity or effectiveness. The third has to do with the already mentioned religious double coding or secondary codes.

Although function systems are differentiated from one another and within the overall society, they are also critically interdependent: they are structured at least in part with reference to one another.[5] One dimension of that interdependence is the relation among their respective binary codes. Above all, this means that two systems cannot operate on the basis of the same primary code, but that the structural logic of these codes in each system will be homologous. Religion, as system, therefore, is under a certain pressure to build itself up not only around such a code, but also around a different code than the other systems, one that differentiates it.

Yet that code will bear structural similarities to the others. The situation is complicated for religion – as it is for other systems – by the relatively lesser differentiation of religious forms in past societies, and thus also of those distinctions that now operate as system-specific binary codes. One symptom of this altered context is that religions today have difficulty operating on the basis of those codes that centrally inform other systems but with which less differentiated religion was clearly associated in the past, in particular true/false (science), enlightened/ignorant (education), ill/healthy (medicine) and legal/illegal (law). This does not exclude attempts on the part of religious instances to do just that. The above-mentioned Islamic valorization of *halal/haram* is one example, as is the widespread emphasis on healing in different religions like Pentecostal Christianity or African Traditional Religion. Yet the possibilities are quite limited and such distinctions can at best operate as secondary codes in religions. The primary code will be different. My observation of blessed/cursed as the central religious code is an attempt to put that operative difference into the most appropriate English words. It is not to suggest that Abrahamic categories are determinative in the global religious system.

Since the core role of a binary code is to precipitate a boundary between the operations of a system and its environment, the prime symptom of a weak or inoperative code is therefore that this boundary will be vague to non-existent. The recursiveness of communication will be compromised. Such a situation is not hard to imagine for other systems. For instance, if there were no tension between owning and not owning, an economy built on commodification and exchange would literally have no purchase in the societal environment. Money and prices would have no consistent meaning. As an example, a utopian communist society, where the ownership of everything was held in common, would not have an economy in that sense. The power to use things would be constructed and thereby distributed in other, non-exchange, economic ways. Similarly, without the difference between government and opposition or out-of-government, between in-power and out-of-power, the political state would have no bounded existence. In such a society, a radical anarcho-syndicalist commune for instance, there would be no state, not in the sense of a bounded territory, but in the sense of a regulating authority structure. Analogous statements could be made for the domain of education if everyone were guaranteed credentialling and everyday life were allowed to count as instruction, for sport if no one could lose, or a scientific discipline in which anything could be said as true and all theories were beyond testing. I introduce all these examples to show how code problems are real possibilities with real consequences; and how the problems are more often than not with the clarity and seriousness of the negative pole.

In the realm of religion, the parallel issue has often been discussed under the heading of secularization, and specifically secularization of reli-

gious institutions as opposed to the secularization of individual consciousness or other social domains outside religion (cf. Dobbelaere 1981; Kelley
1972; Stark and Bainbridge 1985). Much of the literature on this subject
expresses the problem as a loss of 'tension' between the religious institution and the surrounding society. Thus, for example, the decline in
membership and attendance in liberal Protestant denominations in the
West is attributed to the fact that these are no longer in sufficient tension
with the world around them, that they do not ask their charges to make
sufficient anti-worldly sacrifices. Although this diagnosis does correctly
point to the problem as being one of boundaries, the term 'tension' is inadequate for two reasons: it is too strong because it implies that viable
religion can only be constructed as opposition to the rest of society, to the
'world', when that is not the only possibility. It is also too vague because
the physical metaphor does not tell us how this tension is to be observed.
Seeing this issue as a problem with the religious code shows more clearly
that it is an insufficiency in the reflexive construction of religion itself: not
just construction 'in opposition to', but rather construction as such, as religion. It is this which undermines the differentiation of religion within
society. From this perspective, the difficulty which these liberal denominations face is that they have undermined the negative pole of their religious
code, namely the possibility of consequential religious failure, in particular
damnation, being or becoming cursed. It is not just that everyone is
redeem*able*; that is necessary if the code is to operate at all. It is that the
real possibility of hell is missing. Without an effective negative pole, much
of what happens in the world will not be susceptible of translation into
religious communication. Engaging in religious communication will less
likely be perceived to make a difference, thus undermining the boundary-
constructing recursiveness of the system. Much potentially religious
determination will dissipate into non-religious or less clearly religious categories and communication. The situation is similar to a court of law which
can only declare innocence, but not guilt; or a sports competition in which
there can be winners, but no one can lose. Code problems of this sort in
religion can undermine the differentiation of religion. Their solution,
however, does not necessarily have to be the revival of the code in question
or even resort to the code of another system. This brings us to the matter
of secondary codes, above all the moral distinction between good and bad.

The historical relation between religion, in particular contemporary religions, and morality is so well established that a great many religious and
non-religious people alike consider the two to be more essentially related.
Yet even though contemporary religions all style themselves as the foundation and guarantor of morality, it is also clear that moral judgements in
today's social world occur very frequently without any religious reference
whatsoever. Looked at from the perspective of binary codes, what this situation indicates is that the moral code of good/bad plays an important

supportive role in today's religions, but that it is not a code that religions have been able to claim unequivocally for themselves. Religion is in fact more than morality, and morality also operates outside religion, including in other function systems, for instance under the heading of 'ethics'. The moral code is in this sense a secondary code for religions; it does not structure their recursiveness so much as aid in the transformation of communications into religiously significant communication. In situations where the more clearly religious code is or has become problematic, however, this secondary code can offer a potential 'back-up' code. Thus, for example, in Christian denominations that no longer place much emphasis on the possibility of damnation for their members – and here I have in mind more than just liberal Protestant ones – we see the increasing or at least the more visible religious importance of moral judgements. If hell and purgatory are less threatening, issues of justice, the sanctity of life, and sexual control can attain a correspondingly higher profile. Such a development or strategy is nonetheless not without its problems because we are dealing with a secondary code, one that also operates very much outside the religious system. Religious institutions that orient their communication too much in this direction thereby risk weakening or even losing their specificity, which is to say the basis of their differentiation. In a society where the principal power structures are differentiated function systems, that result will have consequences for the relative importance of religious communication and religious power. It is therefore perhaps not surprising that the most striking religious developments today, such as for instance Islamic resurgence or the explosion of Pentecostal Christianity, take different routes, generally trying out different secondary codes than the moral one.

The binary code by itself does not already constitute religion; it is the operative distinction around which religions actually crystallize, the point of reference through which religions construct their self-reference or operational closure as systems. Put differently, the blessed/cursed code (or whatever alternative rendering one wishes to use), much like any binary code in other systems, is potentially religious but requires additional and elaborate specification for it to become the organizing principle of socially real religion. This is the role of religious programmes. For all intents and purposes, the programmes are the religions. They represent the stable patterns through which communications that constitute each religion refer to one another and thus achieve the closure or identity of the religion. If the code affords the differentiated identity of the religious system as a whole, the programmes lend form to the subsystems of that system, the religions. With regard to direct programmatic relations among religions, these are in the case of this system still rather minimal, a fact that does not exclude the (re)construction of these programmes with reference to one another. Further description of the programmes is thus virtually the same as elaborating on what each religion is. The main problems associated with programmes concern contestation over orthodoxy/orthopraxy, namely what does and does not belong: over authenticity, or what is central or peripheral; and authority, that is, the question of how the other two are determined. Rather than try to present a convincing summary of the programme of each religion, something that would automatically raise all three of these questions, I instead turn my attention to the matters of orthodoxy/orthopraxy, authenticity and authority themselves in two contemporary religions, Judaism and Buddhism. I choose these two deliberately because neither, for reasons purely of space, receives extensive treatment in the chapters below.

In spite of contestations about boundaries and authority, certain key constituents of programmatic Judaism are still comparatively easy to list. They are what the vast majority of those who consider themselves religiously Jewish and who are considered as such have in common. There is an all-powerful personal God who is deemed to be the creator of the universe; and there is the self-revelation of that God contained in the Torah, the Hebrew Bible and the 'oral Torah' as manifest above all in Mishnah and Talmud. The core purpose of religious communication (observance) is redemption, personally from sin but just as importantly the collective redemption of the people of Israel and therewith of the world. There is the possibility of heaven or hell for individuals depending on how well they conform to the will of God; collectively the theme of exile from or restoration to the promised land plays an equally critical role. Generally, somewhat unlike its Abrahamic cousin, Christianity, there is less emphasis on right belief and correspondingly more on correct practice, for Orthodox Jews especially obeying the set of God's commandments or *mitzvot*, all based in the Torah. Religious practices vary from one subdivision of Judaism to another but very frequently include regular group meetings at synagogues, during which set rituals are performed, Torah study, daily prayer, observance of dietary and commensality rules, and ritual ceremonies in the home, especially surrounding meals on the Sabbath and on holy days. Beyond these commonalities, there exist a significant variety of different groups, organizations, movements and networks with a variety of emphases, styles, specific practices and views of what is and is not properly Judaic. As with all the religions, there are numerous disputes and contestations over what is correct or good Jewish belief/practice and what is not, who belongs and who doesn't, and so on. Many of the subgroups define themselves in terms of different answers to central questions about orthodoxy and authority especially.

Overall, Buddhism lacks an easily identifiable revelatory or core programme, except in some of its subdivisions. Where the Tripitaka may occupy a central authoritative position for some Buddhist segments, for others it is the Pure Land, the Lotus or other East Asian sutras; and for yet others, such as Chan/Son/Zen Buddhism, it is none of the above. Although it is possible to argue that certain features, such as the three jewels of Buddha, *dharma* and *sangha*, or the four noble truths and eight-fold path, indicate a programmatic Buddhist core, these are probably far more along the lines of formal theological elements put forth in an effort to present Buddhist singularity than they are descriptive of the religious programme that most Buddhists actually follow. What counts as Buddhism among Buddhists in fact exhibits a wide variety, including vari-ations on monastic Buddhism, Buddhism centred on master/disciple relationships and specific lineages, and popular or lay Buddhisms such as Pure Land, Soka Gakkai or the typical lay practice of Theravadin regions. Much as, for instance, Christianity exhibits main subdivisions in its Protestant, Catholic and Orthodox versions; Judaism in its Orthodox, Conservative and Reform branches; Islam in its Sunni and Shi'a variants; or Hinduism in its Vaishnavite and Shaivite directions; so Buddhists often divide themselves according to whether they exemplify Vajrayana/Tantric/ Tibetan, Theravada/South-Southeast Asian or Mahayana/East Asian versions. Although such labelling does indeed describe some of the main lines of variation, it is in all cases also partial and artificial. It represents ways of understanding how manifest difference can nonetheless be consti-tutive of identity. The quest for a programmatic core is an aspect of the modern formation and reformation of religions. Synthesizing such a core for Buddhism, as for other religions, reflects the effort to imagine Buddhism as a singular and distinct religion. Such singularity is as much a product of programmatic unity as the programmatic unity is a result of the quest for identifiable singularity. Yet that quest is constitutive of Buddhism and the other religions quite as much as Anderson's 'imagined communities' are constitutive of nations. Programmes, far from settling the issue of what constitutes the religions, are actually a name for their ongoing construction and therefore of the need constantly to reproduce them as religions.

While codes and programmes are the most important aspects of reli-gions through which the religious function system achieves its particularity, they are by themselves still too abstract to understand how this system achieves concrete social reality. The codes and programmes have to be put into communicative practice. For this we need to know which communications are religious and how these communications are effective as religion. This is to ask about the religious elements or building blocks; and about the religious medium of communication or what consti-tutes religious power. Much like the religious code, for there to be a differentiated religious system beside other function systems, its *core* elements and its medium must be clearly distinct from those of other systems. A consideration of religious elements and religious medium or power is therefore best done in comparison with other function systems.

Perhaps the most clearly differentiated such systems in today's world are the capitalist economic system, the political system of states and the empirical scientific system. What we are asking is whether there exists a religious parallel to the core elements of these (and other) systems and a religious analogue to the characteristic ways of having power in these systems. What occupies the place of selling/purchasing, of deciding/regulating, or of generating data in religion? What corresponds to money, political power and scientific truth in religion? How is one religiously 'rich', 'powerful' or 'knowledgeable'? And what does one do to become so? The fact that we often speak of religion in terms of economic, political and scientific (not to mention health, artistic and even sports) metaphors not only shows that the answer to these questions may not be all that straightforward; it also indicates that the differentiation of religion as system depends on the answers being, in the final analysis, different.

In seeking to isolate typical religious elements, we are looking for those communications that both participants and outside observers consider to be centrally religious. I say 'centrally' because any communication can be drawn into the system as religiously significant, just as, for instance, any action can have economic, legal or political relevance. Yet certain kinds of communication reproduce the system at its core; they are a sort of *sine qua non* of religion and religions. In this place one can only put religious ritual or practice, in particular the sort which is structured as communication either imparted or understood by non-empirical or transcendent partners or realities. These postulated beings or realities (cf. Spiro 1987) are, in one form or another, characteristic of all modern religions quite as much as supply/demand or scarcity is characteristic of the capitalist economy, the idea of the common good of the political system, or falsifiability of the scientific system. They are a core and even axiomatic assumption upon which religion is constructed.[6] As such, they are not the same as what constitutes the system, whether that be codes, programmes, elements, power media or other features. They are, however, a prime condition for the possibility of these. Codes such as blessed/cursed (or alternative formulations as indicated above) operate in terms of this assumption; programmes are structured on the basis of it; it is invariably conceived as the basis of religious power, as well as being a defining feature of the most central religious elements or communications.

Given the status of the moral code of good/bad as a secondary code in virtually all of today's religions, it is perhaps not surprising that moral communications can have the quality of either core religious elements or as communication that is simply subject to religious interpretation. As core religious elements, the good or bad action would itself be seen as communication involving transcendent realities. It is an imparting of information that is understood. Thus, for example, the idea that God sees all that one does and thinks or the notion that an action has automatic karmic consequences structures such events as communication with God or ultimate reality. On the other hand, the understood moral quality of human communication and action can be merely the occasion for the performance of religious communications, as in the case of confession or meditation: moral interpretations in such cases induce and inform the core religious elements.

As the latter example illustrates, beyond core and constitutive 'communication with the gods', a great deal of other communication is just as important for the reproduction of the religious system.[7] This includes above all communication about these postulated transcendent realities and about the communication with them. This other communication is not only important, it may in certain cases comprise the majority of communication that we understand as religious, just as in other function systems much communication hovers around the core sort of communication, preparing for it, dealing with problems associated with it, reflecting on it, and so forth. Thus, communicating about God or the spirits, about revelation or dreams, about the religious significance of otherwise non-religious (for example, moral) behaviour, or about the correct way to pray, meditate or conduct ritual is in various ways just as important for the reproduction of core religious elements – ritual and practice – as is that communication itself. Similarly, government officials and members of the public communicate a great deal about political decisions and regulation before and after they are enacted; business people and customers communicate about production and consumption so that actual economic transactions may proceed; and lawyers, judges and witnesses communicate sometimes at great length and in complicated fashion before and after formal legal proceedings take place and legal decisions are actually rendered.

The relation of elements and programmes on the basis of the code(s) constitutes the recursiveness and thus the integrity or delimitation of the system. Three issues require further clarification in this regard, namely the role of adherents in this reproduction, how exactly religions operate in this way, and the relations among the thus constructed religions. Each of these is critical for understanding contemporary religion and religions as a function system.

Observing religion as communication removes human bodies and individuals from the centre of the picture. They become key conditions for the possibility of religion rather than defining building blocks. What constitutes religion is instead religious communications, the elements, which construct themselves with reference to each other according to a religious programme. Thus, for example, Muslim *salat* in a mosque or a Roman Catholic mass in a church obviously needs human beings to carry out the religious communication, but it is the communication itself that constitutes religion socially, not the bodies (which are important symbols or 'props' like the *mihrab* or the chalice) or even the 'faith' of the individuals participating. Turning around the prevailing idea, as represented for instance by Schleiermacher, James, Otto or W.C. Smith, it is the performance of the communication that constitutes religion socially, not the conscious attitudes of the human participants, relevant as the latter may also be. Accordingly, it is the communicative elements that refer to one another on the basis of the programmes. *Salat* refers to Qur'an, Sunna, Shari'a, *halal/haram*, salvation/damnation and other programmatic components, all of which in turn refer to *salat*. It has its meaning in that closed network of meanings. Muslims perform their prayers primarily with reference to that circular system of significations: a Muslim prays because it is the will of Allah, because it expresses the submission of humans and creation to Allah; all other motivations are *programmatically* strictly secondary, even irrelevant. The individual Muslim can, of course, make different, even unorthodox connections, say, for instance, in order to assure that others consider him or her as a good Muslim. But, given that it is the communications that reproduce the system, that does not matter unless such an attitude becomes thematized in other religious communication, for example, as transgression. Similarly, the throngs that participate at one of the pope's large open-air masses may not all approach their participation as a religious performance; they may perhaps understand it as entertainment, as art, or even something they are doing out of simple curiosity. What matters for the reproduction of the Catholic Christian religious system, however, is the performance of the mass with such a large participation. The attitudes, again, only gain relevance if thematized in this or other religious communication which operates meaningfully within the recursive network of self-referential programmatic communication.

Similar analyses could be carried out for a wide variety of rituals and other religious communication, from the chanting of a Buddhist sutra or Torah reading in a synagogue to Pentecostal glossolalia or Hindu *puja*. Their status as elements that generate and reproduce a particular religious system depends on their meaningful reference to a programmatically closed set of other communications. This characteristic, or even 'requirement', immediately points to another area of potential ambiguity concerning the systemicity of the religious system: is the referential range of any given set of elements sufficiently closed? The only way to answer this question in a specific case is to look at how the same or other religious communication observes them. Sometimes the connections are contained in the communication itself, for instance in the words that form part of the ritual (e.g. a liturgical formula in a Christian communion ceremony, 'Take, eat, this is the body of Christ given for thee'). In other cases, subsequent or previous communications impart the connections, as in the case of an exhortative sermon, the telling of a sacred story, the singing of religious songs, or in public theological reflection. Such connecting or referring need not, of course, be undisputed. Differing interpretations and controversy surrounding them, as I have already emphasized, can be the occasion for the communication that establishes and reinforces the connections. This sort of activity is itself symptomatic, even if not by itself sufficient, of systemicity or system formation. That said, in the absence of such overt self-reference, religion as operative social system becomes questionable, a matter at best of outside, perhaps scientific, observation. Indeed, the apparent lack of clear recursive connection of much communication that has the structure of core religious elements is the main reason that arguing for the existence of a global religious system is less than straightforward. Above all, the tremendous variety of what is often called 'popular' religious practice begs the question of whether and how these communications are incorporated into particular religions, let alone into a single and globally extended religious system. Addressing this issue leads to a consideration of the relation of the religions among each other, to the way that they together might constitute a single system. It also introduces the related question of outside observation or thematization of these religions, to the issue of recognition.

In the previous section, I focused on a historical analysis of the modern formation of different religions. Subsequent chapters provide much greater detail in this regard for some of these religions. An important aspect of these developments is that, like the states of the political system, the religions that did take on modern form did so to a significant extent with reference to one another, sometimes in reaction to one another. Movements to re-form Islam or form Hinduism and Sikhism in late nineteenth- and early twentieth-century South Asia, for instance, did so in response to and in a context that included Christian missionizing in the same region and each other. Earlier twentieth-century movements in China, such as that led by Tai Hsu, sought to strengthen and unite Buddhism at least in part with an eye on the forms that Christianity took, even seeking to do better than the latter. While such developments can be seen as a mere 'aping' of Christianity, as in the parallel case of modern state formation, the differences that they generated among the religions are just as important as the similarities. The movements reinforced, reformed and generated recursive structures for each religion, to some extent with reference to parallel processes in other (re)forming religions, to a larger degree in terms of each religion's received traditions or 'resource' base. It is this formation of religions that is at the root of the contemporary global religious system quite as much as the formation of modern states founded the corresponding political system. States are not religions and vice versa, but there has been this similarity in how the two systems have come about. Among the many differences between the two, however, is that in the case of religions, inter-religious relations, along with the institutions that lend them form, are far less developed than in the case of international relations among states. Thus, what together constitutes the different religions as a single system is largely the parallelism in form that I am discussing here: parallelism at the level of codes, programmes, elements, and as I will address shortly, power media.

The coherence of the religions into a single system does not rely entirely on religious instances themselves restructuring and observing their religions in this way. Outside observation helps, especially thematization in the communicative processes of other major function systems such as the political and the educational. I discuss this matter in greater detail below and in Chapter 6. Here it is sufficient to point out that the recognition of the religions in government legislation, in legal decisions, in educational curricula, and so forth, is an important contributor to the formation of the religions and to their coherence as a single system: they are treated as different manifestations of a single social modality and this is a significant dimension of their being just that.

If such arguments address the question of the singularity of the religious system, the many potentially religious elements that escape recursive incorporation in one of the religions are another matter. The capacity of the various religions to include these elements is somewhat limited; unlike states, religious authorities do not have at their disposal effective religious mechanisms to enforce their orthodoxies/orthopraxies. Instead, they tend to rely on the capacities of other systems, notably but not exclusively the political, legal or educational where such resort proves possible; and on family socialization of the young. Beyond these, religion seeks to persuade, to convert or to exhort their putative adherents to conforming practice. Such efforts seek to reduce religious elements that are not integrated into the programmes or to reinterpret and reform those elements so that they do conform. The degree of success that recognized and restructured religions have had in this task of course varies from place to place and from religion to religion. At the end of the day, the domination of the global religious system in its domain is not nearly as complete as is the case for the capitalist economic system or the global political system. It is relatively easy to 'print' one's own religious 'currency' and religions do not have an effective monopoly on the legitimate use of sacred power. It is to this last issue that I now turn.

It will be noted that thus far in this section I have not spoken a great deal about religious beliefs. These are, of course, of great importance in the structure of the religious system and its subsystems, the religions – and not just Christianity. They are not, however, directly constitutive of it the way elements are. This fact is only too evident in most of the religions, which clearly put the emphasis on right action, or orthopraxy – that is, programme conforming communication – and comparatively less on the cognitive aspect of this action. The main role of belief in today's religions is not as the core elements of these religions but rather as something close to the name for the peculiarly religious medium of power (Beyer 1997;

Gössman 1971; Luhmann 1977, 2000b). Belief in this sense is not just intellectual assent to one or more propositions, but also and more importantly 'faith' in the efficacy of the communications that flow from those propositions, however precisely or vaguely formulated. The person who prays, meditates, performs ritual sacrifice or speaks in tongues does so in the *belief* that these religious performances or communications are effective in bringing about certain religiously defined results, consequences defined through the religious codes and programmes. The religious performances are believed to sanctify, bless, heal, liberate, bring in harmony or create merit and thereby to diminish the polar opposite result. The reverse holds for improper action or communication. To be sure, the precise way in which this religious power medium is structured and understood varies from religion to religion, and my use of rather Christian-sounding words like 'belief' and 'faith' is more an artefact of historical Christian influence on the English language that it is a claim that such words are the most appropriate for describing the power medium of the global religious system. Words like 'piety' or 'devotion' or, to borrow in a way from some contemporary neo-Pagans, '*magick*' might be just as or even more accurate. In this light, the still common idea among some scholars of religion that religion is fundamentally about beliefs and that these beliefs are primarily a matter of cognition or explanation (cf. Stark 1999) is a modern Protestant Christian peculiarity – an aspect of certain religious programmes – that has its roots in the European Reformation and in the differentiation of religion from science in that same socio-historical context. Yet even in this division of Christianity, belief by itself does not reproduce religion but rather the acting out or communicating of that belief in specifically religious performances, including regular professions of faith. Here again a comparison with how power media operate in other function systems may help move the analysis forward.

The corresponding medium in the capitalist economy is money. Money buys commodities; it is the embodiment of economic power. Yet the value of money is, like all social power, constructed or imagined. It is also a matter of faith. Money has value because we believe that it does, because we consider it to be effective in generating economic communication. For money to have value or power, it has to show that by being capable of buying something. The use of the medium in economic communication reproduces the power or value of the medium; failure to use it, the ceasing of its circulation, amounts to the diminishing of this power. Similar statements could be made about political power in the political system or scientific truth in the science system. The respective media are generated in their use and continued 'circulation' such that governments that do not enact regulation or legislation are not effective governments and often will lose authority, legitimacy and power as a result; and research that does not inspire further research tends to be forgotten. This is the case at the level of the systems themselves. For individuals involved in these systems matters are not quite so drastic: one can 'strike it rich' and be wealthy for the rest of one's life. One can see one's political star rise comparatively briefly and gain a lasting legacy; or publish one outstanding piece of research and live off the reputation for an entire career. The situation in the systemic realm of religion is analogous. Religious power is made manifest and reproduced in 'acts of faith' (or piety or devotion or sacrifice), in the continuous and preferably increasing generation of elements of religion that are deemed efficacious in terms of the central religious code. Much as in the other systems, while there is room for and even the systemic necessity of concentrations of systemic power – for example, in charismatic leaders, in monastic, sectarian or other virtuosity, in exceptional visions granted to ordinary people – the dominant emphasis is on the constant increase of the medium through an increase in the production of elements. Accordingly, the modern religious system, *like the others*, tends towards mass participation; and religious vitality more often than not is measured – even and especially by religious people themselves – in terms of how many 'acts of faith' (that is, religious communications) are performed by how many people. The quality of these acts, their programmatic conformity, matters; they have to follow the rules. Yet the self-referentiality of the system, its auto-logic, encourages strength and vitality to be measured largely through the volume of religious power generated, which is directly proportional to the rate of production of elements.

This comparison of the religious power medium to those of other systems is more than a question of imaginative illustration. As with codes and elements, the quite deliberate implication is that the parallels exist because these systems have historically constructed themselves to some degree with reference to each other. As I have noted before, the modern religious system is historically peculiar in many ways; and not the least of these ways is that its very existence and visibility depends in large measure on the simultaneous emergence of the other function systems. The latter help structure what religion is *not*. Accordingly, in order to understand the operation of the religious system better, we must explore its relation to these other systems more directly. Oddly enough, in the scientific literature on modern religion, this matter has until relatively recently held a preponderant place, specifically under the heading of secularization, which usually carries the connotation of some sort of religious decline. It is to a consideration and reinterpretation of this aspect of the religious system that I now turn.

Secularization, privatization and the orthogonality of the religious system

In the classic social-scientific literature of the later nineteenth and early twentieth century, religion often held a central place, but most authors also felt that it was somehow at odds with the dominant features and tendencies of modern society (Durkheim 1965; Freud 1985; Marx and Engels n.d.; Weber 1992 [1930]). This notion that modern society was a prevailingly or at least increasingly secular or non-religious society held sway in the literature until the post-World War II period (Beckford 1989), and in the 1960s experienced another temporary dominance, especially in the writings of authors like Peter Berger, Thomas Luckmann, Harvey Cox and Bryan Wilson (Berger 1967; Cox 1965; Luckmann 1967; Wilson 1966). Since the 1970s, however, the idea that modernity somehow implied an absolute decline in the presence and social importance of religion has gradually faded such that by the end of the century the pendulum seemed to have swung the other way, with scholars across the Western world, especially in the United States but also in Europe and elsewhere, declaring that the thesis was simply wrong and always had been (Davie 2000; Stark and Iannaccone 1994). All along this trajectory, however, a significant number of authors insisted that the question of the relation between religion and modernity could not be subsumed under the simple option of decline or maintenance, that the question of secularization or sacralization was more complex, had more than one dimension, and was subject to different answers depending on what one meant by religion, on region, historical period or social location (Dobbelaere 1981; Martin 1978; Simpson 1988). Secularization meant more than one thing, had more than one outcome, and was more about religious change than it was about either decline or resurgence. Observing religion in today's global society as a function system very much adopts this latter view of the situation. Accordingly, in consonance with other observers such as José Casanova (Casanova 1994) and Luhmann (Luhmann 1977), to mention only two, I view secularization primarily as a question of the consequences of differentiation, specifically as the outcome of the historical development of a plurality of function systems as global society's dominant subsystems, one of which is for religion. From this perspective, secularization refers to the non-religiousness and hence secularity of the *other* subsystems and to the effects of this situation on the form, function and importance of religion. Secularization is about the relation between the religious system and the others. Whether that means 'weaker' religion or 'stronger' religion is a question of comparison with these other systems, and only in that light with the situation in past societies or of today's society as a whole.

Comparing the religious to other function systems involves two sorts of consideration, namely the relative efficacy of religion as a system in comparison with the others, and the degree of conditioning or constraining effect that the religious system has on the others. One might phrase these as two questions: how powerful is religion as a system? and how much does the religious system affect the others? Although these two questions are related, it is important to stress that they are not the same. The former has more to do with the internal structures of the religious system, the latter with the incorporation of religious criteria into the internal structures of other systems. Thus, just to take the example of the economic and political systems by way of illustration, the capitalist economy is not only powerful and pervasive in its own right, its criteria are incorporated significantly into the processes of the political system which not only must see to its own finances but cannot regulate economic matters in disregard for what the economic system dictates. The reverse is also the case, in spite of claims that 'globalization' implies the decline in the power of states. How then is it with religion?

I deal with the question of the internal coherence of religion as system first. The question we are asking here concerns the efficacy of religion as a societal system, and not directly the presence or absence of communication that could be considered religious. Religion is at issue, not just religiousness. Thus, as I emphasized in the previous section, the number of people engaging how frequently in religious communication is important since the system cannot persist without elements; yet even more critical is how well such communication coheres into a recursively structured system. Another way of approaching the issue is to look at the nature and extent of religious convergence or authority. If anyone and everyone constructed their religious communication in whatever fashion suited them from time to time, we could speak of religiousness but not of religion. The high and increasing pluralism in today's religious world as well as the great degree of variability in the practice even of the formed religions makes this a real issue. Adapting Thomas Luckmann's analysis of the 1960s (Luckmann 1967), if religion really did become purely or even dominantly a matter of individual *bricolage*, then this would amount to a fairly radical 'secularization' of our society. Religiousness might be broadly present in the consciousnesses of individuals, but it would have a great deal of difficulty having any real social effect. This is more or less what Bryan Wilson (Wilson 1979) meant by secularization and, as Luckmann's title aptly put it, such religion would be invisible. Comparing such a situation to other systems, it would be the equivalent of everyone being able to print their own money, raise their own armies, enact their own laws, declare their own truths according to their own criteria, or certify their own qualifications. Yet, even though this sort of atomized religious expression is undoubtedly on the rise in various parts of the world today (cf. Heelas *et al.* 2005), convergent or authoritative religion is also very much present and in many places dominant. This is religious expression that follows programmatic patterns and these programmatic patterns are the religions. As I noted above when discussing religious programmes, while the religions may not be all that there is to the global religious system, they do constitute it quite as much as the sovereign states together make up the global political system. Without the religions there would in effect be no religious system. Indeed, the radically individualized sort of religious practice just mentioned can only appear socially as religion by virtue of its resemblance to the forms that the religions take.

Even if we can accept for the moment that religion has sufficient convergent form to warrant its observation as a societal system, that by itself does not settle the question of efficacy. In the absence of any logical or defensible criterion by which this could be measured absolutely, the only way to address the issue further is on the basis of comparison, not, as I said above, with other societies, but with other function systems in today's society. From this perspective, we have to consider more than one factor. First, although religion clearly has a power dimension, as I discussed above, its power medium does not have the sort of clarity that is typical of some other systems. Here the fungibility of money or the clear delimitation of political office, among others, can serve as notable contrasts. How much economic power exists can be measured in terms of money; whether or not one has political power is a matter of occupying defined positions which have jurisdiction in precisely defined territories. Similarly, educational attainment translates itself into grades and diplomas, prowess in sport through records (hence sport's obsession with statistics), and even health through the absence of clinically defined disease. Religion, in comparison, has quite modest possibilities in this respect, at least as far as fungibility and precise delimitation are concerned. Relatively few mechanisms for measuring piety and devotion have been developed, and these are in any case not comparable from one religion to another, often not even from one subdivision of a religion to another. Various religious 'offices' also exist and these quite often carry with them the attribution of elevated levels of religious power. Priests, preachers, gurus, sadhus, rabbis, ulama, pirs, lamas, monks and nuns usually represent significant concentrations of such power; their religious communication often carries more 'weight' than that of individual 'lay' devotees. And yet the power distinction between religious virtuoso and lay adherent has, if anything, diminished in the modern historical process of religion formation, as the above-discussed massification of contemporary religion indicates. That said, however, this relative vagueness of religious power or piety does not necessarily pose a problem for religion as concerns its efficacy and societal influence. Other function systems, notably that for art and entertainment or perhaps increasingly that for mass media, display a similar vagueness in how systemic power is acquired and recognized; but this does not detract from the pervasive influence and presence that these systems have. Nonetheless, in comparison with the other systems, religion does have certain peculiarities that can be understood as a comparative weakness or disadvantage. These concern the relative difficulty in instrumentalizing religion and, borrowing another term from Luhmann, its orthogonality vis-à-vis the other systems (Luhmann 2000b).

Even a cursory look at the more prominent religions in today's religious system shows a consistency in their structures which we can describe as an emphasis on holism. These religions claim relevance to virtually anything having to do with human life and the universe because they purport to offer a perspective that grounds or makes possible the whole. Analyses of religion such as that of Berger or Luhmann, with their respective emphases on distinctions between cosmic and nomic or transcendent and immanent, treat this feature of (modern) religion as more or less definitive. The cosmic or the transcendent are the proper domain of religion, but the function of this domain is to render the opposite pole, the nomic or immanent, meaningful. The 'other world' is the condition for the possibility of meaning and power in 'this world'; and religion is that which allows access in this world to the source of power and meaning in the 'other world', even if that 'other world' is conceived as an intimate dimension of 'this world' (cf. Beyer 1994). Thus, to illustrate from a number of the religions, in the Abrahamic religions, God creates, renders possible or communicates the world. In Hinduism the Godhead, whether Brahma, Shiva, Devi or Vishnu, is ultimately the source, the reason and indeed the only underlying reality of this world. From a core Buddhist perspective, all worldly existence is a product of dependent origination or previous causes, the entire edifice resting on, not so much nothing at all, as upon that which it is impossible to say anything about but which is nonetheless the only reality, namely nirvana or Buddha consciousness. Not all religions are in such a principled way 'monotheistic' or 'monothetic', but all of them have in common the idea of this fundamental realm that is the condition for the possibility of everything worldly, nomic and immanent.

While this may be an accurate description of a central feature of these modern religions, we have to ask why this is the case, above all when one considers that these religions as modernly reconstructed as well as their religio-cultural antecedent forms in past societies were very often also or even predominantly directed towards much more 'this-worldly' concerns and religious communication. Their aim is and has been, for instance, healing the sick, bringing rain, ensuring success in war, legitimating regimes, controlling one's neighbour, encouraging fertility, picking a marriage partner, acquiring wealth, assuring a good hunt, and so on: practical everyday issues, not just ultimate goals. The answer to this question lies in the practical limits to the instrumentalization of religion, but this only in comparison with the other systems. In terms of having concrete, visible, 'this-worldly' and empirically recognizable effect, religion seems to have more limited possibilities than do many or most of these others. For the sheer production of goods and services, that is wealth, the mechanisms and instrumental structure of the capitalist economy are noticeably more effective than prayer and sacrifice to the gods. For healing illness, medicalized health is verifiably more powerful than reliance on faith or shamanistic voyages. And empirical science with its logical procedures and experimental techniques produces results that no religious technique has shown itself capable of doing. Put into the terms that I used in the previous chapter, the 'adaptive upgrading' that has been such an important feature of the construction of these modern function systems has resulted in the unprecedented production of instrumental power for many of these systems; but for religions, it seems more to have favoured the enhanced development of their 'other-worldliness' (cf. Weber 1946). This may very well be by default; other systems have taken over, developed and sought to monopolize the production and reproduction of social power media like truth, law, political power, wealth and even beauty. Religion appears to be unchallenged only in the operation of faith or piety (cf. Simmel 1959).

This peculiar specialization of modern religion does not, however, spell the irrelevance let alone disappearance of the religious mode in modern global society, as perhaps certain versions of the secularization thesis had it. It does, however, point to particular consequences which might be interpreted precisely as indicators of a decline in social significance. One of these is a high degree of privatization, which here means that it is relatively more difficult to enforce religious authority and therefore to ensure a concentrated degree of orthodoxy/orthopraxy (see Beyer 1994). Another way of putting this is to say that religion in the context of the modern global system is not only prone to pluralism, it also lacks much in the way of effective means for limiting that pluralism. In the political system, by comparison, the physicality and set amount of territory on the globe supplies a ready-made way of restricting the number and, to some degree, the size of states; as does the force that states typically have at their disposal. Moreover, the religious power medium's lack of fungibility makes it difficult to translate that medium from one religion to another. An apparent result is therefore increasing pluralism both within religions and between religions, a tendency that if it develops sufficiently could threaten the systemicity of the religious system as such. At the moment, this outcome seems unlikely; and short of that result such privatization and pluralization does not imply that religion ceases or will cease to be an effective and highly present domain in modern global society. The system of art and entertainment, after all, suffers from similar lack of instrumentalization and consequent pluralization of its forms. This system is nonetheless very effective world wide, perhaps because it has found a synergistic – which is to say mutually reinforcing without de-differentiating – relation with the incontrovertibly instrumentalized, convergent and powerful capitalist economic system and more recently with the mass-information media. Such a linking, at least of economy and religion, seems unlikely. The linking of mass-information media and religion has, by contrast, been somewhat of a constant at least since the nineteenth century. In another direction, it is probably because of the advantage of such relationships that there has also been a historical tendency to politicize religion, to try to establish such synergistic relations between a state and a particular religion. I shall return to this question shortly.

A further apparent consequence of religion's comparatively low instrumentality is what Luhmann has called its generally orthogonal relation to the other systems (Luhmann 2000b). I have elsewhere tried to analyze this same feature in terms of religion's affinity for addressing 'residual problems', which is to say problems that either other systems do not address or which they create without being able to solve (Beyer 1992, 1997). What this means is that, while the power media of the other function systems are mutually reinforcing, access to and distribution of the religious medium seems to bear far less, if any, relation to that of other systems. It runs perpendicularly or orthogonally to the pattern of access and distribution of the other systems. Symptomatic of this divergence is that, while people in today's society who have money generally also have greater access to health care, education, scientific knowledge, legal recourse, political power, sport participation and even artistic performance, access to religious power is much more easily available even to the poor, powerless and marginalized. The richest and most powerful regions of the world are not also mostly the ones where religion is most present; one might even be tempted to say that the exact reverse is true. While that would be going beyond what the evidence indicates, undeniable is that religious power is distributed differently in global society than is the power of other systems. Religion, it appears, is relatively easy to produce without simultaneous access to the highly technicized and specialized means that are typical of most of the other systems. Religious 'virtuosi' or religious 'experts' are still possible and very much present in today's society; they are just as important for the reproduction of the religious system as are corresponding specialists in the other systems. Yet even religious expertise does not require a high level of access to the power of the other systems; it only needs 'calling', 'dedication', 'study', 'inspiration' or 'charisma'. This does not rule out religious expertise as the result of expensive and scientifically rigorous academic training or of mass-media savvy; but those routes are not the only or perhaps even the dominant ones.

Religion's character as an orthogonally constructed, almost alternative, system further gives it a peculiar status as a system that seems more local than global, and more non-systemic or even anti-systemic than systemic. Accordingly, religions tend to locate themselves largely in the gaps left by the more dominant systems. They found oppositional movements, they take critical stands towards the dominant systems, often locating the roots of local and global problems in the operation of these systems. They gravitate in their operation towards the marginalized people and regions of the world. They create opportunities for sectarian flight from the world of the dominant systems. They have been peculiarly suited for founding movements that define and assert the exclusive *difference* of particular groups and cultures in the face of the seemingly homogenizing and imperialistic tendencies of the dominant systems. And they are among the most important institutions for helping the more marginalized, but not excluded, people structure rapid changes such as those that typically occur with migration (see e.g. Ebaugh and Chafetz 2000; Geschiere 1999; Gifford 1998; Martin 2002; Meyer 1999; Vásquez and Marquardt 2003).

Examples of these sorts of role for religions are not hard to find. The Christian World Council of Churches and various divisions of the Roman Catholic church involve themselves heavily in environmental issues, in peace issues, in population issues, and in issues of poverty and exclusion, often styling themselves as among the few consistent voices for the poor and the voiceless. Islamic movements such as certain Black Muslim groups in the United States or the Muslim Brotherhood in Egypt see it as their role to provide support services in health, education and welfare for the marginalized within their countries. In several countries of sub-Saharan Africa, religious organizations are among the only effective ones in providing these sorts of service to entire populations. Most of the so-called religious 'fundamentalisms' are not so much movements to preserve threatened religious and cultural traditions as they are neo-traditional but innovative movements that seek to establish a particular region or culture as clearly different from all others, and above all from those in their own territories and outside it that seek to succumb to the relativizing and even homogenizing influence of the dominant systems. Religions offer very suitable resources for asserting such differences, especially in the form of modes and codes of behaviour that are solidly rooted in the very differently structured societies of the past and therefore more likely to appear as sharply contrasting today. In this regard, forms of dress and sharply patriarchal gender roles are frequently used symbols of such difference, being prominent in Islamic, Christian, Judaic, Sikh and Hindu forms of such identifying religious movements (Riesebrodt 1993; Van der Veer 1994b). Finally, whether one is looking at rural/urban migrations or global migrations from one part of the world to another, religious institutions and above all reconstructed religious institutions are notoriously among the most important ways in which migrants establish continuity in the face of fairly radical change. It is under this heading that one might include movements as diverse as the Soka Gakkai and other new religious movements in post-war Japan, the Buddha Light International/Fo Guang Shan in North America, and the countless temples, mosques, churches and gurdwaras that have sprung up in Europe, Australia, Canada and the United States as expressions of new and recent immigrants.

All these examples, however, only show the degree to which religious institutions are *also* suitable for filling in various gaps and running counter to dominant trends. Overall, however, such activity is only the minor part of what religion does. Most religious formations, organizations, activity and movements around the world are much more a part of normal everyday life, reproducing themselves like the typical action of any other social system. In other words, the bulk of religious activity around the world simply reproduces the religious system and does not concern itself consistently or directly with such compensatory applications.

The orthogonality of religion vis-à-vis the other systems is a consequence both of the specialized and differentiated structuring of religion – as Weber put it, its penchant for 'rejection' of the 'world' – and the different composition of the other systems. 'Other-worldly' tendencies in religious forms, while not at all unique to the modern and globalized circumstance, take on a different significance when religion becomes the focus of one function system beside others with a much higher degree of 'this-worldly' instrumentalization or technicization. That historical outcome, however, only implies a serious weakness of religion in comparison with the other systems if the result is that religious criteria have little effect on the latter's operations. Here we move to the second question introduced above, namely the degree to which religion informs the operation of other function systems. To the degree that science, economy, state, health and so forth can and do ignore what happens in the realm of religion, one can speak of a relative decline in its social importance. If they ignore it entirely, then that would be equivalent to a very 'secularized' society. An important empirical question is therefore how much religion makes itself felt in other systems, how much it constrains their operation. I say empirical because the answer varies from case to case, from time to time, and from region to region; it is not inherent in the nature of modern global society itself. A very brief look at the relations between religion and the political (and thereby legal) and the economic systems can serve to illustrate.

One of the more constant features of the contemporary world is the intermittent but frequent attempts to politicize religion: that is, to use the power of the state to enforce one or more religious orthodoxies. The examples vary a great deal, ranging from the effort to meld religion and state in the Islamic Republic of Iran and Sabbath observance laws in Israel, to regulations favouring the Russian Orthodox church in Russia and the constitutional declaration of Zambia as a Christian country. What they show is that religious criteria can indeed constrain the political system in many states in contemporary society; but that constraint varies a great deal from place to place and from time to time, and in many countries religion exercises very little such constraint. Currently, this sort of influence is muted to slight in most countries around the world; but that could change, in one direction or the other. The only limits that the functionally differentiated structure of global society seems to put on it is that 'theocracies', or the thorough de-differentiation of religion and state, are just as difficult to maintain as radically 'atheistic' states.

The constraining or conditioning possibilities for religion on capitalist economy would seem to be more limited, but they are far from non-existent. One could begin with attempts to create Islamic economies in countries like Saudi Arabia and Pakistan, but these efforts are better seen as a dimension of the politicization of religion in these countries. Islamic economics amounts to political regulation; otherwise these countries are as capitalist as any other. Where we can detect a more properly religious conditioning of the economy is through religion's effect on the production of goods and services. The question here is: how much is religion the occasion for, or how much does it affect, economic production and consumption? From one perspective, this is Weber's question: does religion encourage or hinder capitalist economic exchange? From another, however, what we are looking for is the degree to which religion generates and thereby influences economic production and consumption. Thus, political states condition economy by their regulations, but just as importantly by their massive expenditures. The systems for art and sport have little to no direct influence on how capitalism works, but their extensive commodification means that they have a substantial indirect effect. Correspondingly, religion may have a certain positive or negative effect on economic motivation *à la* Weber, but the level of economic exchange of religious goods and services is also of significance. That both these vary from time to time and from region to region almost goes without saying; and thus so does the influence of religion.

Similar analyses could be carried out for the relation of religion to other systems, such as the educational, the scientific or the mass media. The results in these cases would be similar: depending on the region or the time, religion can on occasion be seen to be constraining the internal operations of these systems; but on the whole, such conditioning is quite limited. From this perspective, therefore, religion is rarely unimportant or entirely uninfluential; sometimes strong to the point of being a dominant influence; more often than not somewhere in between, of some significance but not dominant.

Religion in other types of social system: lending religions form

The analysis of the global religious system presented in this chapter thus far has frequently referred to the interrelated issues of self-reference, convergence, orthodoxy/orthopraxy and authority. These terms are vital in the discussion because they deal with the very identification of this function system, what generates it and maintains it as a distinct social reality. The ideas of code, programme, element and medium deal with the social 'stuff' of this system, but they do not address directly how one assures the recursiveness, the convergence of this religious matter. What mechanisms, social techniques or social forms keep religious communication within recognized and recognizable bounds? What keeps the possibility of religious pluralism from eventuating in the above-discussed de-systemization of religion altogether? What forms, in other words, does effective religious authority take in contemporary society? I am not referring here directly to the offices or roles of authority, such as in Weber's well-known magician-prophet-priest typology (Weber 1978). These roles are of course involved, but the larger question concerns the forms in which these leadership offices can be effective. In the classic sociological literature, beginning with Troeltsch and Weber, but extensively developed thereafter, the main way to address this question has been through the idea of 'religious organization', namely the church/sect typology and all its elaborations and variants (see McGuire 2002: ch. 5). These typologies can serve as our point of departure, but they also have to be unpacked and taken in a different direction because they pose the question too narrowly; organizing religion is only one way of assuring its authoritative convergence.

In introducing the church/sect distinction, Troeltsch had in view precisely the problem we are addressing here, namely one religious authority structure, the putatively dominant and overarching church, being challenged by one or more smaller and marginal ones in the form of sects. Embedded in that analysis were already a couple of factors that point beyond the twofold typology itself (Troeltsch 1931). On the one hand, the church implied not only itself but also its relation to another powerful social unit, the state. An important aspect of what made the church authoritative was its positive relation to the state, meaning that the church typically looked to the state to back up its authority claims. On the other hand, however, the sect represented a more clearly differentiated religious form, one not 'tainted' with the relation to the state and all sorts of other 'compromises', which is to say non-religious selection criteria. A third type, one which was not subsumed very often in subsequent sociological discussions, was 'mysticism', which is precisely the unformed religiosity that I adumbrated above. Contained in Troeltsch's analysis, therefore, are several of the factors that are germane in the present context: differentiation, authority, recursiveness (clarity of structure), pluralism, and the possibility of de-differentiation or de-systematization.

Subsequent development of the typology really only added one other possibility, namely the denomination as introduced by H.R. Niebuhr (Niebuhr 1929). What this notion contributed to the debate was the idea that religious pluralism could exist in a society without challenging other and otherwise dominant structures; that religion in the modern context could be differentiated from state and society at the same time as it differentiated internally; and that this pluralistic situation could be stable. The

most critical contribution of the denomination is that it shows how organization itself can be the key to pluralistic religious convergence, this latter
being a vital feature of today's global religious system. In this light, it
becomes clear that this typology of religious organization refers primarily
to that modern situation of religion and only very poorly to others in
which religion is much more marginally organized and differentiated as
system. That said, the typology also has to be unpacked if it is to be useful
for understanding, not just modern religion but also global religion.

Transposing the church/sect/denomination typology into a Luhmannian
social systems key allows the broader perspective required. In this mode,
we ask not what are the possible types of religious organization but rather
through what kinds of social system does religion attain authoritative form
in contemporary society. From this perspective, organizations are only one
such kind of social system, not a general term for all the ways that religion
is given form. As discussed in Chapter 1, three other possibilities exist
beside organizations, namely social movements, societal systems and interactions. The four types are not mutually exclusive in that each type
conditions the operation of the other three: social movements rely on interactions, organizations are critical for social movements, societal systems
influence the structure and content of interactions, and so forth.
Accordingly, religion and religions gain form in contemporary society in
four ways: as (1) organized religion (including denominations, churches,
and sects); (2) social movement religion; (3) religion thematized in societal
(namely function) systems, including of course the religious system itself;
and (4) as social network religion (networks of interaction). The last category includes what one might call 'community' religion; the third
encompasses the use of societal systems beside the religious to support religious authority.

Organized religion

One of the more notable features of contemporary global society is the
proliferation of organizations in virtually every sphere of social life.
Although these are certainly not evenly distributed in this society, any
more than is wealth or power, they affect social life in all parts of the
world. The most powerful of these are economic and political organizations. Yet, both at the national and the international level, an ever
increasing number of non-business and non-state organizations make their
presence felt in our daily lives. Among these is a complex array of religious
organizations of greatly varying power, size, internal structure and degree
of stability. More than any of the other forms, it is organizations that give
religions the recursive presence that is at issue here. Although the Christian
Roman Catholic church is no doubt the largest and most evident of these,
every other recognizable and recognized religion has them. They range

from Buddhist monasteries to Hindu temple organizations, from Muslim Sufi brotherhoods to Christian Pentecostal churches, from organizations that run major Muslim, Hindu or Christian pilgrimage centres to international Daoist societies. Their span can be anything from extremely local to worldwide, from the storefront church in Brooklyn, New York to the international Orthodox Jewish Agudat Israel. Moreover, organizations are one of the two most important mechanisms for giving form to a new religion, or for concretizing variations in already recognized ones. Thus, for example, the much discussed religious pluralism of a country like the United States is primarily an organizational pluralism; religious organizations can lend form to the most minimal variations, enhancing the appearance of pluralism even when the underlying religious programmes are comparatively uniform. Some relatively new religions such as the Baha'i faith or the Church of Scientology, as well as old ones such as the Roman Catholic church, locate organization at their theological core and have successfully established themselves or maintained their presence largely through their concerted organizational strategies. In other cases, such as that of the Hindu Rashtriya Swayamsevak Sangh and Vishva Hindu Parishad, the greater organization of religion has been a deliberate strategy in order to 'compete' with other religions. Many states and legal systems, such as that of countries as diverse as Japan, Indonesia and Canada, encourage the organization of religions as a condition for their recognition and thus for the application of freedom of religion provisions.

Social movement religion

Social movements offer another way of giving concrete social form to religion. I discussed their basic characteristics, especially in comparison to organizations, in Chapter 1. They do so in varying degrees. Thus, the many religio-national movements in regions as diverse as North America, the Balkans and South Asia have incorporated themes and semantics from particular religions as part of their visions of nation and as concrete aspects of their mobilizing events. These movements therefore profile religion, give it social visibility, without themselves being primarily religious movements: which is to say, without generating significant amounts of core religious communication. Religious movements do of course also occur, but most of those things commonly called religious movements in the sociological literature, especially the new religious movements, are in fact not social movements in the sense just described, but rather organizations that are founded at a particular time and seek to spread in terms of membership. This is the case with new religious movements like the Brahma Kumaris, the Church of Scientology, Falun Gong, the Unification church or Soka Gakkai, religious organizations originating in India, the United States, China, Korea and Japan respectively. In contrast, religious movements that would fall under this type quite clearly are, for example, Transcendental Meditation, New Age, neo-Paganism (Wicca), Tai Chi and Qi Gong.[8] In each of these cases, although there may exist organized expressions of these movements, the dominant form of participation is episodic, occasional, largely uncontrolled by any sort of central authority, and to the extent that it is regular, as often individual as it is collective.[9] In certain instances, such as Transcendental Meditation, there has been a move towards the clearly organized form in recent decades as the movement itself faded. In others, such as notably the example of Western neo-Paganism or Rastafarianism, the movement ideology rejects organization as illegitimate concentration of what is for them a basically individual religious authority. Neo-Pagans of this sort will therefore congregate for specific events like festivals and local circle meetings, but there are few if any 'rules of membership', let alone well-defined offices of a stable organization. Thus, typically, when the festival or circle is over, its space (but not necessarily time) reverts to 'normal' or non-religious use just as is the case for other episodic events that constitute the nodal points of a social movement. This comparatively evanescent quality is characteristic of this type of social system. Its reverse side is the tendency for social movements, at some point, to disappear or have their concerns reconfigured in the structures of other types of system, notably, but not exclusively, organizations. Indicative of this aspect is that even those religious social movements that wish deliberately to avoid this fate, namely greater convergence, organization, recognition by the state and other social agencies as a 'religion', seem to find themselves under a fair amount of pressure to go just in these directions. In some cases like the neo-Pagans, the primary reason may be the 'freedom of religion' that such congregation and recognition typically bring. In others like Transcendental Meditation, the difficulty of maintaining the dynamism and constant mobilization of a movement may make the concentration and regularization of organization seem an attractive strategy to follow. In still others, such as several of the New World African religions like Candomblé and Rastafarianism, the perceived need to assert one's authenticity and value in the face of other religions introduced such pressures.

In light of their various qualities, it is evident that social movements are of significance in this question of forming religion because they, along with social networks, lend definition to what one might call non-institutional religiosity, including much of what seems to be highly individual religiosity. From this perspective, what seems like an entirely non-convergent and therefore non- or even anti-systemic religiosity shows how it is nonetheless formed. Truly individualized religiousness, such as in the 'Sheilaism' of *Habits of the Heart* (Bellah *et al.* 1985), may actually be to a large extent part of these (and indeed other) social forms or systems, and only appears 'individualistic' and unsystemic when one takes the individual her/himself as the criterion of definition rather than the religious communication in which she/he participates. One could say something similar about the religious involvement of most people in the world. And to repeat, avoiding this sort of ambiguity of perspective is one of the main advantages to observing religion strictly as communication.

Religion in other function systems

One of the reasons that religion is a contested category in today's society, as noted in the introduction, is that the carriers of religion sometimes resist the categorization of their activity as religion because this implies acceptance of the secularization of non-religious domains and thereby the restriction of religion to its own domain. A common direction for this resistance to take is the politicization of religion, which is to say making the state and its legislative, legal, administrative and military structures instruments for collectively enforcing the precepts and practices of the religion in question. This direction can yield a distinct social form of religion in contemporary society to the extent that religious structures become an express aspect or arm of the state; or, what amounts to the same, the state becomes an expression of the religion. The capacity of the state to set collectively binding norms for the people within its territorial boundaries and thus its ability to make a particular religion an unavoidable part of these people's daily lives lends the religion a clear presence as a religion over and beyond what non-state religious organizations can do in this regard (Beyer 1994). Today, this way of giving religion form is most radically evident in certain Muslim countries like Iran and – between 1996 and 2001 – Afghanistan, but varying degrees of it can also be found in a number of other countries where state identities or ideologies include a particular religion. Examples of the latter would be Israel, India, Pakistan, Bangladesh, Zambia, Sri Lanka, Thailand, Indonesia, Russia and, to an increasingly less effective sense, European countries like Great Britain, Sweden or Germany. One should note, however, that in none of these cases does the religion in question, whether it is Islam, Christianity, Judaism, Buddhism or Hinduism, lack organizational expression as well. State religion, or the use of the state to give social form to a religion is in that sense a supplementary form. Only through the extreme use of this possibility, such as was the case in Afghanistan under the Taliban, can the politicized or state form of religion become the primary form. In other instances where organized religion is weak or contested, for example Hinduism in contemporary India, the involvement of the state apparatus in a vague and general way does relatively little for the differentiation of the religion beyond giving its name a certain public symbolic prominence.

There is, of course, another side to the state giving form to religions, and this involves the efforts of states to regulate religions and control what counts as religion. In most countries around the world, religion and religions have become a political issue in this sense. Some states, like Indonesia, China and to a lesser extent Russia, currently expressly limit what may count as religion to a restricted list. In most other countries, what counts as one of the religions is not that clearly spelled out, but disputes over new and marginal religious movements in countries as varied as Japan, Argentina and France point to at least an implicit model of religion in operation, one that favours heavily the 'world religions' and those with a long history in the country in question. I deal with this matter in greater detail in Chapter 6.

Such translation of religious criteria into the terms of political and legal systems is, however, only an example of the broader possibility of assisting the formation and convergent authority of religion through the mechanisms of other function systems. One way to look at this relation of the religious to the other function systems is, as in the last section, to speak about the conditioning influence of religion on their operations. From another perspective the effect is in the reverse direction. Political and legal control of religion is an example. Although one can regard this as a restriction of religion, it is by that very token also the formative observation of religion; it contributes to its consolidation as a recognizable, differentiated and effective social reality. Much like any identity, the identity of the religious system is the consequence of both 'inside' observation, which is to say self-reference, and 'outside' observation, namely the recognition of religion as religion by other social forms or systems. Moreover, state and legal control or recognition are not the only ways that religion is formatively observed, as it were, from the outside. Other obvious and important societal systems that engage in such observation are the scientific, the educational and the mass media systems. That scientific observation of religion has had an effect on what religion has become is at the centre of the contemporary critiques of the category that I discussed at the beginning of this chapter and in the introduction. Scientific endeavours do tend to regard religion somewhat differently than do theological observers or 'insiders'. The partial incommensurability of these perspectives is a reflection of different systemic criteria or interests (see Beyer 2003a, for a more thorough analysis). Yet both help determine what religion is in contemporary society. Analogously, religion is often a category of observation in schools around the world; and who controls how or even if religion is taught to students is likewise a contentious issue because of the different systemic interests involved. Mass media attention to religion, whether on radio, television, newspapers or the Internet is similarly a location for contestation between systems. Since all these systems are sites of broader social power, influence and authority, they all have an effect on the form of religion and the religions. They are part of what makes religion what it is. The fact that they are also arenas of contestation only reinforces the point that social conflict is in its own way just as productive of social order as is cohesion or congruence. Moreover, those critiques of the modern category of religion which point out its indebtedness to theological, scientific and political interests are accurate as concerns their analysis, but incorrect in their conclusion that religion is therefore 'not real'. Precisely the opposite is the case, at least in today's global society with its dominant function systems.

Social network religion

There is also a fourth possibility for giving form to religion, but this represents both a fourth way and a boundary 'form' between religion that is institutionalized as such, and that which is religious but unformed as religion except perhaps analytically by outside observers. In terms of social systems it takes place largely in interactions, yet this is really only a way of saying that the systems involved are none of the other three. Interactions, after all, are integral to organizations, social movements and societal systems as well. Thus, in much of the world today, as in times past in most societies, what we now call religion is practised locally, regionally and, given today's communication technologies, even globally, but without a strong sense of the system of practices and beliefs being part of a larger whole or of it being a distinctly identified activity called religion. Contemporary examples may be the local or community religious practices in India, China or different parts of Africa, the religious dimensions of life among various Aboriginal peoples all over the world, the already mentioned individual and often idiosyncratic practices of individuals, small group practices in various places, and a whole array of cultural practices that have escaped incorporation into one of the religions. Examples of the latter would be Western 'secular' celebrations of holidays like Hallowe'en, Easter (bunnies and eggs, not Jesus on the cross) and Groundhog Day. All of these manifestations are religious in the sense that one could and occasionally does observe them as religion. But they do not belong to that category in any consistent fashion because insiders do not seek to have them recognized as religion, do not consider that possibility, or reject such categorization; or because no formed and recognized religion successfully claims them. Much of this sort of activity in fact gets observed not as religion but as some other category, notably culture or custom. Put more strongly, these manifestations can appear as religion only by association with the other forms. It is the formed religions that act as implicit models for such religion; any sort of social activity that bears resemblance to them may on occasion be observed and treated as religion. The category and the system have themselves acquired this expansive capacity, this propensity to 'colonize' communications that otherwise escape its structures. Their presence in today's society, as of course in societies of the past, is what makes the idea of religion as a differentiated and selective societal system or delimited social domain seem inadequate: so much that 'looks like' religion appears to be excluded from such an observation.

This situation with religion can be compared to that with respect to other systems. The modern global capitalist economy seems to have stretched its tentacles, more technically its form, virtually everywhere in the world. And yet there is much that is not commodified or incorporated into this system. We do not acquire all our 'goods and services' through monetary exchanges, even if abstractly or implicitly 'everything has its price'. The capitalist economic mode could colonize everything, but in fact does not. Similarly, governments could regulate absolutely all aspects of all our lives. Some of us may even have the impression that they do. In reality, however, they do not. We could make similar observations for other systems. The science system has not digested all the possible things that people around the world know, and yet this knowledge somehow also counts. It is almost a truism that we do not learn all our competences in schools. Not everything that is artistic counts as art. Illness and healing happen massively outside the medicalized health system, even though modern medicine probably could categorize them all if they were brought for diagnosis and treatment. Information is to be had outside the mass media, and much physical activity does not count as sport. In each of these cases, the effort to arrive at a conception that includes all that could analytically be included leads to the same sort of vagueness and inconclusive discussion as the search for a concept of religion valid for all times, societies and places. Therefore the fact that there is a lot of 'religious culture' out there which neither its carriers nor most outside observers deem part of one of the religions does not lead to the conclusion that religion is simply a misnomer. It does indicate highly selective, even if one wishes, manipulative, impositional, and 'colonizing' structures, as do the categories that name the other systems. These are nonetheless real, at least in their effects.

Summary and conclusion

The chief aim of this chapter has been to present the main lineaments for observing religion as a modern function system. Doing this offers a way of understanding the specificity and selectivity of religion in the context of a society that has become truly global. Definitional wrangling among scholars studying religion in the modern world has one of its sources in the lack of theoretical resources for bringing into focus what precisely is different about religion in this context as opposed to what we may choose to call religion in past societies. The chapter took two approaches to presenting this difference. First it outlined the formation of the religious system in historical narrative form, paying particular attention to socio-structural and semantic transformations in Europe and the rest of the world during the last four to six centuries. Then it applied a series of Luhmannian theoretical categories in order to show how religion operates as a differentiated system beside others. In this regard religious binary codes, programmes, elements and power were the principal foci of analysis. In the process various important issues regarding this religion could be addressed. These included matters such as secularization, privatization, religious authority, religious pluralism and the ways that religions take visible form in our society.

A number of related concerns also informed the presentation. The more significant of these are that religion, although 'invented', is also socially real and effective; that religion is both a category of Western imposition and one institutionalized in all other regions of the world such that it is no longer simply a Western, let alone just Christian, notion; that religion is in certain respects at odds with globalization while at the same time being constitutive of it; that modern religion is both in continuity with what went before and also radically different; that the development of the religious system is not the outcome of some inevitable evolutionary process, but rather something historically arbitrary, constructed, and in that sense even odd; and finally, that the religious system as described exhibits a number of ambiguities, including the possibility that it may dissipate or dissolve in the future.

This summary outline also points to what remains to be done, and this is to put much more empirical flesh on these arguments. Although I have in these first two chapters tried to illustrate the various main points, these have of necessity had to be very brief, selective and incomplete. The following four chapters, therefore, represent more detailed case studies that elaborate and concretize the main theoretical observations of these first two.

Notes

1 Cf. J.Z. Smith's claim to the contrary in Smith 1982: xi. To quote, '*there is no data for religion*' (italics in original).

2 Cf. Feil 1986: 138–59, 191–208; Haussig 1999: 47–52. Below, in Chapter 5, we shall see that Japanese and Chinese elites of the nineteenth/twentieth centuries also adapted an indigenous Buddhist monastic term to mean what the modern sense of religion means.

3 Or, following Pandey's analysis (1992), between 'communalism' and 'secular nationalism', but again showing the close relation between religion formation and nation formation in this case.

4 The grammatical form is important; the two poles have to indicate states, not how one gets to those states. Blessing/cursing would be incorrect since these indicate the communicative processes, parallel to buying/selling in the economy or deciding/regulating by governments, through which the states come to be determined. See the discussion of religious power and elements below.

5   Luhmann's theory would insert the idea of 'structural coupling' at this point. See Luhmann 1997. My intention here does not require the detailed introduction of this concept, important though it may be if one were to tie up all theoretical loose ends.

6   In Luhmannian theoretical terms, the appropriate concept here is 'contingency formulae'. These are the understandings that, as it were, 'make a system necessary'. See Luhmann 1977, 2000b.

7   See Beyer 2001 for a more detailed discussion of how this distinction derives from Luhmann's own view of the matter.

8   These latter two can also fall under Daoism, just as Transcendental Meditation may under circumstances be claimed by Hinduism. Since the text is dealing with social forms rather than again the question of the boundaries of specific religions, I leave that issue aside here.

9   Comparing the distinction I am using here to Stark and Bainbridge's typology of sects and cults, social movements would correspond to their audience and client cults, but cult movements are for the most part organized religion. See Stark and Bainbridge 1985. Yet, since social movements include social movement organizations, the line cannot be drawn that sharply. To some degree, as noted above in the text, the typology outlined here and the received typology of religious organizations are incommensurate.

Chapter 3

Formation and re-formation of Abrahamic religions
Christianity and Islam

Introduction: Abrahamic modelling

The global religious system is a relatively recent, contested and highly selective construction. Its practical historical origins in early modern Western European society, combined with the critical role that the global spread of Western power and influence has played, may make it seem that the whole idea of a religious system is nothing more than the projection or imposition of Western and Christian notions on to the rest of the world. A gentler way of putting the same point might be to say that, to the degree that the sort of religious system I have been describing does indeed exist, it uses Christianity as the implicit or explicit model for what a religion looks like and therefore for what can count as religion. Although it would be senseless to deny the importance of Christian religion in this process, that perspective is inadequate in at least two critical respects. First, it assumes that the Christian model, whatever that is, exists logically or historically prior to the development of the *global* religious system. Second, it fails to take seriously both the extent to which other religions have followed different paths in their reconstruction, and how these other religions themselves have come to serve as models for what can count as religion in this system. In sharper formulation, the 'Christian imposition and projection' thesis fails to take into account how Christianity itself only formed as a modern religion in the process of its globalization; how that formation happened in dialogical relation to other reconstructing religions and not in some sort of splendid and self-sufficient isolation; and how the other modern religions are the expressions of analogous dialogical processes, in many respects quite different from Christianity, and just as determinative of the global model for religion.

From this point of departure, the present chapter looks in greater detail at the historical (re)formation of two of today's almost universally recognized and self-identified religions, Christianity and Islam. I choose only these two because of their global preponderance and because space does not permit the inclusion of all possible cases. A similar analysis could be carried out for the third almost universally recognized member of the

Abrahamic trio, namely Judaism. Indeed, an analysis of Judaism could serve to profile further the contingency of the historical paths that Islam and Christianity have followed. For neither Christianity nor Islam has simply manifested some sort of 'inherent identity'; another close cousin has taken a direction that looks 'Christian' in some respects (for example, its denominationalization along a liberal/conservative continuum), 'Islamic' in others (for example, emphasizing in certain of its variants a religious system of law with corresponding binary code), besides necessarily exhibiting features that constitute its dialogically constructed uniqueness (for example, the centrality of the physical Land of Israel). Treating these three religions together suggests itself because of their closely intertwined history and programmatic similarity as the three 'Abrahamic' religions. Two aspects of this kinship are significant in the present context. First, as the expression of their principled monotheism, they share a stress on exclusivity, meaning that they all use the symbolic device of the human individual as a prime strategy for delimiting themselves: a person cannot be Christian, Muslim or Jew *and* religiously something else, especially not one of the other two. Although individual adherents of all three may occasionally violate this principle in their personal religious identities and lives, and there do exist small movements, such as Messianic Jews, that do combine Christian and Jewish identity, these exceptions do not contradict the prevailing, exclusive self-conception of these religions as systems of communication. It does, however, show that exclusivism is not a necessary strategy, even perhaps eventually for the Abrahamic religions. That, in turn, shows the influence of alternative, non-exclusive ways of constructing a religion and thus helps to invalidate the thesis that the global religious system is nothing more than Christianity (or at most the Abrahamic trio) writ large. In reverse, of course, and as I emphasize in Chapter 4, Abrahamic exclusivism also influences the way these other religions construct themselves. Distinguishing one religion from another through the shorthand of human bodies is not the only way, but it is a very effective one. One might even say that it is the closest thing religions have to the artifices of precisely delimited territory and corresponding citizenship that have been so critical for the construction of the global political system of sovereign states.

A second and related aspect of Abrahamic kinship is that all three religions have a long history of mutual identification, not in the modern sense of seeing themselves as three alternative religions, but certainly as mutually exclusive religious communities. Christians have historically defined themselves over against Muslims, Jews and (Graeco-Roman) Pagans; Muslims in contrast with 'people of the book' and infidels; Jews as a religiously defined people apart. The fact that these historical contrasts more or less coincide with the modern differentiation of three of the world's religions makes it both easier to recognize them and for them to present themselves as such, but it also tends to disguise the degree to which all three are the subjects of significant *re*construction in recent centuries, at least as communicative subsystems of a single global religious system. The situation is complicated by the fact that almost all of today's religions, including the Abrahamic ones, use the past as a resource in their self-understanding; they see themselves as traditions. The continuity with the past is more definitive for current identity than relatively recent discontinuities.[1] The latter, in fact, usually justify themselves not as innovations, but as a 'return' to the past, as a recovery of their myth of origin. In this chapter as in this book as a whole, however, the emphasis is on the discontinuity, on the reconstruction, rather than on the continuity. That corresponds to my scientific – and not, for example, theological – purpose and perspective.

Two further matters need discussion by way of introduction to the narratives that follow. These concern the question of the models for a religion in global society, and the relation between religions and other prevalent categories for constructing difference in that society, above all the closely related notions of culture/nation/ethnicity.

As outlined in the previous chapter, it is a thesis of my overall argument that the model for a religion in the global system is not some abstract, overarching pattern to which all religions more or less conform; nor is it simply and consistently one of the institutionalized religions, like Christianity. Instead, what ends up counting as one of the religions and thus what can effectively operate as one of them is the outcome of a historically contingent and selective modelling and mobilization process that refers primarily to one of the religions, to a subset of them, or at the logical extreme to all of them. The set of such operative religions is not consistent across the different regions of global society, nor is it clearly delimited. There are quite a number of ambiguous cases, religions in formation or potential religions resisting formation. The religions that serve as implicit or explicit models therefore vary, historically and today. That said, however, there is also little question that certain religions are more consistently and widely included in such selective modelling than others. Certainly Christianity, especially in its Protestant and Roman Catholic variants, given its role in the global expansion of European influence and its consequent global presence, serves as perhaps the most widespread such model. Yet at least since the middle of the twentieth century, Islam has emerged as a serious challenger to this pre-eminent role of Christianity. In countries and regions where Muslims are dominant or at least strongly present, it has in fact become the clearly prevalent model. And even in areas where Muslims are relatively tiny minorities, they spawn movements which seek to assert 'the Islamic way' as the proper way of operating as a religion. Here is perhaps one reason why many people in the culturally Christian West are suspicious of or even fear Islam. It challenges a way of seeing religion that they have come to take for granted. Speaking metaphorically, if there is currently only one political superpower left in the world, there are now at least two religious ones. One reason for treating the reconstruction of Christianity and Islam in the same chapter, therefore, is to look more closely at the different features of these religions that have brought about their nearly global, but not exclusive, status as 'what a religion should be'.

The relations between religion and culture are complex, not least because both categories have become prime ways of constructing difference within the identity that is today's global society. Both ideas have undergone a similar transformation of meaning over the past two or three centuries, from singular qualities to inherently plural, reified entities (for culture, see Williams 1983). They are both ways of asserting collective identities or exclusivities in terms of which one can contest for power and influence. I have already in several places discussed the close historical relation between religion formation and nation formation, the modern nation being culture manifested in a political mode. In most of the scientific literature on such issues as international migration, globalization and ethnicity (another variant on the idea of culture), religion is not so much totally ignored as assumed and subsumed under cultural headings. Yet religion is not simply a dimension of culture. Unlike culture, religion has been structured in modern society as a differentiated system of communication, albeit one whose symbolic resources are also frequently and consistently incorporated into other systems, including the state, law, education, art, mass media and those systems that carry or embody cultures.[2] In light of this relationship, one way of tracing the differentiation of the religious system is therefore to examine the ways that religion has, like culture, formed as a generalized category of difference on the one hand; and, unlike culture, as one of the function systems on the other. This contrast allows a better understanding of many of the ambiguities surrounding the nature and role of religion in global society. In this chapter, as in the next, the closer look at the (re)construction of Christianity and Islam illustrates this equivocal relationship between religion and culture. As becomes evident from such an analysis, the relation is both symbiotic and one of tension. It shows some of the historical and structural peculiarities of the religious system as well as the difficulties attendant upon selectively reconstructing such a foundational modality as a 'mere' function system.

From Christian religion to globalized Christianity

A comparison of Christian religion in the period before the later Middle Ages and the Reformation with what Christianity is today would show that the two have a great deal in common. Moreover, the differences between Christian religious expression of, say, the seventh century and that of the thirteenth century would probably be at least as remarkable as those between medieval and modern versions. Thus in asserting that Christianity as a religion is a relatively recent development I am claiming neither radical discontinuity with what went before nor that pre-modern eras were not witness to equally or perhaps even more significant alterations in religious forms. The task is therefore not to demonstrate some radical and unique discontinuity between before and after, but instead to show more precisely in what the changes consisted and how they contributed to the formation of a systemic religion in a global religious system.

As an introductory illustration of the sort of transformation that is at issue, I take a somewhat curious argument by two American scholars, Rodney Stark and Laurence Iannaccone. In a 1994 article (Stark and Iannaccone 1994), challenging the idea that medieval Europe was an 'age of faith', a time when people and society were very religious, they point to evidence which shows that relatively few people during that time actually went to church very often, and that when they did, more often than not they didn't pay attention or take the Christian rituals being performed all that seriously. What is curious but also revealing about this evidence is, on the one hand, that it fails to count religious performances and orientations 'outside the church' as proper religion. Diffuse, 'popular' (as we would now call it) religiosity does not receive the same weight as 'churched' religiosity.[3] The implication is that the 'vitality' or strength of religion in a given society is to be measured by the level of social resources (in the terms I am using, the amount of communication) devoted to the reproduction of specific, differentiated and usually organized institutions for religion. Religious activity outside that framework, while not irrelevant, is less significant because it does not contribute towards the building up of 'church' or equivalent expression for differentiated religious institution. Moreover and on the other hand, another potential measure of religious strength that Stark and Iannaccone seem to leave out of the equation is the level of broader social influence of religious leaders and virtuosi. Or, perhaps more accurately, this influence is to be measured by their degree of success in increasing the amount of churched religious communication, not, for instance, in how much wealth their institutions have acquired or more generally in the importance of their 'non-religious' roles such as guardians of knowledge or purveyors of political legitimacy. In sum, for these authors, the social presence of religion is to be measured in terms of differentiated, more often than not organized, and mass-participatory religious communication. The fact that Stark and Iannaccone seem to take these criteria for granted, combined with their rather obvious deficiency for understanding the medieval European context, points to the discontinuity that is at issue here. A form of, in this case Christian, religion has institutionalized itself in the world of these modern authors that is sufficiently different from what went before that applying its standards to those bygone contexts can make the religion of those times appear weak in comparison. And, be it noted, this example is entirely an inner-Christian one; the modern criteria are inadequate for understanding Christian religion before the transformation, not just non-Christian religion. The projection is on to the foreign country that is the past, not immediately on to the foreign countries of today.

The Reformations and national churches

A theoretically and historically defensible place and time to begin the narrative of the construction of modern Christianity is Western Europe of the Reformation period. The reasons are much the same as for beginning the globalization discussion roughly there and then. An important effect of this decision, however, is that the Eastern Orthodox branch – as seems so often to be the case – becomes a more marginal concern and only enters the story at a late stage, in most respects not before the nineteenth century. I return to this exclusion from time to time below.

As I outlined in the previous chapter, the transformations under discussion are first and foremost ones of social form, of 'repackaging' received religio-communicative resources rather than developing radically unprecedented ones, a *Re-formation* (whether Protestant or Catholic), not a new revelation. Typically, the reformers justified their selectivity with reference to the myth of Christian origins. They saw themselves as 'going back' to the original religious impulse and to the forms that this supposedly warranted. The strategy is common to every one of the (re)inventions of religions that are the subject of this and the next three chapters. Moreover, although the Reformation era resulted in the institutional fragmentation of Western Christianity, the reformers actually differed relatively little as concerns the content of their belief and practice, the religious programme. Luther and his Catholic opponents, for instance, agreed that 'justification' was by 'faith alone' and that scripture was the final authority. Where they differed was in the relative emphasis they gave to these items, and in how this faith and authority were to receive concrete expression. For the Catholics, the institutional church had to have a key mediating role; Luther saw a far greater role for individual consciousness of faith and direct individual understanding of the biblical writings. Similar differences in emphasis occurred with respect to the core communicative elements, the ritual and other religious performances in terms of which a soul arrived at its final religious state in the afterlife. If Calvin asserted that this transcendent fate was predestined in the absolute foreknowledge of the sovereign God, the Catholics and other Reformers did not disagree. Where they differed was in the sort of religious communication that was to realize this religious truth. For the Catholics, church-mediated sacraments had to play a key role. For Calvin and his followers, this smacked too much of 'working' salvation and therefore the behaviour itself became much more of a religious performance. The place of the Catholic sacraments therefore faded in importance, and other rituals such as bible reading and preaching, which were also Catholic practices, received a correspondingly more central place. Where they all agreed, however, was in the need to purify Christian religion and the church.

The challenges were different for Catholics and Protestants. The Catholic church at the time of the Reformation was already a very well-developed hierocratic organization administering a complex and integrated programme of ritual (sacramental) communication, plus an array of organized religious orders and institutions of learning. These structures were, however, of a highly elite nature; they did not penetrate consistently into the lives of that many people or did so only to a limited degree. The religious lives of most Europeans were nominally Christian, but in actual practice what that meant was not particularly uniform (orthodox/orthoprax) or even visibly Christian according to the church's standards. The religious programme was neither consistent nor broadly effective. The Roman church was a powerful institution articulated across much of Western Europe, but its power was largely comparative: it had no effective religious rival if this wasn't varied local custom. As an overarching presence, only the developing states within their respective territories and, even more locally, certain towns and cities had anything close to its level of societal influence. The Reformation era demonstrated not the weakness of the church, but rather signalled the rising strength of old and new rivals, especially the political states and, in its wake, the Protestant churches. The Catholic response was not to change direction, to 'admit the error of its ways'. Instead its carriers intensified the directions the institution had been pursuing for centuries. The Catholic or Counter-Reformation of the sixteenth century embarked upon a concerted campaign of building up church structures, and of bringing greater clarity and uniformity to the performance, belief and administration of religion. A key part of this effort was to spread the thus promulgated religious programme more consistently to the great number of people that were supposed to be Christian and Catholic. Not by accident were older orders like the Dominicans and newly founded ones like the Jesuits among the most outstanding organized carriers of Catholic reform. Among their many tasks, the former, the Order of Preachers, were the prime movers in the Inquisition which sought to enforce orthodoxy to the level of the mass of European inhabitants; their role had from their origins in the twelfth century already been to 'combat heresy'. The Jesuits undertook extensive missions also well beyond Europe and played a key part in enlisting the cooperation of as many states as possible in the execution of this expansive project of orthodoxification. In consequence, those portions of Western Europe that remained Catholic became so more consistently and thoroughly at the same time as what Catholic religion meant achieved an unprecedented level of coherence.

Unlike the Roman Catholic church, the Protestant churches of early modern Western Europe had no pre-Reformation institutional history, except as part of the Roman church. In addition, the anti-institutional and even iconoclastic way in which the Protestant reformers often proceeded gave them no sure alternative basis for concrete institution building. Under those circumstances, the prevailing outcome, at least until the later eighteenth century, was the establishment of a number of 'national' Protestant churches whose sphere of operation was defined by the boundaries of the respective Protestant state. Internally, these churches most often adapted the Catholic system of parishes or similar geographical divisions; just as all citizens or subjects of the state were deemed to belong to the established Protestant church, so did one belong to the local church where one happened to live. The churches were in effect what we would today call 'governmental organizations', similar in some respects to the position of the Russian Orthodox church in the rising Russian empire of about the same period (Ware 1964: 112ff.). The religious institution was in this way endowed with differentiated form, but with the full support of the regulatory structures of the rising state. The new churches were able to build their structures and resources under the protective aegis of their respective states at the same time as the latter solidified their hold on their territory, in part justifying their regulatory power through the religion. As concerns religious programme, each of these national churches adopted or developed its own version of Protestantism. Sometimes this meant identifying with one of the main branches of the Reformation. Scandinavian countries, for instance, established Lutheran churches, adopting the Augsburg Confession of 1530 as their programmatic core. The English Reformation produced its own variant, a mixture and even juxtaposition of Catholic and Calvinist features as perhaps most typically represented doctrinally in the 39 Articles and ritually in the Book of Common Prayer, both promulgated in the middle of the sixteenth century.

The close association between Protestant churches and rising states also had implications for the subsequent imagination of nations. Especially in the later eighteenth and nineteenth centuries, as the absolutist states gave way to nation-based states, these churches, like the Catholic church, in many cases came to be identified as an important dimension of the national culture. In certain instances, such as notably the Nordic countries and the Netherlands until well into the nineteenth century, the correlation was quite straightforwardly between one church and one nation. The former were Lutheran, the latter was Reform (Calvinist). In other cases, such as Great Britain, the transition involved more than one nation and more than one church. The Church of England and the Church of Scotland were both resolutely Protestant. They emerged as separate entities, however, not only because they represented respectively more 'Catholic' and more 'Calvinist' versions of that Protestantism, but more importantly because Scottish and English national identities maintained their distinctiveness throughout the history of British state development. In other instances, notably that of Germany in the later nineteenth century, nationhood included the establishment of both Protestant and Catholic churches. The ambiguities contained in these examples, however, show that the identification of culture or nation and religion was never nearly so complete as to imply the reversal of the institutional differentiation of religion. As in the parallel case of the developing educational systems in these same European countries, the differentiation of function systems has been a process of mutual support and reinforcement, not of autarchic dissociation. Indeed, as Stichweh has shown admirably for the science system (Stichweh 1996), each of the function systems has at the very least gone through a 'national phase', a period when the systems nurtured their structures largely within the boundaries of states and as part of projects of building 'national societies'. This has been the case with religion as with the other systems. The national established churches are the obverse side of this historical development; the reverse side is the concomitant emergence of religious forms significantly more independent of the state and other systems.

The organized Protestant churches of national establishment were the dominant form that succeeded the Reformation movements. On the European continent, they still have a certain pre-eminence. Yet, from the beginning, another direction far less trusting of formative alliances with states asserted itself, especially in the Anabaptist wing of the Reformation and in certain Calvinist directions as represented, for instance, in the English Puritan movement. These orientations had, in effect, to reinvent the church institution so that it could carry what for them was a purer religious impulse. In light of their more sharply anti-institutional bias, they reached behind the era of the Roman church to the pre-Constantinian early church where they found a more decentralized and small community form that in the modern context has come to be called congregational or sectarian, one not tied to the state and, on the contrary, sometimes even seeking radical separation from it. These 'dissenting' movements and their organized churches developed to some extent in most Protestant countries, often experiencing significant difficulty with the now 'established' churches. Such was the case for the sectarian Mennonite and Hutterite groups as well as for English Quakers and Separatists. Many of these incorporated the local congregational form as an integral part of their religious programme and theologies in a way quite parallel to the way that established Protestant churches regarded their relation to the state, and to the Roman Catholic church's progressive theologization of its own organizational structure. This quality of religious organization as a dimension of religious programmes is a key feature of the modern reconstruction of Christianity as a religion. The organizations have served as the principal social forms into which adherents have been incorporated as a way of concretizing and controlling the recursiveness of religious communication as a differentiated system.

The Eastern Orthodox churches were not overly affected by the transformations attendant upon the sixteenth-century Reformation in Western Europe. In the nineteenth century, however, the logic of modern nationalism spread to the Eastern regions as well. Given the strong coordination between the imagining of nations, the building of states, and religion in the West, it is perhaps not surprising that this logic also led to a partial redivision and reorganization of Orthodoxy in Eastern Europe along modern national lines. I say partial because, much as the national organization and identification of the Roman Catholicism in the West did not substitute for its previous transnational character but was simply added on to it, so in the Eastern church new national churches arose, but without negating the older, transnational structure or ideal.

The Eastern churches also had a long history of organization, as represented in the four Patriarchates of Constantinople, Antioch, Jerusalem and Alexandria, with the first having the status of the 'first among equals'. In the context of the successful maintenance of a traditional imperial political structure in these eastern regions – until 1453 Byzantium, and thereafter the Ottoman Sultanate – the Eastern churches existed in much closer coordination with those powers in what is often labelled a caeseropapist relation, or *symphonia*. That logic was only extended with the establishment of the Moscow Patriarchate in 1589, reflective as it was of the creation and expansion of the Russian empire (Ware 1964). The rise of the modern nationalist movements did not negate this structure; all the Patriarchates still exist. They have at least the symbolic leadership of the Eastern churches and represent its unity and historical continuity. Much as in the West and elsewhere, however, several of the movements incorporated Orthodox religious identity into the construction of their respective nations, giving this direction institutional expression by successfully erecting a number of new national Orthodox churches whose membership was deemed identical with that of the respective nations. The first of these was the Greek Orthodox organizationally autonomous church in 1850, followed in the twentieth century by others such as the Serbian, Romanian, Bulgarian, Macedonian and Albanian. Of equal importance, this strategy of setting up organizationally independent churches was not limited to the cases of the Orthodox nationalisms. In the context of the transition, independent, sub-national churches also emerged, giving organizational form to Eastern Orthodoxy in majority non-Orthodox countries such as Finland, Estonia, Poland, the United States and even Japan (Agadjanian and Roudometof 2005; Roudometof 2001).

The spread of independent Orthodox churches to various other countries demonstrates that this primarily organizational transformation has not been simply a dimension of nation-state formation; had that been the case then there would have been little call for independent non-nationalist organizations to arise. The entire development is rather a further instance of how the Christian religion has constructed its modern differentiation with the help of the organizational system form, a feature that I discuss in greater detail below. Nowhere is this aspect clearer than in the case of 'New World' diaspora churches, some of which are branches of the new autocephalous European churches, a couple of which are for the time being still under the jurisdiction of the Moscow or Constantinople Patriarchates (but see Kourvetaris 2005; Volkov 2005), and one of which is itself independent, the Orthodox Church of America. This combination of a (symbolically) core transnational church, numerous national churches with often transnational divisions, and more or less non-national, simply Orthodox churches shows both 'Catholic' with 'Protestant' features and thereby demonstrates the flexibility that organizing religion allows. It permits self-described unity and independent diversity. Churches can have close ties with states or be separate from them. They can be centred and identified with nations or transnationally oriented. Finally, as all three main branches of Christianity demonstrate, organization is an excellent strategy for combining ardent localism and rejection of the relativizing implications of globalization, with both universal aspirations and global extent.

Christianity as a single religion: code, medium, programme

The symbiotic relations of church and state in Protestant, Orthodox and Catholic cases do not exhaust the ways in which the development of the different branches of Christianity was similar and thus how they have come to constitute a single religion. Such affinities also do not detract from the many salient differences within that identity. One can analyze both convergences and divergences in systemic terms, namely as concerns the core religious code, the nature of the religious programmes, the character of the most important religious elements or communications, and the ways religious power or the religious medium has been structured. As one might expect, there has been substantial congruence with respect to code and medium, with contrasts being located much more in the areas of programme and corresponding central elements.

A look at how the various main Christian branches conceived the religious code shows a very high degree of correspondence. The construction of specifically religious communication crystallized around the difference between salvation or damnation of human souls. Religious communications, however styled, gained their meaning in terms of whether or not they contributed to or were indicative of the prospect or state of salvation. They either blessed or cursed (damned). Secondary codes, whether the moral distinction between good and bad or the cognitive difference of truth and error, were relevant only in so far as they assisted in operationalizing the core code. In this regard, Protestants, Catholics and Orthodox agreed: correct belief (truth) and correct behaviour (good) manifested themselves in or as correct religious communication; and this brought about or revealed the state or prospect of salvation, namely the state of grace. Damnation was the direction if such belief, behaviour or communication was absent or negative. As concerned religious power, all branches were in accord as to the centrality of faith or grace, even if their detailed programmes apportioned this power medium somewhat differently. Especially the Catholic and Orthodox sides saw a closer relation between ritual performance (e.g. taking sacraments, venerating icons) and the degree of religious power or grace; and they also allowed the partial exception of the possibility of mystical possession, but this medium was generally treated as programmatically suspect, subject, for instance, to control by a 'director of conscience' who made sure that its operation did not contradict or take the place of faith. Below, I discuss the later emergence of more 'enthusiastic' media from Wesleyan Methodism to twentieth-century Pentecostalism and Charismatic Christianity.

Although the differences that developed in the various branches of Christianity are largely to be found on the level of programmes and the corresponding elements that these produce, this is not to say that they did not maintain a basic programmatic unity. As I indicated in the last chapter, the religions of the world distinguish themselves primarily on the basis of different programmes, and therefore it would be surprising if Christianity had maintained its singularity, both as concerns self-conception and external observation, if there were not a discernible programmatic commonality. Accordingly, the centuries since the Reformation have indeed been replete with religious controversy between Catholics and Protestants, among Protestants, and among Catholics, as there had been between Western and Eastern forms of Christian religion before this period, and perhaps again today (Agadjanian and Roudometof 2005). There have been numerous new religious movements and new religious organizations, particularly on the Protestant side, movements and organizations that were the concrete expressions of such controversies. Nonetheless, certain programmatic features have throughout this period remained so central that religious directions which negate them generally end up being considered and even considering themselves as non-Christian or as a different religion. These programme items include above all the monotheistic creator God, Jesus Christ as this God as saviour, the Holy Spirit and hence Trinitarianism; the unique validity and divine inspiration of the Christian Bible, above all the New Testament; the centrality of sin as the violation of God's will; redemption as the atonement of this sin through divine grace; the fate for each individual soul of salvation/damnation in a single afterlife; faith (including repentance and right belief) and grace as the central religious medium; exclusivity of religious identity; and the close linking of the moral code with the core salvation code. Movements that have deviated from any of these core programmatic items have tended to be excluded from the Christian fold. These include, for instance, the Church of Jesus Christ of Latter-day Saints or Mormonism (adding sacred scriptures with attendant unique programmatic additions), the Jehovah's Witnesses (non-Trinitarian), Unitarian-Universalists (non-Trinitarian, non-exclusive) and perhaps, at certain earlier stages of their history, some African Instituted churches like certain South African Zionists (additional 'saviour' and hence non-Trinitarian). Even these, however, are often considered as – at least somewhat – Christian in as much as they still include most of the core programmatic items.

'Churching' through organization

This programmatic core, along with the singularity of code(s) and medium, provides sufficient common material for patterning the identity of Christianity as a societal system. Religious communications get their fundamental meaning with reference to this core and thereby refer to one another, constituting the recursiveness which defines the boundaries or identity of the Christian religious system. That self-referential context, however, still permits a large amount of variety in terms of how elements are constructed and what further elaboration the core programme is given. Such flexibility allows the consolidation of the various subsystems of Christianity itself. Just as critical as the identifying core, in other words, are the ways that difference is constructed within the Christian religious system and with reference to other societal systems, both religious and non-religious. It is here that organizations and social movements have played such a central role. Organization was, of course, the prime basis of differentiation for the medieval Catholic and Orthodox churches; and the Protestant Reformation itself began as a set of social movements. Ever since in the history of the modern reconstruction of Christianity, these two types of social system have been instrumental in generating concrete and variant forms of this religion.

Pointing out the close relation between the Roman Catholic version of Christianity and its organizational form is certainly nothing new. What I want to underline here is how the Catholic religious programme and Catholic organizational structure together have produced a mutually reinforcing, highly flexible, but also stable religious system. It is a model of how religion can operate as simultaneously highly differentiated and thoroughly interdependent with other social structures. Moreover, to a large extent, the analysis that I now give of the Roman Catholic church also applies to the Eastern Orthodox churches. The chief difference, as already mentioned, is that Eastern Orthodoxy churches did not undergo a sixteenth-century renovation in response to the functionally differentiating situation of the Western church. In the nineteenth century, that context changed also for the Orthodox churches with corresponding transformations, above all nationalizations. Yet in many of their dominant areas, the contextual pressure, as it were, was again 'delayed' by the 70-year incorporation into the twentieth-century Soviet empire, the last of the traditional empires. In a certain sense, this segment of Christianity is only now having to deal with the global context head on (cf. Tomka forthcoming).

Beginning with the medieval period, but especially with the Tridentine reforms of the Catholic Reformation, the Roman church has become a strongly hierocratic organization which centres on the production and administration of religious communications according to an integrated Catholic religious programme. At the core of this programme are the sacraments. These have long been defined as not only necessary for salvation but also as the monopoly of the church: *extra ecclesiam nulla sallus*. The primary way of translating this double programmatic claim into organizational terms has been to distinguish clearly and religiously (sacramentally) between two types of members, 'religious' (priests, nuns, monks) and 'lay'. The religious communication of both is defined as member communication, but control over the production of this communication rests primarily in the hands of the former and these, in turn, are much more subject to church discipline, which is to say a supplementary programme of rules and expectations. The distinction is thereby instrumental in assuring the recursiveness of the Catholic system. Far from being atypical in this respect, the Catholic church has here developed a religious version of a structure that is at the core of several of the other function systems, namely that system communication depends on, usually organized, 'professionals' to whom non-professionals have to come to partake in and benefit from the system. Parallel arrangements are to be found in the educational, legal, health, political and scientific systems. Not all function systems operate in quite this way, and typically the line between professional and lay is not that clear in those cases, nor is it as difficult to cross. Notable examples are the economic, artistic, mass media and sports systems, but also other subsystems of the religious system, including many Protestant Christian churches and several other religions.

As in those systems which operate similarly, the Catholic – and Orthodox – structural emphasis on the professional/lay distinction has shown itself to have both typical advantages and challenges. Clarity of structure and control over the recursiveness (that is, orthodoxy) of communications is certainly among the former. In a social context in which function systems become dominant, however, such clarity has to combine with a more or less constant increase in their characteristic communication. How both to delimit and to spread systemic religious communication presents a challenge to all religions, but in particular to a subunit such as the Roman Catholic church. Historically, this church has responded through seeking alliances with states and their regulating and enforcing mechanisms: Catholic religious observance could become mandatory, or at least alternatives suppressed. This is also the path that Eastern Orthodox churches have taken. In the Catholic case, with its different situation, however, beginning especially in the nineteenth century, we witness the intensified pursuit of a different strategy, one that sought to incorporate lay Catholics more directly and consistently into the organization, and to have them express that incorporation through greatly increased religious, above all ecclesial, practice. The Catholic devotional revolution of the latter part of that century is particularly notable in this regard. Through various programmes such as preaching campaigns, the accelerated creation of and intensified recruitment to religious orders, the worldwide missions (see next section), the significant expansion of Catholic schools, hospitals and social service agencies, the founding of devotional associations such as pious confraternities, the expansion and further rationalization of the Catholic diocesan and parish structure, and, be it noted, the further sacralization of the religious organization itself, the Roman church tried and succeeded in intensifying the prevalence of its typical communication wherever it was significantly present. This development, as much or more than anything that preceded it, brought about an unprecedented level of religious communication as Catholic 'churched' communication. The effort continues to the present day, albeit with a subtle but important shift in emphasis from routine, regular communication by members to occasional, episodic, but for that much more intense communication: regular mass attendance and confession have to an extent given way to more pilgrimages, religious rallies and special ritual occasions, all with mass participation. Whether these typically social movement forms will lead back to the high lay involvement Catholicism of the earlier twentieth century remains to be seen.

As already discussed, many of the national Protestant churches took a path similar to the Roman and Orthodox churches with a strong reliance on alliances with state power. The established church model also adopted a comparable organizational focus with strong centralized institutions, a specially trained clergy with control over a defined orthodox programme including both doctrinal and ritual elements, and a subordinate but still integral member role for lay people as belonging participants in church-oriented communication. If a critical distinguishing feature of the Catholic and Orthodox versions in this regard was that its 'national' churches were also at the same time part of a 'transnational' church, then in the Protestant case it was almost the opposite: the state churches were not the only

Protestant churches. From early on, as indicated, they faced the challenge of *dissenting* churches and movements. The basis of such dissent is instructive. It recapitulates the differences that brought about the divergent streams of the Protestant Reformation in the first place. Questions of authority loomed large, above all as concerned the sacred texts and their interpretation. Who, ultimately, had the right to decide what those texts said about Christian belief and practice? At one end was the Catholic position: it was the hierocratic church as embodiment of 'tradition', a parallel if strictly related source of instruction. At the other end were those Protestant dissenters who insisted that *sola scriptura* necessarily meant individual interpretation, the 'priesthood of all believers', along with a commensurate ecclesial arrangement. The established Protestant churches fell somewhere in the middle of this spectrum. But for many of the dissenters, their close ties with the state were a central part of the problem because such linking set up a this-worldly counter-authority to the individual believer's direct access to authoritative scripture. For these Protestants, the independent and absolute authority of God was at issue; and this called for a correspondingly independent institutionalization of the relationship with God, namely religion. The dissenters could not and did not thereby abandon the notion of collective authority. Their alternative social forms were principally sectarian flight from the world such as adopted by several Anabaptist groups like the Mennonites; and religious organizations on an episcopal, presbyterian or congregational model. The former favoured rural communities separated from the rest of society; the latter insisted especially on separation from the state. What they all represent in the present context is organized ways of forming many more sub-Christianities. This the Catholic and established Protestant churches are as well; the non-established Protestant churches have added significantly to the variety of possibilities and thus to the adaptive potential of Christian religion to the different local circumstances of a globalizing society.

Like the Catholic church, the various Protestant versions also faced the task of expanding their characteristic communications, of bringing about the prevalence of religious communication as church communication, in this way producing and reproducing Christian religious subsystems. Given their organized forms, that meant, as with the Catholics, incorporating adherents as involved members. The story is different depending on whether one is looking at the established state churches or the independent dissenting ones. For the state churches, the pressure towards 'churching' the masses as the only way of generating and expanding their systems was generally not as urgent, even if they were by no means complacent about the regular ritual participation of the populations which they claimed as theirs. Yet with state support they did not have to 'cater to the masses', which in effect meant they could insist on a tighter orthodoxy and orthopraxy, a more elite Christianity, if one wishes. As a result, with respect to 'churching the masses', most of these state churches claimed more members than they actually ever succeeded in incorporating on a more than occasional or superficial level. This does not mean that they were without influence over the lives of most of those whom they did claim, nor that their church services were poorly attended. Quite the contrary.[4] At times they made concerted efforts to incorporate the masses, with varying degrees of success at various times (McLeod and Ustorf 2003).

For the dissenting churches, by contrast, incorporating members as regular participants was the basis of their existence. As long as they remained separate from political institutions, they were 'voluntary' organizations, meaning that people could either join or *leave*, as it were, taking their religious communicative potential with them. That meant two things: a much higher percentage of their members were involved members; and non-established Protestant churches tended to multiply or exhibit far less centralized organization. Historically, the possibilities and dynamics of this way of forming church organizations received its clearest and most extensive expression in countries of Protestant European colonization, in particular originally British colonies like Australia and Canada, but above all the United States. In these countries established Protestant churches never achieved the position that they did in the European countries. Instead, what has since been analyzed as denominationalism prevailed (Finke and Stark 1992; Niebuhr 1929; cf. Noll 1992), namely an emphasis on a plurality of voluntary church organizations, some with closer ties to states such as what David Martin has called 'shadow' establishments (Martin 2000: 26ff.), others more practically independent and often theologically separatist. More generally, this pattern of religious organizations as 'non-governmental organizations' has turned out to be the prevailing form in which Christianity has institutionalized itself in most parts of the world, a process that includes the Roman Catholic church in those regions where Catholics are a minority and where states have brought about a clear separation of church and state. In this regard, such separation has not necessarily meant the irrelevance of religion in political processes – as the history of the United States, for one, clearly shows – any more than the prevailing organization of economic production as 'private' firms has entailed the removal of economic matters from government concern. Organizations, whether tied directly to state apparatuses or not, have emerged as the most important way of institutionalizing the differentiation of the Christian religious system, including its differentiation from other function systems. But to repeat, such differentiation does not mean mutual irrelevance, let alone autarchy.

The global expansion of the Christian religious system

Organizations have served as a prime way of giving Christianity form in today's society. Their precise structure and the justification for these structures have not been religiously irrelevant matters; they have been the subject of the variable religious programmes themselves, a symptom of which is the continued presence and development of the theological subdiscipline concerned with these matters, ecclesiology. As I have been indicating, however, organizations are not the only important type of system that has been instrumental in the construction of this modern religion. Social movements have also played a significant role. There were, of course, the Reformations, both Protestant and Catholic. On the Protestant side, sixteenth-century English Puritanism produced a number of separatist churches. Seventeenth- and eighteenth-century German Pietism, an originally Lutheran movement, spawned such organized forms as the Moravian church. Eighteenth-century English Methodism led to the formation of a number of Protestant denominations, some of which developed a worldwide presence. The nineteenth century was the century of Evangelicalism, which influenced the programmatic structure of most Protestant denominations in Britain, North America and around the world. A related version of this movement was the nineteenth-century Holiness movement, from which sprang organizations such as the Salvation Army and the Jehovah's Witnesses. Emerging from this movement in the twentieth century has been the powerful Pentecostal movement. Perhaps more than any other modern Christian movement, Pentecostalism has manifested itself in all corners of the Christian system. It has generated myriad of its own organizations; but, as with the earlier Evangelicalism, most already well-established Christian denominations have witnessed the formation of their own Pentecostal wings, often called Charismatic to signal that they regard themselves as remaining within their respective church organizations, not as separate from them. That includes, in this case, the Roman Catholic church.

As concerns their influence on the make-up of Christianity, the various movements exhibited the typical features of this type of social system. Their identity has been primarily programmatic, motivated and structured by certain goals and ideas such as an emphasis on individual and experientially based conversion or on particular forms of church polity. They have been fluid, delineated only by their leading notions and manifested in characteristic events such as revival or devotional meetings and sometimes through characteristic religious performance such as the Pentecostal glossolalia or speaking in tongues. In addition, these movements have either disappeared after a time, translated themselves more fully into particular Christian organizations, or become absorbed as programmatic changes in already existing churches. In this regard, Pentecostalism has even affected the way the dominant Christian power medium is conceived and translated into ritual elements. For much of Christian history, and certainly during the period of formation as a modern religion, the exhibition of religious power as individual trance has been absent, or at least treated with great suspicion as a too ready source of heterodox views. As easily the most rapidly growing trend in contemporary Christianity, the Pentecostal movement has changed that pattern significantly.

Yet of all the modern Christian social movements, one variety deserves special attention in the present context because it has been so central to the globalization of Christianity and thus to the Christian model for constructing religion. These are the different missionary movements. Mission, like the connected idea of conversion, has been something of a constant in Christian history, a key programmatic item among others and an ongoing organizational policy rather than the basis of identifiable and self-identified social movements. In certain instances, however, this feature has, as it were, taken on a life of its own, constituting the guiding kernel of a significant and distinct mobilization of resources, affecting a number of Christian organizations at the same time, and manifesting itself in recognizable events, discourses and often clearly separate social movement organizations. Like all social movements, Christian missionary movements have therefore been episodic, rising and waning, sometimes leaving behind stable religious structures, sometimes permanently altering the character of religious organizations, but also sometimes simply disappearing without much long-term effect on patterns of religious communication at all. They have also arisen periodically throughout the two thousand years of Christian history. Indeed, the earliest Christian form was arguably as a missionary movement. In the course of the modern development of Christianity that is my focus here, missionary movements have been evident at various points, but without doubt two of the strongest have been the Roman Catholic movement of the sixteenth and seventeenth centuries and then the much more dominantly – but far from exclusively – Protestant movement of the nineteenth and twentieth centuries. These missionary movements are to be distinguished from the straightforward expansion of religious organizations such as happened when the European Catholic or Protestant churches followed their members on their colonizing, political or economic migrations to other parts of the world. Critical as these developments also were for the global expansion of Christianity, they followed a different rationale than did the missions. A chief indicator of the difference is that the success or failure of the two sorts of enterprise varied independently; mission succeeded or failed where colonizing did not, and vice versa.

A closer examination of the two missionary movements just mentioned reveals some important features of the Christian religious system and its historical process of differentiation, both from other function systems and as a distinct system within global society. The first includes the differentiation between religion and state and between religion and education. With regard to the second, the key distinction is that between religion and culture or, what amounts to the same, the question of the indigenization of

Christianity in various regions of world society. Although the trajectories and particular characteristics of Roman Catholic, Protestant and also Eastern Orthodox missions during the two periods differ somewhat, observations about one frequently also apply to the others. It is the commonalities that I want to stress at this point, and therefore in the illustrations that follow what is notable about Roman Catholic missions also applies, *mutatis mutandis*, to Protestant or Orthodox ones, and vice versa.

The European Reformation and Counter-Reformation occurred during the first intense phase of modern European imperial expansion. It was also a period of ardent religious revival or intensification of religious communication. Under those circumstances, it is not at all surprising that the Reformation spawned as one of its dimensions a concerted movement for truly worldwide Christian expansion. That, at least, was the case for the Catholic Reformation, both because Catholic countries like Spain and Portugal were the dominant expansionary powers at this time; but also because the Protestant churches were only in their formative periods and for the most part tied to particular states. The Roman church's much higher degree of independence vis-à-vis states gave it a comparative advantage in the sense that the more purely religious impulse of a missionary movement could mobilize more effectively there. The resources of the state-controlled churches were far more restricted in how they could be used because, although state authorities in France and Spain or in England and Russia took up the cause of religious expansion as part of their imperial projects, this had to find its place in conjunction and coordination with the purposes of economic and political aggrandizement. Typically, the expanding states were more than willing to provide for the religious needs of their agents, soldiers, merchants and settlers. The fundamental *raison d'être* of missionary movements, however, was the conversion of the 'heathen' and the 'native'. For this purpose, state attitudes, while sympathetic in principle, tended to be inconsistent, hesitant and even hostile if the activities of the missionaries threatened to compromise the other goals. This ambiguity can easily be documented in the experiences of the Spanish missions in the New World, the Russian Orthodox missions into Siberia, and much later in the eighteenth and nineteenth centuries in the British Protestant missions to India and Africa. In each case we find restriction or unevenness in the allocation of resources for missions, or in the ability of the religious organizations to put missionary resources into the field not just because of church but also because of state policies (cf. Neill 1986).

This observation, however, only concerns how many communicative and other resources the carriers of the movements could muster. It is not a statement about the differential success of these missionary movements, which varied somewhat independently of the intensity of mobilization. In the sixteenth and seventeenth centuries the result was that the Catholic missionary movement was very much in evidence whereas Protestant missions were vestigial in comparison. Catholic success or failure in 'converting the heathen', on the other hand, bore no clear relation to the level of mobilization, whether subject to European state control or not. Indeed, what constituted success or failure was itself an elusive question. Put into social systemic terms, the missions could engage in their characteristic communication of 'spreading the Gospel', but that only constituted the reproduction of mission as a social movement system. For the Catholic Christian system itself to spread, the movement had to achieve three results: it had to incorporate target peoples into the movement, participating in its communication; it had to translate itself into the regular communication of another system less dependent on the mobilizing communication of the European missions, in particular indigenous or local Christian religious organizations; and the Christian systemic communication had to maintain its programmatic integrity as Christian. None of these would have been achieved by the fact of the missions themselves, irrespective of the dedication, resources or piety of the missionaries.

The sixteenth- and seventeenth-century Catholic missions illustrate these observations in interesting ways. Prime among these is the degree to which the missions tried, succeeded or failed in the indigenization of Catholic Christianity, which is to say its particularization to local cultural ecologies while at the same time maintaining its systemic recursiveness or recognizably Christian communicative integrity. Two examples show representative strategies and outcomes.

In the New World domains conquered in the name of the Spanish crown, the Catholic church was in effect a department of the respective state and therefore subject to its policies. This attachment to the state gave it access to resources and to the people of the new domains. In that context, missions to the indigenous peoples were a priority, but in certain respects, under the imperial state's aegis the outcome was that the church remained more the church of the Spanish and Portuguese European colonizers and representatives than it became the religion and church of the indigenous people and those of mixed ancestry. In particular, the Spanish New World church largely failed to indigenize its professional corps, whether among the regular priests or in the religious orders. As a result, while the church religion maintained its orthodox character, that was largely within the social core, not so much at the periphery. The farther one got from this European core, whether geographically in terms of city and hinterland or ethno-culturally in terms of a continuum from pure European to mixed race to purely indigenous, the more the particular Iberian orthodoxy gave way to the typically mixed phenomenon of what today we call 'popular religion'. This situation calls into question the extent to which Latin American religion became 'churched' Christian Catholic religion during the centuries after the European conquest. The seemingly Catholic character of Latin America may well have been as much the absence of a rival formed religion as it was the Christianization of religious communication. Only in the later twentieth century does this situation appear to be changing with the growth especially of Protestant Pentecostalism and, in Brazil at least, Afro-Brazilian religions like Candomblé. Still, the Catholic missions of the sixteenth and seventeenth centuries in the New World were largely successful in spreading the Christian religious system, even if it was as much a case of the Spanish church spreading with the power of its state as of successful mission to the indigenous peoples.

The situation of Catholic missions on the other side of the world, this time in China and East Asia, was different, and so was the outcome. The efforts of the Jesuits in this vast region are paradigmatic. In contrast to the New World Spanish situation, these missionaries could not rely on state resources, but they made great efforts to indigenize Catholic Christianity, seeking to incorporate Asian elites into a religion packaged in conformity with their cultural styles. So assiduous were some of them in this aim that their European superiors called them to account for 'heretical' deviation from the orthodox programme, a consequence exemplified well in the famous 'rites' controversy. In permitting Chinese Christian converts to honour their ancestors in ritual fashion, certain missionaries argued that this was 'culture', not 'religion'. One notes the critical distinction, a mark of differentiation as religion. Rome eventually disagreed: this was religious 'worshipping' not cultural 'honouring'. The ancestors were being treated in effect as transcendent partners in communication, as loci of the understanding and imparting of information. As such, the rituals in which they were deemed to participate constituted religious communication subject to the criteria of a Catholic Christian programme which could have 'no other gods'. Symptomatic as this episode is of the dynamics of the religious system, however, it would be difficult to argue that the limited progress that these Catholic missions made in East Asia during these centuries was directly on account of such limitations on indigenization. Rather, their relative and, as in Japan, absolute failure was much more a consequence of the powerful social systems that prevailed in this part of the world, in particular the Chinese imperial state and localized family/clan systems, and the rising Tokugawa Shogunate in Japan. To the degree that the Christian religious system introduced by the missionaries claimed differentiated functional independence, to that degree it clashed with the dominance of systems constructed more on stratified and core/periphery principles. Accordingly, the Christian missionaries and their converts were deemed not religiously evil, wrong or heretical; rather they were simply and unalterably foreign, contrary to the Chinese or Japanese way of social order.

In both these earlier cases of missionary movements, the Christian system spread either somewhat superficially, to a very limited extent, or not at all. Although the next great Christian missionary movement of the nineteenth and twentieth centuries would have to confront many of the same obstacles, it took place in a much altered situation, one characterized by the much stronger development of globalizing function systems, including the religious. At this point, these systems were at the high point of their European domination; this was the era of European colonial empires – including the Russian – which ruled directly or enforced their interests in virtually every corner of the world. Europeans ran the states or bent them to their will; they controlled global capitalism, went unchallenged in the pursuit of empirical science, established their schools and enforced their laws wherever they could. The penetration of these systems into the communication of everyday life was in a great many areas and among most peoples still quite superficial, but their power was effectively present everywhere. In this context, Christian missionary movements were a major feature of the imperial landscapes. They sought out every part of the inhabited world and implicated all three of the major Christian subdivisions.

The serious beginning of a global Protestant missionary movement had to await the end of the eighteenth century. It grew from there and reached its peak in the late nineteenth and early twentieth centuries. As with the Roman Catholic missions of the same time and of earlier centuries, the differentiation of this movement from the corresponding religious organizations was marked by the foundation and development of distinct and often independent missionary social movement organizations. Where in the Catholic case this role was mostly filled by the old and new religious orders ranging from the Jesuits and Franciscans to the Oblates of Marie Immaculate, the White Fathers and the Maryknollers; in the Protestant case these were denominationally affiliated, interdenominational and even nondenominational organizations formed expressly for worldwide mission. Among many examples were the Swiss-based Basel Mission, the English Church Missionary Society, the American Board of Commissioners for Foreign Missions and the China Inland Mission (Neill 1986). And as in the Catholic case, the broader religious context in which these organizations emerged was not just one of colonial expansion, but just as importantly of internal religious revival in the sending countries. Above all the evangelical revivals in North America and Europe, beginning with the first Great Awakening in the United States and the Wesleyan movement in Britain during the eighteenth century and continuing into the nineteenth century with, among others, the second Great Awakening and the Holiness movement, marked an acceleration in the development of the Christian religious system analogous to what was happening in virtually every other function domain. The worldwide mission movement was a prime expression of this increase.

The considerable independence of the Protestant missionary societies from their national churches and local denominations also meant a significant level of independence from the resources and control of the colonialist states. This does not mean that the progress of the movement was unaffected by colonial state policies of support or resistance, any more than it escaped the restrictions imposed by state and political authorities in the target regions. The movement organizations did not, however, have the additional challenge of having to conform to state-political priorities and were even in many cases reasonably free from the organizational agendas of their home churches. The situation of the missionizing and missionary orders in the Roman Catholic case was similar. What the latter gained in programmatic integrity and resources by being attached to a centralized organization, the former compensated in flexibility for localizing adaptations. As in the Catholic case of the sixteenth and seventeenth centuries, however, although the relations with states and churches were important and had their effect, the success or failure of the missions in effectively expanding the system was usually more contingent on other factors. One fairly consistent outcome was that the middle and upper strata of the more complex civilizations – namely those exhibiting a dominance of stratified or core/periphery differentiation – were far harder to convert to Christianity than were the marginalized in those same regions or those civilizations exhibiting a dominance of segmentary differentiation and, be it noted, non-literate cultures. Whether we are speaking of Catholic, Protestant or Orthodox missions, the 'success' areas in the late nineteenth and twentieth centuries were prevailingly among 'tribal' peoples, whether in South Asia, the Americas, Siberia, Oceania or sub-Saharan Africa. Another and very much related consistency was that Christian missions had far greater difficulty in areas that already had the sort of religio-cultural resources and traditions out of which the major religions of today's religious system have been formed. Where 'religion construction' was in any case half complete, requiring only the sort of re-formations that occurred in the emergence of Christianity, there the Christian missionaries met with relatively little success in extending their religious system. In those regions, among Muslims and Jews, Buddhist and Hindus, they were more likely to inspire religious counter-formation movements – thereby furthering the global religious system by inspiring the construction of additional religions – or, as in the case of China, even the rejection of the notion of a differentiated religion, than they were to gather large numbers of converts. The conclusion one can draw is that it was the efficacy of an integrated, organized and differentiated religious system that attracted converts at least as much if not more than it was the content of the Christian message itself.

The effect of the Christian missions was not just to spread the Christian religious system. The missions were one dimension of the broader expansion of European influence which implicated and furthered the development of the other function systems as well. Among those more closely intertwined with the religious was the educational system. Christian missionaries, of whatever stripe, tried various strategies for the incorporation of their potential converts, including often building model Christian villages designed for more effective resocialization. They also set up schools. These aimed to teach the young a Christian (and usually also European cultural) outlook, and for the Protestants especially, the ability to read the Christian Bible. Mission schools, however, also became in many places a way for indigenous elites to gain the training deemed necessary for participation in the power structures of the colonial regimes. On that basis the schools grew to become effective instruments for proselytization, but also more than that: they provided the beginnings of a differentiated academic education system in these areas. Often enough, they gave the impetus for the same indigenous elites to set up their own, non-Christian schools, whether in imitation of the Christian ones but with, for instance, a Hindu or Buddhist orientation; or as re-formations as modern schools of long-standing educational traditions such as in East Asia. Just as Christian missionizing inspired in several regions the appropriation of the religious modality to re-imagine local religious traditions as one of the religions, so did the mission schools play a part in leading to the particularization of the global educational system in these same regions (cf. Ramirez and Boli 1987). The spread of the medicalized health system could be analyzed in a similar way.

The spread of these systems, of course, does not mean a simple diffusion of European religious, educational, health and other forms to different parts of the world. Universalization has always also involved particularization by which the universal spreads, but in so doing transforms itself. Thus, although the missionaries were instrumental in transplanting the Christian religious system, what that system became concretely in the different regions, and thus what global Christianity has become, is different than what the missionaries imagined and even could have imagined. It is also more than what the missions accomplished. The indigenization of Christianity in the non-European cultural settings has to an extent engendered new versions of this religion, ones that have also influenced and are influencing the directions that European variants are taking. New particularizations of the Christian universal are themselves becoming more universal. This leads us to the critical question of the contemporary global composition of the Christian religious system, in particular to the role that variants play in the coherence of this system. Put in somewhat different terms, we must ask if and how different particularizations contribute to the singular construction of Christianity in global society and not, logically, to its dissipation in myriad disconnected forms or to the emergence of more distinct religions beside Christianity.

The institutionalization of globalized variants and Christian social movements

If the spread of Christianity to the non-West had been nothing more than the extension of missions, then we could not properly speak of the globalization of Christianity. The missionary movements were critical for that globalization, but they are historically and logically only the first moment. As with the formation of the global religious system more broadly, the process of religion formation includes indigenous appropriation, particularization and thereby transformation and further construction. In the case of Christian globalization, that meant the development of Christian social forms in which religious communication was more under the control of the 'targets' of the missions and in which that communication also expressed itself in the inherited and constructed cultural idioms of those targets. In concrete terms that meant the creation of indigenous Christian movements and organizations both carried and directed by local people, the reformulation and specification of the Christian religious programme in tune with local cultural patterns, the generation of new theologies as the reflective self-descriptions of those new programmes, and the corresponding reconstruction and even invention of religious practices or elements. As a final moment in this dialogical process, these new forms of Christianity have sought to project themselves beyond their local bases, whether through transnational organization, social movement or social network. The particularizations have engaged in their own universalization. All this is the recapitulation in non-European idiom of the European-based phase that the narrative has described thus far.

A great many examples could serve to illustrate this particularization and re-universalization of Christianity in the process of its globalization. Each of them would have its own peculiarities and its own complexities. I shall focus briefly on three examples: African Christianity, including the African Independent or Instituted churches (AICs); Latin American liberation theological movements; and Pentecostalism, both as organizations and movement. Many other examples could be drawn and would focus on different aspects of an overall development that has resulted in the institutionalization of a large number of globalized Christian variants. A subsequent section then concludes with a brief reconsideration of how this variety nonetheless still can constitute an effective sense of Christian unity, which is to say the operative singularity of Christianity as a subsystem of the global religious system.

African Christianity and the African Instituted churches

In most of sub-Saharan Africa, the arrival of Christianity coincides with European expansion and the sending of European Christian missionaries to these regions. Ethiopia was the only significant exception, and its variation has even today not spread substantially to the rest of the continent. Indeed, the southern two-thirds of the continent became aware of this ancient form only after and in the context of the arrival of the Europeans. The first of these were the Portuguese who, beginning in the later fifteenth century, established various coastal outposts from Cape Verde in the northwest to Mombassa in the east. Certain of these efforts resulted in long-lasting Luso-African Christian communities, but for a number of reasons they declined or remained very marginal presences by the middle of the eighteenth century (Hastings 1996: 71–129; Isichei 1995: 45–73). Thereafter, Africa, and its sub-Saharan regions in particular, became a prime target for the Evangelical Protestant and Catholic missionary impulses of that period. Especially with the end of the trans-Atlantic slave trade and the progressively greater incorporation of African regions into the globalizing colonial system in the nineteenth century, we see the acceleration and intensification of such efforts to cover almost all southern areas of the continent. As much of the literature on the subject exposes, these missionaries came to spread versions of their religion that were heavily characterized by European cultural features and by the religious movements, such as the ones that I have had occasion to mention, which arose in the European context (Clarke 1986; Neill 1986). Although success was until the twentieth century quite moderate, the Europeans did manage to set up their respective churches in the areas that they targeted; and these churches bore many of the characteristics of their sending versions (Hastings 1996; Isichei 1995).

The construction of particular African variants of Christianity did not occur solely or even predominantly outside the churches that the missionaries planted. In fact, such 'Africanization' began seriously already with the rapid growth of these missionary churches at the beginning of the twentieth century. The missionaries and their supporting organizations were critical for the initial introduction of the Christian religion, and for providing key resources such as translations of the Bible and catechetical material into vernacular African languages. Yet Africans themselves were the ones who transformed Christianity from a colonial implant of Europeans into a mass religion of Africans. All over sub-Saharan Africa, it was African teachers and catechetists, often independently of missionary oversight, who spread Christianity beyond the mission stations, founding churches that included a rapidly increasing number of Africans as converts and members, but that were also for the most part still extensions of the European denominations that the missionaries had introduced (Hastings 1996: 437ff.). Nonetheless, virtually from the beginning of the mass expansion, many of the new African Christians adapted their new religion to their own and different cultural forms and priorities, for instance through the incorporation into Christian worship of local musical styles, or by putting a far greater emphasis on the ability of the Christian God to bring this-worldly benefits, particularly personal healing. Since the Protestant missionaries set translation of the Bible into local languages as a high priority, their new adherents learned to read the Christian scriptures relatively early and inevitably interpreted them in ways somewhat different from their European mentors. They could, for instance, find biblical precedent for important elements of certain African cultures that the missionaries did not approve, in particular the practice of polygamy. Other issues, such as female circumcision, attitudes towards witchcraft, and especially African leadership of the new churches also became broadly contentious. The net result of many complex developments is that the African Christian churches of today, when they still belong to or still identify themselves with historically European denominations, show their own distinct characteristics in emphasis, in biblical interpretation, in ritual form and style, and in ecclesiastical governance, to mention only some of the most obvious. In this regard, even the Roman Catholic church in Africa, one which perhaps experienced its greatest growth in the middle parts of the twentieth century, shows characteristic distinctiveness. It conforms in organizational structure, internal discipline and core belief and ritual to the Roman pattern, but has adapted Catholicism for African sensibilities in various ways nonetheless, from liturgical music and dance, to an emphasis on healing, to its own indigenous Catholic religious orders.

This difference is perhaps even more pronounced in African churches that are independent of the originally European sending denominations, the African Instituted churches, or AICs. In many cases, such as the Harrist churches of Ghana, the Aladura churches of Nigeria, the Kimbanguist churches of the Congo, and the Zionist churches of South Africa, these were founded by independent prophets or leaders whose movements ended up breaking away from the Europeans – whether they actually intended this or not – because these did not seem to offer the Christian message in a sufficiently African form, or simply because Africans found European missionary control too restrictive and unnecessary (Maboia 1994; Ositelu 2002). Far from being simply and purely imposed on them by the colonizers, a great many Africans proved only too eager to adopt and adapt the Christian message in the rapidly changing circumstances in which they found themselves (just as a parallel statement can be made for Islam in many parts of sub-Saharan Africa). Not surprisingly, however, they wanted to lead their own churches, or at least have the possibility of leadership and advancement in them; and they wished to stress those elements in the Christian tradition that most spoke to their situation and their inherited way of understanding the world. Christianity offered a way of adaptation that promised the necessary continuity within discontinuity, a universal that overarched the European and African worlds but that could be readily particularized to the Africans' concrete

circumstances and cultural proclivities. The AICs were only one manifestation of this possibility. At least until the post-World War II era and the
period of African state independence starting in the late 1950s, what made
them different, along with distinct interpretations and combinations of
Africanized Christian elements, was precisely their independence, the fact
that they were instituted and run entirely by Africans. Accordingly,
throughout the earlier part of their history, many of those who represented
the European-based versions suspected them of not being sufficiently
Christian at all, of being less than 'orthodox' or of leaning too much in the
direction of African Traditional Religion. This is a question of religious
boundaries: whether the AICs are genuine versions of Christianity, another
religion, non-religion or even anti-religion (i.e. 'heathen'). It is typical of a
religious system in which mutual identification of religions from each
other is an important structural feature (cf. Mndende 1998). It cannot
really be decided on the basis of some neutral or general criteria because
none exist, or at least they have to be formulated in the very process of
making the mutual identifications; and this is what was at issue in this
African debate. What exactly was the status of a Simon Kimbangu or an
Isaiah Shembe vis-à-vis Jesus Christ? Was monogamy essential to Christian
faith and practice? How does one assess the claim to perform miracles or
the taking seriously of witchcraft as a reality to which Christian means
have to be applied? Such questions concern the core features of the general
Christian programme. They touch critically on the moral code that plays
such an important structural part in this religion, and they involve the
difficult issue of how the religious power medium is to be understood. On
the whole, the answers have been in favour of AICs as authentically
Christian: today, they are generally considered part of the Christian fold,
even though these sorts of issue still remain quite controversial, among
African as among non-African Christians. The cases of the Kimbanguist
and Aladura churches being accepted as members of the World Council of
Churches (WCC) would seem to be the clearest cases where this question
has been answered organizationally in the affirmative (Pobee 2002). The
parallel cases of the Southern African Zionist churches and many others
remain somewhat more ambiguous, but not that much more controversial.
The other side of the coin, of course, is that for many Africans the AICs
can never be *African* enough precisely because they are so clearly
Christian, the religion of the outsider.

The significance of the WCC and parallel ecumenical bodies in these
matters is a subject that I discuss below, but here it is important to underscore the degree to which the formation of different versions of
Christianity in sub-Saharan Africa has almost automatically raised the
practical question of Christian unity, and that this question tends to be
addressed not by the older hierarchical means – if you do not recognize a
particular central authority, you are outside the fold – but rather in typically

modern fashion of trying to include the variety in a multi-centred, plural-istic and, be it noted, organizational as well as theological way.

Like virtually every other form of Christianity today, African versions have not remained confined to Africa. One could begin with the Christianities of the descendants of Africans transplanted to the Americas in the context of the sixteenth- to nineteenth-century slave trade. African-American and African-Brazilian Christians, for instance, played important parts in bringing Christianity to the sub-Saharan African continent and also influenced its development in several areas. But their variants origi-nated in the New World, had different if in certain ways related characteristics, and have had a separate history. They are, in effect, yet more chapters in the overall modern Christian story, different particular-izations undertaking their own universalization. As concerns the African Christianity that is the current focus, some of these churches too have by now moved well beyond their continent of origin, mostly as their African carriers have migrated to other parts of the world. Thus, to take a few examples, West African Christians from countries such as Ghana and Nigeria have transplanted a variety of their churches to European coun-tries and to North America, where they not only minister to their migrant core population but also missionize among the larger population of these countries, sometimes considering their new lands as un-Christianized as the earlier European missionaries considered the Africa of their time (Adogame 2000; Ter Haar 1995, 1998). In addition, the African prophetic impulse that has been so important for the foundation of the African Instituted churches has also made its way to the historically Christian heartlands, as exemplified in the case of the Zambian Archbishop Milingo's healing ministry in the Italian metropolis of the Roman Catholic church to which he claims steadfast allegiance (Lanternari 1998). Another, perhaps more subtle but equally effective, road that this out-migration of African Christianity takes can be seen in those originally Western churches where Africans, or at least non-Westerners, now constitute a very sizeable proportion of the global membership – sometimes, as in the case of the Seventh-day Adventists even the majority – and occasionally also in the 'home' countries of such denominations (Lawson 1990, 1999). The African presence in organizations such as the Seventh-day Adventists, the Jehovah's Witnesses, and even or especially the Roman Catholic church can be expected to have a significant influence on the Christianity in these variants, just as the African forms have been so heavily influenced by what the missionaries originally brought.

The importance of such 'reverse-flow' phenomena in my argument is not their size or their level of overall influence. Rather, it is that they illus-trate a significant dimension in the dynamics of contemporary religion construction: particular versions of, in this case, Christianity spread through missionary activity or migration to other parts of the world, where they are adopted and partially transformed by indigenous people there. These new and different versions establish themselves and gain over time broad legitimacy precisely as authentic Christianity, a process that expressly includes an often high degree of contestation. Then, these now institutionalized forms engage in their own spread or universalization beyond their territories – and not infrequently populations – of origin, thereby becoming a more globalized part of the overall picture and having a certain influence on what Christianity becomes also in the areas to which they have expanded. One particular example of this influence is the greater prevalence of 'ecstatic' forms of Christianity around the world, with more emphasis on such manifestations as healing and (Holy) spirit possession. For this Africans are certainly not solely responsible, but they have contributed; and this observation leads us logically into a consideration of our second example of the generation of globalized Christian variants, namely the case of the Pentecostal movement.

Pentecostalism

The case of the worldwide Pentecostal movement thus has a certain conti-nuity with that of African Christianity, but it also illustrates some quite different aspects of global religion construction. Above all, Pentecostalism began and has continued to be a much more multi-centred movement than most others. None of its localized versions claims even symbolic priority as the historical, theological, power or demographic centre from which all other Pentecostalisms ought to draw their legitimation.[5] One symptom of this attribute is that Pentecostalism still shows characteristic social-movement features, including a more vague sense of membership or adherence, a strong sense of 'narrative' identity (based on a Christian biblical story of a movement of the Holy Spirit), and greater stress on what Thomas O'Dea famously called 'movement effectiveness over organizational elaboration' (O'Dea 1966: 90ff.). Indeed, the identification of the movement does not stress organization in the way that is so typical for most other branches of Christianity; even though organization is nonetheless fairly important, above all at the level of the local congregation or church, but also through denominations like the American-based Assemblies of God. The dominant bond which identifies Pentecostalism is instead the presence of *individual-ized* demonstrations of religious power in ritual settings, especially ecstatic utterances (prophesying, glossolalia), other bodily possession, and ritual healing.[6] Correspondingly, the programmatic aspects of Pentecostalism stress the interpretation of these events as manifestations of the Christian Holy Spirit and as justified only in terms of the Christian Bible. No other modern Christian movement of this magnitude has put such great stress on the religious power medium, a trait that perhaps helps explain some of its rapid and globally extended growth in the twentieth century. Centred on power instead of an elaborate programme promoted or enforced through organizational authority structures, Pentecostalism has proven attractive to a wide variety of peoples in different cultural settings. It is easy to adopt and above all easy to adapt. As Harvey Cox has put it, 'Its potent combination of biblical imagery and ecstatic worship . . . [enabled] pentecostalism [sic] to root itself in almost any culture . . . It was a religion made to travel, and it seemed to lose nothing in the translation' (Cox 1995: 101f.). Not surprisingly, therefore, the Pentecostal movement has in its relatively short history produced a great number of local and globalized variants. These, however, do not put the unity of the movement into question. Instead, together they configure the singular identity of Pentecostalism; they are differences which construct themselves with reference to a common, but ultimately abstract, identity.

The combination of plasticity with clarity of Pentecostal form and identity are reflected in its historical origins. In a strong sense, it was a continuation and outgrowth of Methodist, Evangelical and Holiness movements of the eighteenth and nineteenth centuries. Yet, although associated with various strong individuals, it had no clearly recognized founder as do other Christian forms that arose more or less during the same period, movements and organizations such as the Salvation Army (William and Catherine Booth), the Jehovah's Witnesses (Charles Taze Russell) and, somewhat earlier, the Seventh-day Adventists (William Miller, ultimately), Christian Science (Mary Baker Eddy) and even the Latter-day Saints (Joseph Smith and Brigham Young). To be sure, the self-description of the movement very often locates its beginnings in 1906 with the Reverend Seymour's revival meetings on Azusa Street in Los Angeles (Hollenweger 1972 is a classic example). This origin story is an element of the movement's identity, but only as part of the narrative. Azusa Street has symbolic importance; it is not a fount of authority and authenticity. In this regard, there is evidence to suggest that twentieth-century Pentecostalism in fact had its beginnings among Christians in multiple geographical centres ranging from India to Britain to the United States (Wilkinson 1999). This in itself is not all that surprising, given that the sort of enthusiastic and ecstatic ritual expression along with its understanding in terms of the biblical Pentecostal story have been a somewhat constant if irregular and controverted feature of Christian history. What Azusa Street furnished was a necessary focus through which the contemporary 'charismatic' impulses could come together as a self-identified movement, one key dimension of which would be precisely its global presence and spread.

From an analytic perspective, Seymour's key role in the Azusa Street story further points to the substantial admixture of African and African-American religious style in Pentecostalism. Even though the details are quite different, aspects of Pentecostalism are also a reflection of the earlier 'forced universalization' of certain African religious styles in the context of the Atlantic slave trade. The slaves and their descendants before the twentieth century almost all became Christian, but they nevertheless preserved elements of collective African religious memory, some of which manifested themselves in the twentieth-century Pentecostal movement. Another side of this observation is that the Spirit emphasis of Pentecostalism resonates with a great many forms of historical and contemporary African Christianity including, of course, African Pentecostal churches. From this perspective as well, the movement shows a globalized face. It has been an expression of religious globalization from early on, both in its geographical reach and in the sources of many of its recombined elements.

In consonance with its movement-like form and strong combination of narrative self-description and experiential power-medium emphasis, the spread of Pentecostalism also did not proceed predominantly along centre/periphery lines. Certainly Pentecostal churches have from the beginning engaged in missionary efforts in many parts of the world. Yet its history is also replete with stories of individuals who happened to be visiting somewhere, witnessed what was happening, perhaps experienced Pentecostal spirit-possession themselves, and then brought the movement and the message back to their own places where they helped found a new Pentecostal church or churches. Or they simply heard about it, read about it and, as if they had been waiting all along for the message to arrive, almost spontaneously kindled the movement in their own backyard (see Hollenweger 1972, for many examples from around the world). At least this is the way the stories are told. Far from indicating that Pentecostalism as a movement has not stressed mission and evangelism, this aspect of its global spread is actually much more a further symptom of its inherent multi-centredness. The frequently used metaphor of 'fire' is therefore not inappropriate (Cox 1995; Martin 1990), both because the spread was quite rapid and because it seemed to arise almost spontaneously in multiple locations, at the same time or one after another.

In sum, then, Pentecostalism, while defining itself internally (as well as being observed externally) as a singular movement of the Christian Spirit, has in practice been a multi-centred one from the beginning, never defining itself in centre/periphery terms or with respect to one or even a very few clearly privileged centres of authority and authenticity. There are today, and have been virtually from the beginning of the movement, multiple Pentecostalisms; not just regional versions, but different theological and programmatic directions such that, if it were not for the deliberate and conscious self-identification of so many of its manifestations around the world as part of the same thing, one would be tempted to say that the word 'Pentecostal' describes a general type of Christianity rather than a defined movement. As it stands, there is such identification: Pentecostalists read each other's literature, attend worldwide Pentecostalist conferences, have their leaders visit other Pentecostal churches around the world, and thematize the global nature of their movement in their local practices, publications, sermons and discussions (Coleman 2000; Cox 1995; Martin 1990). Different local Pentecostal churches establish transnational links and have founded branches in other countries, thus globalizing localized versions translocally. In this they are similar to many other, more tightly organized Christian denominations. Nonetheless, and this is a point of special importance, the variety of Pentecostal forms of religious expression is also quite wide. The typical Pentecostal church in say, Latin America, can in style, ritual practice, theological orientation and emphasis be very different from Pentecostal churches in Sweden, Korea, Ghana, Ethiopia or Sri Lanka. And these all can in turn be quite different from each other. This 'internal' variety manifests itself again when the adherents of these different Pentecostalisms migrate to other parts of the world, thereby transplanting their particularized versions such that the different versions are not only aware of each other, but exist geographically in the same place and often belong to the same local umbrella organizations (Wilkinson 1999). The interrelations, far from undermining the differences, actually are part of the process of constructing and preserving them, such that there seems to be no serious trend towards homogenization as a result. Quite the contrary. In spite of the fact that the majority of Pentecostal churches do not belong to the large 'mainline' umbrella ecumenical organizations and movements, they nonetheless demonstrate in their structure and practice how religions in today's global society, and Christianity in this case, are fundamentally multi-centred in terms of programmatic emphasis, ritual style and reflective theology; but remain singular in practice, and this not just from the perspective of analytic observation. Thus Pentecostalism, like Christianity, is not just a label of convenience, but an operative singularity in the social world that we inhabit.

That said, and as a transition to the next section, Pentecostal Christianity is also, from a slightly different angle, a name for a commonality of style, for a particular trend in virtually all defined Christian subdivisions like denominations and churches, not just those that identify themselves as part of the Pentecostal movement. For this broader perspective, the literature generally reserves the title of charismatic Christianity (Poewe 1994). What is involved, however, is more the particular ecstatic form of religious practice than either the typical theological interpretations that characterize the self-identified Pentecostal churches or the practical sense of belonging to the same overall global movement of the Spirit. While charismatics, or non-Pentecostalist Pentecostals, typically affirm a certain kinship with their co-religionists, they also maintain their adherence to their respective churches, whether Catholic, Protestant or Orthodox.

Liberation theology

There are, however, movements within Christianity that are more purely particular trends, with far less of this additional form. Under this heading one could put, as examples, liberation theology, Evangelicalism, as well as the just mentioned charismatic impulse. Here I want to focus on liberation theology precisely because there is no distinct and unified liberation theology movement in the sense of representative churches or denominations; but there is or has definitely been, a liberation theological social movement of some importance. Treating it will allow me to focus more closely on this issue of form, especially as concerns the difference between social movements and organizations.

With antecedents in post-World War II political theology centred in Europe, liberation theology emerged out of Latin America in the 1960s, in part a product of the ferment of the early post-Vatican II era (Berryman 1987; Christian Smith 1991). Like Pentecostalism, therefore, the impulse towards liberation theology occurred in more than one region, even though in terms of the trajectory of the movement, much more clearly in one region. Latin America has a historical as well as narrative primacy. From the late 1960s up to the early 1980s especially, this theological orientation became a practical movement within the Latin American churches to which its proponents belonged, mainline liberal Protestant ones, but especially the Roman Catholic church. In Latin America, one might say that it had its heyday during these approximately one and half decades, receiving particular impetus and visibility from its roles in promoting social change and even revolution in various countries ranging from Brazil and Chile to El Salvador and Nicaragua. Today this movement is not as visible as it once was, yet liberation theology remains an important option within many of the churches, now both in Latin America and elsewhere (Sigmund 1990). Indeed, its relatively early spread beyond Latin America is what makes it peculiarly apt for illustrating the main point I am trying to make here. From North America, the Caribbean, and Europe, to southern Africa, India, the Philippines and Korea, liberation theology has been adopted and adapted by Christians in a whole range of regions and countries (Ferm 1986). The emphasis is always recognizably the same, an understanding of Christian faith and an interpretation of the Christian sources as the grounds for bringing about practical social change aimed at a more just society with more equitable distribution of power, influence and life chances. Liberation theology has in this form become a kind of global universal that receives expression in various particular and localized variants. This is the case for all manifestations of this Christian direction, including the liberation theology of Latin America. It too has evolved or re-particularized over the decades (McGovern 1989). Above all, no more than in the case of American Pentecostalism does Latin American liberation theology today set some kind of implicit or explicit standard of authenticity for the other versions. It thereby parallels in its way of realizing itself the religion as a whole: globalized localizations at the same time as localized globalizations, neither being primary, and no sub-variants having anything but symbolic priority of authenticity or authority.

What does, however, make liberation theology different in the current context is that it has not succeeded in, or perhaps has eschewed, taking on the sort of distinct institutional forms that would allow it to systematize itself as a regular, dare I say, routinized variant of Christianity. This is exactly what has occurred with Pentecostalism and Evangelicalism with the explicitly Pentecostal and Evangelical churches. Neither of these latter impulses is to be limited to those kinds of churches; but in both cases the organized churches provide the most visible and effective manifestations in terms of ongoing, recognizably charismatic or evangelical religious communication. Liberation theological movements never took this extra step. The basic ecclesial communities (CEBs), which at one point became both theological and practically typical of the movement, were a beginning, but have thus far not continued a more clearly organizational path. In consequence, a combination of events has conspired to maintain the liberation theological direction as an established theological orientation in many churches, and as a resource for mobilization as particular circumstances arise. One thinks in this latter regard of the more recent events in Chiapas, Mexico. Yet overall, perhaps in the wake of persistent efforts on the part of the Roman Catholic authorities to tame and control it (a strategy also adopted successfully in the case of Catholic charismatics), and above all after the collapse of the socialist block and thus the severe weakening of socialist analysis as a politically practical alternative, liberation theology has, for the time being at least, lost much of the visibility that it had only two decades ago. Like all social movements, it awaits renewed opportunities for mobilization on the basis of its characteristic cause and message; and these may not be that difficult to find.

Christian unity and ecumenism

I turn now again, in more focused fashion, to the question of how all these Christian variants, whether they take the form of regionally based particularizations, globally extended religio-social movements or globally articulated organizations, nonetheless all contribute to the overall identity of an effective and singular subsystem of the global religious system, called Christianity. To some degree, I have already answered this question with the above discussion of code, programme, elements and power medium. The reverse aspect is also of some importance, namely that these Christian manifestations consider themselves and are treated by others as *not* one of the other religions, nor as belonging to the realm of non-religion or, from a religious perspective, the secular. Such negative identity, however, points to positive ways of asserting the unity of the Christian diversity, overt structures, processes and strategies which reflect and thematize the operative unity brought about by the self-referential communications themselves. Certain major subdivisions of the Christian system, most especially the Roman Catholic church, accomplish this through the ecclesial symbolism of their organizations. Yet for the overall unity of Christianity, a better place to begin is with a main organizational manifestation of Protestant unity, because it is this branch which has historically engendered the most Christian variants.

The World Council of Churches is largely a creature of many of the world's Protestant churches, but Eastern Orthodox churches are also members and the Roman Catholic church has often been a close collaborator. It is a prime expression of the theological and practical urge towards a larger Christian identity. That said, its importance in the current context lies as much in what it is not as in what it is. As perhaps the largest organization representing the broad ecumenical movement within contemporary Christianity, it had its antecedents in the missionary movement of the early twentieth century and took on its present form as a international non-governmental organization of some note in 1948 (Lefever 1987; VanElderen and Conway 2001), at around the same time as quite a number of other global organizations, including the United Nations. Its similarity and difference with respect to the latter is instructive. On the one hand, the WCC, like the UN, had global pretensions from the very beginning, even though it was in its earlier period largely the expression of only the large, mainline or national Western churches. In addition, beginning in the 1960s, this pattern of domination gradually altered to a degree as an increasing number of 'Third World' churches gained fuller membership and succeeded in putting many of their concerns among the priorities of the organization. The WCC is always open to the inclusion of new members, its criteria being somewhat loose and certainly not including any really meaningful test of orthodoxy. Moreover, like the United Nations in the political sphere, the WCC also has more of a consultative, even symbolic importance than it has any real authority in world Christianity. On the other hand, the WCC is also unlike the United Nations in critical respects, the most important of which is that, without the artifice of territorial states with precise and contiguous boundaries that cover the entire globe, Christianity, like religion more generally, has no equivalent of territorial-based sovereignty, and therefore no handy mechanism for symbolizing the inclusion of all its subdivisions. Many churches and Christian groupings are not and do not want to be members of the WCC, in particular a rather large portion of the Evangelical sector. In addition, the Roman Catholic church has never become a full member of the WCC, even though it has participated in its activities and collaborated with it on a number of fronts. The WCC, therefore, can justifiably claim to represent churches that cover the entire globe, but it cannot and does not claim to represent Christianity as a whole. Nor does it claim broad religious authority or to be able to determine questions of Christian authenticity. Its importance in the present context is nonetheless precisely in this combination: it expresses the unity of Christianity without thereby constituting or assuring it. The different particularizations of Christianity, both within and outside the WCC, are the real and effective centres of authority and authenticity, the localizations are the concrete manifestations of the global reality, or in Robertsonian fashion, social reality in global society is for the most part primarily glocal (Robertson 1995). To the extent that the WCC exercises influence in the Christian world, it is only as yet another localization or particularization. Just like those Christian churches that claim to be the only centre of orthodoxy, the whole that is the WCC is also but a part, not even the sum of the parts and especially not more than the sum of the parts. And yet, having said that, the WCC is also important because it embodies the self-conception of Christianity as a singular religion and not, in the final analysis, as either more than one religion or religion in general.

The other side to Christian unity is, of course, that which is not Christianity, most importantly but not exclusively the other religions and the other function systems. The Christian religion constitutes itself to a certain degree through the self-referential unity provided by its binary codings (above all salvation/damnation, moral/immoral), its faith power medium, and core aspects of its programmes, especially the mythic complex of God, Jesus and the Holy Spirit in the context of its Bible. Its reproduction is also brought about by the mutual reference, in practice, in theology, in networking, in movements and organizations, of its different versions to each other, whether positively in ecumenical spirit or negatively in criticism, dismissal or sometimes still in anathema. All this, however, would ultimately be insufficient if it were not for those other systemic identities in the Christian system's environment, entities which Christian theology and discourse recognize and reflect. These are concretely what Christianity is not. It is not the other religions; it is not or no longer, except in a minority of its self-conceptions, religion in general; it is not the state, the schools, the hospitals, the economy or the research and development centre. This distinguishing in no sense means that the Christian system has nothing to do or to say about these other systems, that it does not 'interfere' in their affairs. Quite the contrary. Moreover, these other systems also thematize Christianity in their communication. And, of course, other religions can thematize their own identities positively and negatively with reference to Christianity. All these 'external' references contribute to Christian unity quite as effectively as do 'internal' self-references. They are thereby a critical illustration of my central argument in this book. The global religious system operates in and as one function system among others. It is historically and socio-structurally peculiar to that context and makes little operative sense outside it. Christianity is a single religion because we, whether inside or outside observers, treat it that way.

Islam: orthodoxification and the global emergence of an alternate model?

In turning now to another major Abrahamic religion, I will try to show how the situation of Islam is both similar and different to that of Christianity. What follows will therefore have some of the same emphases as the previous section. In many respects, however, the approach is of necessity rather different because of the different details of Islam, certainly, but almost more critically because of the different position it has acquired in the modern globalizing context. Above all, Islam has not been the religion of hitherto dominant centres of the global system; more consistently the contrary.

As with Christianity, the historical process that is of interest in the present context is not a matter of the invention of a religion called Islam nor of its original construction out of disparate but already existing social structures and cultural traditions. Just as the idea and an institutional reality for the Christian religion predated the modern era by many centuries, so was a self-identified, institutionalized and recursively structured system of communications called Islam an important and in many regions highly determinative social reality from about the ninth century CE. As with Christianity, therefore, the issue at hand is not the invention of Islam but rather its re-construction, re-imagination and thereby (renewed) differentiation. The key question is what forms Islam takes in a socio-historical context in which differentiated and globalized function systems, including for religion, dominate.

The key to understanding the sorts of transformation and reconstruction that are at issue here is again the notion of differentiation, that is the differentiation of Islam as a religion beside the others and as a subsystem of the religious system beside other, non-religious systems. As an illustrative symptom of this double differentiation, one can refer to the frequently heard insistence on the part of devout Muslims today that Islam is indeed a religion, but it is at the same time more than that: it is a complete 'way of life'.[7] The recognition of its status as a religion implies comparison with other religions: Islam is a religion and thereby a different religion. Not surprisingly, Muslims sharing this recognition differ greatly on the issue of exactly how this religion relates to the others. Opinions range on a continuum between those who assert that Islam is the only true or universal religion, and those for whom it is a religion on a par with other religions, but happens to be 'my' or 'our' religion. The insistence that it is also a way

of life makes the additional claim that this religion is not limited in its relevance to only one domain of life. It is a way of living all aspects of one's
life, whether religious, familial, cultural, political, legal, economic, physical,
emotional or intellectual. Although from one perspective such a statement
may seem redundant – after all, is that not what the devout adherents of
any religion might claim – in the contemporary societal context it points
directly to the issue of the secular character of other, 'non-religious'
systems. Claiming that Islam is also a way of life amounts to a problemati-
zation of the institutional differentiation of other functional spheres.
Implied is that the latter should be grounded in and structured in consonance with the values and priorities of the religious system of Islam, that
the system of Islam is expressly not a system like the others but rather the
system that should have operational primacy over any others. Even though
this is a question for every one of the other religions and for the religious
system as a whole, in contemporary Islam, it has moved much more into
the foreground as a way of declaring and structuring the specificity of Islam
as a religion. This is not to say that Islam in the modern world is simply
defined by this problem of delimitation vis-à-vis other, putatively 'secular',
systems. For the most part, as with all the other religions, the everyday
practice of Islam proceeds without much attention to this issue, which is to
say that the communicative practices that recursively constitute Islam do
not constantly thematize it. Just as Christians today do not constantly talk
about, let alone pray about, questions like Christian unity, and Hindus are
not in their religious practice endlessly obsessed with how Hindus are not
Christians or Muslims; so Muslims generally just go about their religious
business of praying, fasting, reciting or preaching without worrying exces-
sively about whether capitalist, state, educational or sport structures in
their region or in the world are sufficiently 'Islamic'. Nonetheless, in terms
of the social forms (especially social movements) and theological emphases
that have restructured and re-imagined Islam for the contemporary modern
and globalized context, the question of Islam's boundaries of social influence appears to have been among the most important.

Islam, Islamic civilization, Islamic religion

The main question is thus one of the restructuring and re-imagination of
Islam for a different, namely globalized, context. As in the Christian case,
therefore, it is well to begin the further discussion of these developments
with a look at aspects of the institutional and conceptual realities of Islam
before the modern and global era. The key points concern the nature and
degree of institutional differentiation, both with respect to 'other religions'
and to 'non-religion'.

Its core mythic narratives in both Qur'an and Sunna, as well as the
practice of historical Muslim societies, seem to indicate that religious

plurality is rather more foundational to Islam than it is problematic. Other religious revelations to other peoples are discussed and accepted as authentic in the Qur'an; to these corresponds a concept, *din*, which, although not used in the Qur'an, does have a plural form, *adyan*. The systematic way of living in the world that the Qur'an calls Islam is an example of a generic category *din*, albeit the best example (Wilfred Cantwell Smith 1991: 81). Moreover, historically Islamic societies are well known for tolerating other religious groups, especially the so-called 'people of the book', Jews, Christians and others such as Zoroastrians. That phrase, 'people of the book', however, indicates that this tolerance is not the same as the clear recognition of differentiated religions in the modern globalized sense discussed here. The Qur'an, in fact, presents itself as the single and only revelation of the one God, as 'the' book revealed *as such* to different groups of people through different prophets, albeit in their own languages. The difference of the Qur'an is not so much that it reveals a different religion to Muhammad and the Arabs, but that it is the Arabic and undistorted rendition of the single revelation revealed to the final prophet, the seal of the prophets, Muhammad. Religion, on this view, is singular, and contained in its pure form only in the Arabic Qur'an. The tolerance is therefore not of other religions, but of other peoples, in the plural, who have a different but distorted version of that one religion. It is a way of underscoring the uniqueness of the religion of Islam, not a decla-ration of the plurality of formally equal and alternative religions. Indicatively, those people not deemed to be in possession of a version of this single revelation are, in Qur'anic terms, people without religion, not people practising a different religion. This understanding in most ways resembles that prevailing among contemporaneous Christians: Christian religion is the name for the authentic religious path in comparison with which 'other religions' are imperfect approximations or not religion at all, even anti-religion.

Although the Islamic understanding of *din* has historically been singular in this sense, the differences in comparison to the roughly contemporary European meaning of *religio* are just as instructive. Perhaps most critical among these is that the Islamic *din* contains the meaning of an encompassing system of life-conduct 'in this world' (Gardet 1960 [1980]). Unlike the founding narratives and early history of the Christian movement with their eschatological emphases on a 'kingdom that is not of this world', on 'rendering unto Caesar', on 'two natures', on what we today would call sectarian organization, the Islamic movement, likewise in its founding narratives and early history, featured a union of eschatological and this-worldly political orientations, such that it was from early on a religio-political movement in the largest sense of that term. It informed empire more fundamentally, much earlier in its development, and above all more seamlessly than the Christian movement did even in the centuries after the Constantinian turn. Just as suspicious of mystical trends and renewed propheticism as its Christian neighbour, Islam also stressed a rejection of renunciatory asceticism and monastic flight from the world. Hence the pre-modern European meaning of *religio* as referring to the monastic 'way of life' contrasts with this Islamic sense of *din* as referring to the 'way of life' of all Muslims.[8] This early established pattern received institutional expression not only in the form that Islamic empires or states typically took, for instance in the Sunni idea that the caliph was ideally both the religious and political head of the community and not just legitimated on religious grounds. It further manifested itself in the refusal to allow the development of corporate institutional entities that were not also an expression of this seamlessness, in modern Islamic parlance, this *tawhid*.[9] Correspondingly, for example, the Christian collective term, 'church', from early on carried an organizational, communal and even somewhat sectarian meaning, whereas the parallel term in Islam, *ummah*, denoted only the communal self-descriptive dimension. All this is definitely not to say that the Islamic conceptual ideal actually manifested itself straightforwardly and consistently in concrete Islamic social reality, that institutions operated quite so seamlessly. It is, however, to say that this conceptual ideal had a powerful and persistent presence in Islamic societies, making its use for restructuring Islam in the context of the developing global religious system of recent times as likely as that Christians would resort to an organizationally inspired strategy in that context. At issue are the ideational resources that Muslims have had at their disposal for engaging in the re-imagination of Islam, not some putative 'essence', let alone 'fundamentals' of Islam.

Nonetheless, the *tawhid* conceptual emphasis present in Islam should not lead one to think that Islamic societies did not exhibit important structural differentiation. There was always such institutional differentiation. The seamlessness of Islam as a system (*nizam*), however, points to the fact that this will not have been primarily functional differentiation. Indeed, the notion of *din* as encompassing life system contains the express negation of the conditions for a primacy of functional differentiation. Instead, the form of differentiation implied in the recognition and toleration of other religions or other religious communities is rather hierarchical or stratified, and therefore *dhimmi*, or 'protected people', status in Muslim societies has historically been 'second-class' status. A good example of the institutional expression of this understanding can be found in the Ottoman *millet*[10] system, by which Jewish and different Christian groups were accorded their own legal and educational, as well as religious, institutions, but were barred from full participation in the power structures of the empire, notably high state office and the military. Although the *millets* were distinguished as religious communities, they were not just religious divisions, but rather something much closer to class or strata divisions defined in religious terms. Analogously, the society as a whole was considered Muslim, as the House of Islam in which the prevailing ideology dictated that powerful functional institutions were to be Islamic, something that did not prevent the sort of practical differentiation between especially religious and political/state structures that also prevailed in premodern Christian society. Correspondingly, the other side of the functionally defined House of Islam (*dar al-Islam*), namely the House of the Infidel (*dar al-kufr* or *dar al-harb*), had no positive place in this understanding: to recognize the other side would have been to lend functional distinction primacy, as of course is the case in the contemporary global religious system.

The issue of Islam's relation to 'non-religion' before the modern and contemporary eras must be seen in a similar way. It is not that there was no institutional differentiation according to function. Political, economic and religious leaders were most often not the same people; there were 'specialists' in each domain. State and imperial structures were not also those of the religious scholars and Sufi adepts. The distinct development of especially these two streams is standard stuff of the history of Islamic societies (Esposito 1999; Lapidus 1988: Part I). Yet this was not the primary form of institutional differentiation, core/periphery, stratified and segmentary forms being rather more critical depending on the time and place which one is considering. Thus, political leaders relied on explicitly Islamic legitimation to justify their rule, incorporated Islamic scholars into their law and administration as a matter of course, and the scholars usually saw themselves as the natural occupants of these positions. At least as critically, these societies did not exhibit the clear institutional differentiation of various other functional domains, for instance the scientific, the educational, the legal, the economic, the health or the media. Practically, the failure of these domains to develop is attributable to the fact that the religious experts and institutions saw to those functions, especially the first three. But part of this practical reality was the conceptual and semantic dimension: they were understood functionally as aspects of the system of Islam. Thus, although the relation of Islam to the world was definitely also an issue (*din* vs *dunya*), it did not and could not present itself as one of the relation of functionally defined institutional spheres, one of which was religion. In practical terms, the traditional Islamic societal situation is quite similar to others such as the South Asian and European: religious leaders were the knowledge providers, the educators, the judges and arbitrators. Yet in Christian Europe the notion and concrete institutional reality of functionally differentiated institutions had much more solid precedent, as we have seen. In developed form, it is a peculiarity of the modern and now global situation in which function systems dominate.

Islamic reform and the challenge of Western power

As in the case of Christianity, the starting date for a narrative of modern Islamic reconstruction must of necessity be a bit arbitrary. Following John O. Voll's oft-cited treatment (Voll 1982, 1999), I begin with developments in the eighteenth century not because little of importance transpired before then, but rather because the more significant reform impulses that characterized this century provided key thematic resources and emphases for the numerous reformers and intellectuals that followed in the nineteenth and twentieth centuries. The eighteenth century was not a time during which Western presence was all that overwhelming in most Muslim dominated regions. British, Dutch and French forces especially were definitely present in most areas, such as South and Southeast Asia, but their ultimate hegemony was far from evident at the time. Islamic reform movements of the time were responses to more regional and local developments, such as the gradual and roughly simultaneous decline in the efficacy of the three dominant Muslim empires of the time, the Ottoman, the Safavid and the Mughal.

A more nuanced understanding of the different Islamic reform impulses of that time would have to examine different regions, different movements and the orientations of the various leaders that spearheaded them. For the present purposes, however, one can limit the discussion to three dominant themes typical of many of them, namely a distrust of conservative imitation of received tradition in favour of re-appropriation of core religious sources, an emphasis on what Voll calls 'socio-moral reconstruction', and a particular understanding of the unity of Islam. The three themes mutually inform one another. The first, expressed for instance in a rejection of imitation or *taqlid*, stressed the degree to which then prevailing forms of doing Islam had become corrupted, were unreliable or at least had to be re-examined rather than just imitated. Thus was the door opened for a reformulation of the programmatic core of Islam on the basis of the selectivity of the reformers, namely their ability to engage in independent interpretation, or *ijtihad*. This breaking free from received tradition, however, meant anything but openness for eclectic borrowing from a wide variety of sources or radical invention of new traditions. The dominant eighteenth-century trend circumscribed the possibilities quite sharply. Neo-Sufi impulses such as that of the Naqshbandiyyah order or more austere directions like the Wahhabis agreed that reform had to consist in a recovery of the Qur'an and the traditions of the prophet, the Sunna, as the obligatory and only reliable sources. As so often in religious reform movements, reinterpretation of the core religious programme proceeded by way of a putative recovery of the mythic origins. It was structured recursively, presenting itself as a winnowing or purification rather than an adaptation or augmentation. Thus, corresponding to this positive 'return to the origins' was the rejection of those aspects now deemed to be illegitimate accretions, or of the obligatory nature of anything not traceable to the origins as the reformers understood them. In the Islamic reform impulses of the eighteenth century, that meant practically the rejection of a large portion of accumulated Sufi belief and practice, especially that related to the veneration of Sufi saints and direct personal religious experiences as a reliable source for doing Islam (cf. Gellner 1969). The Wahhabis represent the most extreme form of this direction. In general, the reformers were inclined to reject notable historical Islamic figures that represented these tendencies, especially Ibn al-Arabi, in favour of the more 'scriptural' and rule-oriented Islam of figures like al-Ghazali and Ibn Taymiyyah. The prevailing tendency was in favour of obeying God's commands and away from a stress on a devotional and quasi-pantheistic search for closeness to God. Yet this submission (Islam) as obedience to God was not to be done on the basis of imitating a human authority, thereby creating another intermediary between God and the human being. It was rather the respon-sibility of the individual Muslim using only the reliable sources of Qur'an and Sunna.[11] To this 'socio-moral' emphasis corresponded a notion of Islamic unity that eschewed a more pantheistic understanding of *tawhid* as the unity of everything *in* God in favour of one that stressed God's tran-scendence and therefore unity of the world under God. Hence the critical role of the communicated 'texts' as opposed to experience or persons as the medium between the two. In this context, a final critical aspect is that these reform impulses in no wise represented or took the form of a kind of sectarian rejection and flight from the world. Rather, the idea was that all aspects of the human social world should be conducted under the aegis of *tawhid* based only on the core sources.

The eighteenth-century reform directions thus combined a wish to 'purify' Islam, to bring it back to what was deemed to be its essential core, and yet also to expand the purview of this purified form to include all of society. In systemic terms, they sought to consolidate Islam as a functional and clearly recursive programme that nonetheless encompassed all aspects of social life and thereby claimed to subsume all potentially rival func-tional forms. It is precisely in this aspect that the socio-structural logic of the European society of the time had been developing in the opposite direction. Although the European presence in the eighteenth-century Muslim world was not yet inescapable, in one critical respect it was already making itself felt, namely in the economic realm. As Wallerstein's analysis makes clear, a key aspect of the development of the European world economy was its shift to a worldwide trade and production market, not just in luxury but also in basic goods like food and cloth (Wallerstein 1974–80). The merchants of the Muslim empires were at that time already increasingly involved in this growing new economic system, building rela-tively independent bases of social power that the central imperial authorities could not control. The relative 'chaos' that such diffusion of power created was part of the social context in which the Islamic socio-moral reform movements arose.

By the end of the eighteenth century, the European presence in Muslim-dominated regions had begun to reach much more serious proportions, not only in the increasing influence of the European-centred world economy but also now in the political realm. The apogee of Western imperial presence came in the following roughly 150 years. Some regions, like South Asia, Southeast Asia and most of Africa became express colonies of European empires; others, like most of western Asia, found themselves subject to direct or indirect political control while maintaining a nominal political independence. In colonial areas especially, the European powers sought to introduce other functional institutions such as legal, educational and media structures. This they attempted in different degrees and with varying success, with or without the collaboration of indigenous elites. Not surprisingly, both the European colonizers and the indigenous colonized understood this imperial success in what one might call societal, cultural or civilizational terms, attributing it, for instance, to the supposed superiority or 'genius' of the Europeans as a people; or, what amounts to the same in reverse, to their barbarity. In other words, both sides saw this expansion on the, to them, familiar model of past empire-building projects such as those of the Romans, the Mongols or the early Arab Muslims. In social systemic language, they understood it in terms of core/periphery or stratified differentiation, not primarily in functional terms. From the perspective of the present, however, it becomes possible to see that this success was different in precisely this respect.

The Europeans were more powerful because, in the shift to a structural dominance of function systems, they had differentiated and upgraded distinct forms of social power based on function, the development of which had always been kept in a certain check in societies – including their own before the modern period – where other forms of differentiation dominated. The issue was not just one of more power as opposed to less, but also of different forms of power, in several of which the Europeans had the advantage and the socio-structural logic that would keep that advantage as long as their opponents/victims/others did not also adopt it in some fashion. With that in mind, it is highly significant that one of the functionally specialized domains in which the Europeans did not succeed in making inroads in Muslim-dominated regions was precisely religion. The dominant reconstructed religion of the Europeans, Christianity, hardly had any success in regions where Islam was already dominant, a result that again points to the orthogonal character of religion discussed in the last chapter. In responding to European hegemony, therefore, two sorts of functionally oriented strategies have historically dominated. State-centred nationalism is one of them and by far the more common. Religious reconstruction, however, is another. And nothing prevents a combination.

Islamic responses: *tawhid* and *ummah* through social movement

In his already cited work on modern Islamic movements, Voll adopts an analytic typology of what he calls Islamic styles of action. He distinguishes adaptationist, conservative, fundamentalist and personal-piety styles (Voll 1982: 29–31). These he presents as informing all periods of Muslim history, not just the modern era; but they are useful for discussing Islamic responses to the context characterized by European hegemony because they help one to appreciate both historical continuities and discontinuities in how modern Islamic movements have structured their responses and thereby contributed to the restructuring of Islam as a religion in the global religious system. Briefly, *adaptationist* styles allow for Islam to change, to incorporate new ideas and forms that present themselves in the environment. The Mutazilite incorporation of Greek philosophy or Akbar's eclecticism in Mughal India can serve as examples. *Conservatism* wishes to preserve and rely on what has been received; it is a kind of 'default' style that reacts against movements of more radical change. Those who defend the status quo at any given time or place would be its representatives. The *fundamentalist* style insists on a reduction or return to what is seen as the authentic core of Islam; it is past-oriented but often radical in its proposals for change and can include important innovation in areas that are not deemed as part of the core. The position of Ibn Taymiyyah or the Wahhabis already mentioned would be pre-modern examples. Finally, the *personal-piety* style focuses on the individual or restricted group practice of Islam, much of devotional and mystic Sufism of times past being one example. The utility of this typology in the present context is that it identifies four strategies that have been typical of Islamic responses to the modern and global circumstances: reforming or modernizing Islam, simply continuing as before while allowing the gradual incorporation of changes once well established, redefining Islam in opposition to what are perceived as the dominant modern and global forces but thereby also introducing radical change of the Islamic status quo, and the privatization of Islam with varying specific emphases. The adaptationist and fundamentalist responses have received the most attention in the literature on modern Islam (see e.g. Donohue and Esposito 1982; Esposito 1983; Kurzman 2002), probably because they have in fact been the most visible and effective. The possibility of conservative and personal-piety varieties should, however, be kept in mind. They may offer better prospects of longer-term stability in the global and modern contexts. All four styles can inform the kind of dissolution of received elements out of old structures and their recombination with new elements in new forms that is typical of the reconstruction of religions in contemporary global society.

Voll's styles of Islamic action are useful as heuristic devices for classifying the different basic orientations that Muslims might use to respond to whatever historical situation they happen to find themselves in. How these styles manifest themselves in a particular circumstance, however, will depend, among other factors, on which sorts of social system they inform in any given historical period, and that again will depend on which kinds of system are dominant or available. In the past the segmentary system of the tribe, the clan, the family, the quasi-organizational brotherhood or core/peripheral and status group societal systems occupied this place. Islam and Islamic styles therefore incarnated themselves in and through these sorts of system. The increasingly preponderant place of functional societal systems, organizations and social movements in the globalizing society of the last two hundred years would, however, lead one to expect that the modern reconstruction of Islam as one of the major religions of the global religious subsystem will take place by way of these types of system. Interaction systems, of course, are universally present, whether in past or today's societies. Above, I argued that the organization has been particularly critical in this regard as concerns the modern reconstruction of Christianity, but that social movements and other function systems have also played important roles in concretizing and controlling the recursiveness of this religious subsystem. In the case of Islam, the same sorts of system have been involved, but the order of priority has been somewhat different. For the reconstruction of Islam as one of the religions, the social movement and other function systems, especially the political and the legal, have been more important, the organizational strategy having thus far played more of a supportive role. In consequence, for instance, the literature on modern Islam is currently dominated with analysis of various modern Islamic social movements, especially with the ideology and mobilization strategies of these movements (because that is what largely constitutes such systems); with the incorporation of Islamic meanings in the political and legal systems of various states; and relatively less, or primarily in that context, with express organizations such as the Egyptian Muslim Brotherhood, the Indonesian Muhammadiya or the South Asian Tablighi Jama'at, and even here as social movement organizations. Less movement-specific organizations, for instance various now more formally organized Sufi tariqats, Muslim student organizations or local mosque organizations, are beginning to receive more attention, however, indicating either a rise in the importance of the organizational form or simply greater attention to organizational responses that have been there for quite some time but ignored for various reasons.

The explanations for this different emphasis in comparison with Christianity are somewhat speculative. Part of an answer, however, undoubtedly lies in the already discussed Islamic precedents of the past, both the beginning ones and those of the more recent past, namely the eighteenth-century reform movements. Above all, the critical position of *tawhid* and the very unorganizational stress of *ummah* make it more likely that reform will seek to engage society as a whole as its primary system of reference, and not one or more social subsystems of whatever type. The fluidity and restlessness of the social movement and the collectively binding quality of political and legal forms of power are better suited to such an emphasis than is strong reliance on the organization with its ability to carve out well-defined, even institutionally complete, but thereby also somewhat 'sectarian' social spaces. In combination, the resort to the broader and more nebulous forms easily confirms the impression that Islamic reform has sought anything but the differentiation of a specifically Islamic societal subsystem beside others. Meaningful intent, however, as modern revolutionary movements from the French and American to the Bolshevik, Maoist and Iranian show, does not usually translate directly into corresponding socio-structural consequences. Social systems have an independent logic of their own. Thus, the characteristic challenge for Islamic reconstruction has been, not the realization of utopia, but the translation of social movement impulses into available and more stable systemic structures which will perpetuate Islamic religious authority and operative recursiveness of Islamic communication. As with modern Christianity with its more clearly organizational emphasis, the alternative to such translation is a gradual dissipation of religious communication into the cultural ecological landscape, into individual bricolage, communitarian patterns and radical privatization.

In what seems like the majority of scholarly presentations of Islamic reform since the beginning of the nineteenth century, certain movements and certain historical figures appear again and again, even though, globally, the field of such movements and figures is, as one might expect, exceedingly complex (Donohue and Esposito 1982; Kurzman 2002; Lapidus 1988; Voll 1982, 1999). The most frequently discussed nineteenth-century responses have been the adaptationist ones associated with names such as Sayyed Ahmad Khan in South Asia and Mohammad Abduh in Egypt, and fundamentalist movements represented especially by the more latter-day Arabian Wahhabis and the more personal-piety oriented Deobandis in South Asia. While far from presenting a complete picture, these movements can serve as representative examples of the sort of reconstruction efforts that dominated at that time. In looking at them more closely, however, it must be kept in mind that these were not express efforts to reconstruct Islam as one of the religions in a global religious system. As noted, in a real sense they sought to avoid that outcome. Yet in the context of the parallel construction of other systems, especially other function systems like the state or capitalist economy and other religions like Christianity, Sikhism and Hinduism, that is what they have contributed to accomplishing. More specifically, given the holistic

emphasis of most of these movements, they have to be understood in relation to the parallel arising of more non-religious movements of response,
especially nationalist ones. Whether in adaptationist or fundamentalist
form, holistic Islamic movements, through their universalistic or pan-
Islamic stress, have inevitably had to contend with nationalist movements,
a critical factor in the parallel institutionalization of the modern political
state system in Muslim majority areas as elsewhere. Although not unique
to Islam, the ambiguous relationship between religion and state has been
especially evident in this case, a symptom of two function systems
constructing themselves with parallel meanings (e.g. *ummah* vs nation,
tawhid vs the common good or nationalism) but with incompatible strategies of delimitation (Muslim bodies, wherever they are, vs sovereign
territory). Thus the perpetual question has been whether Islam is for the
nation or the nation is for Islam. Concretely, the only systemic ways of
avoiding this outcome would have been to rely on other system types more
heavily, above all, as in the Christian case, the organization.[12]

The South Asian reform direction represented by Sayyed Ahmed Khan
(1817–98) in the latter half of the nineteenth century took very much
Voll's adaptationist direction. In the wake of repeated failed efforts to
defeat British power and influence in India, ranging from the Barelwi
revolt of the 1820s to the 1857 general Indian uprising, this member of the
Muslim elite advocated acceptance of British political rule while at the
same time promoting Muslim religious and cultural distinction. The relation of his vision to the emergent functional prioritization represented by
the British is instructive in the current context. Sayyed Ahmed Khan
advanced a kind of scriptural 'fundamentalism' which, in typical fashion,
rejected historic accretions to claim the Qur'an and the 'indisputable'
Hadith as the only true sources of Islam. Those sources, however, had to
be understood as being in consonance with human nature, meaning that
true Islam could not be in contradiction with modern empirical science. It
was not thus reduced to science, but rather re-imagined as a functionally
resonant domain, as precisely not orthogonal. In tune with this refash-
ioning of Islam, a main concrete institutional expression of this movement
was the founding in 1874 of the Muhammedan Anglo-Oriental College at
Aligarh, today Aligarh Muslim University (see http://www.amu.ac.in). This
institution aimed to train the modernizing elite that could restore Muslims
to positions of power, a kind of Indian Muslim Eton and very unlike the
traditional Islamic madrassa (Voll 1982: 112–13). The possible implications of this direction for the understanding of Muslim religion appear
with particular clarity in the orientation of Khan's associate, Chiragh Ali
(1844–95), who made a clear distinction between Islam as religion and the
social system in which this religion was embedded, defending Islam as religion especially against Christian criticism and rejecting the idea that
Shari'a was anything like a codified, positive law or legal system (Donohue

and Esposito 1982: 38–47). If one adds the fact that neither Khan nor Ali advocated for a Muslim state and even eschewed a Muslim nationalist direction, then we have a revisioning of Islam very much in tune with a social context in which function systems dominate the societal structures. Religion remains important, even vital, but it is a domain beside others with which it is interdependent.

While Khan's orientation demonstrates one possibility of Islamic reconstruction, and the movement that he represented was not without influence, other directions were just as consequential. Among these was that associated with the foundation of another school, the reform college at Deoband in 1867. Like the Muslim college at Aligarh, this school was structured along modern lines with a defined curriculum, institutional accreditation and a fixed professional faculty. Unlike Ahmed Khan's institution, however, it took a neo-Sufi direction, stressing the traditional Islamic sciences of Qur'an, Hadith and law without nearly as much attention to non-traditional subjects like empirical science. The school was in fact the central institution in a much more communal, and even sectarian, response that sought to recreate as much as possible a Muslim society, but without the mechanism of a Muslim state. Beside establishing and running a growing system of schools, Deoband ulama encouraged their movement followers to consult them on all aspects of life, and were well known for the volume of legal rulings that they issued (Metcalf 1982). To re-form the Islamic community, they had to reform the practice of Islam, which meant, in Voll's terms, a fundamentalist return to the sources and then the selective rebuilding of an authentic Islamic practice. In systemic terms, they sought to re-establish and strengthen the operative recursiveness of Islamic communication through their reform programme. This purified Islam, in conjunction with the schools as the central modern institution and, be it noted, organization, was to be at the centre of a Muslim community, a kind of status group like an Ottoman *millet* or even a Christian sect, that sought precisely to avoid the dominance of function-based institutional systems and thus the differentiation of Islam as one of them and as one of the religions. What is particularly instructive about what one might thus call the Deoband option, however, is that it actually accords quite well with the re-ordering of social structure towards a dominance of function systems because it does not effectively seek to interfere with their development: it works towards the solidification of the Islamic religious system, leaving the political, economic and other systems to do likewise. The one system where it does 'interfere' is in education, but even here the segmentary differentiation of this system, as elsewhere in the world, allows parallel development of schools, in their own way as functionally coherent as any other, without requiring control of all schools. The efficacy of developing the Islamic religious system in this 'pillarized' fashion should not be underestimated, yet it immediately points to a further possibility, and that is to do what Deoband tried to do, but expand the effort to, as it were, 'colonize' other developing function systems in addition to the educational, namely and especially the political and legal, and thereby also as much as possible the others within the borders of a particular state. This option is in fact the one that became most visible in the latter half of the twentieth century in the form of various 'Islamist' movements in numerous states. Its history in the modern period reaches back further than that.

Three movements will serve to illustrate this option and some of its variations: the movement associated with Abu al-Ala Mawdudi (1903–79) and the Jamaat-i Islami in South Asia/Pakistan, the Muslim Brotherhood of Egypt, and twentieth-century Wahhabism in Saudi Arabia. In each case, the relationship with their respective states has been different and, in the present context, instructive of how the differentiated construction of other function systems pushes religion in the direction of a parallel systemic development, even when religious ideology and state practice adopt a de-differentiating orientation. In all cases, this outcome is substantially the result of the fact that, even when Islam wants to be religion as such and not one of the religions, the parallel and global construction of other religions makes that aim impossible to attain. Likewise, a state can become 'Islamic' to a significant degree, to the point even that it uses religious communication as the basis for many of its political decisions, much of its legislation, and to structure its legal system. Yet because that state is in fact a differentiated segment of a global function system that is the system of sovereign political states, it is also under substantial pressure in other respects to operate like any other state that is not Islamic, and thereby contribute to the reproduction of that differentiated system as well.

Like the Deobandis and others taking a more, in Voll's terms, funda-mentalist direction, the twentieth-century Islamic revival movement associated with Mawdudi insisted on a recovery of Islam based on the original sources, but was also more or less open to modern techniques like empirical science and academic education, so long as Islam established their limits. Unlike the Deobandis, however, Mawdudi and the modern type of movement organization that he founded in 1941, the Jamaat-i Islami, took up the principles of *tawhid* and *ummah* in a broader and less sectarian fashion. This different orientation manifested itself above all in opposition to the Muslim nationalism represented by the Muslim League and its leaders like Ali Jinnah and Muhammad Iqbal. The League, some-what ironically, represented the main direction that Ahmed Khan's more adaptationist direction had taken by the end of the nineteenth century. For Mawdudi, their idea of a modern Muslim state contradicted the societal holism reflected in *tawhid* since it in effect set up the nation with its state as the primary institutional domain, not religion. Correspondingly, by including only some Muslims within this state-centred understanding of society, it also contradicted the notion of *ummah* as the community of all Muslims. Translated into the terms used here, Mawdudi opposed the League because its functional priorities were for him wrong: it set up the political system as a structural domain with an independent (Western) logic at least on a par with the (Islamic) religious system, if not frankly superior. In the historical context of the early to mid-twentieth century, however, Mawdudi's direction did not have at its disposal the structural means that could put his vision into practical effect. An Islamic conquering army, for instance, such as the Barelwis had tried in the early nineteenth century, was not an option. The closest that he could come was to found a kind of 'vanguard of Islam' party in the form of the Jamaat-i Islami, a political organization that, like the communist parties of that time, could operate nationally but with international, here pan-Islamic, aspirations (Adams 1983). Again somewhat ironically, however, by the mid-twentieth century the viability of that option in the South Asian region already depended on the prior existence of just the sort of nation-state that Mawdudi opposed. In those circumstances, the Muslim League, which of course had a modern territorial state as its prime objective, succeeded first. Pakistan was founded only six years after the creation of the Jamaat-i Islami. Not surprisingly, Mawdudi moved to this state after Partition and it is there that his organization became an important political organization, albeit with continuing wider ambitions. Once his movement had a political state in which to operate, it could be and was much more practically effective.

An analogous experiment further west took the form of the Muslim Brotherhood of Egypt. Here again, one encounters the stress on the fundamental sources of Islam, the Qur'an and the Sunna, and on the functional comprehensiveness of Islam as a system. The organization that Hasan al-Banna founded in 1928, although critical to his purposes of revival, was not to be limited in its aims to just Muslims, as in the case of the Deobandis in India. It was to be the spearhead for establishing an entirely Islamic society and hence also an entirely Islamic government. Since the Egyptian state was already formed, the Brotherhood from the beginning could and did act primarily on that national stage. It did set up schools and tried to offer various social services, much like the Deobandis; but the political arena also quickly became a prime domain of operation because the collectively binding power of government was so central to its vision of what Islam was. In the postwar period after 1945, it eventually clashed head on with the functionally analogous orientation of the Arab socialists who in fact succeeded in taking over that government. Since then, it has been the target of successive Egyptian governments as a politically subversive organization, but has also transformed itself into something resembling more a political party that also runs educational, health and other social service organizations. It has survived to some degree because it has maintained the social form of the organization as its core form, allowing adaptation to changing social and political contexts. Like other organizations, it can expand its activity beyond the borders of the Egyptian state, but only to the extent that it is careful to respect state boundaries. Accordingly the primary way of expanding the Islamic movement for which it is the most important movement organization is for other Muslim Brotherhood organizations to establish themselves in other states. In principle, it recognizes no functional differentiation between political and religious spheres. In practice it has to because the political system in its environment, much like the economic, is so well established. Thus, while its influence on how state and economy operate in Egypt or elsewhere is quite limited, its effect on how Islam is viewed, understood and to some extent practised, is by comparison considerable, although not necessarily dominant.

The Wahhabi movement in Saudi Arabia presents a more directly successful variation on this theme. With its origins already in the eighteenth century, the alliance between this, again in Voll's meaning of the word, fundamentalist reconstruction and the Saud family – an interesting case of a family system eventually substituting for what in other countries was 'the party' – permitted the creation of a state in which Islamic religious system and political state system were significantly de-differentiated. In this sense, Saudi Arabia has been analogous to socialist states like the Soviet Union or Maoist China, except in those cases it was the capitalist economy and the state system that were thus intertwined.

At its inception in the eighteenth century, the Saudi-Wahhabi alliance followed the older strategy of imperial state-building through core-to-periphery military conquest. The experiment was only partially successful, rather short-lived as a significant presence, and then for most of the nineteenth century restricted to the inner peripheral regions of the Arabian peninsula. The Saudis had some success in repeating the experiment in the early twentieth century, but by that time the modern state-political system was well on the way to solidifying in the Middle Eastern region, especially after World War I when most of it was carved up into spheres of European state influence. Accordingly, although they could still conquer the important Hijaz region for their state in 1925, the other boundaries were the result of treaty and negotiation with surrounding states. Saudi Arabia became a state much like any other, with sovereignty within its more or less precise boundaries. Within that territory, it could pursue policies and establish structures that in various ways melded political and religious communication. Had it not been for oil and the exploding importance of that sector of the global economy after World War II, it may have remained a marginal presence of little broader geo-political importance. That economic incorporation, however, has made all the difference. Not only could the Saudi state continue its de-differentiating option internally, it could even hope to 'export' it on the back of its oil revenue. The way that this has happened is instructive in the current context.

In effect, Saudi resources have sought to assist other Muslim states, but even more importantly to finance independent Islamic organizations, including social movement organizations, wherever in the world this proved possible. From mosque organizations in London and New York to military factions in post-Soviet invasion Afghanistan, this technique for expanding and reproducing Islam, and preferably the Saudi-Wahhabi version of it, has done so in a way that essentially respects the differentiated structures of the global system, most especially the political state and capitalist economic systems that are its most powerful and visible features, but just as importantly the religious structures. The outcome has been to assist the construction of Islam as a global religion beside the others, not the export of the Saudi political-religious model as such. As the history of the Islamic Republic of Iran[13] shows, such direct export is fraught with difficulties in the current global context, not the least of which is the danger of being slotted into the 'axis of evil' by the remaining political-military world superpower. I shall return to this question below in the section on forms of Islam in global society.

Islamic programme, codes and power

Perhaps the most obvious consistency among these nineteenth- and twentieth-century reform movements is their virtually complete agreement on certain rudimentary features of what constitutes Islam, features that hark back to the eighteenth-century movements as well. While no more surprising than in the case of Christianity as outlined above, it is well to point these out explicitly because they are critical to the operational recursiveness of contemporary Islam as a religious system. These are the core programmatic features that determine what Islam is, as opposed simply to what it is not. Accordingly, from Ahmed Khan to Mawdudi, internal understandings of Islam centre on these programmatic characteristics: there is a single God, Allah, who is the only God, unrepresentable, and the creator of everything that exists. He is constantly and everywhere present, sustaining his creation in every place and in every instant. He has communicated with human beings through a special and verbal revelation which is given to particular individuals or prophets, the last and final of which was Muhammad in the seventh century CE. This final communication is the Qur'an, the recitation that was transmitted through Muhammad in Arabic and consists of the literal words of Allah. In addition to the Qur'an, however, there is another almost as completely reliable source of divine instruction, namely the reported actions and sayings of the Prophet Muhammad himself, embodied in the Hadith, the collection of such traditions authenticated within the terms of the Islamic religious programme.

From these two sources, Muslims recursively derive and legitimate their entire religious programme, including above all the so-called 'five pillars' of declaration of faith (*shahadah*), prayer (*salat*), fasting (*sawm*), alms (*zakat*) and pilgrimage (*hajj*), as well as various other rituals, beliefs, practices and ethical standards for behaviour in all aspects of human life and society. This is the way (*Shari'a*) of Islam. The justification and the purpose of this way of Islam is contained within itself: this is the way to be fully human because Allah made it that way: 'There is no God but God and Muhammad is his messenger.' All the individual elements lead back to that origin and do not need any justification outside that recursive circularity. Ultimately that dependency and reflexivity expresses itself in the idea of the Last Judgement, when each person's eternal fate will be determined by their degree of conformity in this life to the God-willed way. Moreover, as with Christianity during the same modern period, adherence to Islam is exclusive of other religious loyalties and practices; although it should be stressed that such exclusivity and what constitutes it are features of the religious programme, not something that can be established by standards outside that system.

Within this broad agreement, however, as in any religion or any social system, there is significant room for variation. The illustrative nineteenth- and twentieth-century Islamic movements discussed in the previous section show some of the possibilities. Thus could the adaptationist and fundamentalist responses, again in Voll's meaning of those terms, agree on these basics and yet diverge sharply in critical ways, including with respect to the relation of the Islamic system to the other systems and other religions. One could put such variation down simply to the different programmatic emphases and derivations from the core sources that characterize each movement. An advantage of the Luhmannian conceptual apparatus used here allows one to understand these divergences in more strictly sociostructural terms. It is at this point that the notion of binary codes as fundamental features of most modern function systems again comes to the fore. As with the other religions examined in this book, these codes are by far not the only features that constitute religions. Yet they do play a vital role in establishing, maintaining and determining the system because all the communications that constitute the system ultimately refer to them. Like central processing units and binary coding in computers, everything passes through them and can in the final analysis be expressed in terms of them. One might say that, with reference to Islam, they play a central role in 'operationalizing' Allah. It therefore matters which ones (plural, but always mutually self-referential) a religious system uses and what order of emphasis a religious variant gives them. While I argued in the previous chapter that the general core code for religions in the modern world is something like the distinction between blessed and cursed, each religion in actual fact expresses this basic code somewhat differently. In the Islamic case, as with Christianity, salvation/damnation is still in a certain sense core, but also often rather remote in the day-to-day reproduction of religious communication. More critical, again as with the other religions, are secondary codes, ones that render the basic code more immediately applicable for everyday religious life. In the case of (modern) Islam, distinctions like *halal/haram* (permitted/forbidden), lawful/unlawful and of course the moral code of good/bad (including here just/unjust) have tended to fill this role. Rather than continue to discuss these abstractly, however, I turn to a brief discussion of an illustrative sample of twentieth-century Islamic thinkers, namely Fazlur Rahman, Tariq Ramadan and Sayyid Qutb. I make no claim that these three are somehow representative of all the contemporary movements. As with the nineteenth- and twentieth-century movements outlined in the previous section, their choice is justified because they show what is at issue, in this case how different emphases among secondary codes translate into different sorts of relation with other systems, above all other religions and other non-religious function systems.

Among twentieth-century Islamic thinkers, Fazlur Rahman generally counts as one of the more 'liberal', in Voll's terms, something much closer to an adaptationist than a fundamentalist (Kurzman 1998: 304). Among his primary concerns was to reform the understanding of Islam so that it could be effective in the modern world. This is the sort of reconstructive impulse that interests us. He was convinced that modernity as represented in the dominant West lacked a necessary spiritual and moral foundation which Islam could provide. Religion therefore had a critical functional role to play in the health of contemporary society, but it could not be either by voiding Islam of all its particular content so as to secularize it to Western ways, nor could it simply be a reaction against the West in the style of Voll's fundamentalists, among whom Rahman definitely counted Sayyid Qutb. Like the latter, however, and like the nineteenth-century reformers before him, Rahman insisted that Muslims had to go back to the 'normative' sources of the Qur'an and Muhammad, not the historical, traditionalist Islam that had developed in the intervening centuries and which was inadequate to the modern context. Like the eighteenth-century reformers, he therefore saw the solution in this return to the sources, but also in combination with a stress on socio-moral reconstruction and *tawhid*.

The consistent and unifying concern of the Qur'an and Muhammad's mission was for Rahman the 'founding of an ethical sociopolitical order in the world' (Rahman 1982: 15). Islam is thereby about all of human life in society and the connection between the message and the sociopolitical order is an ethical or moral one. Although he recognized that the basic tenets of the Qur'anic message centre on the one God, and the Last Judgement as the mechanism of human accountability or relation to that God, Rahman insisted that the fundamental aim of it all was socioeconomic justice in this world:

The basic élan of the Qur'an – the stress on socioeconomic justice and essential human egalitarianism – is quite clear from its very early passages. Now all that follows by way of Qur'anic legislation in the field of private and public life, even the 'five pillars' of Islam that are held to be religion par excellence, has social justice and the building of an egalitarian community as its end.

(Rahman 1982: 19)

In terms of coding, what this means is that, while the duality of salvation/ damnation is indeed foundational, the more practical code of good/bad is more critical: it expresses the fundamental Islamic principles through which the whole religious enterprise is constructed. Moreover, what distinguishes Rahman as a reformer/adaptionist and what, as we shall see below, contrasts him with Qutb especially is this moral, as opposed to legal (permitted/forbidden) foundationalizing. This ordering becomes clear in how Rahman sees the derivation of Islamic laws. Rather than assuming that these can be taken or derived directly from the Qur'an and the Sunna, he insists that one must first abstract from the 'concrete case treatments of the Qur'an – taking the necessary and relevant social conditions of that time into account – to the general principles upon which the entire teaching converges'. These principles are essentially ethical. Only from this basis can Muslims then move to 'specific legislation, taking into account the necessary and relevant social conditions now obtaining' (Rahman 1982: 20). It is this subordination of the legal 'obedience' code to the moral code that is at the heart of the adaptationist or liberal difference of Rahman vis-à-vis the fundamentalist position of Qutb and his many followers. It lends religion its specificity, giving it a domain and an orientation in which none of the other function domains specialize. Thus can Islam claim essential relevance for modern society and in all other aspects of that society, but without claiming to subsume them. The allowance of other systems that are in themselves non-religious is a critical consequence.

In a recent volume, Tariq Ramadan (Ramadan 2004), a very contemporary European Islamic thinker, sets himself the task of outlining how Muslims in the West can go about leading authentically Islamic lives. The task is very much parallel to what Rahman envisaged in his somewhat earlier work. Ramadan's vision insists on full integration and participation by Muslims in their Western societies, and thereby excludes sectarian isolation. He does not advocate what one might call a '*millet*' or 'pillarized' option. The effort asks precisely the functional questions at issue: how can Islam be an integral and socially consequential system of religious communication in a context where other religions exist, and where globalized function systems prevail as the dominant structures of society? His answers are instructive because they are clear on both counts, on the integrity of Islam and on the relation of this Islam to other function systems. Moreover, given that he is also clear on how his option differs from other contemporary Islamic possibilities, one can compare him to the other two thinkers discussed here also on his own terms.

Ramadan sees himself as representing what he calls a 'reform *Salafist*' orientation, one that derives its Islam directly from the two authoritative sources, the Qur'an and Hadith, without necessary adherence to intervening traditions of interpretation such as one of the schools of jurisprudence (for example, Hanafi or Jafari). Reform refers to the necessity of reinterpreting the core sources, of renewed faithful and rational effort or *ijtihad*, so that Islam will be relevant, integral and effective for the present day. He contrasts this position with what he calls the 'scholastic traditionalists', essentially those who insist on the continued validity of intermediary traditions of interpretation like the juridical schools; two types of 'literalist *salafists*', who insist on a passive or political isolationist stance for Muslims: the 'liberal/rationalist reformers', who reduce Islam to at best a private spirituality or cultural orientation; and the 'Sufis' who, while not necessarily isolationist, stress the spiritual life, mystical experience and community (Ramadan 2004). One may note the rough similarity of this scheme to Voll's distinction between traditionalist, adaptationist, personal-piety and fundamentalist styles. Ramadan's option, in that classification, may thus be considered a kind of adaptionist fundamentalism (i.e. 'reform' plus '*salafism*'), in the conceptual terms I am stressing here, one that insists on the integrity of the Islamic religious system but accepts that this system exists among others and must adapt to that environment.

Ramadan sees his option as very much a middle way, one that steers between secularizing privatization and isolationist sectarianism (see especially 2004: 29, Fig. 1.1). Like the eighteenth-century reformers discussed above and like Rahman, he stresses a return to the core sources (*salafism*), 'socio-moral reconstructionism' and *tawhid*. His interpretation of the latter idea, however, does not require that Islam be the only core organizing force of a society. Above all, he rejects the division of the world into the *dar al-Islam* and the *dar al-harb*. *Tawhid* in this vision means the relevance or applicability of Islam to all areas of life in all regions of the world; it refers to the universalism of Islam. Accordingly, Ramadan asserts that it is the business of Muslims to bring Islamic *principles* to bear on all aspects of society, wherever they may be living. The relation he sees between binary coding and this task is instructive. In effect – he does not himself use the category of codes – the code closest to the religious heart of the matter is salvation/damnation, but this is the subject of rather little discussion; it is not so directly relevant for Ramadan's task of showing Muslims how to live Islam as fully integrated in the Western (and more broadly, modern) world around them. He pays much more attention to what is permitted and forbidden through Islam, especially through an ongoing process of interpreting anew (*ijtihad*) the primary religious texts (communications) for modern contexts. Yet the actual application of Islam to other spheres Ramadan accomplishes more immediately through what he calls Islamic principles as opposed to derived regulations. These principles, as with Rahman, are largely ethical ones; the operative code that links purely religious practice with applied practice is again the moral code of good/bad, in particular through notions of justice, equity, fairness, peace and solidarity. Islamic law, *Shari'a* and *fiqh*, provide the intermediary mechanisms through which Muslims arrive at what is correct within the Islamic system. Yet it is not such regulation that is directly applicable to the other systems. *Shari'a*, unlike for the political literalist *salafists* like Qutb, does not need to become the law of the land. For Ramadan, the principles of Islam provide the way for judging the systems in the environment of Islam by way of a moral code informed by a religio-legal and a salvific code. In this way, Ramadan can accept the operation of other function systems according to their own criteria, as well as the other religions,[14] albeit not without sometimes sharp criticism. Thus, for example, he condemns the operation of the global capitalist system as violating the principles of Islam, the ethical principles just mentioned, but he does so on the basis of an interpretation of *salafi* injunctions for *zakat* (almsgiving) and against *riba* (interest). The result is a view of the role of religion and the application of religion to other function spheres that is not at all unlike that exemplified in Christian liberation theologians or, even more clearly, in the letters and encyclicals of the Roman Catholic popes since John XXIII, with their combination of social justice critique and personal moral conservatism.

Rahman and Ramadan therefore present variations that are in many ways quite similar, especially as concerns the prioritization of the different Islamic binary codes. While they both see a role for other possibilities, above all permitted/forbidden (*halal/haram*) and salvation/damnation, these codes operate much more strictly *within* the religious system of Islam; they are not the codes which mediate the relation between the Islamic system and others. That said, Ramadan does seem to tie the legal code more closely to the moral one and therefore can perhaps be seen as the more 'fundamentalist' (again in Voll's sense) of the two. Both in prioritization and in this critical question of the relation to other systems, however, Sayyid Qutb presents a clear contrast. Especially in his later writings, this chief ideologue of the Muslim Brotherhood and highly influential twentieth-century Islamist laid out a vision of Islam which, in the spirit of Mawdudi and most eighteenth-century Islamic revival movements, rejected the very idea of Islam as a functional sphere of society beside others, whether religious or non-religious. The results are instructive, especially when compared to what Rahman and Ramadan have advocated.

For Qutb, Islam is an encompassing system that derives directly from God through the Prophet Muhammad and the Qur'an. In addition to this stress on *tawhid*, like the others, he insists on a return to the original sources, rejecting the normative character of intervening accretions of Islamic tradition; and on socio-moral reconstructionism as a primary aim of Islam. Where he differs sharply is on what these fundamental points imply for Islam in today's global society. Unlike Ramadan, Qutb embraces the distinction between the *dar al-Islam* and the *dar al-harb*, but in this case, the whole world falls into the latter category because nowhere, according to him, is Islam currently established. The world is under the sway of *jahiliyyah*, the state of ignorance or denial of God's guidance (Qutb n.d.: 11). For any part of it to become Islamic, it must first be conquered through *jihad*, which Qutb insists necessarily includes offensive war and is not restricted to defence, inner struggle and preaching. Although he puts great stress on the essence of Islam as the universally valid personal path of religious and moral orientation and practice, such personal pursuit is only possible once the Islamic system has been socially instituted in the surrounding society. For this condition to obtain, the society must be governed by God, which means through *Shari'a*. 'When, in a society, the sovereignty belongs to God alone, expressed in its obedience to the Divine Law, only then is every person in that society free' to follow Islam (Qutb n.d.: 94). Qutb insists that this law is not limited to 'legal matters', but includes legislation of 'the attitudes, the way of living, the values, criteria, habits and traditions' of people (n.d.: 95). In other words, law is not a differentiated and thus limited domain beside others but rather the concrete expression of an encompassing and totalizing system. By centralizing *Shari'a* in this way, Qutb is clearly giving 'obedience to the law' a fundamental place. In terms of binary coding, this means a prioritizing of the distinction between that which is permitted or forbidden as the practical dichotomy which establishes the conditions for the other possibilities, like good/bad or salvation/damnation, to operate.

Qutb's rejection of any functional differentiation of Islam has logical consequences for the form that he advocates for Islam in the global society of today. While he foresees Islam taking over society entirely in the future, the current reality is for him the dominance of *jahiliyyah*. Concretely, this takes the form of communism (he wrote during the Cold War era) and capitalism, the latter sometimes conflated with Christianity and Judaism as 'international Crusaderism' and 'international Zionism' (Haddad 1983: 80). These are rival encompassing systems for Qutb, not alternatives that can co-exist in the same world. Again, since the nominally Muslim countries of the world are also under the sway of this *jahiliyyah* because their rulers and elites try to copy one of these rival systems, there is no state to which he can point as even an approximation of an Islamic society. Accordingly, the social form that Islam must take in the current circumstances is that of the social movement:

Islam cannot fulfil its role except by taking concrete form in a society, rather, in a nation . . . In order to bring this about, we need to initiate a movement of Islamic revival in some Muslim country. Only such a revivalist movement will eventually attain to the status of world leadership.

(Qutb n.d.: 9, 11)

The practical goal is to have Islam embodied in the whole world by way of a state through a social movement. The core of this movement for Qutb is the equivalent of the party, a vanguard for which he sees the precedent in the Prophet Muhammad and the formation of the original Islamic community. Although this party or *jamaah* (see Haddad 1983: 87–8) can take organizational form as did the Muslim Brotherhood in which Qutb was involved, this is less critical than the movement itself. Thus like so many Islamic revivalists before him, he resorts to a kind of social system that is not structured by central dichotomies or even a highly elaborated programme, let alone seriously identified with one or more organizations. Qutb is very short on the details of what an Islamic society would actually look like, what precisely, for instance, would be permitted or forbidden. Instead, he focuses on an ideology of mobilization, and thus, for him, Islam must be a constant attempt to bring about the dominance of its system, and certainly not 'reduced' to regular personal or community practice and faith, which is to say differentiated as (a) religion.

Qutb's extreme Islamist focus indirectly also points to the question of religious power, the particular form that social power takes in his and, by comparison, others' visions of Islam. As I discussed above for the case of Christianity and as will become evident also for Hinduism in Chapter 4, the specific power medium for religion in today's world tends to be ambiguously developed, if at all, even though the religious domain often bears a direct relation to the broader issue of social power. Rahman, Ramadan and Qutb illustrate this general situation nicely. In the case of the first two, there is an almost total absence of discussions of power, except implicitly as faith that the Islamic religious system is at least potentially effective: without the practice of Islam, without the putting into effect of Islamic principles in society, that society is lacking in a way analogous to if it wanted for economic wealth, political order or scientific knowledge. The dimension that, for instance, Rahman states is needed in secular Western modernity, what he calls the 'sanctity and universality of . . . all moral values' (Rahman 1982: 15) is what only religion, in particular Islam, can provide. For Ramadan, this is substantially also the contribution that Muslims can make irrespective of where they live. Qutb, by contrast, specifically rejects the adequacy of such a vision. For him, Islam is not possible only on the basis of moral suasion, individual belief and practice, or missionizing preaching. In keeping with his functionally de-differentiating perspective, the first order of business is for Islam to be expressed in political and legal forms of power. That is the implementation of *Shari'a* which is for him the condition for the possibility of the other forms. A differentiated, peculiarly religious, medium of power is a contradiction in terms. Qutb is not alone among religious observers to have come to such a conclusion. His rationale points to a prime *religious* reason for the frequent politicization of religion in our world: it offers a *powerful* way of lending religion and the religions concrete and consequential social form.

Social forms of Islam in global society

Sayyid Qutb's vision of Islam continues that historic tendency that I discussed above, namely a modern emphasis on giving Islam form through social movement systems. There I noted that this corresponded well with the encompassing and undifferentiated understandings of *tawhid* and *ummah*, and that the challenge of transforming social movement impulses into more stable systemic forms has led to a variety of developments, including attempts at sectarian or pillarized separation in the surrounding society and seeking the Islamization of particular modern states. This latter direction has certainly been a constant feature, especially of the later twentieth century, and has garnered the bulk of scholarly and popular attention regarding Islam in our contemporary world. Without denying the historical significance of this latter outcome both for the religious system of global society and for Islam as one of the dominant religions of that system, Islamic social movements, unlike by comparison Christian organizations, do not actually include or capture the bulk of the religious communication that reproduces the modern global system of Islam. While it may be argued that the various Muslim and Islamist movements, from the somewhat 'pietistic' Tablighi Jamaat to the jihadist militarism symbolized by the moniker 'al-Qaeda', are having a significant influence on how Islam is conceived both within and outside its fold, the bulk of Islamic communication occurs in the context of other social forms, notably interaction networks, but also organizations of various sorts. These forms deserve some attention; they are perhaps less visible to the outside (often Western) observer, but that should not detract from their importance.

In most parts of the world where Islam is the dominant religion, its reproduction proceeds primarily by way of regular interactions that can be observed as social networks of such interactions, but not as distinct types of system like a social movement with its typical goals, narratives and mobilization events, or like an organization with its defining member/nonmember distinction and rules of membership. The system to which communication in these networks contributes is primarily the societal system of Islam and the interactions themselves. These latter can be ritual interactions with Allah as they are in core ritual performances such as daily and Friday noon prayers, hajj and other pilgrimage, Eid celebrations, Qur'an recitation or pious fasting during Ramadan. Or they can be strictly human–human interactions in which the structuring themes are Islamic, such as in sermons, religious discussions, religious education, and so forth. What controls the recursiveness of communication in such interactions is a variety of factors, including internalized tradition which continuously reproduces the same Islamic performances; 'community expectations' in the form of the expectations of potential or actual interaction partners; and authority structures such as are found in imams, ulama, pirs, teachers, parents or print and electronic media. In this context, Islamic organizations also play a role, but only to a certain extent does this religious communication directly reproduce those organizations as social systems. I return to this point presently. Another critical aspect of this recursiveness is the self-understanding or self-description of this communication as Islam, as programmatically coherent Islamic religion in particular. Although it need not be constantly thematized, the idea that what Muslims are doing when they engage in these interactions is in fact Islam is a regular part of such communication: if asked, almost all the Muslim participants will acknowledge that this is Islam. Add to this that outside observers (including myself and most likely you, the reader) also understand it as Islam, and we have two effective contributors to making it precisely that: social reality as communication is also, by that token, observation.

Although organizing Islam has globally not been a dominant strategy for supporting and guaranteeing form to this religion, its contribution in this direction should also not be underestimated. As noted, the bulk of Islamic organizations do not operate in the style of those many and often still dominant Christian or (North American) Jewish denominational organizations in which religious communication is at the same time organizational communication. Islamic organizations like some Sufi tariqats, the Muhammadiyah organization in Indonesia or certain mosque organizations in the North American diaspora do substantially take this direction, but globally only a minority of Muslims are thus 'organizationally incorporated' (in Christian terms, 'churched'). The more general role of Islamic organizations is to provide venues for ritual performances, especially the great many organized mosques around the world. Then there are those which render Islamic services of all sorts. These include education in madrassas, Qur'an schools, universities and other such organized institutions. There are the many advocacy organizations like the government-linked Organization of the Islamic Conference or the Muslim Society of North America; and many others like the various Muslim Student Associations, the social movement organizations already discussed, and those which provide Islamic social, health, relief and other services. All these provide supportive context for the reproduction of Islamic communication, often serving as venues for core communication involving Muslims who are not, strictly speaking, members. Global Islam would certainly lose a great deal of the power to assure its own recursiveness and thus systemic reproduction if it were not for these Islamic organizations. Thus, there is a great deal of Islamic organization in the world today; but Islam as a religious system is only somewhat organized.

Returning now to the strategy of Islamization, like other religions Islam is also given form through thematic incorporation into other function systems, notably but not exclusively the political, legal, educational and mass media. The conceptions of Islam and the Islamic conceptions that are integrated into the communication of these systems influence how the religious system of Islam is able to reproduce itself in different parts of the world, without thereby necessarily also constituting more religious communication. As already discussed at some length, however, many of the reconstructive directions that Islam has taken during the last two centuries have placed quite some emphasis on precisely this latter possibility: not just thematization of Islam in the communication of these other systems, but Islamic communication as the communication of these other systems. They have envisaged significant functional de-differentiation. In several Muslim countries, such efforts appear to have had a fair amount of success. The example of Saudi Arabia has already been discussed, but countries as different as Indonesia, Pakistan, Iran and Nigeria, to mention only a few, could also be discussed under this heading. Here, to very varying degrees, Islam is part of school curricula, informs what laws are made and how they are enforced, is reproduced through media broadcasts and, in the case of Iran at least, has a significant role to play in how governments are formed and how they engage in their regulation once formed. All these incorporations help to reproduce Islam as religion, to lend it its contemporary systemic form, even as they also help to reproduce these other systems. The larger issue, of course, is to what extent such incorporation actually amounts to de-differentiation of function systems, to what extent the political or legal systems of these countries, for instance, are 'part of' Islam as opposed to merely being influenced in their operations by Islamic themes, concepts and selection criteria. It is that question which I address in the following section.

Islam as alternate globalized model?

I began this section on Islam with the idea, often heard, that Islam is indeed a religion, but that it is also more than that, a total way of life. Translated into the theoretical terms used here, that claim poses the question of whether that means that Islam can escape the logic of contemporary functional system differentiation, which is to say whether it can avoid or negate the secularization of the other function systems. The ambition is certainly there, embodied in religio-social movements such as the ones discussed above. In countries like Iran and Saudi Arabia, the reality also seems to be there, at least to an extent. Yet one must be careful not to confuse the influence of a religion on other non-religious systems with de-differentiation. All function systems are influenced by all other function systems in their operations; that is a feature of their interdependency. Thus government policy in all countries is influenced by economic criteria just as the operation of the capitalist economy is influenced and even constrained by the regulatory activities of governments. The situation is similar for the relation of any other pair of systems. The operative question as concerns differentiation is not the fact of such influence but rather whether and at what point it prevents a given system from recursively reproducing itself substantially through its own criteria.

Asking this question with respect to Islam as a contemporary religious system, one notes that, most often, what is meant by Islam being a way of life beyond a religion is that explicitly Islamic programmatic elements ought to condition other aspects of life. There should be a way of acting in all realms of life which is in conformity with Islam. Most often this refers to Islamic moral precepts which dictate the limits of how one can use one's body, how one should treat other human beings, what it is good to strive for in one's personal and in public social life, and so forth. These sorts of determination, however, are what one would find in any religion or version of a religion. They do not necessarily require the sort of constraint on other systems that would amount to de-differentiation of Islam and those systems. The visions of Fazlur Rahman and Tariq Ramadan outlined above can serve as examples. Where various movements in modern and contemporary Islam – those following more closely the example of Sayyid Qutb or Mawlana Mawdudi – do go significantly further is in the idea that Islamic programmatic elements should be used to run the other differentiated institutional domains. Thus, to take the most common examples, there should be Islamic law as the law of the land, Islamic government as the way a state is organized, or Islamic economics as the way to conduct business affairs. The implication is more than that Islamic principles should exercise a morally grounded influence in these domains: it is that Islamic precepts taken from the religious sources (above all Qur'an and Hadith) should themselves directly structure these domains; that, for instance, Islamic sources provide the actual laws and legal proceedings, dictate how government is formed and how it is carried out, or determine the financial structures that regulate such key areas as banking, investment and credit. That is the ambition. Closer inspection of what this amounts to concretely in the various countries where such ambition has been implemented tends to show, however, that the range of applicable Islamic precepts in these domains is in fact quite limited. Beyond various symbolic clusters like the Hudud ordinances, inheritance regulations, *zakat* (government taxation understood as almsgiving), *riba* (proscription of fixed interest rates) or the principle of *shura* or consultation in government, most of what gets done in these domains even in the most Islamic of countries is really no more Islamic than law, government or business is Christian in predominantly Christian countries, Buddhist in Buddhist countries, or Hindu in India. By and large, the legal, political and economic systems operate on their own logic. And where this has not been the case, such as in revolutionary Iran of the 1980s or the Taliban regime in Afghanistan in the 1990s, the consequences seem to have been to weaken the efficacy of all the institutions, including the religious. Put into slightly different terms, in those instances where the 'interference' of religion in other domains has been kept within limits – thus essentially maintaining institutional differentiation – Islamization has been, certainly controversial, certainly not irrelevant, but arguably more a matter of making things look Islamic than of actually having religious practice run other institutions. In those instances where matters have gone further, the institutions have tended to break down or to lose their credibility. The Ayatollah Khomeini may have been correct when he asserted in his version of Islamic government that, for genuinely Islamic government to happen, the religious experts would have to exercise direct rule. In this he succeeded, but the outcome was that a lot of mullahs became politicians, with the result that both their political and religious legitimacy was, if not destroyed, then certainly weakened (Khosrokhavar and Roy 1999). Similarly, the Taliban under Muhammad Omar certainly tried to carry out the complete Islamization of Afghan society as they saw it. The 'government' that they set up, however, was in most areas completely ineffective, and their religion had to be constantly enforced (Rashid 2000). What these outcomes suggest is that differentiation is rather more constitutive of Islam as a religion, and thus of its social efficacy, than even many ardent religious practitioners would allow (cf. Roy 1992). Put in somewhat paradoxical terms, it may be that the vitality of this religion, like the others, depends to some extent on the secularization of society in the sense of the institutional differentiation of other, non-religious domains, precisely because these are so well-institutionalized in most of global society. The efforts of many Islamicists to go in the opposite direction only end up confirming this conclusion. The de-differentiation of religion and society, far from implying the 'religionization' of society, in this case may actually have the reverse outcome, the de-institutionalization of religion.

Does Islam, then, offer an alternative model for doing religion in contemporary global society, one that rivals the otherwise dominant Christian model? The answer to this question must be yes and no. On the one hand, the various efforts at the reconstruction of Islam in the modern era have brought about the particularization of Islam as a religion in ways that are distinct from other religions, notably Christianity, but also Judaism, the third of the Abrahamic subgroup. Aside from the obvious programmatic and elemental differences, there is also the far more concerted resistance to the sort of privatization of religion that has been a hallmark of many Christian and Jewish denominations. The widespread efforts at societal Islamization are a manifestation of that difference, and it is arguable that this different orientation has had an encouraging effect on similar reassertions of public influence in other religions, including this time Hinduism and Buddhism in countries like India and Sri Lanka (cf. Jaffrelot 1996; Tambiah 1986). In this sense, Islam may well be offering an alternative. On the other hand, if by alternative we mean a religion that avoids the fate of reconstruction as but one of the modern religions, that avoids differentiation as religion beside other religions and other, non-religious systems, then, notwithstanding important and continuing efforts in this direction, one would have to conclude this has not been the prevailing direction for Islam in modern times. In this sense, Islam does not offer an alternative, a different universal as opposed to the particular-ization of the same universal as the other religions. Such an alternative would require the dismantling of the most powerful, non-religious systems, especially the political, economic and scientific; as well as – and this should be emphasized – the dismantling of the other religions. Such a result does not seem to be the direction in which we are headed. Put into the terms that Tariq Ramadan uses, seeing the goal of Islam in the world as the creation and assertion of the *dar al-Islam* against the *dar al-harb*, while possible, is also pretty much futile. Far more effective is it to see the entire world as the domain of Islam, as the house of mission or preaching, *dar al-dawa* (Ramadan 2004).

Summary and conclusion

Since the analysis of a global religious system becomes very quickly the analysis of particular religions, this chapter has been devoted to the two religions that, together, present the most influential models of how a reli-gion can be constructed in the contemporary global context. This is not to say that they are straightforwardly determinative. All the reconstructed religions, including some globally speaking rather minor ones, help to give social shape to this system. Even among the so-called Abrahamic religions, Judaism offers a third highly influential model that is a regular part of the religious field in many parts of the world. Had space permitted the extended inclusion of it in this chapter, that would have been easily demonstrated. At least three factors, however, give Islam and Christianity special weight. The first is that (again, along with Judaism), they have the longest history of differentiation as religion even in societal contexts not characterized by a dominance of function systems. Their institutional 'reification', as W.C. Smith put it, is for them a historical as well as a contemporary resource, making reconstruction as one of the religions in the modern global context comparatively more straightforward. Second, Islam and Christianity make up the majority of global religious communication incorporated into specific religions: they are by far the 'biggest' religions and thereby the most visible. The fact that many of their variants are also among the more publicly assertive in global society only enhances this visibility. Third, Christianity has been the religion of the dominant segments of global society, especially the Europeans and their North American relations. The missionary efforts of the Europeans that were such an integral part of their expanding global influence over the past centuries not only were instrumental in the shaping of that religion, Christianity also thereby came to represent, in religious mode, the challenge that all other regions of the world had to face in dealing with European power. Just by token of this power position, Christianity has more often served as the model which others have appropriated or rejected.

Given the thus preponderant position of these religions, it remains now in the next two chapters to take a more detailed look at the historical construction of the global religious system in portions of the world where they have not been the dominant form of religious expression, namely South and East Asia. These two regions not only represent over 40 per cent of the world's current population, they have also been witness to two rather different responses to the globalizing context as far as religion is concerned. In spite of the global dominance of Christianity and Islam, developments in South and East Asia show how the religious system is substantially more than either of these writ large or simply projected on to the rest of the world. Accordingly, in the following two chapters I analyze these two possibilities of religious system construction that contrast with and profile the reconstruction of the Abrahamic trio.

Notes

1   In Chapter 6, I discuss the corresponding difficulty that genuinely 'new' religions have in being recognized as religions, and the corresponding strategies on the part of some of them to present themselves as 'recoveries' of the past, in other words, as tradition.

2   With regard to the question of whether there is also a global function system for culture, the answer would have to be no. Although one can certainly, along with Geertz (1966), speak of cultural systems, and describe religion as one of them, these are not function systems of the sort I am describing for religion. Rather, cultures are systemic only in the sense of referring to ecologies of themes, memory (Luhmann 1997) and communicative styles. Accordingly, it is difficult to isolate a code for culture, what culture is all about in contradistinction from such systemic domains as art, politics, education or mass media. A peculiar or core cultural element or type of communication is also hard to

discern unless one uses culture in the sense of art. Ironically, therefore, it would be more accurate to say that cultures manifest themselves only as dimensions of other systems, including the religious, rather than religions being subsumed as dimensions of cultures. On the other hand and as a corollary of this hypothesis, it is correspondingly easier to observe a global culture than it is a global religion. The latter does not exist; the former is at least arguable as an ecology of themes, models and communicative styles. See Featherstone 1990; Stichweh 2000.

3 Cf. Finke and Stark's well-known reconstruction of American religious history under the title, *The Churching of America* (Finke and Stark 1992), where 'churching' is synonymous with strong religion.

4 And there were correspondingly fewer churches, certainly not enough to receive the entire population on a Sunday morning. Building too many churches or ending up having too many churches in areas of relative out-migration could, in fact, lead to the impression that there was a problem if those churches were not well attended as a result. For the idea that this sort of phenomenon was at the root of later nineteenth-century 'secularization' in England, see Gill 2003.

5 Cf. Cox 1995: 102 and Dempster *et al.* 1999, who both use Cox's phrase, 'a religion made to travel', to point to this same feature of translocality and multi-centredness.

6 See, for example, Hollenweger's classic work (1972), the title of which names the individuals, the Pentecostals, not the movement, Pentecostalism. It also gives priority to medium and programmatic content (Chapter 1.2) as well as discussing the ambiguous view of organization (Chapter 3). Cox's well-known work (1995) also begins with narrative (Part I), passes to discussion of medium, ritual and programme (Part II), and ends with the movement's spread and globalization (Part III). To the extent of my research, these features are typical of the literature on this subject. See also Poewe 1994.

7 As one illustration of how widespread this assertion is, entering the combination of 'Islam' + 'religion' + 'way of life' into an Internet search engine like *Google*™ yielded fully 121,000 hits. Sampling these randomly showed that most of the sites declared that Islam was *both* a religion and a way of life. Date of search: 4 August 2004. Virtually any other way of sampling public Muslim opinion reveals a similar result. See, for illustrations of contemporary Muslim intellectual opinion, Esposito and Voll 2001.

8 It may be noted, that this sense is different from the 'this-worldly asceticism' that Weber ascribed to Calvinist Protestantism, precisely in that the asceticism is missing. See Weber 1992 [1930].

9 For an analysis of the consequences of this orientation in the domain of 'science', see Huff 2003.

10 An alternate, albeit apparently less prevalent, word for religion in the Qur'an and in Islamic usage is in fact *millah*, from which the Ottoman *millet* is derived. *Millah* (Wilfred Cantwell Smith 1991: 294, n. 86; Ursinus 1960 [1980]) has come to be a modern Turkish and Persian word for 'nation', a usage that can serve as one of many examples in today's world of the fluid boundary between 'group culture' concepts and the idea of religions.

11 Developments in Iranian 12er Shi'ism of the time present a variation: here the eventually dominant *usuli* school of thought and reform stressed the authoritative interpretive capacity of the leading *mujtahids* (practitioners of *ijtihad*) and the necessity of *taqlid* for ordinary Muslims, the *mujtahids* being sources of this imitation. Indicative of the similarity of reform impulse, however, is that such sources had to be living *mujtahids* (Arjomand 1984).

12 The case of Hinduism, and Hindu nationalism in particular, offers striking parallels. In this case, however, given the strong presence of Islam in South Asia, there has been more than a little modelling by the Hindu nationalists on the example provided by Islamic movements. See the discussion of this issue below in Chapter 4.

13 For an analysis of the Islamic Republic and its fate in the theoretical terms used here, see Beyer 1994.

14 Ramadan 2004. See especially the figures 'Tawhid, Ethics, and the Sciences' (p. 59) and 'Muslim identity' (p. 83) with their corresponding discussions. Chapters 6, 7 and 8 discuss relations with particular function systems; Chapter 9 with other religions.

The realization of Hinduism

Introduction

The more recent criticism of the concept of religion that I discussed at the beginning of Chapter 2 attacks the application of the term to some civilizational regions more than others. To some extent, a rough distinction between West and non-West informs the debate, the former being the usual source of error, imposition or projection; the latter more clearly the target. Thus, the more common empirical examples are drawn from those peoples and areas where the three Abrahamic religions were not dominant before the era of European expansion, especially the eastern half of Asia and sub-Saharan Africa.[1] Hinduism is a frequent theme in these contexts. Scholars such as Timothy Fitzgerald, Robert Frykenberg, Romila Thapar, Ursula King, S.N. Balagangadhara and Richard King have, with important different nuances and emphases, offered cogent analyses to the effect that Hinduism, like the modern notion of religion, is a modern, invented and imagined construct which has arisen not accidentally in the context of Western imperial expansion and the formation of global society.[2] The present chapter in many ways recapitulates their arguments, but it adopts the theoretical framework of this book for understanding the same historical developments. From this perspective, the invention of Hinduism has been an important moment in the emergence of a global function system for religion. It represents the selective, contested and relatively recent recombination of mostly received but also in part newly devised features in a new form, one that resonates with the modern context of a world society structurally dominated by function systems of this sort.

In this modern construction of Hinduism as a differentiated religion beside others, Western imperial expansion and the actions and understandings of Western observers are certainly elements in this story; but they are not the only or even the most important ones. As critical are the self-observations and self-understandings of those who consider themselves, in one way or another, 'insiders' to Hinduism. The ideas and influence of people from Hariscandra or Rammohun Roy to Vishva Hindu Parishad activists, from

Dayananda Saraswati or Swami Vivekananda to the Maharishi Maheshyogi, from the members of the Hindu Temple Association in Ottawa, Canada to the members of the current Supreme Court of India, are ultimately more significant than those of H.H. Wilson and F. Max Müller because they have more concretely brought about the actual social construction of Hinduism rather than just provided imaginative suggestions. To be sure, this construction is far from a uniform, uncontested, unambiguous and completed process. There are and have been different visions of what counts as Hinduism, different ways of ordering the variations. There are many 'insiders' who contest the whole notion. That incompleteness and contestation, however, is a dimension of the systemic process I am describing; it is a feature of all religions, including most especially Christianity and Islam, as discussed in the previous chapter. Moreover, beside the fact that not all those whom one might consider to be Hindus practising Hinduism would recognize themselves in this claim or have actively joined in this imaginative reconstruction, the notion of Hindu has also during the same historical period acquired more than religious meaning. The line between Hinduism as religion and Hindu as broader cultural and national identity is often vague or contested, especially in India; but neither are the two the same. As elsewhere in world society, the construction of the religion has been bound up with the rise of nationalist and 'communal' (in the sense of culturally identified group) movements. The two processes have been mutually reinforcing and their combination is widespread, not at all unique to the South Asian situation. Finally, the whole idea of Hinduism as a religion beside others is not simply a self-evident and permanent fact. It may eventually reveal itself to have been a historical development that did not last. After all, as I detail in the next chapter, China, if not also Japan, provides good examples of the non-necessity of such modern reconstructions. That outcome, however, given the present state of the evidence, seems extremely unlikely. Far more probable is that the realization of the category of Hinduism in concrete social institutions will continue.

The pattern of presentation in this chapter follows more or less that of Chapter 2. Thus, the next two sections offer aspects of a historical narrative of key developments and movements in the construction of Hinduism from the late eighteenth to the end of the twentieth century. Two further sections then analyze the different dimensions of this reconstructed Hinduism using the Luhmannian scheme. One section focuses on codes, programmes, elements and power; another looks at social forms. The conclusion, besides summarizing the argument, pays particular attention to the difficult question of whether too much currently escapes from systemic Hinduism for it to operate as anything more than a, strictly speaking, minority religion of the urban, middle/upper class and diaspora elite.

Orientalist imagination, colonial structures, indigenous reconstructions

As has been the case in general with the entire globalization discussion and more specifically, in the last chapter, with the (re)formations of Christianity and Islam, a historical narrative of the (re)construction of Hinduism could begin at a number of points, including somewhere during that important millennium between 500 BCE and 500 CE, or at later times such as the sixteenth to seventeenth centuries. My choice of the end of the eighteenth century as an effective starting point is therefore again a bit arbitrary, justified primarily because it is at that time that British orientalists began to 'discover' what later came to be called Hinduism (see Marshall 1970). They did not operate in a vacuum, of course. Typically, like the Jesuits in China of the previous century, they observed existing cultural forms and components in selective and particular ways. The texts that they selected, the Brahmin pandits that they consulted, as well as the ritual complexes, religious groupings and institutions that they admired or rejected as barbaric or decadent were already there, the products of ongoing and complex historical trajectories entirely independent of European influence. Yet unlike the Jesuits in China (or earlier in India, for that matter), the British observers of the late eighteenth-century India were the representatives of an increasingly dominant colonial and imperial power. Their imaginative reconstruction of 'Hindu' culture and religion had a much more powerful and long-term impact. In this context, the structures of British colonial power were at least as important in providing the conditions for the invention of Hinduism as were the ideas of the orientalists. That context of power is what enlisted new and old indigenous Indian elites in the production of new social forms and new knowledge that was both continuous and discontinuous with what came before. These forms and that knowledge, in turn, while related to the British constructs, did not just ape them; rather, they appropriated them, creating social realities that the colonial observers neither foresaw nor likely intended. Only one of these is the contested complex of Hinduism; another is the equally contested idea of an Indian nation.

The British were not the first 'external' imperial power to rule in India. Immediately before them, the Mughal empire, succeeding the Delhi sultanate period, had extended its influence over most of the subcontinent; and for at least the first hundred years of their presence there, during the seventeenth and early eighteenth centuries, Portuguese, Dutch, Danish, French and British trading interests competed with one another under Mughal suzerainty, exerting but limited colonial power in small littoral enclaves. Only in the later eighteenth century, after the decline of Mughal power and the elimination of their European rivals, did effective British rule or *raj* begin to spread. As the British East India Company, in conjunction with the British state, arrogated to itself the responsibility for administering a larger and larger territory, it fostered the institutionalization of social power structures that were different than those typical of the Mughals and other previous imperial regimes. They were also quite consequential in terms of how indigenous Indians responded. Among the most important of these are several of the modern social systems that I have been discussing: capitalist economy, a centralized and increasingly invasive regulatory state, courts administering positive law, academic education, mass media and differentiated religion. These arose gradually, implicating especially indigenous elites more and more. Their construction characteristically encouraged the proliferation of social movements and organizations as the most typical social forms for expressing these systems and for countering their hegemony. Religious movements, religious organizations and a religious system featuring distinct religions were among these. They exhibited both continuity and discontinuity with what went before. They amounted to a re-formation and re-imagining of cultural traditions and resources; but they also constituted ways of Indian appropriation and particularization of the general forms, and thereby contributed to the overall construction of the global systems.

By the late eighteenth century, the British had begun seriously expanding their control inland from previously established 'beachheads' in India, notably around Madras in the southeast, Bombay in the midwest and Calcutta in the northeast. At the beginning of the period, the more significant were those in Bengal and Madras. Later on Maharashtra, the northwest, notably Punjab, and other areas took on similar importance as British hegemony consolidated. For ease of presentation, I will alternate between these various areas, treating them somewhat as variations on a theme, since developments in all areas to a large degree reflected more or less uniform, but also shifting, British company and colonial policy.

In accordance with that policy at the turn of the nineteenth century, among the many concerns of British colonialists was the training of British civil servants who would staff the many offices that administered the company's affairs and to a degree rule the indigenous people. From the late eighteenth to the very early nineteenth century, the prevailing notion which guided successive governors-general was that, in order to rule well, British legal and administrative functionaries had to understand the local people, their languages, their culture, their religions. They therefore set up training institutes, in Bengal, for example, the relatively short-lived but important College of Fort William in Calcutta, which would teach the British candidates the right knowledge (see Kopf 1969). The British teachers and other associates, above all members of the newly formed Asiatic Society, a scientific organization, had the task of deciding what that was. They did not simply take whatever happened to prevail among the local indigenous elites. Like most British colonialists, they saw the local society as degenerate, in need of revival, if not simply of civilization. In consequence, people like H.T. Colebrooke, William Jones, Charles Wilkins, H.H. Wilson and quite a few others set about researching and recovering the 'authentic' India of the past which would serve as the proper basis for training and, some hoped, revival. Relying on the local Brahmin literary elite whose responsibility was to transmit them, they 'discovered' the importance of, among other things, key religious texts such as the Vedas, the Bhagavad Gita, the Dharmashastras, the Puranas; and the corresponding 'golden ages' of their origin (see examples in Marshall 1970). In thus selectively reconstructing the history of Indian civilization, these scholars helped to fashion models for what that civilization essentially was; or at least favoured and enhanced certain already existing models over others. It was this that they sought to pass on to their students, who would by and large perpetuate and develop their initial reconstructions. They also created a situation in which their visions were associated with power.

As regards the effect that these British orientalists (Kopf 1969) had on segments of the indigenous elite, one must be careful not to project it too far. As Peter Marshall points out (Marshall 1987: 172ff.), the Bengali intelligentsia who carried what some have called the Bengali 'renaissance' were a restricted group, in most cases directly connected to the colonial power structure. The British may have influenced them quite a bit, but that did not translate into a corresponding influence on the larger Hindu elite, let alone the larger population. The importance of figures such as Rammohun Roy, the Tagores, Henry Derozio, Keshab Chandra Sen, Radhakant Deb and many more was not, however, that they simply carried forward a British impulse to (re)fashion the Hinduism of Bengal and then the subcontinent. Rather, it lay in aspects of both the content and form of their responses, elements that, in effect, set some of the precedents for the future.

Probably the most well known of these men, Roy, provides good illustration. Roy founded what eventually became the Brahmo Samaj with the aim of reforming Hindu society, fairly closely in the image of certain of the British observers. His version of the essential Hindu worldview was what has since been called neo-Vedantic, giving priority to the Vedas as its textual foundation and stressing a unifying monism, even monotheism. He was, however, sharply critical of prevailing Hindu ritual practice as superstitious and, in the Abrahamic sense, idolatrous (Kopf 1979). The Brahmo Samaj and other organizations inspired by it, such as the Maharashtran Prarthana Samaj, are also significant because they expressed its 'Hinduism' precisely in *organized* form (cf. Gold 1991). As such, its purpose was to do just what is under discussion here: present or reform Hinduism, and also more broadly, Hindu culture, in a coherent and convergent way not only to and for Hindus, but also to outsiders.

The earlier nineteenth-century neo-Vedantism of the Brahmo Samaj was not the only sort of response among indigenous elites with significant colonial contact. At least as important, both in Bengal and in other regions, were largely opposing conceptions that corresponded much more to the religious practice then more widely prevalent among the elite, especially those that held that 'idol worship' was justifiable and authentic; and that various cultural practices such as those associated with caste regulations were genuine aspects of what being Hindu was all about. Representative of these alternatives in Bengal were less famous figures such as Mrytyunjay Vidyalankar (see Chatterjee 1995), and less discussed organizations such as the Dharma Sabha associated with Radhakant Deb (Kopf 1969). These, it should be stressed, were not simply 'reactionaries' defending an ostensible status quo. Rather, they were other members of the Bengali intelligentsia whose vision of Hinduism was also not without resonances among the British. H.H. Wilson in particular is well known for his view that not Vedic but, roughly speaking, Puranic medieval Hinduism represented the most authentic version. His vision and that of Deb's Dharma Sabha, no less than the neo-Vedantism of Colebrooke and Roy, was a way of presenting Hindu religion and culture as a whole, an alternative identification in a context where British activity helped to make this question important. In fact, one could go so far as to say that these contrasting visions began the critical process of imagining and establishing a unified Hindu 'orthodoxy', what has since come to be known more generally as *Sanatana Dharma*, a vision of Hinduism which could claim to be the 'received tradition' against which reformers such as Roy and most of the British orientalists would be seen as reacting. In the historical process of religion construction, it has been just as important to construct such 'orthodoxy' as it has been to 'reform' this projected religion for the new contexts of the present. This is an aspect that I stressed in the section on Islam in the previous chapter.

A further significant dimension of the response of the Bengali intelligentsia had to do with schools and with printing. Here the nature and purpose of the Calcutta School Book Society, Sanskrit College and Hindu College, were symbolic if not in themselves determinative. These were, respectively, joint, British and Bengali foundations of the early nineteenth century whose purpose was to upgrade indigenous education, in effect to prevailing British standards, both in native languages and in English. As with the Brahmo Samaj, there was as yet in these institutions relatively little British/Indian or Christian/Hindu antagonism or contrasting identification: they were intended to contribute to the mutual project of 'uplifting' local society. The further development of both schools and presses in Bengal and elsewhere would, however, become instrumental in making just such distinctions paramount. Mass printing was, for India, a new technology which British administrators and most especially Christian missionaries used to formulate and to propagate particular visions, whether religious or otherwise. Schools were nothing new to India; but their prevalent form changed and their importance grew enormously from the beginning of the nineteenth century. Together they were to provide, not the only, but certainly two prime avenues for asserting, propagating and institutionalizing different versions of what the Hindu or Hinduism was in contradistinction to other worldviews or identities, in particular Christian and Muslim ones, but also of course other Hindu claims. I return to this issue shortly.

Around 1820, the broad direction of what one might call British cultural policy took a new direction, one destined to make religious distinctions much sharper and of greater consequence. Put simply, the doors were opened for Christian proselytization, the respect for even 'authentic' Hindu civilization declined, and, not incidentally, the degree of British control in Bengal as elsewhere on the subcontinent gradually increased. In effect, from a more universalistic policy that sought to revive Hindu culture as a branch of an essentially single human civilization, we witness a notable shift towards one that sought to replace it. As the weight of British power on Indian lives increased, the local elites responded with a great variety of initiatives whose consequence – if not always conscious intent – was to identify and strengthen what was Hindu (or Muslim, or Sikh, or simply Indian) as part of the attempt to gain and regain power. Far from excluding 'intra-Hindu' competition, these responses rather included them and helped structure them.

Several dimensions are worthy of mention in this context. The much greater entry of Christian missionaries brought in its wake similar reactions all around the subcontinent. As these spread their message and made converts among the indigenous people, Muslims and Hindus especially counteracted in various ways: they engaged the missionaries in polemical debates so as to discredit them and their religion. In the process, they acquired and used printing presses to disseminate their counter-claims, often thereby crystallizing in uniform and relatively stable fashion what they thought were the essential features of their own religion. Examples from various areas include Vishnubawa Brahmachari in mid-century Maharashtra (Conlon 1992), Arumuga Navalar slightly earlier in the Tamil regions (Madras presidency) (cf. also Frykenberg 1976; Hudson 1992); and, in the latter part of the century, Dyananda Saraswati in the northwest (Jones 1976). To a great extent, it was because the missionaries represented a manifestly alien power that overtly denied the value of local culture, that the Indians formulated defences. The print medium, whether in the form of books, pamphlets or newspapers, was one of those institutions that helped to solidify and spread those defences. We do not therefore have the rise of a uniform vision of Hinduism (or Islam or Sikhism), because no one version came to dominate as a result. But in large part because the Christians presented themselves as followers of a single, same religion (also with meaningful, to say the least, internal differences), the Hindu responses had to take on a corresponding appearance. The situation illustrates a central moment in the entire process of 'religion identification' in modern global society: we declare who we are as much in response to parallel declarations on the part of others, as we do positively to reflect on who we are. And, to emphasize once again, that exercise is not just one for the sake of meaning; it also aims at power.

Returning to the question of schools, in effect, the construction of Hinduism as a religion within a global religious system was interdependent with the emergence of an Indian academic educational system. Accordingly, in a great many places where religious controversies took place, participants also set up explicitly Hindu schools, institutions intended to counteract the many schools that the Christian missionaries had founded (Frykenberg 1976; Hudson 1992; Jones 1976). The aim of these Hindu schools was not to offer a completely different education, one perhaps harking back to what schooling was in pre-British times. Instead, it was to provide an education roughly similar to that offered in Christian schools, differing primarily in terms of the religion taught. Like the Christian schools, the idea behind the Hindu ones was to provide students with an education that would allow them to have access to the systemic power structures as they were developing under British hegemony. The Hindu schools, however, were also there to teach their charges whatever was deemed to be Hindu, and in the same stroke prevent them from becoming Christians. The issue was not simply one of *who* taught in these schools, British/Western or South Asian, or even the religious identity of the teachers, since examples of all categories could be found in all types of school. At issue was rather the Hindu or Christian character of the school and its curriculum. To be sure, throughout the nineteenth century, the majority of 'modern' schools in India remained Christian schools, namely run by Christian organizations and representatives. Even today, these schools are still an important part of the Indian educational sector. Still, the Hindu schools, comparatively few as they were, formed part of the attempt by indigenous elites to counter the control of the British and the Christians, by offering a Hindu and consciously Indian alternative for the children of the elite.

A further set of developments interdependent with the process of religious identification concerns the political/administrative and legal systems. Law and the courts, along with increasingly complex political and administrative institutions, played their roles in encouraging the more precise delineation of what counted as Hinduism and who counted as Hindu. Key aspects here have to do with features of modern positive law, the elaboration of politico-administrative regulation, and the gradual setting up of representative government structures. The specifics of British policy, of course, affected the more precise ways in which these systemic institutions would impinge upon the process that interests us. I pay particular attention, therefore, to the questions of religious law, the administration of religious festivals and sites, the regulation of religious authority, the ownership of religious property, the census, the civil service including the army, and consultative assemblies.

In the early nineteenth century and even before, the British adopted the policy of letting indigenous law operate as much as possible. The idea was to change only what had to be changed for efficient extraction of economic resources and revenues; the rest they deemed best left to operate in the traditional manner so as not to cause unnecessary upset and resistance. This policy included religious law up to the point of British enforcement of aspects of Hindu law and religious practice. In Madras after 1817, for instance, the British administration itself enforced public Hindu practice and controlled the temples and holy places (Appadurai 1983; Frykenberg 1976). In Bengal, already in the eighteenth century, British scholars and civil servants like Nathaniel Halhed and H.T. Colebrooke in cooperation with local twice-born literati were instrumental in deciding what Hindu law should be enforced by British courts. Yet such deliberate fostering of continuity did not change the fact that the British altered the operation or administration of law in consequential ways. Chief among these differences were the greater codification of law, gradual expansion of the possibilities for litigation, and greater precision in its application. For religion the results were several. To begin, far from seeking to abolish religious law, whether Hindu or Muslim, the British policy was to solidify its jurisdiction, but in more precisely restricted areas such as family and inheritance matters (see, for example, Chandra 1995). Doing so, however, required decisions about what the religious law was and what it was not; and therefore the British administration and courts required the selection of certain law texts and not others, certain interpretations of those texts and not others. The insistence on a procedurally more formalized administration of law thus necessitated just the sort of selection that is at the heart of the reconstructive process at issue, namely deciding what counts and does not count as Hindu and Hinduism. Equally as important, the people who did the selection were not just the British, but more significantly the high-caste Hindus who were the carriers of the textual traditions that the British favoured (cf. Bayly 1988: 675f.). This is not to say that such codification and formalization happened uniformly and all at once, only that it did so in proportion as the British expanded and elaborated their control in the subcontinent. Even after independence in 1947, the role and definition of religiously identified law has remained a consistent issue (cf. e.g. Conrad 1995).

In other respects, the sort of legal procedures and structures that the British instituted encouraged resort to the courts to settle all manner of civil affairs, including religious matters. The courts become an additional arena for carrying out religious controversies between, say, Christians and Hindus or Muslims and Hindus; they also helped to settle disputes among Hindus. Some of these concerned the control of important temples, pilgrimage sites and the organization and running of public festivals; others centred on matters touching religious authority and Hindu ortho-doxy/orthopraxy itself. With regard to the latter, the famous Maharaja Libel case of 1862 is indicative of the possibilities. Even though legally this case centred on the supposedly libellous allegations of a member of the Pushti Marga *sampradaya* against its leader, the Maharaja, it was at root a more purely religious controversy over the proper form of Hinduism (cf. Saha 2004). The plaintiff, Karsondas Mulji, represented the movement for reform of Hinduism, its restoration to the 'original religion' (see Clémentin-Ojha 2001: 193f.). He argued that the Vallabhi Maharajas ruled over a corruption of that religion. The Maharaja of course sought to assert the contrary. According to Lütt's analysis, the case not only embarrassed the Maharaja, it also contributed to the larger transformation of Vaishnavite Hinduism and to a recasting of the legitimate range of Hindu religious authority (Lütt 1995).

The sort of law and procedure introduced by the British put great store in questions of jurisdiction, and in this context, ownership. To the degree that temples and other religious sites were property, they had to have an owner, whether personal, corporate or public. The courts therefore tended to give exclusive ownership of such religious property to particular people or to organizations that claimed to be responsible for them. This certainly was a way of settling disputes efficiently, but it also favoured control by people who had the wherewithal and the organization to resort to the courts. Resort to litigation and legal private control of temples and religious properties was not just a matter of creating new possibilities which someone was bound to pursue. British administrative policy, especially in its later, less tolerant phases, encouraged them. The more polemical and exclusivist atmosphere of the post 1820s era made the courts another place in which Christian–Hindu and Hindu–Hindu disputes could be settled and lines of demarcation clarified (Appadurai 1983). A recognizable and socially influential institution called Hinduism emerged in the process, not just as some observers' idea, but as a socially operative entity. As Frykenberg states with respect to South India of the mid-nineteenth century,

> All sorts of issues pertaining to '*the* Hindu' religion and 'Hinduism,' *as this now became known and ever more reified*, were settled in this manner. The structure of precedent law which now emerged served as the foundation for a new kind of court enforced 'corporate Hinduism' the likes of which had never before been seen.
>
> (Frykenberg 1989: 37, second emphasis added)

Another aspect of the shift in British administrative policy in the second third of the nineteenth century concerned the civil service. Where before, as noted, such policy favoured civil servants at all levels drawn from Britain, now more and more only the higher positions were to be thus reserved, all others to be filled with members of the educated indigenous elite. This change made it even more important that the children of these elites be educated in the growing school system in order to qualify for these positions. Thus the religious implications of these schools became more, not less important. In addition, British attitudes at the time tended increasingly to divide all people, including Indians, into specific races each of which ostensibly had its particular characteristics. These distinctions could be 'ethnic' or 'religious' and thus included categories such as Sikh, Bengali, Maratha, Hindu, Muslim, Rajput or Gurka. Their importance lay in that they affected how the colonialists staffed their civil service, including the British army in India. Certain races were martial, others were not. One of the more important administrative surveillance procedures that concretized such classification was, from 1871 on, the census (cf. Barrier 1983). Not only did these surveys ask questions about linguistic, religious and caste identity, the results became an instrument for apportioning administrative positions according to the size of a corresponding population.

Towards the end of the nineteenth century and into the twentieth, such questions took on an extra dimension after the British introduced representative political institutions. Here again, the colonialists showed a willingness to ensure that the different 'communities' of India were all properly represented. And the censuses told them who and how large these were. Under the circumstances, numbers became important: it mattered how many people identified themselves as Hindu, Muslim, Sikh, Christian or other religious community. Various significant religious movements and organizations during this era were in part a response to the situation. The Singh Sabha movement, and later the Akali movement among the Sikhs in Punjab; the Arya Samaj, especially in its *shuddhi* or Hindu reconversion campaigns; and the Muslim League itself have to be seen at least to some degree in this light. Quite aside from *what* counted as Hindu, Sikh, Muslim, Jain or whatever else, the colonial political context of the time encouraged at least clearer distinctions among these categories of religious identity. It required people to declare or be declared as belonging to one community or another. Although 'Hindu' functioned in all this somewhat as a residual category – if you were not something else, you were Hindu by default – within that category there was debate and controversy over what were its positive characteristics.

Putting Indian 'communalism' in its colonial context is not, of course, the same as saying that these distinctions are *only* a reflection of that context, the symptom of a British policy of 'divide and conquer', for instance. The distinctions between religious communities were, for the most part, already there (Pandey 1992; Thapar 1989). What the British colonial context did was to favour some such distinctions over others, to encourage subsuming certain categories under others. Hinduism in this situation became one of the umbrella concepts without this determining what positively defined it. Such matters were not only open for debate and controversy; they also did not have to be precisely determined so long as almost everyone agreed that there was such a thing. The fact that, as the presentation thus far has shown, a fair amount of concretization happened anyway does not detract from the degree to which the self-description of Hindu and Hinduism was negative: a matter of knowing what it was not.

We can clarify the issue further by looking briefly at the simultaneous rise of Indian nationalism, both in its nineteenth-century cultural and then later expressly political phases. The open question with regard to the idea of an Indian nation has always been whether that notion necessarily means, when all is said and done, a Hindu nation (cf. Embree 1990). Certainly the Indian National Congress movement consistently sought to avoid this identity, evidence for which is, among other things, the rise of organizations and movements that resisted such inclusivity. The appearance in the first part of the twentieth century of the Muslim League, the Hindu Mahasabha and the Sikh SGPC, attest to the difficulty that the Congress movement faced. Indeed, as Pandey argues in his well-known work, Indian 'communalism' in the twentieth century is probably better seen as expressive of alternative visions of the nation or of polity than as a matter of religious oppositions (Pandey 1992: esp. 233ff.). In that context, unlike the 'religious' communalist movements, the 'secular' Congress movement had little traditional material at its disposal with which to define the new nation; at least not material that was not more easily appropriated for religious, caste or regional identities. Perhaps the best evidence of this is the clearly 'Hindu' appearance of the Gandhian vision, complete with its central emphasis on the tolerance of many religious ways and on principled non-violence. Only in post-independence India under Nehru do we find a period of ascendancy for a national vision which was neutral with regard to religious, linguistic and regional distinctions; and this did not survive much beyond the life of its highly influential carrier. Nonetheless, with the notable and very significant exception of partition along 'communal' lines in 1947, the Indian state was created and has survived quite well, this in spite of rather persistent internal conflicts structured precisely along religious/communal cleavages. The Indian state, however, has to its advantage the clear political, legal, administrative and military structures that are at the heart of the modern and globally institutionalized state (cf. Thomas *et al.* 1987). It can survive without a conception of the nation that is of comparable clarity. There is thus an Indian nation whose precise nature is both vague and a matter of constant debate or disagreement; but that concept of nation has a 'real presence' in the form of the Indian state, and therefore its vagueness is not a fatal detriment. It may even be an advantage. What, however, does this imply for the very parallel concept of Hinduism? There is no obvious parallel structure on which Hinduism can rest the way the Indian nation can rest on the Indian state. The implications of this comparison bring us to a consideration of whether Hinduism has become or has remained primarily a rather vague cultural identifier, or whether we can also speak of an effective and institutionalized entity that is the Hindu religion; whether Hindu is effective mostly as a cultural moniker, or has in fact also been reconstructed as one of the religions.

Institutionalized Hinduism in the nineteenth and twentieth centuries

To this point, I have tried to show how the construction of Hinduism in the nineteenth and twentieth centuries has been contingent upon the presence and consolidation of the other systems, notably the political, the legal, the scientific, the educational and that for mass information media. Institutionally, I have therefore talked about, among other things, scientific societies, law courts, state administrations, schools and print media. All of these served as institutional locations in which and through which the idea of Hinduism as a distinct cultural and religious entity could and did receive expression. Yet none of these systems are differentiated as religion; they only thematize religion. We must therefore ask what specifically religious institutions have formed as the carriers of Hinduism as such; what parallel and concrete social structures specialize in the production and reproduction of Hinduism as religion?[3] Continuing the political/national comparison, it was ultimately not enough for the Indian nation to be expressed as a cultural theme in nineteenth-century nationalist literature, to be a subject of discussion in newspapers and journals, to be a question of historical research. Eventually, the crystallization of the Indian nation required concrete political embodiment, first in nationalist organizations, then in representative bodies under the British raj, finally in the form of the Indian state. Similarly, Hinduism, if it is to be a single religion beside the others, has had to find its characteristic and specialized institutions. In point of fact, much of the ambiguity surrounding the notion of Hinduism and the hypothesis I am presenting here has to do with insufficiency in this regard. Hinduism today at the beginning of the twenty-first century still hovers uneasily between being a clear religion beside others and serving only as a cultural resource for various purposes. The standard pattern in other religions, of course, is that it is both. An examination of some important religious movements of the later nineteenth and twentieth centuries can serve to clarify what is at issue. I turn therefore to analyses of the role played first by the Arya Samaj and the Ramakrishna Math and Mission as representative of so-called Hindu reform movements; then to consideration of the Hindu Mahasabha and the Rashtriya Swayamsevak Sangh (RSS; National Volunteer Organization)/Vishva Hindu Parishad (VHP; World Hindu Council) as exemplifying politically motivated movements of Hindu demarcation; and finally to the broad Sanatana Dharma movement and various modern Hindu 'sectarian' movements as illustrative of important variants in contemporary institutional Hinduism. Most of these take the form of organizations; others demonstrate the characteristics of social movements. By themselves, these organizations and movements do not constitute all the social forms that together have thus far institutionalized Hinduism as a religion. They do, however, illustrate some of the main lines of this institutionalization. It will be for a subsequent section to look more broadly at how and to what extent the multifarious forms of Hindu religious expression actually do constitute a single self-referential religious system.

Both Swami Dayananda Saraswati and Swami Vivekananda carried forth and transformed the neo-Vedantic vision of Hinduism that emerged in the early nineteenth century (see, from among many, Brekke 2002; Jones 1976; Radice 1998). Dayananda's Arya Samaj presented a significantly more 'puritan' or iconoclastic version than did the Ramakrishna Math and Mission. The Ramakrishna Math, as the name indicates, formed itself much more around a monastic core; Arya Samaj put more stress on schools and mass recruitment campaigns. Both were organizations intent on not only religious but also broader social reform: they were worthy successors to the Brahmo Samaj which, by the end of the nineteenth century, was already waning in influence and presence. Although one cannot be sure, it is likely that this fate had to do with the perception that Brahmo Samaj was not 'Hindu' enough, that it did not display enough continuity with received tradition and too much with that of the colonizers. Be that as it may, both the Ramakrishna movement and Arya Samaj were expressly *organized* forms of Hinduism which have maintained themselves throughout the twentieth century; and which carry a vision of a single Hindu religion (cf. Gold 1991). Nonetheless, neither these nor any other group of organizations – monastic or otherwise – dominates the Hindu religious landscape the way, for instance, denominations and organizational groupings do in Christianity or Judaism. They also do not represent nodal points of authority or orthodoxy as one finds in the Islamic world; or in the monastic traditions of Buddhism. This feature is symptomatic of the wider question of how exactly Hindu manifestations can or do converge as Hinduism.

Further examination of the effect and the limitations of these expressions of a new Hinduism can proceed by looking at the origin, purpose and historical fate of one of the most intriguing endeavours of the Arya

Samaj, namely its *shuddhi* or conversion campaigns. The double meaning of *shuddhi* is instructive. Traditionally, *shuddhi* refers to the purification rites for twice-born Hindus who have been outcaste after violating caste norms but wish to regain their previous status. One notes that in this meaning it is a ritual of expiation, not a way of conversion, a way of becoming Hindu. It is also a rite of passage restricted to the twice-born. To the degree that this meaning of *shuddhi* implies defined boundaries for what Hinduism might be religiously, it is that only the twice-born can be 'real' Hindus. Here the status of being twice-born would occupy a similar place to concepts of 'religious community' in other religions: *ummah* in Islam, *sangha* in Buddhism, 'Israel' (as people) in Judaism, 'church' in Christianity. The meaning that the Arya Samaj gave to its rite of (re)conversion was originally quite compatible with this since it targeted high-caste individuals who had converted to either Islam or Christianity. Later, however, when the practice came to be applied to whole communities of low-caste Muslims, Christians and even Sikhs, the meaning changed to one that sought to incorporate into the Hindu fold positively and ritually any South Asian about whom there might be doubt: Christians and Muslims, but also 'untouchables' and 'tribals'; those who were positively something else or negatively not clearly Hindu. Part of the motivation for the direction thus taken was the importance that communal numbers took on in light of British administrative practice, as discussed above. A further reason, connected with this, was the nationalist dimension of Arya Samaj efforts: *shuddhi* was to consolidate and protect the Hindu nation (cf. especially Jones 1976, on this aspect). Another was the wish to make Hinduism into a single, mass religion. It is important to understand that these motivations are very much related, but not just different ways of saying the same thing.

The Arya Samaj thus sought to transform the meaning and practice of *shuddhi*. The movement wished to dissolve it out of its received contexts and re-embed it in a new frame of reference characterized by the aim of Hindu solidarity and self-assertion in the face of other religions. Both the ambiguity and the consequentiality of this gambit can be read from the pattern of reaction to it by the 'orthodox' twice-born over time: that is, by those who might be seen as representing *shuddhi's* meaning and practice *ante quem*. As Christophe Jaffrelot has argued (cf. Clémentin-Ojha 1994; Jaffrelot 1994), this segment of the population was never consistently opposed to the Arya Samaj campaigns. Until relatively recently, their reaction varied between support or acquiescence and resistance, depending on whether or not they also perceived that 'Hinduism' was directly threatened by other religions, notably Christianity and Islam. In other words, if the issue was one of 'internal orthodoxy', then the Arya Samaj appeared as deviant, even heretical. If, on the other hand, the salient issue was one of Hindu versus other religions, then the Arya Samaj were regarded as 'in the

Hindu fold'. Significantly, according to Jaffrelot, by about 1980, the acquiescence seemed to have become general and positive even from the
'orthodox' quarter. Rather than such conversions being viewed primarily
as the move of people who are already Hindus into a new and, for some,
questionable form of Hinduism, that is, as 'sectarian' conversion to Arya
Samaj, they are now more or less accepted as a change from one religion
to another, from Christianity or Islam to *some form of* Hinduism. This
sense is much closer to the idea of conversion in other religions. Yet that
does not mean that the 'orthodox' – or perhaps better the Sanatana
Dharmists – have accepted the specific Arya Samaj vision of what it means
to be Hindu. Jaffrelot notes that, as he puts it, the 'individual and spiritual
dimension' (Jaffrelot 1994: 92) is largely missing from these conversions.
The rites involved in this *shuddhi* are indeed religious rites and seem to be
accepted as effective for making Hindus; but their application does not
necessarily mean initiation into a particular version of Hindu belief and
practice. Thus, the support of the orthodox twice-born may well be an
indication of the lack of necessary religious content in these conversions.
They establish the boundaries between Hindu and Christian or Muslim,
but say little about the actual content of the Hindu. In spite of such ambiguity, however, Arya Samaj *shuddhi*, like the generalized Hindu activity of
many other groups such as the explicitly Hindu nationalist organizations
to which I turn shortly, has in fact aided in delimiting a specifically Hindu
identity, defining more precisely *who* is a Hindu while avoiding the more
difficult question of *what* a Hindu does or believes. That does not mean
that the latter has no consistent answer, that 'Hinduism' is therefore little
more than a convenient label devoid of content. Rather, it sets important
parameters for arguing or deciding precisely this question. Not only the
Arya Samaj has its version of that content: so have the 'orthodox', the
Sanatanists, had to construct their variants more clearly in order to
counter organizations like the Arya Samaj and the Ramakrishna movement, and to be clear about what Hinduism is in contrast to other
religions. The 'orthodox' is not just what has been received; it is what has
been asserted as received, as tradition, as authentic in the new context of
mutual religion construction. I return to this point below.

   Mention of the nationalist motivation in the Arya Samaj campaigns of
proselytization and conversion brings us to a brief consideration of two
other Hindu organizations which demonstrate the ambiguity under discussion even more clearly: the Hindu Mahasabha and the Rashtriya
Swayamsevak Sangh (RSS). The former was an expressly Hindu nationalist
organization whose main purpose was to promote the idea of a Hindu
nation as opposed to the more inclusive or even 'secular' version represented by the Congress movement.[4] Here again, the communal as opposed
to the religious nature of the category of Hindu is most evident (cf. Pandey
1992): the Hindu Mahasabha did not insist on a particular vision of

Hinduism, especially in its practical details, but rather wished the nation to be self-consciously Hindu without being too specific about what that meant (Jones 2001). The RSS, despite its reputation as an extreme, even fanatical Hindu movement, is actually of a very similar nature. As essentially a training and mobilizing organization for the Hindu nation, the emphasis in the RSS has always been on producing able and motivated militants in the broader cause of the nation (Andersen and Damle 1987). Religious symbols and at least quasi-religious ceremonies have been very visible parts of that effort, but unlike the Arya Samaj or the Ramakrishna movement there has been little effort to present the RSS as a complete way of doing Hinduism. Correspondingly, the RSS has been, more than anything else, a resource base for other types of organization, especially political ones like the Jan Sangh and now the Bharatiya Janata Party; and more expressly religious ones like the Vishva Hindu Parishad (VHP). Only the latter is directly concerned with the sort of convergence or 'orthodoxification' of Hindu religious practice that would make Hinduism recognizably different and yet look like other religions;[5] and even here, the aim is not to decide among the different versions, but rather to have them collaborate for common purpose and present them as essentially interrelated.

At least in the Western-language literature on modern Hindu developments, the emphasis has been on reformist movements such as the Brahmo Samaj or Arya Samaj, politically oriented ones like the RSS, along with new, charismatically led groups like the Swaminayaran and Satya Sai Baba movements (see, as examples, Andersen and Damle 1987; Babb 1986; Brekke 2002; Dalmia and von Stietencron 1995; Embree 1990; Larson 1995; Radice 1998; Sontheimer and Kulke 1989; Williams 1984). This stress is understandable given that these most clearly highlight points of discontinuity with the past and therefore what is particularly modern and new. It would, however, be a mistake to adopt, even implicitly, a too sharp distinction between 'modern' and 'traditional' in this regard. On the one hand, movements like the ones just mentioned are in many ways also continuous with developments before the nineteenth century. On the other hand, the vast panoply of Hindu religious forms that antedate this era and which are the subject of a far greater literature have themselves undergone discontinuous adaptations and transformations in the modern context. Thus to take but a couple of interrelated examples, the Ramakrishna Math and Mission or the Swaminarayan *sampradaya* have constructed themselves in many ways along the lines of a typical Hindu monastic movement or order, for example in adopting the familiar distinction between ascetics and householders with different sets of rules for each and with their emphasis on the high authoritative status of the founder(s). Correspondingly, monastic movements with their origins much earlier than the nineteenth century, such as the different divisions of the Madhva or

Vallabhi *sampradayas*, have themselves undergone transformations during the modern period, for instance in the establishment of clearer distinctions between the authority of the leaders (*maharajas*) and the property (*havelis*) of the organization in the latter; or even in the creation of exportable and missionary variants in the former (Babb 1986; Dalmia 1998; Radice 1998). Overall, the transformed social context featuring such structures as modern states, law courts, mass media and self-identified or missionizing other religions (especially Islam and Christianity, but also Sikhism and Buddhism), as well as the discourses on Hinduism introduced by the reformers in that context have had a powerful effect on the 'received' forms of Hindu religious thought and practice, at least as concerns what Agehananda Bharati has called the 'Sanskrit/Vedic Hinduism' of the largely urban middle and upper classes.[6]

This discontinuous continuity is perhaps nowhere more evident than in the greater promulgation of 'orthodox' Hinduism, what its representatives often call *sanatana dharma*. The assertion or reconstruction of this 'eternal religion' has a history quite parallel to that of the various modern Hindu reform movements, often in direct response to these movements. Thus, for example, following Kenneth Jones' overview of modern religious movements (Jones 1989) in each of the major regions of nineteenth-century India, both neo-Hindu reformist and corresponding 'orthodox' movements arose, the latter usually at least in part as a direct response to the presence of the former. Above, I discussed that relation between the Bengali Brahmo Samaj and Dharma Sabha associated with Radhakant Deb. To this example, Jones adds similar complementarities between the Arya Samaj and the movement represented by Sraddha Ram in Punjab, and between the Bharat Dharma Mahamandala and Vivekananda's influence in the Hindi heartland of Uttar Pradesh (see also Jones 1998). In other areas such as the Dravidian south and Maharashtra, according to Jones, the orthodox Brahminical reaction and strength were instrumental in making the atmosphere for reformist movements like the Prarthana Samaj less than hospitable. Into this category of 'orthodoxifying' response movements one could also place movements to reform and reassert Vaishnava and Saiva directions as Hindu orthodoxies. Hariscandra's efforts to unite north Indian Vaishnava *sampradayas*, but at the same time assert bhakti Vaishnavism as 'the' *sanatana dharma* in opposition to the reformers, serves as one important example (Dalmia 1995, 1998).

As noted, the nineteenth and twentieth centuries have also been witness to a number of new religious movements in various parts of India. Here again we can observe both continuity and discontinuity. The history of the subcontinent is replete with the rise (and decline) of numerous sectarian religious movements; some of these are still important features of the Hindu landscape today. Prime examples are the various monastic schools and movements that in one fashion or another trace their lineage to great founders, notably Sankara, Ramanuja, Nimbarka, Madhva or Vallabha (Clémentin-Ojha 2001; Dalmia 1995, 1998; Hardy 2001; Lütt 1995; Pinch 1998; Zydenbos 2001). These have a strong presence in most parts of India, so strong that it is precisely the leaders of these that the founders of the VHP sought to bring together to 'represent' Hinduism (Jaffrelot 1996; Van der Veer 1994a). One could also include under this heading different *panths* or movements such as the west Indian Dadupanth (Horstmann 2000; Thiel-Horstmann 1989). Yet, during the last two centuries, a number of new movements have become important features of the South Asian Hindu landscape. In this group, one could place, beside those already mentioned, the Swaminarayan movement founded by Swami Sahajananda, the Satya Sai Baba movement, the Radhasoamis and even the Brahma Kumaris (Babb 1986; Juergensmeyer 1991; Schreiner 2001; Williams 1984). Although these movements are all of relatively recent origin, they also share important features of continuity with those of longer standing, not least of which is the absolute centrality of the founding guru, and in many cases the continuing authority of charismatic successors.

While this variety of broader organizations and movements is important for the contemporary institutionalization of Hinduism, a number of other manifestations together probably constitute the bulk of what ends up counting as actual Hindu practice in South Asia. Under this heading, one would have to include the many important pilgrimages such as the Kumbh Mela (see http://www.kumbhmela.com [consulted 3 April 2003]) of Allahabad, and important temples such as the Vaishnavite temple at Tirupati in Andhra Pradesh (see http://www.tirumala.org [consulted 3 April 2003]). These kinds of institution not only feature a high degree of organization and therefore defined social form; they are also of ever increasing popularity, a fact not least made possible by the networks of modern communication and travel. Without necessarily being centres of convergent religious authority, these and many others like them do have the effect of linking the religious practice of a larger and larger number of Hindus in a way analogous to how *hajj* operates among Muslims or large pope-centred events among Roman Catholic Christians. To such 'macro' institutions should then be added the myriad smaller temples in India and around the world, and the everyday practices that take place in Hindu homes. These latter may seem largely non-institutionalized and disparate, but even at this level the twentieth-century growth in the pan-Indian spread of rather standardized religious paraphernalia such as pictures of deities (Babb and Wadley 1995) is having the effect of weaving these together into a broader Hindu tapestry as well. Under this heading, one might also put the articulating effect of mass media events such as the television serializations of both the Mahabharata and the Ramayana in recent years (Malinar 1995). It is these connections among the variety that are as instrumental in generating a single Hinduism as are the organizations and movements.

The networks of Hindu institutions and practice, of course, also reach beyond South Asia, notably into the sizeable and globally extended Hindu diaspora in countries from Malaysia to South Africa, from Western Europe to the Caribbean and North America (Baumann 2000; Bilimoria 1996; Burghart 1987; Dessai 1993; Kumar 2000; Sekar 2001; Vertovec 1992; Williams 1988). Although a small minority when compared with the overall Indian population, for the question of the formation of Hinduism these Hindus and their institutions take on a significance beyond their numbers, and this for two basic reasons. First, a large majority of them, to the extent that they participate in Hindu religious practice, do so in what Bharati (as noted above) calls 'Sanskrit/Vedic Hinduism', precisely the sort of Hinduism that is at issue here. Reflective of this characteristic is that a large proportion of them have relatively high communicative power, which is to say their socio-economic status, level of education and overall incorporation in the dominant global systems of power is well above the Indian average. Second, however, these Hindus everywhere form a small minority of the surrounding populations; they have therefore had to construct their specifically Hindu institutions much more clearly and much more deliberately, leading to a greater delineation of what exactly belongs to Hinduism and what does not. In particular, because they live in parts of the world where the majority populations participate in or at least take for granted more clearly convergent religions – notably Christianity and Islam – these Hindus are under greater contextual pressure to do likewise: to decide what Hinduism as a distinct religion is and how to put this Hinduism into practice. Thus, without in the least claiming that they have a determinative influence on the contemporary construction of Hinduism, the 'NRIs' (non-resident Indians) find themselves in a relatively privileged position in this regard.

This significance of NRIs does not mean that Hindu diaspora forms are somehow more convergent or uniform than those in India. Many of the South Asian Hindu organizations and movements already mentioned have been international for quite some time. These include the Ramakrishna Math and Mission, the Arya Samaj, the Swaminarayan movement, the RSS, the VHP, the Satya Sai Baba movement, to mention only a few. The variety that they represent has therefore globalized geographically, and the followers of these forms outside India are overwhelmingly NRIs as opposed to converts from other ethnic origins. More importantly, however, the sorts of temples and other Hindu organizations that have formed more or less independently among diaspora Hindus themselves take on a great diversity of forms. In some cases, such as the multiple deity temples that are common in countries from Canada to Germany and from Australia to South Africa, these are quite different from almost anything one would find in India. Migrant Hindus have found ways of allowing different versions of Hinduism to be represented in the same temple or organization, thus creating new 'hybrids' which may or may not become models for the future, whether among migrants and their descendants or in South Asia itself. In other cases, especially where the diaspora populations are sufficiently large or dominated by people originally from particular South Asian regions (e.g. North or South India, Tamil Nadu, Gujurat, Sri Lanka), the temples and systems of belief and practice are reasonably faithful recreations of what existed in the 'homeland' (Baumann 2000; Burghart 1987; Dessai 1993; Rukmani 1999). If there is a degree of uniformity among the migrant Hindu communities, it is only in the afore-mentioned comparable context: they are minority populations who often feel a greater pressure to circumscribe their Hinduism more clearly and more thoroughly than would be possible or necessary in South Asia itself.

The general picture that emerges from this very brief consideration of modern and contemporary institutionalizations of Hinduism is that, in the absence of powerful orthodoxifying forces such as exist in the three Abrahamic religions, the diverse Hindu organizations and movements together delineate a broad range of possibilities for doing Hinduism. Yet the question that is critical in the present context is how and whether this diversity in any real and socially effective way converges to constitute a recursive social and religious system. Symptomatic of the difficulty in this regard is not just the great diversity itself, but the fact that efforts by Hindus (and, for that matter, outsiders as well) to observe or to assert such a convergence so often shortcircuit to the question of who is or is not a Hindu, leaving the issue of what set of communications reproduce this Hinduism open for the sake of having any chance at rough agreement. Not surprisingly, the exceptions to this pattern are to be found in some of the organized forms and among Hindus in minority situations. In South Asia itself, the difficulty of seeing the unity even in terms of bodies, let alone with respect to content, has led to a kind of negative 'majoritarianism': Hindus are all those who are not something else, especially Christian or Muslim. Positively, the possibilities are limited. One is forced to answer the question in a minimalist fashion, perhaps as does the Hindu nationalist movement, referring to a small set of symbolic issues such as 'cow protection' and 'Ram temples'. Or, to take the example of the recent pronouncement of the Indian Supreme Court, one resorts to sufficiently vague criteria like Veda-centredness, inherent multiplicity of paths to salvation, and a plethora of divinities (see below).

Such indicators would seem to show a fatal lack of convergence as far as the social reality of a single Hinduism is concerned. Embedded within them, however, are other, more centripetal factors. Above all, what is evident among a great many Hindus in India as elsewhere is the conviction that, in fact, Hinduism does constitute a unity; that Hindus, in spite of their differences participate in a singular 'something' with the name of 'Hindu'.[7] Hindu nationalists tend to give this 'something' much more of a cultural-national – in India, 'communal' – flavour, and yet even here what content there is to this vision is centrally religious in the systemic sense that I am using that word; and on the other side of the sacred Hindu form are, as I have just indicated, other religions, not other nations. Moreover, both the vision of a singular Hindu religion and the provision of content to that vision have been the aim of a number of the most influential figures in modern, including twentieth-century, Indian history: notably Swami Vivekananda, Rabindranath Tagore, Sri Aurobindo and Sarvepalli Radhakrishnan (see the various contributions in Baird 2001). These men did not share a unified vision; they demonstrated the diversity as much as any of the institutional manifestations already discussed. Yet all of them sought to observe and to promote a Hindu religious unity. Not coincidentally, their visions generally included consideration of how the different variants of Hinduism related to one another, and how these related to other religions. In terms of the present analysis, they imagined Hinduism as a single systemic religion within a system of many religions. Although, more often than not, they ordered the different Hindu versions and the other religions hierarchically, with their version as the 'best', in this they were no different than the majority of parallel inside observers in other religions. Now, while the level of influence that the visions of these luminaries or the Hindu nationalists have over the actual communicative practice of Hinduism is debatable, they at least show that the unifying enterprise is something much more than the misconceived projection of Western outsiders. It is on this basis that it makes sense to proceed to the next portion of the presentation, namely an attempt to observe that unity from the theoretical perspective that informs my efforts.

Code, programme, elements and power in reconstructed Hinduism

As in Chapter 2, the analysis of the Hindu religious subsystem now moves from an emphasis on historical developments to an attempt to observe the recursive structuring of the communication that supposedly constitutes and reproduces this system. To do this, I again apply the central Luhmannian concepts that have informed the earlier efforts. If one can identify which features of contemporary Hindu religious communication fit into these categories, that will contribute to demonstrating how such a system operates effectively in contemporary society. Nonetheless, important caveats have to be kept in mind. First, the aim is not to force these analytic concepts on actual Hindu realities, but rather to use them to see how Hindus themselves observe what it is that they are doing. It is external observation, but primarily *of* self-observation. The second limitation is that even the examination of Hindu self-observation is no more than suggestive, because of the absence of any sort of centralizing Hindu authority, the corresponding diversity of versions, and the fact that those Hindus who make their versions public are generally members of a relatively small elite who may or may not be representative of the way Hindu communication works 'on the ground'. At the end of the day, the best that I can do in this presentation of theory is to demonstrate the plausibility of the hypothesis. Third, the hypothesis does not require or claim that everything that could be construed as the 'religious communication' of people called Hindus needs to be incorporated into the Hindu religious system for that system to be an operative social reality. The religions are selective reconstructions.

In order to address the questions of Hindu code, programme, elements and medium, one needs to select a sample of Hindu self-observations regarding belief and practice. These can act as representative efforts to observe Hinduism as a self-referential system of communication, even if they cannot also claim to be determinative or authoritative in this regard. Although one cannot assume a clear discontinuity between such self-observations in India and those which are based outside this country, the local context is nevertheless of some importance. As mentioned, the context in regions where Hinduism is a minority religion is more likely to encourage cohesive visions in contrast to the majority religions that surround it. The situation in India is quite different in terms of the diversity of phenomena that might be included and thus in the prevalence of religious expression that might escape such incorporation and yet not be part of another reconstructed religion. Hinduism is in a different sense a minority religion in India. The sort of reflexive observation one is likely to find there may also be different.[8] Moreover, although all such self-observations are likely to be elite observations in one fashion or another, one must also keep in mind that there are different elite contexts, notably academic and non-academic ones. In light of these contingencies, my choice of representative visions includes some of those that it could be argued have had a significant influence among Hindus in India and among diaspora Hindus. They also reflect different elite contexts. As well, within that range of possibilities, I exclude those of the 'neo-Hindu' leaders whose movements I have already had occasion to discuss, notably those of Swami Vivekananda and Dyananda Saraswati. The Ramakrishna movement and the Arya Samaj are important, especially historically, but perhaps a bit too obvious to serve the illustrative purposes called for here. The most important aspect of the selection is to sample the diversity and thereby to see what continuity of vision may exist.

From among sources from the Indian context, I have chosen one extremely well-known representative, Sarvepalli Radhakrishnan (from 1926); two lesser-known figures who have published works in India during the last few decades, V.C. Channa (from 1984) and Chakravarti Rajagopalachari (from 1959); and, on a different plane and of course far more briefly, the Supreme Court of India. From the diaspora context, I have selected two Hindu organizations which have undertaken the task of observing a unified Hinduism but are not expressions of Western academia. Both have an Internet presence and therefore their versions are at least very broadly available to a certain portion of the elite, claiming nothing about their actual influence. One reflects a VHP orientation; the other presents a Saiva perspective, but is also decidedly Western in the sense that its founder is a converted Hindu. What emerges from this diverse sample is both continuity and discontinuity, but within that a consistent structure that demonstrates difference within identity. It is this structure that I wish to highlight.

In 1995, the Indian Supreme Court reiterated[9] as an 'adequate and satisfactory formula' the definition of who is a Hindu put forth by the famous Congress leader of the early twentieth century, B.G. Tilak. Accordingly,

> acceptance of the Vedas with reverence; recognition of the fact that the means or ways to salvation are diverse; and the realization of the truth that the number of gods to be worshiped is large, that indeed is the distinguishing feature of the Hindu religion.
>
> (cited in Hinduism Today 1999)

While this definition is very minimalist, and probably deliberately so to include the maximum number of manifestations, it does contain a kind of skeletal outline for the present question of a Hindu system. First, it indicates a programmatic centre, namely the Vedas, and programmatic diversity radiating from that centre, the ways to salvation. It also points to elemental content in the form of worshipping the myriad transcendent communication partners, the gods. Finally, it declares an ultimate religious goal, salvation and thus at least one side of a structuring binary code. The only feature missing is a statement of the power medium. The significance of this absence is a subject of discussion below.

There are certain figures in twentieth-century Indian history who have enjoyed an enormous prominence among the elite classes and, to the extent that they have pronounced themselves on the question of Hinduism, can be said to have offered highly influential if far from definitive self-observations of this religion. Vivekananda, Aurobindo, and to a certain extent Gandhi, may be counted among these; but so must Sarvepalli Radhakrishnan. In considering his vision next, however, I do not wish to suggest it as some kind of standard to which the others will be held. Instead, it should be seen as representative of those elite pronouncements that have as their prime audience both Hindu Indians and non-Hindu others outside India, including especially Westerners. It is not a Western 'textbook' version written by an Indian,[10] but it does present a kind of 'high Hinduism' which distances itself to some extent from what Hindus might actually be doing in their religious lives in favour of a refined, theologically and philosophically sophisticated neo-Vedantism that can hold its own in comparison with corresponding visions from other religions.

My representative text is Radhakrishnan's Upton lectures, delivered at Oxford University in 1926 (Radhakrishnan 1980 [1927]). For Radhakrishnan, Hinduism is based on monism and monotheism as its guiding principle, Vedanta as its prime source, and tolerance as its chief criterion of elaboration. The assumption is a singular reality to which Hinduism gives insight (*darshana*), at its highest and purest level through Vedanta, textually principally the Upanishads, the Brahma Sutra and the Bhagavad Gita, but also others. In a famous expression, he declares that 'Vedanta is not a religion, but religion itself in its most universal and deepest significance' (18). Yet actual Hindu religion devolves from this source in the form of the myriad deities and related practices. Hinduism, according to Radhakrishnan, has historically become a theistic religion characterized by its ability to absorb over the centuries all sorts of gods, goddesses and cults, all of which are appropriate for someone and all of which reflect the core Vedantic impulse. What is more, he believes that most practitioners of these diverse forms are aware of that underlying source (40). Radhakrishnan's way of ordering this diversity is primarily through hierarchy: there is a hierarchical continuum of forms of religious orientation, from the highest which focuses on the absolute, all the way to animistic belief as the lowest with various theisms in between (24ff.). In this context, he decries some of the superstitious accretions of the masses: the tolerance evidently has limits, else it would lead to the loss of all defining form. To this skeletal structure of unity, Radhakrishnan attaches various programmatic features, including the three principal paths of wisdom (*jnana*), service (*karma*) and devotion (*bhakti*) (58); the chief goals of right-eousness (*dharma*), wealth and power (*artha*), art and culture (*kama*) and spiritual freedom (*moksha*); and the duties associated with four stages (*ashramas*) of life. Although he does not detail the elements through which these programmatic items are carried out, he does stress that the religion is much more a matter of practice than it is of belief. As concerns the question of code, Radhakrishnan, perhaps typically, puts spiritual liberation or *moksha* into the background, even though that is what the insight that Hinduism offers ultimately amounts to. More immediate are questions of right order and conduct, in one version the difference between *dharma* and *adharma* (55ff.). Indeed, correct practice appears to be the core informing principle in his unified vision. On the question of religious power he is virtually silent: insight, order and right conduct are their own reward.

A less well-known but still apparently highly influential rendition is that of Chakravarti Rajagopalachari, published first in the late 1950s in India

(Rajagopalachari 1970 [1959]). Unlike Radhakrishnan's work, this one is intended for Hindus in India primarily. The Indian context is very much in evidence especially in the explicit rejection of conversion, mostly of Hindus to Christianity or Islam (14). Rajagopalachari shares with Radhakrishnan a core emphasis on Vedanta and monotheism. The high gods of the Hindus are in reality but one (31); the Upanishads and the Bhagavad Gita are the main part of Vedanta, the former containing the essence of all religions (42). In terms of coding, Rajagopalachari is explicit: *moksha* is the one goal (69ff.); it is achieved through a programmatic process of purification or detachment centred on the unity of *brahman* and *atman* (47f.). *Samsara*, the other side of *moksha*, is where the soul and God are separated (61). The paths to this one goal, however, are many. These include the three ways of the Bhagavad Gita (knowledge, action and devotion), Vaishnavite and Saivite, *advaita* and *dvaita*, northern Indian or southern Indian versions (41, 72, passim). The programmatic core of all these is not only the cosmological aspects, but the practical ones centred on devotion and right action or *dharma*. Rajagopalachari sees the notions of *karma* and rebirth along with the *dharmic* prescriptions from which these devolve as the central distinguishing features of Hinduism with respect to other religions. Yet he emphasizes the continuities among the religions, saying they all worship the same God and have devotional practices at their centres. Perhaps in contrast to Radhakrishnan, however, Rajagopalachari insists that, although religion is the foundation of all other spheres of life, such as economy, politics and science, it does not replace them. The differentiation of religion is for him important and clear. Finally, just like Radhakrishnan, the question of specifically religious power is hardly touched: Hinduism and religion are evidently matters of meaning and order, of realization and devotion, not of power.

My third textual example is that of V.C. Channa, published in the 1980s under the simple title of *Hinduism* (Channa 1984). The range of influence of this work is far less certain in comparison with the previous two. I have chosen it because of its apparently quite different vision. I say apparently because the basis of the difference is more a question of what is elaborated than it is a fundamental disagreement about the nature of Hinduism. Essentially, where the previous two authors stress the Vedantic unity of their religion, Channa devotes most of his attention to its programme and elements, the matter of coding becoming evident in the process but the question of unity of vision receding partially into the background. Religious power again gets short shrift.

Channa begins his overview in a way reminiscent of the previous two authors, mentioning the sacred texts of the Vedas, Upanishads, the Bhagavad Gita and the Puranas. He speculates that the unity of the tremendous diversity that falls under the title of Hinduism has to do with the flexibility and adaptability of the religion, being capable of adjusting to new circumstances and the proclivities of different individuals without also generating irreconcilable discontinuities: tolerance of variation is a hall-mark of the religion here as well. Where the contrast begins is in Channa's insistence that Vedantic speculation and textual basis are not the main part of Hinduism for the average Hindu: rather, it is idol worship and the performance of myriad rituals (v–viii). Accordingly, the bulk of his book focuses on the presentation of the gods and goddesses, their avatars and other manifestations, and the ritual complexes associated with them. Hinduism, according to Channa, is about the great divinities, about Shiva, Vishnu and Brahma; Parvati, Durga, Kali and Lakshmi; Ganesha, Hanuman and Krishna. It is also about the Ganges and the Jamuna, about god-men like Mahavira, Nanak, Caitanya and Sai Baba; about *rishis*, *munis* and the Matas. Clearly the most important texts are the Epics, the Ramayana and Mahabharata especially, because they directly inform the understanding and worship of the deities. With respect to ritual, Channa focuses on prayer, that is *aarti* and *puja* (82ff.), in temples and outside, to Vishnu, Shiva, Durga, Lakshmi, Kali, Ganesha and Hanuman especially. Calendrical and life-cycle rituals are also prominently treated. Only in several shorter chapters toward the end of his book does Channa treat of the way these elements are programmatically woven together. Here we find discussions of *dharma* and its associated polarity of purity and pollution, of *karma* with its distinction between *pun* and *pap* (what is enjoined and forbidden by *dharmic* rules). Yet these are only uniform in the sense that they all proceed from universal Brahma. In reality, the cosmos is divided according to time; there are different rules for different circumstances. But the principal divisions are social distinctions, above all those of caste and gender. Channa asserts the Hindu validity of the system of four *varnas* and makes no apologies for the subordination and different *dharmas* of women with respect to men. The unity of the system is in its hierarchical ordering principle. *Dharma*, in its differentiated forms, precedes morality, the moral/immoral distinction being meaningful only in terms of its expression through that between *dharma* and *adharma* (150). Although Channa decries what he calls human selfishness and the abuses of this system, its coherence, authority and authenticity are not thereby cast in any doubt.

These are then three Indian and internal versions of Hinduism as a systematic religion. To round out the sampling with versions from another part of the Hindu world, I turn to two Hindu websites from the significant Hindu diaspora. Both the different medium and the different contexts should provide further testing for the idea that a continuity of self-conceptions of Hinduism exists among Hindus and, in this case, also globally.

My first diasporic example is to be found at the website of a Hindu student organization associated with the VHP (Hindu Students Council 2003). It is not without significance that this site and the organization are centred in the United States, that is in the Hindu diaspora where the issue

of declared self-definition is usually more urgent. Nonetheless, its association with the VHP, both as concerns its origins and the sorts of issues with
which it is concerned,[11] makes it less of a purely diaspora affair and therefore more appropriate for the present purposes. The site is replete with
Hindu religious elements, in particular details of numerous *pujas,
samskars, bhajans, kirtans,* pilgrimages (*yatras*), festivals and astrological
forecasting. Links are provided to lists of Hindu temples around the world
and in all regions of India. In typical fashion, it includes Buddhism,
Jainism and Sikhism, but is also careful to distinguish these *dharmas* from
Hindu *dharma* (the indigenous word for modern religion). Other links list
Hindu[12] organizations, providing a very broad range of variants evidently
deemed to belong to Hinduism, from Arya Samaj and the Ramakrishna
Math to the Gaudiya Vedanta Samiti and the Brahma Kumaris. In this
selection, web and worldwide presence seem to be important. The limited
range of organizations may well be a reflection both of these selection
criteria and the limited organization of Hinduism. As concerns beliefs,
sacred writings, deities and saintly personages, these are also given in some
detail. Under beliefs, one finds a list of essentials that include the harmony
of all religions, non-violence, Atman-Brahman, *dharma* as moral code,
karma and reincarnation, and *moksha* defined as escape from *samsara* and
as union with the divine. Scriptures are given as non-exclusive, but include
the Vedas and the Epics. Deities are listed as multiple manifestations of the
same God, and the site adopts the idea of the Hindu Trinity (*Trimurti*) of
Brahma–Vishnu–Shiva. In addition, there is a glossary of Hindu terms
which includes a definition of 'Hinduism' as the 'modern name for the
Vedic teaching'.

In this instance, one again finds most of the relevant dimensions: a
central code, *moksha/samsara*, including reference to a secondary moral
code; a complex set of elements or religious communications; numerous
components of an elaborate and diverse religious programme in the form
of a presumably consistent set of practices and beliefs; and consideration
of social forms, especially organizations and temples. If there is a clear
power medium for this site, it takes the form of karma, although, as with
the previous examples, this concept is not explicitly presented in power
terms. The site evidently considers all these dimensions to be consistent
with one another and even offers a Frequently Asked Questions (FAQ)
section which it claims to be evolving. The framers of this site evidently are
convinced that Hinduism is one of the great religions and endeavour to tell
the visitor as much as possible about it.

A further example, perhaps a bit more suspect for our purposes, is to be
found at the Internet site of the Saiva Siddhanta Church, an organization
founded by a Westerner and based in Hawaii (Himalayan Academy 2002).
Its interest in the current context is limited to the list of 'Hindu basics' that
it suggests, and the degree to which they correspond to the other visions

considered here. These basics include, in Saivite fashion, that the Agamas have a status almost equal to the Vedas, the *karma*/reincarnation nexus, the singular divine principle with its many theistic manifestations, the critical role of the preceptor or guru – an item that only Channa even mentions and no one else locates quite so centrally – the value of ritual practice such as temple worship, the idea of the great cyclical ages (*yuga*) of history, non-violence and the multiple paths to *moksha* but the singularity of this religious goal. The different versions of Hinduism are classified as Saivism, Shaktism, Vaishnavism and Smartism. Other religions are acknowledged (there is even an explicit point-by-point comparison with Christianity) as 'genuine religious paths' (Himalayan Academy 2002, 'Hindu Basics'), although the precise relation among them is left unclear. In addition there are links to various Hindu temple sites around the world, and to numerous Hindu organizations with websites, including a great many of those found in the Hindu Student Council site. The Saiva Siddhantists are, however, less charitable in their range of inclusion in this regard, classifying movements like Satya Sai Baba and Ananda Marga under 'social service/universalism', the Divine Life Society of Sivananda as 'quasi-Hindu', and ISKCON, the Brahma Kumaris and Transcendental Meditation as 'non-Hindu' (Himalayan Academy 2002, 'Resources', 'teachers and organizations').

What is striking about all five of these sources is the degree to which they agree on the 'basics'. *Moksha/samsara* does at least appear as an operative binary code, but closely connected to *dharma/adharma*, sometimes moral/immoral; but manifest in the programmatic notion of *karma/* reincarnation. A certain set of writings is usually central, but there is significant variation on precisely which ones and exactly how important any of them is to the practice of this religion. By contrast, the multiple deities that manifest a single divine principle, and the many legitimate paths for pursuing the central religious goals, are consistent features. Ritual communication, especially in the form of devotional practices and the observance of *dharmic* prescriptions, are common emphases to all five examples. Only the two diaspora websites put emphasis on organization, but here these receive extensive attention. There are also other important differences, including the range of manifestations included, but perhaps the most critical among these are the differences in emphasis. Clearly none of these sources takes a radically exceptional direction. Indeed, given the level of overlapping self-description, the degree of convergence of vision would seem to be at least as great, and perhaps greater, than it would be in comparable cases of Muslim, Christian or Buddhist self-representation.

On the basis of various examples of Hindu self-description, I want now to present a brief analysis of what may plausibly be defended as the contemporary, systemic convergence of Hinduism as one of the religions that compose the global religious system. I begin with the question of code.

I have suggested in a number of places that *moksha/samsara* acts as the core binary coding of contemporary Hinduism. The exemplary self-observations of Hinduism that I have just outlined more or less support this idea, whether salvation is conceived in monistic fashion as ultimate union with Brahman or in a dualistic manner as entering into the permanent presence of the ultimate deity. As in other religions, however, this Hinduism also avails itself of key supplementary codings, ones that specify the general code further, thus rendering it more immediate. Although the moral code of moral/immoral is plausibly one of these, as it is in most other contemporary religions, it is far from the most important one. More critical are the distinctions between *dharma* and *adharma* and, one could add by extension, the differences between auspicious and inauspicious or between pure and impure (purity/pollution). In the examples that I have outlined, all of these appear. It is these, along with the usually more remote *moksha/samsara*, that render the universal religious code of blessed/cursed into particular Hindu form. The degree of their self-referentiality is, of course, largely a matter of Hindu self-observation. As in other religions, the precise articulation of the primary and secondary codes may not be a foremost consideration in the enacting of most religious communication: the average Hindu religious communication is probably performed much more immediately in terms of the secondary codes, the primary one being more often than not a remote consideration. The situation is similar in other religions. Most Christians or religious Jews, for instance, engage in their religious communication only indirectly with their eternal fate in view; more immediate blessings, religious duty or moral rightness are as or more likely to serve as motivating considerations. Similarly, Hindus performing *pujas* or *bhajans* will do so more in search of more immediate divine blessing or out of a sense of religious duty; *moksha*, like many high gods, may only inform the larger scene.

Unlike in a religion like Christianity or Islam, the programmatic core of contemporary Hinduism is not to be found in certain sacred writings such as the Bible or Qur'an. To be sure, Hindus mostly pay a certain homage to the Vedas and Vedanta; the Epics and Puranas along with other writings such as the Saivite Agamas are probably of more immediate significance for most Hindus, but even these do not function as infallible sources to which the devout consistently resort for deciding (and disputing) what is proper. Aside from certain principles like tolerance of different paths, divine monism and such notions as *dharma* or *karma*, more central to Hindu reality seem to be a relatively small number of divinities, transcendent personages to which most practitioners of this religion direct their ritual devotions. These include above all Vishnu and Siva, but also avatars and consorts of these such as Rama, Krishna, Lakshmi or Parvati; one or another form of independent high goddess such as Durga or Kali; and lesser but no less important adjuncts to the high gods such as Ganesha,

Hanuman and others. The stories and rituals that surround and refer to these divinities together constitute a kind of central programme to which individuals and subgroups will add others from a truly large selection. It is because the programme centres on these divinities and not on texts (as revelation, for instance) that reference to sacred writings is as inconsistent and variable as it is. The Vedas and Upanishads, for instance, while holding a central symbolic position, are actually the direct source of very little determinative mythology and even less ritual practice; they function much more as a kind of concrete guarantor of Hindu programmatic unity than they do as source of obligatory instruction. They are the real primary reference of certain elite but minority versions of Hinduism, above all Vedanta and others such as Arya Samaj. The programmatic core material, as Tilak's famous and judicially approved formula has it, is actually the many gods/goddesses and the many paths, most of which focus on the divinities, some of which abstract from them. To all this, for many Hindus, one might add a central role for the guru or spiritual preceptor, the line between the divinities and which can at times become quite blurred.

Corresponding to the many deities and many paths, Hinduism exhibits a wide variety of typical elements. These as well, however, exhibit a certain reconstructed unity or at least particular kinds of elements appear to be the most widespread and consistently present in Hindu practice. Among these *puja* and *aarti*, whether in the home or at the temple, are singled out in almost all of the self-descriptions. Along with these rituals of divine presence (*darshana*), less consistently mentioned but probably of comparable importance are the rituals of sound (*mantra*), above all repetition of *mantras* and singing (*bhajan/kirtan*). To these should be added various others, for instance processions (*yatra*), pilgrimage, astrological prediction, divine service of various sorts (*seva*), meditative or yogic practice, and the various seasonal, life-cycle, and daily observances that usually include the other elements as core features.

As indicated, the five selected self-descriptions pay scant attention to the question of religious power in Hinduism. It is not so much that power is entirely absent; there is instead a lack of explicit thematization. Radha-krishnan, for instance, makes comparisons of Hindu spiritual insight (*darshana*) with the Christian idea of 'faith' and Rajagopalachari parallels 'grace' and *karma* (Radhakrishnan 1980 [1927]: 14; Rajagopalachari 1970 [1959]: 85), but the power dimension of these notions remains muted and at best implied. As with the other religions, the power medium or media are present but relatively undifferentiated as such. The medium hovers close to being simply the dynamic dimension or the consequential aspect of the binary codings (cf. Luhmann 2000a). Thus Rajagopalachari puts emphasis on the *karma* consequences of *dharma*, Channa stresses the purifying outcome of Hindu practice, and Radhakrishnan speaks of levels of spiritual development with reference to which *moksha* represents spiritual freedom. Power is there, yet it is virtually identical with the reproduction and intensification of programmatic religious communication as such. In this regard, it is perhaps instructive that Radhakrishnan includes in his presentation of the Hindu 'view of life' the common Hindu paralleling of different social power pursuits, namely *artha* (wealth and political power), *kama* (artistic and cultural power), *dharma* (righteousness) and *moksha* (spiritual freedom) (Radhakrishnan 1980 [1927]: 56–8). Although his aim is to underline the completeness and unity of this way of life, elaboration is almost entirely on the side of the last two as the bases of the other two and not as distinct forms of power. One might conclude that, although Hindu practice includes ideas of mystical or ascetic power, even arguably of possession and trance in certain of its variations, although Hindu vocabulary contains possibilities for naming an explicitly religious power medium, for instance as *karma*, *pushti* (grace), *shakti* or *balam*, self-descriptions such as the ones I have outlined tend to underplay or ignore these possibilities in favour of seeing the religion as a guarantor of meaning and order, in Parson's terms as primarily a matter of 'latent pattern maintenance' (Parsons 1971).

The social forms of Hinduism

The general theoretical question of the systemicity of the Hindu religious system needs more than a consideration of the structural features that provide for the singular recursiveness of Hinduism. The components just discussed need further to be embodied and reproduced in recognizable social forms that carry them. These other social systems are not simply another way of looking at the religious system but rather additional systems that help to lend concreteness or 'localization' to Hinduism. There are, as discussed in previous chapters, four basic possibilities in this regard: organizations, social movements, social networks of interactions, and other function systems. Here it is important to highlight the way that they, together, contribute to the concrete social realization of Hinduism as a religion.

Contemporary global Hinduism is not a religion that exhibits a very high degree of organization, especially in its dominant heartland, India. As in several other of the most prominent religions, organization plays a significant role, but the strategy of addressing the problem of boundaries through a heavy reliance on 'membership' in organizations has not been particularly pronounced. The sorts of organizations discussed in previous sections do incorporate a fair number of people. The various *sampradayas* and other orders can count on the regular and significant participation of a great many devotees; the major pilgrimages and temples have millions of regular and irregular attenders or 'clients'; many gurus have a regular and devoted following; and, especially but not exclusively in diaspora situations, temple organizations are often the centres of Hindu religious life and practice. Overall, however, when one considers that vast amount of religious communication that constitutes the 'Sanskrit/Vedic Hinduism' that is the point of focus here, a great deal of it escapes these organized forms partially or entirely. Nonetheless, organizations are of critical importance because they provide social centres for the structuration of Hindu variants. Not everyone or even most of those who consider themselves to be practitioners of Hinduism necessarily have to follow the organizations or participate in them on a very regular basis. Their concreteness, their resources, their visibility, in short their presence as nuclei of authoritative authenticity make them model forms for the orientation of religious practice, of self-observations and of outside observations. More than any other type of social system, Hindu organizations provide venues for the recursive structuring of religious communication that is recognizable and recognized as embodiments of Hinduism. They are not alone in this regard, but without them a socially effective religion called Hinduism would continue to exist only with great difficulty.

As in other religions, religio-social movements have also played and continue to play a conspicuous role in lending Hinduism concrete form. These include many of those that express themselves in the organized forms just discussed, such as the continuation of Saivism, Vaishnavism, neo-Vedantism and, perhaps more broadly, *sanatana dharma* movements. Not to be forgotten is also the highly visible and much commented Hindu nationalist movement with its various historical predecessors, although here we are dealing with social movements that have been and are quite overtly political as well as religious. The degree to which they have reproduced Hinduism in the sense used here is an open question requiring more focused research. Certainly that contribution is not insignificant. Particular manifestations, from the earlier cow protection movements to the currently ongoing Ayodhya-Ram temple movement to diasporic Hindu student movements, incorporate and highlight important Hindu symbolic elements, rendering them, and therefore, one can assume, the practices associated with them, more visible and perhaps more frequent. By comparison, however, the former, more purely religious, variety embodies the religion of Hinduism much more directly and consistently. Core movement ideas such as that Siva or Vishnu is *the* high god to whom devotional activity should be directed; that Vedanta is that from which all Hindu activity should take its orientation; or that there is an 'eternal' and 'orthodox' Hindu practice which must be preserved and furthered in the face of various compromising heterodoxies; these give shape to broad Hindu tendencies of which various organizations, celebrations, festivals, pilgrimages, conferences, publications and other events can be and are the expressions. As such, these movements may be associated with organized Hinduism, but they are not co-extensive with them and therefore deserve separate mention when discussing the various forms that embody contemporary Hinduism.

In the broad scholarly literature on Hinduism, a form that receives frequent and focused attention, especially from anthropologists and ethnographers, is what I here call the Hinduism of social networks of interaction. This is where 'community' Hinduism would fit, the religious practice of particular villages, towns and regions, especially in India. These are not organized, nor do they take the form of deliberate socio-religious movements with explicit narratives of justification and characteristic movement events. They are simply regular configurations of religious communication that prevail in specific areas. It is the tremendous variety that such local patterns of religious action exhibit which has been among the key reasons for questioning how anything so diverse could actually constitute something singular and coherent called the Hindu religion. And, indeed, as I indicated above in restricting the system of Hinduism to Bharati's 'Sanskrit/Vedic' variety, one must be careful not to try to see too much of this sort of South Asian religious tradition as necessarily or self-evidently part of Hinduism. To be sure, there exist today, and have occurred for quite some time, elite-led efforts to see these 'village Hinduisms' as expressions of the larger religion; and it may be that representatives of some of them occasionally concur in these aims and assessments. Yet, by and large, failing solid evidence to the contrary, such inclusion remains the province of outside observers, having little effect on the religious practice of the people concerned and on their understandings of what it is that they are doing. Without self-observation (that is, observation from the same sources as perform the religious communication) as specifically Hindu religion, half the construction of these forms as such is missing.

The final possibility for forming Hinduism is through other, non-religious systems such as the state, law, education, art and mass media, to mention only the most relevant other function systems. I leave consideration of the first two of this list for Chapter 6, where state and legal conceptions of religion are the subject of an entire section. Here I want to point out the particular importance of the last three. In the history of the construction of modern Hinduism, it would be difficult to overemphasize the significance of education and mass media, the latter often overlapping with the world of art. Already in the nineteenth century, elite reformers set up schools among the aims of which was to perpetuate a specifically Hindu identity among their students. Hindu religion is a regular part of education in a great many schools in India today; and diaspora communities are noted for the special attention that they pay to the religious education of their second generations. Moreover, the texts that in the previous section I chose as examples of Hindu self-descriptions have for the most part also served at least as university-level readings and texts, perhaps owing a good portion of their reproduction to these markets. As concerns the mass media, we have seen that, since the latter part of the eighteenth century in India, the expansion of print technologies was instrumental for the success of the various reform and response movements. Today, one would have to add television, film, video/audio media and the Internet to that list. As exemplified in the television serializations of the Ramayana and Mahabharata, and in Internet sites such as those discussed in the previous section, mass media are peculiarly suited for 'broadcasting' structuring visions of Hindu programmes in their different variants. To the degree that these reach the mass of nominal Hindus in India and around the world, they will contribute to the effect of further articulating Hinduism as a single and self-identified religious system.

Conclusion: Hinduism as ambiguous reconstruction

By way of summary, and in light of frequent admissions to this effect, it may seem to many readers that the evidence I have presented for my central hypothesis with regard to Hinduism is somewhat inconclusive. This ambiguity, I would suggest, stems from two sorts of factors, one specific to Hinduism, the other not. The latter derive from certain characteristics of the overall religion-formation process itself, above all the lack of clear instrumentalization combined with the unavoidably plural pattern of religion construction. Religion also seems nebulous by comparison with other systems, notably the political with its neatly delimited territorial states and the economy with its precisely quantified power medium, money. Contemporary Hinduism exemplifies these general features quite well. First, Hinduism does not have at its disposal a history of authoritative convergence but only a large number of these, all of them perhaps interconnected, but none of them definitive except for some of their adherents. Without such institutional convergence that defines one or a relatively limited number of 'orthodoxies', the identification of Hinduism will always seem lacking because both what is included and what is excluded seem rather arbitrary. Second is the comparative lack of pervasive religious organizations in the Hindu sphere. In both these respects, however, Hinduism is not all that different from other religions. If 'multiple centredness' and a muted level of organization are to be arguments against the existence of Hinduism as a distinct systemic religion, then this is a general problem with observing the religious system, not something peculiar to this religion.

More specific, but not unique, to Hinduism is a characteristic to which I have thus far given scant attention. It concerns the question of belonging. Unlike the 'clearer' religions (if one wants to consider Christianity, Islam and Buddhism as exemplary), Hinduism is not in its own self-descriptions to any significant degree a proselytizing religion: many paths lead to the ultimate goal common to all religions; proselytizing is more of an affront than a religiously laudable activity; and correspondingly, conversion from the incontrovertible outside to Hinduism is still quite uncommon. Partial exceptions are 'export' movements such as ISKCON, Transcendental Meditation, Divine Light Mission and Rashneeshpuram or Osho. For the most part, however, to be Hindu is to be born into it, meaning that ethnic or national identity, while not identical, overlap to such a degree with the religious that Hinduism may indeed seem to be more appropriate as a name for the religious dimension of a broad cultural identity than it is the designation of a distinct self-referential system. Although one cannot completely deny this peculiarity, it is also arguably just that: a peculiarity of Hinduism (but not *just* Hinduism). As the Arya Samaj's *shuddhi* campaigns illustrate, this 'cultural identity' aspect of Hinduism is also understandable as an integral feature of its religious programme. Hindu conversion, as it happens, is not a contradiction in terms; rather, it tends to take certain forms rather than others. Specifically it more often than not takes the form of a 'return' to Hinduism, a purification and 're'-incorporation, albeit of persons that in most cases, outside the perspective of this religious programme, have never in their lives been Hindu before, much like any new convert to Islam or Buddhism. The situation has a parallel in Islam, an incontrovertibly proselytizing religion. Here one also speaks occasionally not of 'conversion' but of 'reversion', under the Muslim programmatic notion that we are all born Muslims but that many of us are as yet unaware of that basic state. Accordingly, the ambiguity in the idea of Hinduism as a separate religion that refers to its characteristic as simply a name for a particular cultural way of life is better seen as evidence of Hinduism as a particularly constructed religion, *beside others*. In the final analysis, like the common protests that 'ours is not a religion' heard from representatives of most religions, the issue is less one of the existence or not of religions than it is one of the ambiguities inherent upon differentiating religion at all. This, however, can be said for any of the function systems.

Notes

1   See Chidester 1996; Fitzgerald 1990; McCutcheon 1997: 158ff.; Peterson 2002. Asad (1993) is a partial exception as is W.C. Smith (1991) since they include and even focus on Islam.
2   Balagangadhara 1994; Fitzgerald 1990; Frykenberg 1989; King 1999; Thapar 1989. Ursula King (1989) offers a very similar analysis but does not assume that this invention is somehow illegitimate. Important statements are also to be found in various contributions to Dalmia and von Stietencron 1995.
3   The question is quite similar to that posed by Appadurai (1983) with respect to control of South Indian temples and using the Geertzian distinction between cultural and social system.

4 A very good parallel is to be found in Zionism or Jewish nationalism: whereas the World Zionist Organization represented a decidedly secular and often socialist vision of the Jewish nation, the Mizrachi were an organization within Zionism consciously promoting a religiously nationalist version. See Beyer 1994.

5 Jaffrelot puts this aspect, which he calls 'stigmatization and emulation', at the centre of his analyses of contemporary Hindu nationalist organizations. With respect to both the RSS and the VHP, see especially Jaffrelot 1996.

6 I take this classification as presented by Gerald Larson (1995: 20–1). By his estimate, the reformers plus the practitioners of this 'Sanskrit/Vedic' Hinduism constitute no more than about 20 per cent of the current 'Hindu' population. Bharati's third type, 'village Hinduism' – what one could perhaps call 'popular Hinduism' in India – would account for the other 80 per cent. It should be noted that Larson excludes the 20–25 per cent of the Indian population often classified as 'untouchable' or 'tribal' from the Hindu category. Accordingly, the sort of Hinduism I am discussing in the text constitutes the religious expression of no more than about 100–150 million of India's approximately 1 billion people. While these numbers are only rough approximations and reflect a heuristic or analytic categorization, it would not be going too far to say that this minority, plus the majority of diasporic Hindus in other parts of the world, are in effect the carriers of the Hindu religious system that is the subject of this chapter. I discuss this 'minority' status further in the last section of this chapter.

7 A similar situation is evident with the Christian fold with respect to Pentecostalism. See the discussion in Chapter 3 above.

8 The situation contrasts with that of Islam where a far stronger sense of core orthodoxy and orthopraxy has developed since the eighteenth century, as intimated in the discussion of the last chapter.

9 Interestingly enough, the context was a case in which representatives of the Ramakrishna Math and Mission wished to be recognized as a separate religion from Hinduism! The court rejected this claim, declaring that the movement wished to do so for political/economic reasons, not because they represented a distinct religion. Many 'authorities' were called upon, almost all of whom denied the plaintiff's claim (Hinduism Today 1995). The list of 'authorities' served as one source for the representative samples that I outline in this section.

10 Compare in this regard the well-known work by Kshiti Mohan Sen published by Penguin in the early 1960s (Sen 1961). Here we have the typical 'historical and textual' approach that, at least until relatively recently, was so prevalent in Western academic visions of Hinduism.

11 Thus, for instance, on 14 March 2003, the banner issues included concern over the Ram temple issue in Ayodhya, and extensive coverage of the killing of Hindus at a temple in Gujarat.

12 The site distinguishes between Hindu organizations and Spiritual organizations (Hindu Students Council 2003, 'temples and organizations' 'home of Hindu organizations'), and most of those indicated in the text fall under the latter category. A close look at the two lists, however, shows that all 'Hindu' and 'Spiritual' organizations are within the broad Hindu orbit that the VHP espouses; and the links to this portion of the site indicate 'Hindu organizations' (as in the reference just given).

Chapter 5

Refusal and appropriation in East Asia

Confucianism and Shinto

Introduction

In addition to the debate about Hinduism in South Asia, East Asia is another prime area for which recent literature (e.g. Fitzgerald 1997; McCutcheon 1997; Paper 1995) has deemed the supposedly 'Western' term, religion, to be inapplicable. Just as for India, this literature argues that using the notion in trying to understand Chinese and Japanese religious culture is misleading and inappropriate, a product of unreflected projection of one's own cultural assumptions on others or an aspect of cultural and political imperialism. As I have been emphasizing, there is certainly much that is cogent in this sort of criticism, especially as regards the history of this region before the modern period. For this modern period, however, the argument can easily become too simplistic and unreflected, itself making unwarranted assumptions and missing a good portion of what has been going on.

That noted, the East Asian regions, especially China and Japan, do present a markedly contrasting case of how the modern idea and social reality of religion have been appropriated. In contrast with the positive construction of Hinduism by people in South Asia, the corresponding Chinese and Japanese elites of the nineteenth and twentieth centuries embarked on a rather different path, not so much of uncomprehending rejection, but definitely of a more negative orientation to the concept and, more importantly, of a refusal to re-imagine what they saw as their most characteristic 'religious' traditions as religions. The Chinese and Japanese cases are, however, only to a limited extent 'the exception that proves the rule'. With respect to the historical construction of the global religious system, particular patterns are not so dominant that the idea of exception really makes any sense. Rather, what we have globally is an array of variations, each of which contributes to the reproduction of the global religious system, and each of which represents a different particularization of it. Among the commonalities in these is the fact that all the variant appropriations *exclude* some things that *could* count as religion analytically speaking, but in practice do not; and *include* a more or less consistent core of religions. In the cases of China and Japan, much of what others, especially people in Western countries, might include, notably Confucianism and Shinto, does not operate practically as one or more religions, or does so only to a very limited extent. The reasons for this difference are only partly a matter of Western projections, impositions and misunderstandings. Only to a certain extent do they reflect the supposed unsuitability of East Asian religio-cultural traditions for such imaginations because, at a limit, all religions can be styled as 'unsuitable'. As critical is the deliberate refusal of people in these East Asian countries to engage in the kind of reconstruction that took place in South Asia and elsewhere. That refusal, however, also includes a practical acceptance of certain religions, notably Buddhism, as religions.

Moving to the more detailed consideration of these East Asian regions, a first section adopts a historical narrative strategy to examine the case of Chinese appropriation and rejection during the nineteenth and twentieth centuries. A second section takes a look at Chinese Buddhism more particularly, and a third focuses on the case of Japan. A final section then reiterates and underscores how these East Asian examples demonstrate the global religious system thesis.

Incorporation and the question of appropriation in nineteenth- and twentieth-century China

In some ways, the nineteenth-century incorporation of China into the then Western-dominated global social system was quite similar to that of other areas. The various Western colonial powers used above all their technological and military superiority to gain a series of concessions from the Chinese imperial state, forcing the signing of treaties that allowed the Westerners to pursue their capitalist economic interests in China, to establish political and military outposts in the treaty ports, and to send their Christian missionaries into various parts of the vast empire. Whenever the Chinese authorities attempted meaningful resistance, their forces were soundly defeated, leading to another round of concessions (see Chesneaux et al. 1976; Fairbank and Liu 1980; Hsu 1995; Spence 1991). China, like other regions, had no practical choice but to accept some form of incorporation. The large question that concerns us here is what that form would be. For, in spite of the similarities with what happened in other regions, the Chinese situation was also unique in decisive ways.

Central among the differences was the size, complexity and longevity of the Chinese imperial system. At the beginning of the nineteenth century, Chinese elites could still see themselves as the heirs of the only truly human civilization, as the leaders of the Middle Kingdom in comparison to which all others were barbarian, not as one nation beside others. The emperor was the Son of Heaven, not just the ruler of the Chinese.

Outsiders, such as the Mongols or the Manchus, could conquer the Chinese territory, but their rule would have to conform to the Chinese model. Unlike the Indians who had already experienced centuries of Muslim suzerainty before the arrival of the British; unlike the Japanese who had been unconquered but isolated before the Meiji Restoration; the Chinese empire encompassed immense territories, over 400 million people, and could be defeated but not conquered. Whatever path incorporation took, it would from the beginning be largely in Chinese hands.

A further factor unique to the Chinese situation was the epochal decline of the Qing dynasty. Western encroachment happened to coincide with imperial decadence. The nineteenth century was not only the time of the Opium Wars and the multiplying treaty ports, it was also a century of significant rebellions in various parts of the empire. The Taiping, especially, but also the Nian and Muslim rebellions were eventually put down by imperial forces, but not before many years and not without devastating losses in the areas concerned. They demonstrated the weakness of the Qing rulers and therefore resulted in severe depletion both in terms of resources and of legitimacy (cf. Chesneaux *et al.* 1976: 38ff). In another era, this dynasty may have toppled even without the arrival of Western gunboats, opium and ideas.

The Qing dynasty did fall in 1911, but not before the imperial state had set in motion a number of important changes. The traditional examination system was abolished in 1905, thus eliminating the key institutional source of the country's traditional elite class. In its place was to be a 'modern' educational system. Already in the late nineteenth century, the imperial government had started setting up new sorts of schools and sending a few students abroad, mainly to Japan, the United States and Europe. As in other areas, the main intent of this and other institutional reforms was to learn from the outsiders what was necessary to allow China to recover its power and thus its greatness. While the imperial system remained, the watchword was, sometimes literally, sometimes in effect, 'Western learning for the applications, Chinese learning for the essentials'. China would borrow content from the West, but not cultural and institutional form. As defeat followed defeat, however, the question became quite different: how much and what kind of Western *form* would have to be adopted to regain Chinese prestige and what precisely were the Chinese *essentials* that should survive? In effect, the Chinese elite and leadership were faced with the question of how to modernize, and this manifestly implied some degree of 'Westernizing' in the sense of adopting ideas, forms and values at that time associated with the West. It is in light of this question that the Chinese attitude to religion and their own religious traditions must be understood.

The main question concerns both the level of ideas and that of institutions. As regards the latter, Chinese society during the late Qing era had plenty of institutions that could fall under the rubric of the modern conception of religion. In this sense, it was not an a-religious society. Beside the imperial cult and the veneration of ancestors, the countryside was dotted with well used temples and shrines of the local, regional, family clan and imperial variety. Ceremony and ritual were an integral part of Chinese lives at all levels. They pervaded official and public structures as much as they did the clandestine, the unofficial and the underworld of *jiang-hu*. Buddhist and Daoist monasteries were plentiful and reasonably healthy (see e.g. Yang 1967). The Christian missionaries had had minimal success, but Muslim communities in certain regions were strong enough to mount significant rebellions. Yet if what one might call the 'stuff' of religion was everywhere present, its position, especially among both the old and new elites of society, was more ambiguous. To understand the fate of the category of religion in modern China and hence its institutional expressions, we must first understand the position and attitude of these elites in late Qing society.

A sizeable portion of the elites in question consisted of the literati, that is, the products of the imperial examination system. They were highly influential, above all as the administrators of the empire, as scholars, but also as privileged local elites. Although they fulfilled various important ritual and ceremonial functions, they were not the sort of religious specialists as were, for instance, the *ulama* in Muslim society, the rabbis of Jewish society, the priests and religious of medieval Europe, the Brahmins of India, or Buddhist monks and nuns. If anything, they were literary specialists and moral generalists, but this did not prevent them from filling a great variety of functions, including military. Their ideal, to the degree that we can speak of a common ideal, was one of individual self-discipline which would generate proper social order by example much more than by technique and knowledge. The key overarching social institutions upon which their influence was based were the imperial state, the imperial bureaucracy and the examination system, all of which disappeared in the early years of the twentieth century. The most powerful cultural elite of late Qing China thus lost its institutional base in the process of Chinese incorporation into the global system. Even if they could have been said to be the carriers of a typical worldview and practice, and even if this life-practice could have been re-formed as a 'Confucian' or Chinese religion, this would have required not only re-imagination, but the construction of more or less new social institutions such as in India, for instance, were provided in part by the colonial structures themselves, in part by new movements and organizations, in part by movements and institutions with an already long history.

Somewhat the reverse situation obtained for those who were clearly religious specialists, that is the Buddhist and Daoist monastics. It is perhaps even too much to call this group members of the elite, for their status was by and large much lower than that of the literati. With the possible exception of a small number of Buddhist monks, few of these were even in a position to guide or seriously influence Chinese response to global incorporation. Their institutional bases, the monasteries, were reasonably healthy throughout the modern period, or at least not in irretrievable decline; but their broader social influence did not match whatever solidity the institutional base had. Indeed, given the imperial government's long-standing penchant for seeking to maintain tight control over monastic institutions, the monks may have had difficulty exercising influence even had they enjoyed higher stature.

Beside the literati and the monks, and of course partially overlapping these, were the new intelligentsia. By the late nineteenth century, this group had already begun to exercise considerable influence. Moreover, given that many of them had received Western or Western-style education in Japan, Europe or America, or had had significant exposure to Western ideas through other means, this group was in the best position to formulate Chinese responses (see Grieder 1981). As a group, they were in fact the ones from whom the most powerful re-imaginings and transformations of Chinese culture came; and therefore, from the perspective of ideas, the group that deserves a fair amount of attention within the present analysis. For the new intelligentsia as well, however, the question of institutional base has to be asked. Typically, what comes into consideration under this heading are publications, voluntary organizations, educational institutions (above all universities) and political parties. Most of these, it will be noted, are also more typically modern, having few or only remote precedents in traditional Chinese culture (cf. Weller 1996; Yang 1967).

Moving to the question of ideas about religion, a not infrequent analysis that one finds in the literature is that the Chinese elite and intellectuals outside the monasteries were, as a group, little inclined to take seriously the sort of belief and practice that is most often meant under the modern concept of religion. Either that or they typically felt strongly that such religion was a highly personal matter not to be made part of a public movement and certainly not a group phenomenon (see e.g. Chan 1978: 217ff.; Smith 1983; Yang 1967: 354ff.). Among the characteristics that compose this negative attitude are, for instance, that the literati and intelligentsia ideally did not believe in the reality of gods, spirits and ancestors as active agents. Ritual practice was for the purposes of self-cultivation, for understanding one's true nature and for upholding the proper this-worldly moral and social order. It was not about actually communicating with super-human partners or another reality logically other than the phenomenal world. Religion as the worship of spirits was something that could at most be allowed the ignorant masses, but it was not for the enlightened elite. Another aspect of this argument is that, with respect to the 'three teachings' (*sanjiao*) from which Westerners derived the category of the 'three religions', although this notion had a long history in China, it was not a major influence among late Qing literati and modernizing intelligentsia: they rather rejected religious Daoism altogether and only accepted aspects of philosophical Daoism and Buddhism (see Brook 1993; Chan 1985; Liang 1959: 115–18).

While such descriptions of elite attitudes cannot be dismissed and undoubtedly formed part of the picture under scrutiny here, they are insufficient in themselves because they argue either from essences or from cultural habits. Both of these are only ways of blocking the question at hand, not of answering it. Essences do not simply exist. Habits change. And in fact, radical transformations of conceptions of indigenous cultural traditions have happened elsewhere, above all, as I have shown, in the West; but also in other non-Western parts of the world such as in India and in Japan. To argue from essence or cultural habit is to miss the key point that the Chinese first had to decide on what was essential and what were defining cultural traits in the modern context. In this respect, their task was the same as that of the Westerners who often acted as their foil, their 'other'. Such defining was and is a positive task requiring a selective (re)construction of 'who we are', and arguably always have been. In tune with this point of departure, therefore, I suggest that a better view of late nineteenth- and twentieth-century Chinese developments with regard to the category of religion must go beyond talk of inherent Chinese cultural tendencies and ask the question of how the category of modern religion fared among the Chinese themselves, how they imagined their cultural traditions with respect to that category and in light of their incorporation into the global system. This brings us back to Chinese elites since they were in position to have a greater effect on the outcome.

In terms of conceptual development, one of the commonplaces in discussions of modern Chinese religion is that, before the later nineteenth century, the Chinese had no indigenous term that meant roughly the same as the modern Western word 'religion'. Prime evidence for this is that, following the Japanese, there arose a Chinese neologism to fill this place. *Zongjiao* was the Chinese equivalent of the Japanese *shukyo*, an originally minor technical Buddhist term pressed into service to translate the Western notion of religion. In the Japanese case, it was first used in treaties between Japan and the West, only gaining consistent usage and wider currency among the Japanese themselves towards the end of the nineteenth century (see Hardacre 1989: 63). The Chinese version apparently established itself thereafter.[1] Of significance at this point in the presentation is that the word clearly carries the hue of the modern sense of religion. Although there is some difference of opinion (see e.g. Yang 1967: 2), both in Japanese and Chinese its literal meaning is close to 'group teaching' or 'sectarian teaching', implying the perspective of a delimited subgroup of society and not something universal.[2] Thus the tension between universal and particular is built into the Japanese and Chinese terms. Moreover, the establishment of the word is symptomatic of a more general appropriation of the category; it is not simply a neologism that indicates something fundamentally alien, inapplicable to Chinese and Japanese realities. In fact, one could argue that the Japanese and Chinese terms help to develop the modern concept in specific directions and not others. They could, for instance, support attitudes to religion that see it essentially as a private, voluntary affair separate from the state or other institutional spheres. I return to this point below.

Beyond the term itself, it is also clear that many if not all of the new intelligentsia had variable but reasonably clear understandings of the idea behind the category along with various of its characteristics. Among the possibilities are that religions form a differentiated sphere in the sense that specific and interrelated institutions express a religion; that religions are therefore systematic, their various aspects relating to each other in a coherent way; that religions have leaders/founders/specialists who, like professionals in any domain, represent the religion in an authoritative way; and that religions have close association with particular nations or peoples. Without question, the clearest early example of one such understanding even before the idea of *zongjiao* achieved wider currency is the effort by Kang Yuwei and his supporters to create a Chinese national and eventually state religion on a Confucian base.

Kang Yuwei's proposals for making Confucianism (*kongjiao,* later also *guojiao* or national religion; or Jensen's (Jensen 1997: 175ff.) suggestive 'Confucianity') the official state religion and styling it as a world religion formally modelled on Christianity, complete with religious specialists and organizations, ultimately failed to capture the imagination and loyalty of very many Chinese; but it shows that the re-imagination of elite cultural traditions in terms of the category of religion was conceivable.[3] Both what Kang proposed and the reasons for its rejection are instructive (Hsiao 1975).

One foundation of Kang's proposal was the transformation of Confucius into a religious founder. According to Kang and the New Text school that he represented, Confucius actually wrote the Classics rather than merely transmitting them: he was the prophetic source of the classical 'revelation' and as such of at least equal status with other founders such as Christ, Buddha or Muhammad. Interpretations like this were not unheard of in Chinese intellectual history (Hsiao 1975: 106), but Kang combined 'Confucius as Prophet' and 'Classics as Scripture' with other features which show that he wanted Confucianism to become a modern religion beside others. The three such features that stand out are his proposal for reform of the Confucian examination system, his attempt to found Confucian 'missionary' organizations, and his push to have Confucianism declared the state religion of China. Before its abolition, Kang wanted to maintain the examination system but change it so that candidates would specialize in different areas. One such specialization would be religious, meaning that some candidates would graduate as 'Confucian priests', while others would become administrators or other specialists (Franke 1968: 32–5). With regard to organizing Confucianism, Kang travelled fairly widely and encouraged the foundation by his followers of Confucian religious organizations or churches that would propagate Confucianism as religion primarily among overseas Chinese,[4] but also among all people. Yet the key organizational effort was the idea that Confucianism should become the official state religion of China. Kang pushed for this 'establishment' of Confucianism both while the Qing were still in power and in the early republican years under Yuan Shihkai. In so doing he was obviously keenly aware that a religion in the modern sense had to have clear institutional and organizational manifestations. These could be voluntary organizations of adherents or state organizations; but a religion could not remain a cultural abstraction, a kind of observer's analytic category. It had to be something socially, and indeed politically, real. In addition, and most important in the present context, Kang considered these religious reforms to be part of much wider reform that was in his opinion necessary if China was to regain its power and take its place in the modern, global world. In this regard, his suggestions in the religious realm can be seen as part of a deliberate modelling on the Japanese strategy, part of which of course included the transformation of Shinto religious culture into a state religion (Howard 1967).

The most frequent judgement on Kang's effort has been to say that it had to fail because it went against what 'Confucianism' actually was, and thus tried to fit Chinese cultural content into a Christian and Western mould. John Shryrock, for instance, accuses Kang and his supporters of attempting 'to read into the ancient literature ideas which they borrowed from Christianity' (Shryrock 1966: 12). This assessment is inadequate in the present context because it assumes that 'borrowing' is somehow illegitimate in a historical context that manifestly called for some kind of creative appropriation. Other critics take a more essentialist path. Wingtsit Chan, for instance, writes with respect to arguments like Kang's that 'all these arguments, reasonable and factual as they are, can only lead to the conclusion that Confucianism is religious, but they do not prove that Confucianism is a religion, certainly *not in the Western sense of an organized church comparable to Buddhism and Taoism*. To this day, the Chinese are practically unanimous in denying Confucianism as a religion' (Chan 1978: 16, my emphasis). This position, far from settling the issue, merely begs the question. Kang Yuwei effectively recognized that Confucianism or *kongjiao* wasn't a religion. The point was to make it one. Moreover, Chan's comment carries unquestioned assumptions which themselves need explanation and which I have italicized: not only is religion a Western concept, organization is the key to belonging to this category;

and, like Kang and most other Chinese intellectuals, Chan has no trouble with slotting Buddhism and Daoism into this category; he refers to these as religions, not just Christianity. To understand the failure of Kang's bid, therefore, we must look more closely at the Chinese reasons for opposing him. Prominent and representative among those who did so was Kang's own early disciple, Liang Qichao.

Although highly influential among his contemporaries, Liang did not maintain a consistent position with regard to the question at hand. Until about 1902, he shared in Kang's enthusiasm for establishing Confucianism as a religion and as a state religion. Thereafter, he went through a period in which he distrusted organized religion as being too likely to engender conflict, only to arrive at a later life position where he saw the motivational aspects of religion as essential, but rather favoured Buddhism as the best religion (Chang 1971; Huang 1972; Levenson 1970). These transformations and their rationale are instructive in the current context because Liang represented well a more general ambiguity and questioning that was occurring among a certain segment of Chinese intellectuals during this entire period.

When Liang parted ways with Kang, he did so both because he was more pessimistic about the role of religion in society and because he felt that what was valuable in the Confucian heritage was not its religious aspects. Like Kang and all other reformers and revolutionaries during this era, Liang's fundamental motivation was to change what was necessary in order that China could become great again. Like Kang, therefore, he sought to adopt and adapt such 'Western' forms as were necessary to accomplish this, but to do it in such a way that the Chinese 'essence' would remain. By the first years of the twentieth century, he had lost confidence in the form of religion because he felt it had created problems for the West. It was manifestly not the path to follow. What was positive about the Confucian heritage for Liang at this time was its 'humanistic' character, its ability to lend cohesive strength to the Chinese people so that they could become a strong nation beside others. Echoing the European experience of the post-Reformation era, organized religion, he felt at the time, was divisive and therefore would militate against this outcome. Put slightly differently, Liang lost confidence in the category of religion for the sake of the category of *nation*, both of them 'Western', but both potentially representing necessary Chinese modernization. Thus another aspect of Liang's criticism of religion at the time was that this was a declining force in the West, and therefore for the Chinese to adopt it would be to lag behind and suffer continued subordination and weakness. One notes that Liang's practical orientation here has little to do with 'essences' as such, and everything to do with the situation that China was facing: the ineluctable incorporation into the global system. When we then look at Liang's subsequent change of heart, we will find the same dynamics at work, only this time the outcome is different with respect to the category that interests us.

Most important in Liang's subsequent change of heart was World War I. With this disaster, the West proved that it was not so clearly superior; that the historical path it had taken led to power, but also to terrible consequences. Close following of the Western path and adoption of its characteristic forms was therefore not necessarily the way for China to go. In response, Liang arrived at a position which saw the West as powerful, but one-sidedly materialistic; whereas China, although materially weak for the moment, was spiritually strong. The proper path for China was to improve upon Western materialism by balancing it with Chinese spiritualism. Such a distinction has not been at all uncommon among non-Western intellectuals over the last two centuries as a way of asserting native cultural value in the face of Western might. The Chinese version of it as represented by Liang and others has its unique features, however.

Chinese spiritual strength did not necessarily mean religion. In fact, Liang reflected a general pattern among those Chinese intellectuals who did not reject the Confucian heritage totally: he saw Confucian philosophy and ethics as superior to religion because it went beyond 'superstition' and thus captured the basic human truth that religions pointed to less clearly. In the theoretical terms I am using here, Liang saw the problem with religion in its core form of communication, in the core elements of a religion. To make of Confucian this-worldly philosophy an other-worldly religion would therefore be to rob it of its unique contribution and insight. The best of Confucianism was therefore a Chinese contribution to the world that neither Western material philosophies nor Western religion could deliver. The later Liang, however, now saw religion again as good, but, as with philosophy, found the Eastern version superior. Religion for Liang was to emotion and motivation what philosophy and ethics were to knowledge; but the best 'religion' of this sort was Buddhism and not a Western one, and this precisely because Buddhism was not other-worldly and 'superstitious' (see Chan 1985: 40–3). Daoism remained condemned throughout Liang's life as misleading superstition.

In short, then, Liang represented a wider tendency among intellectuals deemed more 'conservative' in early twentieth-century China. This tendency saw the value of the Confucian cultural heritage in its this-worldliness and therefore dismissed its capacity to act as the centring focus for imagining an indigenous and unified Chinese religion. Daoism he dismissed almost altogether; and Buddhism, the best exemplification of religion was, aside its Chan branch, a religion that was not Chinese in origin. Liang, like all others, whether Chinese or outside observers, also did not find another name under which this imaginative unification could have proceeded. It is thus that Liang could make the following pronouncement without contradiction:

> [T]here is no religion among the indigenous products of China[;] what makes up Chinese history of religion are mainly the religions introduced from foreign lands . . . Taoism is the only religion indigenous to China . . . but to include it in a Chinese history of religion is indeed a great humiliation.[5]

Significantly, however, he did not reject the concept of religion as inappropriate for China; and he had a fairly clear idea of what counted as religion and what did not. Religion was something real and something important. It just did not constitute something natively Chinese and thus not what made China essentially unique and different.

Even in opposition, however, Liang Qichao's opinion about Kang's effort was generous by comparison with a great many, and probably most, of the early twentieth-century Chinese intelligentsia. For, in the wake of the May Fourth Movement and the subsequent New Culture movement in the 1920s, a more dominant and more negative opinion set in, not only with respect to the notion of religion, but more broadly towards the wider classical heritage. The New Culture group rejected the contemporary value of religion altogether, not only in its Western manifestations, but as such and thus including the 'native religions' like (Chan) Buddhism and Daoism. Their overall attitude towards the classical and scholarly heritage was to consider it obsolete, a prime source of China's 'backwardness' and thus to be replaced, not preserved and hallowed. In the question of modernization versus Westernization, they quite clearly favoured more or less complete Westernization, as they understood the West. With respect to Kang's effort to establish Confucianism as a state religion, all this did for the New Culture intelligentsia was to confirm that heritage as an integral part of the defunct imperial system which had to be swept away if China was to progress. And as concerned religion, these cultural leaders shared the opinion of those Western thinkers who had a significant influence on their thinking. Savants like John Dewey, T. H. Huxley, Bertrand Russell and Herbert Spencer were not known for their high estimation of the role of religion in modern life. New Culture thinkers more or less shared this assumption that modernity implied secularization in the sense of a decline in the importance and influence of religion. They reflected the progressivism and evolutionism so prevalent in Western thinking which located religion in an older stage of evolution, to be swept away by the advance of rationality and science. Thus, presentations of the ideas that dominated the New Culture movement rarely even mention religion (see Chan 1978: 217ff.; cf. Grieder 1981: 203–79, where the subject of religion is hardly even mentioned).

One of the most well-known representatives of the New Culture movement and thus of its orientations was Hu Shi, a man reputed for his agnosticism, but not hostility, towards matters religious and a consistent defender of a liberal modernization that drew few major distinctions between this process and Westernization. Like almost all his contemporaries, Hu was also concerned that China adopt such measures as would enhance its power and position in the world. He saw these as in the interests of progress and fully shared the teleological evolutionism I have just mentioned. And thus, in spite of a temporary conversion to Christianity while he was a young student at Cornell University (Jensen 1997: 369, n. 71), he found a solid place for religion in China's past, but deemed that, both in the present and the past, religion could only serve to block the country's progress towards a 'truly humanistic civilization' (quoted in Jensen 1997: 248). Hu eventually developed a significantly better opinion of the Confucian heritage, but he also rejected the tactic of seeing China as spiritually advanced if materially weak, and indeed was suspicious of all insistence on a native Chinese 'essence'. The idea was that such distinctions and claims only served to preserve non-progressive tendencies in China's development. As concerned both Western and Chinese heritage, whether religious or not, the point was to overcome the irrational, the other-worldly and the non-humanistic in these traditions for the sake of a 'scientific and technological world culture and the spiritual civilization behind it' (de Bary *et al.* 1964: 195).

Further insight into the Chinese appropriation of the category of religion, at least for the pre-1949 period, is available through a brief look at another twentieth-century Chinese intellectual, Liang Shuming. Here we have what in other cultural contexts might have been the perfect re-former of Chinese religious tradition. Early in his life, Liang, like his unrelated namesake, turned to Buddhism as offering the most profound religious insight, yet significantly, perhaps, a highly philosophical form of Buddhism. As an adult, however, he adopted a Confucian outlook that included the highly disciplined life of the traditional Confucian ideal. He looked and behaved as a 'religious sage'. But he also rejected the title of religion for the path he had chosen, using the usual argument that Confucianism was better than religion. His rationale incorporated another dichotomy familiar from other times and places where global incorporation was occurring, namely the difference between particular culture and universal civilization. For Liang, Confucianism represented not just the best and unique in Chinese culture, it was the only truly human approach to the world and to life. To maintain its status as universal rather than merely particular, Liang rejected the limiting category of religion.[6] What is deemed problematic here quite clearly, as in so many other instances around the world, is the compartmentalization and thus secularization implicit in the idea that religion is one domain beside others: that is, the religion/non-religion distinction.

Like Kang and unlike Liang Qichao, Liang Shuming also concentrated on institutional proposals. Unlike Kang, however, Liang's were situated at the other end of the social-structural spectrum. Rather than trying to refashion Chinese society through the state from above, Liang wished to recreate genuine Confucian Chinese society from below. The key to his lifelong effort was rural reconstruction which included a central educational component: the Chinese masses would be taught the previously elite philosophy (parallel to the Vedas being accessible to all Hindus?) and this at the local or communal level. As in traditional Confucian ideal thought, strong social order would be fashioned from the moral example of the sage whose influence would radiate out from his individual and local centre. From here Chinese civilization would resurrect itself and become the centre of the only true civilization that it had always thought of itself as but always failed to be.

In light of his complete dedication to Confucianism, Liang Shuming showed well in what direction this cultural tradition had been taken in twentieth-century China: those who saw it as humanistic, this-worldly and moral philosophy carried the day because this view asserted both Chinese uniqueness and superiority. To refashion it as the centre of a Chinese religion would not have accomplished that distinction and assertion; at least that was the prevailing opinion. As with Liang Qichao, however, the rejection of the religion category did not mean the rejection of all 'Western' categories. Where Liang Qichao and many others might be seen as nationalists, Liang Shuming more or less rejected that category as well, attempting to fashion a more universal one. In this respect, he had far more in common with those who really did carry the day in mid-twentieth century China, the communists. If Liang's scheme for Confucian rural reconstruction bears more than passing similarity to Maoist programmes of cultural revolution and Chinese socialism, that is because both sought to address the question of Chinese global incorporation by resorting to a universalized particularism that was not religion or nation. Liang tried to find this in indigenous and traditional sources; Mao and the communists adapted into Chinese mould another 'Western' category. In the end, Confucianism failed as both a national religion and a universal philosophy. The 'Western' categories of nation and socialism superseded it in both these capacities.

The typical elites who in other parts of the world engaged in the re-imagination of indigenous religio-cultural traditions as one of the religions therefore did not do so in modern China. I have focused on the Confucian tradition, because that would probably have had to form the core of any such reconstructive effort, given its close association with elite imperial culture. As in the case of India and modern Hinduism, it would then have had to find a way of incorporating or claiming much else, including the vast panoply of popular cults and devotions, divination and shamanistic practices, clan religiosity (the 'ancestor cult') and even the shadowy under-world of *jiang hu*. This, of course, did not happen, but what is worth underlining in this refusal is the basis on which it was done. The negative comparison was always Western religion, in particular Western Christianity. China did not have a religion *like that*. And among the key criteria for the rejection was also what I have been arguing is a key feature of the global religious system, namely its core religious elements which take the form of communication with a transcendent realm, whether this be God, spirits, ancestors, the Dao or *sunyata*. Such elements the Chinese elites had no trouble recognizing as religious and even, in systemized form, as religion, *zongjiao*. They did not, however, want to see them as or make them the basis of a self-referential Chinese religious system; they were rather more inclined to keep them in the traditional and negative category, superstition. Correspondingly, no systematizing central binary code could even come into serious consideration. Immortality, enlightenment, even salvation (e.g. in the Western Paradise) were certainly there as positive-pole possibilities, ones identified with *recognized* religions. Something like harmony/disharmony could have, in the abstract, served as such a code for a religion such as Kang's *kongjiao*. Power concepts like *qi* were in wide usage and therefore easily at hand for the imagination of a religious medium. And central programmatic ideas like *Tian* or Heaven were, as the Jesuits among other Western observers had suggested, available for focusing the construction of a programmatic orthodoxy. All this did not happen, however, because those in the historical position to make it happen have not done so. Instead, a long period of attempted rejection set in, one that did not entirely succeed, largely because China had after all by the mid-twentieth century been irrevocably incorporated into the global system. This context we can read even from the orientation of the Chinese communists to religion.

The official policy towards religion in mainland China from 1949 to the present has been one of negation: religion is mostly the opium of the people; eventually it will fade away. In detail, however, there has been far more ambiguity and fluctuation. With the exception of the long Maoist period from 1957 to 1976, the orientation has more or less been one of strategic or grudging acceptance, continuing under some socialist guise directions already present in other forms in the pre-PRC period. This ambiguous attitude is significant for my overall thesis; for even to say it is opium implies a conception of what it is that is supposed to fade away and what it is not. As with the early twentieth-century elites already discussed, it is not that religion is not real and 'out there'; rather, it is that it should not be or that it does not represent the way forward for China. In this post-1949 case, however, we are dealing not with the concept only as viewed by a group of influential but nonetheless non-official intellectuals, but also with an official, government-sanctioned orientation. It is worth looking at this conception more closely since the ambiguity it demonstrates mirrors aspects of the global religious system.

With respect to this question, it is in the post-Maoist period that the more interesting developments occur. Thus, in the *Zongjiao Cidian*, a 1981 dictionary of religion, we still find the typically Marxist definition of religion as a sad illusion which must be overcome (MacInnis 1989: 115f.). The more detailed and concrete view of a 1982 document emanating from the Eleventh Party Congress of the CCP, however, shows us that matters are no longer quite so straightforward. Here the orientation to religion is much more positive, if still very obviously politically motivated and seemingly strategic. 'Document 19' (reprinted in MacInnis 1989: 7–26) implicitly or explicitly presents two sets of important characterizations. On the one hand, embedded in the presentation is the notion that, at root, a religion has three characteristics: it espouses a belief in supernatural beings, it consists in a set of beliefs and practices with relation to those supernatural beings, and it is a group or organized phenomenon. Beyond this general characterization (cf. Yang 1967: 1), the document's conception also exhibits the older 'five characteristics' (first appearing in the 1950s; see MacInnis 1989: 2f.). These are that religion is complex, inherently a phenomenon of the masses, long lasting, with important implications for relations with ethnic groups and with countries around the world (MacInnis 1989: 11). What is significant about this list is that it is manifestly[7] intended to restrict what can count as *legitimate* religions.[7] Some religions are to be recognized for very practical reasons of ethnic and international relations, because they do indeed have a great many adherents, and are unlikely to 'go away' very soon. The policy exhibits a grudging acceptance of an evident social reality that exists both in China and elsewhere. It recognizes a distinct domain which, from the perspective of the state, is subject to regulation. Accordingly, only five religions are discussed as legitimate: Buddhism, Protestantism, Catholicism, Islam, Daoism; and no others. What we have here is obviously a list of the so-called 'world religions' (MacInnis 1989: 23) given official sanction outside the refined atmosphere of religious studies departments. In this regard, although Hinduism and Judaism are not on the list, one suspects that this has everything to do with the party's practical understanding that there are no Hindus in mainland China and that the Jews of Kaifeng are not practitioners of Jewish religion. The list does not have the air of being exhaustive and evidently other religions could count as legitimate (cf. Luo 1991: 32). Yet, for the policy document, other legitimate religions are irrelevant. Religion manifests itself as a delimited set of religions. They are recognized through naming them, not by matching a set of defining characteristics to social phenomena that may qualify as religions.

The Chinese Communist Party is not the only Chinese East Asian agency that tends in this direction. An examination of Taiwanese educational policy reveals a similar list, albeit this time Daoism (*taojiao*) shades over into the category of illegitimate religion and thereby not religion

(Meyer 1987). In this context, Confucianism also has status, but specifically not as a religion. Rather, Confucianism is for the Taiwanese a philosophy and the source of morality, something that all students learn, and not a matter of personal choice either for believing or studying. Here again, we meet the penchant to exclude something from the category of religion explicitly in order to escape the particularism, compartmentalization and voluntariness implied in a concept that is in principle plural. On the mainland, of course, Chinese socialism used to occupy exactly the same position as does Confucianism in these Taiwanese textbooks. Marxist-Maoist philosophy and practice is no more religion than is Confucianism, even though analytically there is no doubt that either could be understood functionally as religious. A further East Asian manifestation of this new solidified concept of religion is to be found in Singapore, which is demographically dominated by ethnic Chinese. Here under Lee Kwan Yew's government, the state pursued a similar educational policy which required all students to study the religion of their choice. Significantly enough, in this case Confucianism was not only one of the choices, but also the choice favoured by the government. In fact, the policy was dropped precisely because not enough students were choosing Confucianism; and other religious groups, notably Christian churches, were using the implied official recognition that the policy gave them to presume to criticize the government on other matters and to make converts (Tamney 1995: 25ff.). Nonetheless, the recognition of the category of religion is clear in this case as well, and once again Confucianism does not quite seem to make it because those who might be considered to be its adherents refuse.

A further significant aspect of the CCP orientation is that it both acknowledges the legitimacy of the category of religion while also considering it to be problematic. A prime purpose of the policy guidelines is precisely to allow the control of religions and religion, while also being able to claim that 'freedom of religion' reigns in China. This is in effect admitting that religion and the religions are 'real' or at least real in their effects, not someone else's mere invention, let alone only a foreign phenomenon. Yet it is also in the character of religion to be problematic and an arena of contestation and the declaration of difference. In this regard, including the characteristics of ethnicity and transnational significance in the five characteristics is important. What the CCP is effectively recognizing is that religion can be, at one and the same time, a dimension of culture and therefore cultural identity, and an independent arena of endeavour (MacInnis 1989: 22). Thus, in spite of the 'self-serving' aspect of this characterization, it does end up according quite well with the way the category of religion gets treated elsewhere in global society, above all in the West. In fact, we might say that the Chinese are ahead in the game because they are explicit about how the category of religion implies a connotation of 'legitimate religion', and this in a way that many Western countries are not. This leads me to a short discussion of the Chinese concept of anti-religion, *xiejiao*, and its Japanese parallel, *jakyo*.

What both these concepts mean is 'evil teaching' or, in the Chinese, more intriguingly, 'heretical teaching' or 'unapproved teaching'. Document 19 deals directly with the difference in a section significantly entitled 'Criminal and Counter-Revolutionary Activities under the Cover of Religion' (MacInnis 1989: 22), implying of course that not all social phenomena that might look like religion will actually count as religion. The section includes within its interdiction 'all superstitious practices which fall outside the scope of religion', 'all banned reactionary secret societies, sorcerers, and witches, without exception', 'those who spread fallacies to deceive and who cheat people of their money', and 'phrenology, fortune telling, and geomancy'. Obviously what falls under these categories is to be determined by those whose job it is to decide what is 'injurious to the national welfare as well as to the life and property of the people'. That evidently includes a great deal of traditional Chinese 'religiosity', including the vast panoply of popular and unofficial forms that any invention of a Chinese religion would have had to include. In addition, the recent proscription of Falun Gong (and *qi gong*) after a period of toleration is instructive, and, moreover, reminiscent of strictly parallel processes in Western countries such as France and Germany. And indeed, the most frequent way of translating *xiejiao* into English, at least as it refers to Falun Gong, is 'cult'. The category of religion, like the societal system that it names, is globally selective. Not everything that could count as religion does so. There is therefore a continuing need for a counter-category, whether a 'secular' one like cult, *xiejiao* or *jakyo*, or an inner religious one like heresy or apostasy.

The role of Chinese Buddhism

Document 19 contains the following justification for the importance of the international character of the world religions it discusses: 'At the present time, contacts with international religious groups are increasing, along with the expansion of our country's other international contacts, a situation which has important significance for extending our country's political influence' (MacInnis 1989: 23). It is quite evident that the official policy of the CCP is to make the People's Republic a major cultural, political and economic force in contemporary world society; and this aim requires dealing with that outside world through a policy other than isolation and rejection. Given the transnational presence and influence of at least four of the five religions that the document discusses, religion is one of the institutional spheres that invites 'friendly contact' across political boundaries. Of course, the CCP wishes to exercise far more control over such transnational links than most Western countries, but the point here is that it sees religion as a distinct sphere in this regard and does so in large part because of the organizational aspect of religion, here the ability of organizations to channel these transnational contacts. Religion thereby represents an opportunity and a danger because, in light of the party's insistence that the political sphere should be supreme over all others, and that the party should be the only legitimate expression of that political sphere, religions can help increase political power by improving China's international image and prestige; but they can also challenge political supremacy if not kept under control.

In this context, Buddhism – and to a lesser extent Daoism – takes on a role quite different from the others because it is both a strong indigenous religion and an extensive global one. Buddhism, in fact, throughout the modern history that I am discussing here, and not just with the CCP, is without doubt the one religious factor that has almost by itself assured that the category of religion would make some self-evident sense to the Chinese elite that have reflected on the matter. Here I repeat the above cited quote from Wing-tsit Chan: 'but they do not prove that Confucianism is a religion, certainly not in the Western sense of an organized church *comparable to Buddhism and Taoism*' (Chan 1978: 16, my emphasis). The characteristic that Chan stresses is organization, the 'group' aspect reflected in the word *zongjiao*, which, as I have mentioned, was borrowed from Buddhism. One can recognize religions primarily by this organizational face, which means in effect that the criteria of what belongs are religious as opposed to national/political, economic, or broadly speaking cultural factors. Organization is here seen as the prime factor through which religions express their difference, from each other and from matters non-religious. Extending Chan's perspective beyond the more narrow question that he was treating in the text cited, organization is an important social structure that allows a religion to appear as such within a country and across countries. Thus, to return to the CCP document, politically motivated as it is – and indeed probably just because of that – it is the transnational factor that in four out of the five religions discussed seals a religion's identity and legitimacy as a religion. Only Daoism does not have this feature; but many other sources, from Liang Qichao to the Taiwanese educational authorities, exclude Daoism from the category. They do so on the basis of its ostensibly 'superstitious' character, yet this might well change to the extent that Daoism acquires a transnationally organized character which would make it far more difficult to dismiss in this fashion. In the other cases, it seems fairly clear that the reach of these religions beyond the Chinese people and the ethnic populations among them contributes significantly to their status as religions. Buddhism, like the two Christianities and Islam, attains its status in this view in part because it has indigenous organizations; and because, as with

Islam, significant ethnic minorities – in the case of Buddhism the Tibetans under the subcategory of Lamaism – identify with the religion. The other half of the designation, however, is the international factor, which is probably why 'tribal religions' do not make it onto the party's list of religions. The difference in each case is that the religion is differentiated from the wider social reality in which people live, that it is in this sense 'reified', regarded as something else and in addition. The other side of the coin, of course, is that Buddhism, like the Christianities and Islam, also thereby attains a certain foreign quality. It comes to be seen as not entirely foreign and not entirely domestic. That status is illustrated in how the same elites that I have discussed viewed Buddhism (Chan 1985). I have already dealt with this question in discussing intellectuals like the two Liangs. For them, as for many members of the modernizing intelligentsia, Buddhism was positively valued, but not precisely as a religion *like the others*. Rather, its utility lay in its character as a useful philosophy which might be able to motivate and unite the Chinese people. The stress was more often on what was perceived as the this-worldly orientation of Buddhist teaching, not on its status as a salvation religion with promises of rewards in a future life.

An analogous tendency and even ambiguity is visible among the Buddhist monks that strove to strengthen Buddhism in China by 'modernizing' it. Here, in the pre-1949 period, Tai Xu undoubtedly stands out as the premier example (Welch 1968). This modernizing monk cuts a strange figure as someone who was both very prominent but ultimately unsuccessful in so many of his endeavours. Tai aimed for the reform of Buddhism in several directions. He tried to institute what were in effect Buddhist seminaries to train monks that would be knowledgeable and representatives of Buddhism the other religious and secular elites would respect. He wanted to unite the various manifestations of Buddhism, above all its Theravada, Mahayana and Vajrayana or Tantric forms into a single religion. He wanted to demonstrate that, as a religion, Buddhism was congenial with modern emphases, especially that it was consonant and even foundational of modern science. The idea was not only to give Buddhism new and vital form in the modern world, but to raise its status as a realm of endeavour of equal value with the manifestly more powerful ones. An integral aspect of his project was to found organizations to help in carrying out these tasks. Notably, these organizational efforts were not to be restricted to national ones: the project had a distinct transnational component. And it is perhaps the failure of these organizations to attain solid institutionalization over longer periods of time that, more than anything else, constituted the failure or at best only very partial success of his movement.

In spite of such meagre results on the domestic front, however, Buddhism has throughout the period under discussion continued to institutionalize itself worldwide as one of the world religions. In this respect the transnational or global aspect is undoubtedly critical. As a religion that its practitioners and carriers recognize as being much more than the religious culture of a particular group, indeed as a religion suitable for all of humanity, Buddhism has not had to depend on the results of such modern re-imagination in one country only. If Tai Xu's efforts did not yield astounding results, Chinese Buddhism could nevertheless benefit in terms of its status as one of the religions by what was going on in a great number of other countries, including the Theravadin countries of South and Southeast Asia, Taiwan, Hong Kong, Japan and of course the various countries of the West.[8] That, of course, contributes to its partial 'foreign-ness', but this in itself can also enhance Buddhism's status as religion to the extent that Chinese 'culture' is conceived as something different.

Japan, State Shinto and religion

Like most other non-European languages, Japanese did not have a word corresponding to the modern Western idea of religion before the nine-teenth century. No more than in China did the development of such a word occur in conjunction with the initial European incursion into Japan, that is, in the case of religion, after the arrival of the Jesuits in the sixteenth century. Instead, less than a century after its introduction, the Tokugawa rulers suppressed Christianity (see e.g. Earhart 1982; Nosco 1996), expelling the foreigners and their ideas. Towards the middle of the nineteenth century, however, aware that isolation was no longer a viable option, the Japanese leaders negotiated treaties with the Westerners, in this case the Americans. For the Japanese versions of those treaties, they needed a word to translate the English word 'religion'; they decided on *shukyo*. Far from catching on immediately, it was not until towards the end of the century that *shukyo* gradually became the accepted word meaning religion (Hardacre 1989).

It was not the treaties, therefore, that 'imposed' the idea on the Japanese. Rather, in their drive to 'modernize', to make themselves a powerful country that could stand up to the Westerners, the Japanese adopted and adapted a number of structures and ideas from their rivals, including the notion of religion and a written state constitution in 1889 that included a provision for 'freedom of religion'. What this 'religion' meant and implied for the Japanese, however, was highly contested, for it embodied the question of how Japanese traditions related to this word. Was there a Japanese religion? Were there Japanese religions? What counted as a religion? Was religion good or bad? To summarize a very complex history, for the Japanese, what was clearly a religion was Christianity (*kirisutokyo*); this was the evident model of a religion and also foreign. Correspondingly, religion, at least for a time, came to be consid-ered as primarily about teaching and belief. Ritual or practice could be separated from the idea of religion. Nonetheless, many Buddhists responded positively to the idea and asserted Buddhism (*bukkyo*) as another religion. Perhaps even more importantly, a number of new religions, like Tenrikyo and Konkokyo, arose claiming freedom and recognition.[9] In that context, it is the concomitant development of what is now known as Shinto that reveals significant particularities in the Japanese understanding and institutionalization of religion.

Before the establishment of the word *shukyo* to mean religion, the word 'Shinto' was also not used with any regularity or consistency to designate a set of indigenous Japanese traditions. That development happened parallel to the promulgation of *shukyo* and points to an indigenous process of constructing Shinto as a re-imagined 'Japanese religion', distinct from, but also parallel to, Buddhism and Christianity especially. With its origins in the eighteenth-century National Learning (Kokugaku) school, there arose already in the early nineteenth century a movement to 'restore' Shinto, lending it more systematized teaching and outfitting it with a more complete set of independent rituals. The movement aspired for Shinto to become the national and state teaching and way of practice. After the Meiji Restoration in 1868, the movement eventually succeeded in its aims, but not before the question of the relation between the co-arising categories of Shinto and *shukyo* was ideologically and institutionally settled. How could one make Shinto *the* national and state religion while taking account of the other – notably Buddhist but also other, sectarian Shinto – claimants to the category of religion? In effect, the solution lay in attempting to make and enforce a double distinction, one between two sorts of Shinto, and a corresponding one between teaching (belief) and ritual (practice). What an eventually dominant segment of the new governing elite and their allies succeeded in doing was to separate two types of Shinto, one 'religious' and one that was not religion. The bases of making this distinction tell us much about what *shukyo* meant and to a large extent still means for the Japanese (see Reader 1991: 1–22). First, what eventually came to be known as Shrine (*Jinja*) or State Shinto was deemed not a religion because it was not a 'group' or 'sect' teaching, meaning that it was not limited to those who voluntarily attached themselves to it. Rather, Shinto was a universal or, what amounted to the same, a *national* teaching (*kokkyo*), about which there could be no sectarian difference of opinion. Second, and strictly related, this non-religion Shinto was not so much about belief as action, and specifically ritual. It was 'orthopraxy' much more than orthodoxy. By contrast, Religious (*Kyoha*) or Sectarian Shinto was a series of recognized and organized Shinto sects which were not national in terms of who was deemed to belong to them and which were identified in terms of distinct teachings with corresponding organizations. With the help of such contrasts, the governing elite during the period from the late nineteenth century to the end of

World War II built up Jinja or State Shinto as a kind of 'civil religion', a nationalist ideology, complete with a vast number of official shrines and ceremonies, that was not a matter of private belief or choice, of 'freedom of religion', but the obligatory expression of patriotism and civic duty (cf. Thal 2002). It was enforced as above and beyond *mere* religion. In this context, *shukyo* groups, including Buddhist, Christian, Shinto and other groups that did not demonstrate their subordination to the overarching and national system were suppressed and labelled 'evil teachings', *jakyo*, in effect as traitorous.

This subordination of religion to a more universal ideology is, of course, neither historically unprecedented nor unique to the modern-century Japanese situation. In imperial and contemporary China, religious sects and movements that did not demonstrate their subordination to the state and its reigning ideology were and are deemed traitorous and dangerous. In ancient Rome, the Christian movement famously opened itself to periodic and severe persecution because it also refused to admit its subordination to a state ideology that sought to enforce its priority. And, as I detail in Chapter 6, various state-supported national ideologies ranging from Indonesian *pancasila* to French *laïcité* claim to provide the universal conditions that determine the limits in which particular religions are to operate. Unlike these latter two, however, nineteenth- and twentieth-century State Shinto was militantly enforced and became the basis of a militaristic and aggressively imperialistic policy on the part of the Japanese government. Perhaps most significant for our purposes here, its active incorporation of a great many existing and invented symbols, shrines and ceremonies that were in form and structure religious from the perspective of the modern differentiated notion of religion amounted to a different sort of refusal of that concept than was the case with the Chinese. The emperor was not just *kami*-like, he was a *kami*. Ise was not just a religious shrine among others; it was a national shrine and a locale for communication deemed quite as political as anything the Diet (parliament) did. Indeed the express aim of the Shinto 'restorationists' was precisely to restore what they perceived as the ancient Japanese unity of ritual and government (*saisei-itchi*) as the foundation of the post-Meiji Restoration state.[10] The typical characteristics of core religious elements, communication between human and 'divine' partners, were thereby to be features of key political communications as well. It is not just that religious orientations, power and communication influenced the operation of the state, some of them *were* state operation. In this respect, the Japanese example can provide a kind of litmus test of systemic differentiation. A country that has an officially favoured and established religion, or one in which religious leaders are influential to the point of being able to affect state policy, does not thereby also de-differentiate religion and politics. When, however, as in Japan up to 1945, the elements, power media and programmatic components of what even in that same country counted as part of some other religions also become incorporated as core elements in the operation of the state itself, then we do have a situation in which religion and the state constitute the same social system. To be sure, Japanese State Shinto was not that different in its style and role from, for instance, the Nazi ideology in early twentieth-century Germany or the Mao cult during the Cultural Revolution period in China. What makes it different and instructive is that it amounted to just the sort of re-imagination and reconstruction of religion that happened in South Asia and was explicitly rejected in China, except that the Japanese fashioned the political system with their efforts rather than a *differentiated* Japanese religion. As such, this Japanese example demonstrates again the historical non-necessity of constructing the function systems in what has come to be the globally dominant way; but the alternative here is not a straightforward refusal. Rather, it is an attempt to draw systemic boundaries along different lines. This effort is also, as we have seen, typical of certain contemporary Islamist movements.

For a while, the Japanese were quite successful in this alternative route. In another, less globalized era, they may have established a fairly long-lasting regional empire. Yet precisely because they not only did this during the contemporary period of intense globalization, but also in response to and with the typically modern strategy of instrumental system construction, the effort led to a relatively rapid clash with an array of global neighbours that their ideology forced them to see in centre/periphery, civilized/barbarian terms. The late nineteenth-century slogan, 'Revere the emperor, expel the foreigner', while appearing to indicate a mere combination of Tokugawa era isolationism with a return to imperial rule, was actually a formula for imperial aggression if only because this slogan also informed the Japanese appropriation of the restless and expansive logic of the modern instrumental function systems. In just these terms of instrumentally systemic power, however, this Japanese strategy of particularization turned out to be a dead end over the longer term. The de-differentiated religio-political system in Japan was partly responsible for this misjudgement: the gods were not just on the side of the Japanese, the gods *were* Japanese. They could not therefore be defeated by mere mortals. And yet, although they ultimately prevailed because they had more systemic resources than the Japanese and could therefore outlast them, the Americans also represented the restless and developmental logic of modern function systems. They enlisted the help of the scientific system with decisive and horrific results, making the Japanese the first and thus far only victims of nuclear weapons, and therewith signalling the end of the Japanese alternative route.

Since the end of World War II, some aspects of how religion is understood and how it is institutionalized in Japan have changed, but others have not. The main change is that, in light of the American-imposed constitution of 1947, 'freedom of religion' has been retained, but Jinja or State Shinto must now operate separately from state support and sanction; and in so doing must be treated like any other religion (see Woodward 1972). In other words Jinja Shinto was to be a *shukyo*, not state. Rather than a 'national teaching', it too had to be treated as a 'sect teaching'. The possibility of a 'national' religion of course still exists. Yet such a religion would have to be voluntary. It would have to be differentiated as one religion among others. In the event, a new national and voluntary religion called Shinto did not develop after 1945. Instead, with the exception of Jinja Shinto now moving into the realm of religion, the particular way that the modern Japanese have engaged in religion construction has continued and prevails. This particularization has three features which, while seemingly uniquely Japanese, are actually of broader application and therefore also useful for understanding aspects of how the global religious system operates. First, in what McFarland has called the 'Rush Hour of the Gods' (McFarland 1967), the post-war era saw the revival, continuation, reformation and foundation of a large number of 'new religions' such as Soka Gakkai, Seicho no Ie or Rissho Kosei-kai. These are sometimes Buddhist, sometimes broadly Shinto, sometimes neither or both. They exist alongside other religions, including Christian ones and older Buddhist or Shinto ones: that is, movements, teachings, practices and organizations that can trace their origins to before the nineteenth century. Today, they are all organized and people belong to them as they would to any other organization. In fact, although only a minority of Japanese belong to one of the new religions, the majority belong to parallel and older Buddhist or Shinto organizations. The largest such organization is the heir to Jinja Shinto, the Association of Shinto Shrines (Jinja Honcho) (Murakami 1980).

If, therefore, we look strictly at the degree of religious organization, then Japan is one of the most organized places in the world. From that perspective, religion in Japan is embodied in a clearly distinct set of social institutions and thereby also constitutes a clearly differentiated societal domain. The communication that these organizations generate is mainly religious communication and is in most cases reflexive or systematized. Organization, however, as elsewhere, is only part of the picture because religious organization is only one way of forming differentiated religion, it is not identical with the construction of religion as a societal system as such. A second notable feature of Japanese religion that might be seen to work in the reverse direction and which continues from the pre-war period is that religious 'belonging' is in a great many cases not exclusive. Typically the total figures for religious adherence far exceed the number for the total population.[11] Given that in so many situations around the world, including Europe, North America and South Asia, counting adherents is a prime technique for asserting the boundaries between religions, this Japanese – and one should also add, Chinese and perhaps even broadly East Asian – way of treating belonging makes religion appear less differentiated there, less of a distinct social domain than it is elsewhere. Yet, as with organization, this feature is also not conclusive and can be misleading. Religion, as a type of social communication, is not simply a matter of 'counting bodies'. Just because Japanese people are not typically exclusive in their religious identification and practice, that does not mean that religion does not operate there as a differentiated social system, any more than that the high degree of religious organization by itself demonstrates the opposite.

A further feature, however, is more consequential in this regard. It concerns again the distinction between ritual and belief, the former being considered not necessarily religious unless it is accompanied by the latter. Accordingly, a great many Japanese participate in an array of recognizably religious rituals, but the majority does not consider that such participation makes them religious people and they do not profess belief in the 'supernatural' realities that give those rituals their religious meaning. From the perspective of the people engaging in the religious communication, therefore, a great deal of what Japanese people do ritually does not for them fall under the category of religion (cf. Hardacre 1989: 143ff.; Reader 1991; Reid 1991: 13f.). It is rather an aspect of their Japanese-ness; which is to say, it is culture, not religion. The understanding of the majority of Japanese people that their belonging to religious organizations and their participation in religious ritual does not make them or their actions religious underscores the degree to which the meaning and belief component, which is to say the way the religious communications are *understood* and *imparted* is important for making such communication religion. For the priests and other religious officials who run the organizations, the temples and the shrines, all this belonging and participation of the public may well be religious in precisely the sense of systematic reproduction of elements with reference to codes, programmes and religious media. Nonetheless, because this understanding is not overwhelmingly shared, the religious system in Japan maintains a socio-structurally nebulous quality. Lest this be thought to stand as proof that religion in this modern sense is in the final analysis but a Western and Christian projection that does not apply well to other parts of the world, it must be pointed out that the situation is analogous in the West, especially in Europe. There the prevailing interpretation has been that religion has seriously weakened in the later twentieth century because so many people no longer participate in regular religious ritual, even though a great many of them still 'belong' to religious organizations, and even believe in the core items of religious programmes. They believe, they often belong, but they do not practise. In Japan, by contrast, the formula is somewhat transposed: the Japanese usually belong, often practise, but a significant majority does not believe. Both combinations have the effect of making religion seem weak or not particularly present. And we can in fact conclude that the religious system, *as differentiated system*, is comparatively weak in both regions. It is less convincing, in light of the parallel situations, to insist on calling one secularization and the other inappropriateness.

Several features of the Japanese appropriation and transformation of the idea of religion are worth underlining because of the parallels in virtually all parts of the world. First, religion and religions self-evidently exist, and they are not all of Western origin or character. Second, religion is something that a person can have or not; it is not an inherent aspect of human existence. Third, much of what analytically could count as religion does not, but falls under another less differentiable category. Fourth, there are both good (or morally neutral) and bad religions. Fifth, religion and culture are not at all tied together in an organic fashion; they may even be contradictory. Religion and religions, in other words, are differentiated social forms. The one area where Japan remains different, and in this respect more like China, is that there religion carries a sectarian or parochial connotation, meaning that for a sizeable portion of the Japanese population, religion is somewhat suspect and narrow, not clearly oriented towards the common good. That attitude has only been confirmed in light of the Aum Shinrikyo affair of the mid-1990s (Kisala and Mullins 2001).

Conclusions: the contingency of the global religious system

Differentiation, as I have indicated more than once, depends on a good amount of reification or objectivation, and this requirement is at the root of the contested nature of this modern category. Put slightly differently, the relatively common assertion that the Chinese are not very religious people, that they in effect have no religion that is typical of them, is just as much a way of using the institutionalized category of religion as a way of doing and declaring difference as is, for instance, the equally common assertion that Islam is not a religion but rather a way of life. In each case, what is at issue is identifying contestation which wishes the basis of identification to be placed beyond relativizing comparison and therefore beyond potentially deconstructive scrutiny.

The Chinese and Japanese modernizing elites of the nineteenth and twentieth centuries both explored different possibilities for conceiving and then institutionalizing the idea of religion in the context of their overall efforts to (re)assert the power of their regions. In each case, they ended up appropriating the category and rejecting it at the same time. Efforts by figures like Kang and Liang aside, the prevailing orientation in mainland China was for a long time a near complete rejection in favour of what was in effect a nationalist ideology in the form of Chinese communism/

socialism. As a result, religion and religions had difficulty institutionalizing themselves as a differentiated system in China, an outcome that may only be changing gradually in the first part of the twenty-first century now that the old ideology has lost most of its conviction. If Taiwan is indicative of what will eventually happen on the mainland, then the future of the religious system in this region looks positive (*The Republic of China Yearbook* 2002: 453ff., Hunter 1991, 1992; Pas 1989). In Japan, the institutionalization of State Shinto up until the end of World War II amounted to a parallel outcome, except that religion and religions were at the same time permitted somewhat of a differentiated existence, but subordinated to the state-centred ideology. In the post-war context, the ambiguities discussed above notwithstanding, modern religion has institutionalized as a much more clearly differentiated domain, notably in the form of the new religions. These will be the subject of analysis in the course of the following chapter because they illustrate the process of 'new' religion formation in the global system and not so much the idea of qualified rejection that has been the focus of this chapter.

The dominant conclusion, then, that follows from the preceding analyses is that the formation of religions as subsystems of a global religious system is indeed a highly contingent affair. Historically and today, it does not necessarily have to happen and it does not have to happen in only certain ways. Formed religions are a definite part of society in East Asian regions, but their construction has taken rather different paths when compared to parallel developments in virtually all other parts of the world, each of which of course demonstrates its own peculiarities. Although on one level this East Asian difference is clearly attributable to the different histories, cultures, social structures, orientations and worldviews that have prevailed here historically, on another level the difference is also one that has been deliberately and historically constructed by local people (especially elites) as they and their regions have incorporated into the global systems that are such a dominant feature of global society. The ways of doing religion and religions in countries like Japan and China evidently diverge from how they are done elsewhere; naively applying the concepts for understanding religion in the West to these regions is both risky and more or less inappropriate. Yet that does not also mean that the religion formation process that is the subject of this book has not taken place there. China and Japan are exceptions; but only in a different way than the United States and Europe.

Notes

1   I have been unable to find works that discuss the Chinese history of this usage systematically. Hardacre (1989: 63) cites several sources to support her contention that the treaty use of *shukyo* did not result in the term's immediate acceptance as a generic Japanese word for religion. This would support Paper's

assertion (1995: 2), one I have heard corroborated by others, that the Chinese version only began to be used at the beginning of the twentieth century. I thank Li Qiang, Wang Jiwu, and Dai Liyong for insightful remarks on this question of the status of *zongjiao*.

2   A Chinese dictionary that traces the meanings of Chinese words mainly used before 1840, *Ci Yuan* (Origins of Words) [Beijing: Shangwu Yinshuguan (Commerce Press), 1986], vol. 2, p. 815, under the entry of '*zongjiao*' explains the term as follows: Buddha's teachings are *jiao*, and his disciples teachings are *zong*; *zong* is therefore a branch school of *jiao*. Together, *zongjiao* means Buddha's teachings plus his first disciples' explanations of Buddha's teachings. I thank Dr Wang Jiwu for verifying this source for me.

3   What C.K. Yang has to say about one previous unsuccessful attempt to do this in late Ming times is instructive for the present argument. Of Wang Chiyuan, the leader of this attempt, Yang writes,

> Wang Ch'i-yuan attempted to promote Confucianism as a religion, regarding Confucius as a prophet sent from Heaven and Confucianism as a comprehensive system that covered all problems concerning 'Heaven and Earth and all things that exist' . . . *Wang's movement was intended explicitly to meet that challenge of the rising tide of Christianity among the intellectuals.*
>
> (Yang 1967: 357, my emphasis)

Significantly perhaps, the movement left little to no trace.

4   See Coppel 1981 for an account of Confucian churches in Indonesia which, while small, still exist today.

5   Quoted in Yang 1967: 5, from Liang's *Complete Collected Works from the Ice-Sipping Studio* (Shanghai, 1929). The longer quote from which I have excerpted the above summarizes well Liang's overall later position as I have tried to present it here.

6   See Alitto 1979. Liang made a tripartite distinction between Western materialism, Chinese culture and Indian culture. The last he believed to be the best form, but for contemporary Chinese circumstances, the operative contrast was between West and East as in Western materialism and Chinese spiritual culture. One is strongly reminded of the sort of neo-Hindu universalism as represented, for instance, by Vivekananda or Radhakrishnan, with the small, but highly significant difference that, unlike the Chinese intellectuals, the latter saw in religion precisely the universal and universalizable category. See Chapter 4 above for discussion.

7   In his introduction to Luo (1991), MacInnis writes of the essays included,

> The nine essays in the appendix use case studies to document the extent of and reasons for revival since 1979 of the five religions: Buddhism, Islam, Daoism, and Catholic and Protestant Christianity. (While passing mention is made of folk religions and superstitious practices, *these are not protected by the constitutional guarantee of freedom of religious belief and so are not included in this research volume.*)

My italics. See the discussion of *xiejiao* below.

8   Dumoulin and Maraldo 1976 provide a modest, if by now seriously outdated, overview. An updating of this effort would require the inclusion of developments in both the traditionally Buddhist regions of the world as well as in Western countries where Buddhism has proved particularly attractive to a not insignificant portion of the population. See e.g. Prebish and Baumann 2002.

9   See the discussion of Japanese New Religions below in Chapter 6.
10   See Murakami 1980: 20ff. Murakami writes,

> The original fountainhead of imperial authority lies in the primitive reli-
> gious function of the emperor as a magical king who is in charge of the
> fertility of rice . . . and who serves as the chief priest for the important rite
> of the harvest festival. In order for the emperor to become the political
> authority of the newborn state featuring centralized authority, revival of
> the emperor's religious authority was indispensable; the revival of the
> policy of unity of ritual and government . . . was an urgent task for the
> new Meiji government in establishing its political authority.
>
> (Murakami 1980: 20)

The echoes of the imperial Chinese situation with its corresponding central
ritual roles for the emperor are evident in this quote, indicating the degree to
which the inability of China to follow the 'Japanese road to modernization'
was at least in part blocked by the requirement that the imperial system had to
be replaced there, not restored. Successful Japanese modernization depended
on maintaining critical continuities as well as making critical changes. This
combination, one might say, is the essence of 'particularizing the universal' in
global society.

11   Reader 1991: 6 cites 1985 figures to the effect that religious belonging to
Shinto, Buddhist and Christian groups totalled about 223 million at a time
when the total population of Japan was only 121 million. The overwhelming
majority of the 'double belongers' were Buddhist and Shinto. See also Inoue
2000.

Chapter 6

New religions, non-institutionalized religiosity and the control of a contested category

Contesting the religious system: issues of boundaries and control

Religion is an ambiguous category, subject to a variety of interpretations and usages. Observing religion as a global societal system has therefore meant dealing with more than a few contested questions, especially those having to do with what counts as religion and what that counting implies. Issues of the boundaries and control of religion arise with some frequency, both for the carriers of religion and for those outside. This chapter deals with areas of dispute that have hitherto received only passing attention, namely how new religions form in the global religious system, and 'religion' that escapes or seeks to escape incorporation in this system. Flowing out of the analysis of these questions, it also deals in more focused fashion with the ways that other systems, especially the political and legal, seek to control religion and religions.

The lines of contestation as regards religion tend to target two sorts of boundary, that between religion and non-religion and that between one religion and another. A closer look at the variety of disputes associated with each of these will serve to situate the relevance of 'new' religion and 'marginal' religion to the present discussion.

The construction of a function system for religion has the consequence of giving religion a sharp social profile, but this also implies greater clarity of that which is not religion. The latter, far from being merely a kind of vague background domain, receives concrete and powerful expression in, among other forms, non-religious function systems with the outcome that differentiation can also result in at least a perceived reduction in the power and importance of religion. The result has been the frequent contestation around the implied limitation of religion to its 'proper sphere'. That includes resistance on the part of carriers of religion to these limitations, but just as importantly attempts by other function systems such as states, courts and scientists to keep religion within these 'proper' bounds, to prevent the 'excessive' interference of religious authority in these other function systems; or to prevent a particular religious authority from imposing itself at all beyond the range of its voluntary adherents. Under this last heading also fall contestations over the convergent form of religion as such. Protesting that a particular set of practices represents 'spirituality' rather than religion is in part arguing against the convergent authority of religion and religions as such; it may also be tantamount to declaring a new religion that seeks to escape the restrictions of all the others. The analyses below of such phenomena as the 'New Age' and 'Aboriginal spirituality' explore this possibility.

The pluralistic nature of the religious system, its segmentary differentiation into religions, makes for analogous disputes, ones in which the boundary between religion and non-religion shades over into that between one religion and another. Under this heading fall contestations over orthodoxy/orthopraxy, namely what is an authentic part of a religion and what is not. Distinctions such as that between religion and apostasy, religion and heresy, religion and superstition, or more generally religion and irreligion are often pressed into service to express such disputes. Quite similar in their structure are conflicts over the boundaries between religions: whether, for instance, a particular religious movement represents an illegitimate aberration or whether it is simply a different religion. These sorts of quarrel are especially relevant for understanding the difficulty that new religions frequently have in gaining acceptance, a consequence that also flows from the comparative lack of clear singularity in the religious system, the fact that worldwide we tend to judge what is religion in comparison with those religions that are familiar and that we already accept, and only in this indirect way with reference to some overarching model. In this respect, invidious distinctions like religion/cult, *zongjiao/xiejiao*, or less severely religion/culture represent attempts to control the proliferation of religions. The seeming necessity of these efforts is, moreover, an indication of the normality and effectiveness of religion in contemporary global society in spite and because of its differentiation. In sum, for some the differentiation of religion implies the undue restriction of religious significance; for others it threatens its uncontrolled proliferation. Indeed, it seems that in all function systems exhibiting segmentary internal differentiation, the problem of 'excessive' unit-multiplication poses itself. One need only think of political separatisms, gold medals at the Olympics or academic disciplines to realize that religion is not unusual in this respect.

The frequency of religious contestation therefore does not cast into doubt the social reality of modern religion and the religious system. What it does show is that this religious system is highly selective in terms of both content and form. Form is of particular importance because modern religion is a particular social form or set of social forms, not some universal human quest that is to be found in all times and places. The recognition or legitimation of new religions and the incorporation or not of marginally but potentially religious communication is from this perspective primarily a question of social form. Phrasing the question in this way avoids dealing with the conundrum of whether something or other *should* count as religion, whether it is *inherently* religious. Instead, we ask only: what has in fact taken the form of religion, what has been historically constructed as religion; and which particular forms does it take? Throughout this book, I have emphasized four systemic forms in this regard, namely interactions (conceived as social networks), organizations, social movements and societal systems. All of these are important for considering the question of new religions and marginal religiousness, but our main attention in the sections that follow focuses on organizations and social movements. The last possibility, taking form through other systems, is more the subject of the final section on controlling religion.

The following sections illustrate these various issues through the brief analysis of selected examples. As was the case for the chapters on exemplary 'world religions', this selection is in part arbitrary and in part a reflection of the different dimensions of the problem under discussion. Accordingly, the illustrations treat two sorts of 'new' religion, those which actually have a longer history but have struggled for recognition as distinct religions, and those which are new since the second half of the twentieth century. Thus I look at Sikhism, the Baha'i faith, and African Traditional Religions under the first heading, Japanese New Religions and Scientology under the second. These examples are primarily located in different regions of global society, they include varying outcomes as concerns gaining broad legitimacy, and they focus both on the contentious religion/non-religion and the religion/religion boundaries. On the whole, all five examples show that 'joining the club' is neither easy nor straightforward, but rather the uncertain outcome of an often long and contentious historical process.

A further set of illustrations then examines what one can call marginal religiousness. These are mostly phenomena which outside observers, especially scholars, have tended to treat as religion, but whose representatives resist that incorporation or have simply not formed their practices as one of the religions. Under this heading, I look more closely at the New Age, North American Aboriginal religion and New World African religions. I also examine the idea of individual *bricolage*, which is to say religiosity that is more or less totally non-institutionalized. From certain perspectives, these all could and sometimes do count as religions; from others they do not reproduce the global religious system. Together, they show very well the ambiguous features of this system, but also its dynamism. Religion, no more than the other systems, is simply a matter of preserving heritages from the past; it is much more about reproducing and expanding a peculiar social modality of the present.

Old new religions: Sikhism, Baha'i and African Traditional Religions

The so-called 'world religions' are all reconstructed and re-imagined religio-cultural complexes that trace their history back over more than a thousand years. This longevity of much of their programmatic cores is a key part of their self-images and of their claims to legitimacy. Each of them includes deeply historical myths of origin which serve as a prime resource for assuring the reflexivity of their programmes and thereby for judging the legitimacy of movements of reform and variation. Their character as 'traditions', in other words, is essential to their identity as religions. Indeed, the characteristic holistic stance of these religions depends in most instances on the claim to be founded in deep historical or mythic time. It is the temporal dimension of the belief in 'eternal' validity. The pluralism of such absolutes is therefore to some degree, if not a problem, then an area of potential ambiguity and contention. In consequence, given that the model for a religion is the combination of all the recognized religions and not some overarching set of features, adding a 'new' religion is consequential for the system as a whole; it changes and challenges the system and does not just expand it. Adding a religion raises the question of the contingency of the entire system, precisely its quality as a humanly constructed social domain. Two symptoms of this property of the religious system are therefore that new religions gain acceptance with difficulty, but that those which can successfully claim roots in time immemorial or at least deep in human history have a comparatively easier time being recognized. As with nations, it is vital for religions to 'have a history', the longer the better. Without it, recognition is an uphill battle at best.

Several of the examples in this chapter illustrate this aspect. In this section, I examine three religions whose carriers have actively and to a large degree successfully sought broad or global acceptance, but for which the road has not been easy or is not complete even today. Sikhism is a religion that seems finally to have gained this status unequivocally at the end of the twentieth century, but the process has been long, largely because its historical roots are 'only' 500 years ago and because another modernly reconstructed religion, Hinduism, has claimed it as a version of itself. The situation of the Baha'i faith is similar, but in certain respects worse: not only is its history only a little over a century old, but the other religion which has claimed it, namely Islam, has usually labelled it as irreligion or heresy, not as part of itself. Finally, African Traditional Religions (ATR), like many 'tribal' religious complexes, have had difficulty establishing their history at all. This once having been achieved, their road to recognition looks to be much smoother since no other established religion has ever claimed them, as part of themselves or as an aberration of themselves. ATR is an example of a 'world religion' (perhaps more than one) which has for clear historical reasons not yet undergone a recognizable and recognized process of invention, of formation explicitly as a religion, but may be doing so now.

Sikhism

The historical context of the Mughal empire witnessed the rise of a number of non-Muslim religious movements that, like the Pushti Marga and Caitanya Vaishnavism, have subsequently become expressions of the Hindu religion. The modernizing and globalizing context of the British suzerainty and then of independent India was instrumental in this second development. Strictly parallel to the emergence and then incorporation of such 'Hindu' religious movements is the story of what was at the beginning just another one of them, but in the second phase struggled successfully to become a separate religion. This is Sikhism. The significance of the Sikh example is therefore in its character as a religio-social movement that shared its conditions of origin with several others and was in many ways much like them; but that in the context of the formation of the modern global religious system took the path of becoming a distinct religion rather than a variation on another reconstructed religion. Sikhism shows not only the comparative difficulty that 'new' or additional religions have in gaining recognition as religions, but just as importantly that the difference between 'subdivision' of a religion and distinct religion is consequential. To reformulate W.C. Smith (see the beginning of Chapter 2), it is a matter of concern for the scholar and the person of faith alike.

The sixteenth-century movement founded by Guru Nanak and developed subsequently under the symbolic aegis of his successors did not conceive itself as a separate religion; such a distinction would have made relatively little sense at that time. What it was was a way of devotion and broader social practice which for at least the first two centuries of its history centred on following the guru and observing certain central precepts such as ritual commensality. If it distinguished itself from anything, it was Islam or the Brahminical system. The early injunctions against caste separation and marrying Muslim women could subsequently be seen as symptoms of either; but the defence of Brahminical conventions by later gurus and the stress on the ineffable oneness of God could be taken as indicating exactly the opposite. The early Sikh movement was indeed a response to a certain historical context, one that included Mughal suzerainty and the importance of caste or jati distinctions. Yet that does not mean that the early version of what we now recognize as Sikhism was from the beginning a religious movement whose self-conception and conception by others was as something different from two clear religious 'others', Hinduism and Islam. The movement's boundaries were not that sharp and not that exclusive (Oberoi 1994: 47ff.).

If the earlier Sikh movement did not found a new religion, as opposed to a new religious movement, neither can we interpret the emergence of the Khalsa at the beginning of the eighteenth century in those terms. Irrespective of the precise conditions of its founding and the undoubtedly dominant presence of this movement among Sikhs in the later eighteenth and nineteenth centuries, the Khalsa did not so much represent a transformation of the entire Sikh movement as the creation of a perhaps more demanding direction among Sikhs, more closely akin to the founding of a religious order like a Sufi *tariqat* than to the launching of a broadly based reformation (McLeod 1989a; Oberoi 1994). What the Khalsa direction eventually provided, and what we can see only with the benefit of historical hindsight, was a gradually developing set of critical programmatic items which were to prove effective symbolic resources in the later nineteenth- and twentieth-century reconstruction and re-imagination of Sikhism as a religion distinct from especially Hinduism and Islam. These include the stress on the outward symbols such as the Five Ks and the Sikh turban, but probably more importantly the Khalsa *rahit* or religious code of belief and conduct (McLeod 1989a: 48ff.). Since one of the key dimensions of religion formation in the modern religious system is the promulgation of one or more programmatic and self-referential orthodoxies/orthopraxies, these and other items such as the importance of the gurdwara, the status of the Golden Temple (Harimandir) and Akal Takht in Amritsar as central holy site, and the Adi Granth as central authoritative sacred writing have afforded the probably inevitable symbolic and conceptual materials for that aspect of the project. The formation of Sikhism as a separate religion and its concomitant 'Khalsa-fication' have thus been of a piece.

As with the invention of Hinduism as one of the religions, the reformation of Sikhism in this direction begins during the British raj, specifically with the Singh Sabha movement of the late nineteenth century (McLeod 1989b: 62ff.; Oberoi 1994: 207ff.). It is in the context of this movement that we hear for the first time the clear enunciation that Sikhs are 'not Hindus'. That statement, of course, only made sense because parallel Hindu movements had for some time been collaborating in the formation of Hinduism over against other religions, especially Islam and Christianity. Aspects of those movements contributed to the urgency and logic of a separate Sikh awareness, for instance when the Arya Samaj applied its 'reconversion' rituals, *shuddhi*, to Sikhs as well as Muslims. Other contributing factors were rooted in British imperial policy such as the census and army recruitment which treated Sikhs as separate and thus helped give the distinction practical consequences outside the area of religious observance. Put somewhat differently, observation by 'others' of Sikhs as distinct helped provide propitious conditions for those tendencies within the Sikh fold which favoured a separatist orientation. That impulse, in the form of various movements of the twentieth century, above all the Akali movement of the 1920s and its politically oriented successors up to the current Khalistan movement, eventuated in the consolidation of distinct national and transnational Sikh organizations such as the Shiromani Gurdwara Parbandhak Committee (SGPC) and the World Sikh Organization, in the development of a more or less definitive Sikh *rahit*, and in the promotion of a distinctly Sikh ritual complex complete with orders of worship and Sikh rites of passage that were reflexively not Hindu (Kapur 1986; Oberoi 1994: 305ff.).

The successful construction of Sikhism further illustrates a number of key points that have arisen in the previous chapters. First, the transition to invention as one of the religions was neither a necessary historical development somehow organic to the nature of the historical Sikh movement, nor was it radically discontinuous with what went before. Sikhism was not created out of nothing in the fevered imaginations of nineteenth-century reformers, nor was it simply the purified continuation of a religion that had existed fully formed since the founding of the Khalsa. Instead the creation of Sikhism was a reformulation of mostly received religio-cultural goods in such a way as to establish more precise boundaries between this specifically religious form and others strictly analogous to it, especially Christianity, Hinduism and Islam. The mutual identification, the fact that all three of these religions generated or reinforced their distinctiveness in the context of nineteenth- and twentieth-century South Asia together, is an integral part of the process. Without it, the identity of Sikhism for Sikhs and for others, just like the identity of the other religions, could not have been realized with anything like the requisite clarity. The self-referential character of a religion needs other religions to help define its form similarly to the way modern states need other states. That mutual identification is not only constitutive of each of these religions, it is thereby also formative of the global religious system as system. Moreover, the Sikh example further illustrates how religion formation is all along its trajectory a matter of contestation, struggle and usually conflict, both internally and externally. Internally, the contest is over the programmatic content of the religion; externally it is a question of recognition as a religion.

The re-formation successfully begun by the Singh Sabha movement in the late nineteenth century did not go uncontested, neither among those who regarded themselves as Sikhs nor even among the core participants in this movement. Included in the controversial questions were the issues of whether Sikhism was really entirely distinct from Hinduism and what was the range of permissible behaviours which allowed one to still count as a Sikh. Those who advocated complete separation more or less won the day. As concerns the broader matter of orthodoxy/orthopraxy, much disagreement still obtains, as in all other religions. Overall, however, the Khalsa identity has gained a dominance significantly greater than was the case before the late nineteenth century (Oberoi 1994). As in a number of other cases examined in this and preceding chapters, the question of recursiveness, of systemic closure, is often translated into one of persons: 'what belongs to Sikhism?' becomes very close to 'who is a Sikh?'(McLeod 1989a, 1989b). While this strategy by no means settles all the contentious issues, like state frontiers, it helps to concretize them.

With regard to external recognition, there political and legal developments have been of particular importance. The Singh Sabha and then the Akali movement in the earlier twentieth century succeeded in having Sikhs recognized by the British colonial government and courts as a distinct religious category. As a result of Akali efforts, the ownership and control of Sikh gurdwaras was transferred to an elected Sikh body, the SGPC, thereby giving critical organizational expression to Sikhism and affording it a quasi-political arm. Thereafter, in the context of the drive for Indian independence from British rule, some Sikhs sought the creation of a separate Sikh state if Muslims and Hindus were to have theirs (Kapur 1986). That effort failed and Sikhs ended up in Hindu-majority India where by the mid-1960s they succeeded in having the boundaries of Punjab redrawn in such a way as to create a Sikh-majority state within the Indian union. Then in the late 1970s and especially after the Indian army's attack on the Sikh holy sites in Amritsar in 1984, the movement for the creation of an independent Khalistan achieved particular prominence and was accompanied by a further consolidation of the Khalsa identity as the core Sikh identity. As has been the case with so many other religions, the coordination of political nationalist and religious identity has resulted in the greater profiling of the religion, not in its dissolution as part of a broad cultural identity. Cultural nationalist movements provide opportunity and resources for religion formation quite as much as religious symbols and resources serve the cause of the nation-state.

In the wake of these highly conflictual events, the recognition by others of Sikhism as a distinct religion has increased. Thus, to take but two examples, in India the ultra-Hindu nationalist organization, the RSS, in spite of claiming Sikhs as members of the Hindu nation, has also admitted publicly that Sikhism is a distinct and separate religion. This was a response to vehement protests on the part of Indian Sikhs that religiously they were not Hindus. Outside India and on a rather different front, in the wake of the violent events of the 1980s, Sikhism now more often than not receives treatment as a separate religion in Western school curricula and in government statistics, whereas in the past it was just as often considered a Hindu variant. To be sure, there remains a measure of ambiguity, as evidenced in the fact that Hindu nationalists still want to claim Sikhs as Hindu and that the Indian constitution implies a similar concatenation (see National Informatics Centre 2001: Article 25, Explanation II, and the discussion below). On the whole, however, the long process of separating Sikhism out of Hinduism and of lending Sikhism a dominant convergent programmatic identity has succeeded, even if it took about a century for this to be accomplished.

Baha'i

The case of the Baha'i faith is in many ways parallel to that of Sikhism. Here as well we have a religious movement that began life within the putative orbit of another religion, Islam, but then in the latter half of the nineteenth century transformed into a self-proclaimed new religion distinct from Islam and all others. Throughout the twentieth century it has been working towards clearer internal convergence through a developed programme and towards outside recognition as one of the 'world religions'. In this latter respect it has also succeeded, at least outside its original Middle Eastern heartland. Beyond such broad similarities, however, the story of Baha'i is also quite different and offers evidence of how very disparate the possible paths to new religion formation are. Baha'i, for instance, by itself does not have nearly as deep a history as Sikhism and therefore has had to develop much more of its programmatic structure during the period of its formation as a religion. Innovations and interpretations proposed as part of this process are thereby visibly more contingent: one cannot argue very easily from origins and original intent because both of these are that much more historically visible. This can give the whole religion more of the appearance of a recent invention as opposed to the carrying on of a time-honoured tradition. In addition, the movement out of which Baha'i emerged, the Iranian Babi movement of the first half of the nineteenth century, was from early on branded an Islamic heresy by dominant Muslim authorities. Its successor, Baha'i, carries the stigma of these origins and has been the subject of periodic suppression in its Iranian heartland both before and after the Islamic revolution of 1979. As a result, the formative periods of Baha'i development occurred, not only 'in exile', but without the movement having its authoritative and demographic centre of gravity in any other place. While that made it comparatively easy for it to fashion itself immediately as a 'world' religion, this de-territorialization also emphasized its de-traditionalized quality. Without either geographical, temporal or even clear 'ethnic' roots, and in the absence of incorporation as a subsystem of an already established religion, this feature of Baha'i has probably contributed to its somewhat more difficult road to 'being taken seriously' as one of the world's religions. It has also removed paths to recognition that other religions, including especially Sikhism, have had immediately at their disposal, namely the possibility of tying religion to nation or of ethno-cultural assertion as vehicles for lending the religion visibility. Put into terms of dialogical globalization theory, Baha'i's path to universalization has not benefited as much as other religions from a prior or concomitant particularization in regional or cultural terms. That said, in several other respects, Baha'i has from early in its development exhibited many of the qualities that would seem to make it a model 'modern religion'. Although it may have lacked in particularizations, it has exhibited strong universalist tendencies, and these qualities are among those that Baha'is themselves have stressed in their quest for world religion recognition. They are worth looking at in a little more detail.[1]

Baha'i's precursor, the Babi movement, was a species of millenarianism not unprecedented in the Twelver or Imami branch of Shi'a Islam. Its founder presented himself as the Bab, the gateway to the soon-to-arrive representative of the hidden Imam. While the reception of his claim was mixed and he was eventually executed as a heretic, his message had deep resonance in Twelver mythology and eschatology. In this form, it was clearly a movement within the programmatic fold of Islam and not something all that new. The subsequent reworking of the movement's impulse by one of his prominent followers, Baha'ullah, did undertake this transformation. Of particular significance here is that this charismatic founder combined the attachment of his followers to his person – he claimed to be the one whom the Bab had announced – with the production and early dissemination of his own writings as authoritative and inspired texts around which a religious programme could be fashioned. Since these texts did not recognize the authority of the corresponding Muslim core, namely the Qur'an and Sunna, let alone the Muslim *Shari'a*, he was effectively founding a new religious direction which could then be developed by his successors and followers into one of the religions. Among the items that Baha'ullah stressed was a concrete global universalism, a politically quietist impulse to unite all religions behind his message. He appealed in writing to the monarchical heads of the world's states for unity and peace, one indication of just how much this religion was forming in a globalizing social context. Abandoning the locally Iranian and theocratic impulses of his predecessor, his orientation was from early on globally universal, with a recognition of the differentiation but interdependence of the religious and the political. Baha'ullah's son and successor, Abdu'l-Baha, continued this direction.

Of particular significance in the developments under Abdu'l-Baha's leadership was the early expansion into the Western world, especially the United States but also Europe (McMullen 2000; Van den Hoonaard 1996). Although one should not overestimate the influence of Western converts on Baha'i, their increasing numbers during the first half of the twentieth century encouraged certain directions rather than others. Included under this heading are the practical universalism of Baha'i, the fact that it is a religion for everyone and not even primarily just for Middle Easterners or Muslims; the corresponding religious liberalism which accepts the validity of other religions, albeit, like Swami Vivekananda's vision of Advaita Vedanta Hinduism, with the proviso that Baha'i expresses the 'highest aims' of them all; and the emphasis on social reconstructionism or engagement in the world. Moreover, the very different outlook of the Westerners, and indeed of other converts in other regions of the world outside Iran and the Middle East, made some kind of unifying authority structure virtually imperative if the Baha'i movement was not to fractionalize and dissipate beyond a recognizable identity. The principal formative contribution of Abdu'l-Baha's successor and last of the Baha'i 'gurus', Shoghi Effendi, responded to this need. Under his leadership, Baha'i became one of the more thoroughly organized religions of the world, and indeed an excellent example of how far organization itself can go to assuring the authoritative convergence and recursiveness of a religious programme.

What Baha'is refer to as the 'Administrative Order' began to be formed in the early 1920s. The two main planks of this structure were Local Spiritual Assemblies and National Spiritual Assemblies which gave Baha'i a hierarchical and geographically based organizational form that could be expanded as missionary efforts and numbers warranted. Relatively early in the process, the Assemblies were legally incorporated, drafted by-laws, and established formal membership requirements for those who wished to participate in their elections. Baha'i became in many senses a formally organized religion and has used this systemic form consistently throughout the twentieth century to develop and enforce its programmatic orthodoxy. During his lifetime, Shoghi Effendi still guaranteed the centre of this authority structure, but thereafter a group of leaders appointed by him, the Hands of the Cause, effectively took over and these have since ceded authority to a permanent rational-legal governing body, the Universal House of Justice, which was established in 1963. Subsequently, other central and functionally oriented administrative bodies have been added (Cole 1998).

The Baha'i administrative structure is deliberately global in its intent, if not in its actual extent, similar to the Roman Catholic diocesan structure. Like the latter, it also has theological justification, being regarded by Baha'is as foreseen and intended by the founder, Baha'ullah; and as the model of a future world government. In this respect, Baha'i sees itself as one of the world religions yet also eschatologically as *the* eventual world religion. Such theologized globalism it shares with a number of other religions and religious movements, but it is perhaps unique in linking its organizational structure so clearly with its universalizing intent.

Baha'i is not strongest in its country of origin, as noted above. The repressive atmosphere of the post-revolutionary Iran has only exacerbated this feature of its distribution. Western countries have been instrumental as sites for the elaboration of the administrative structure and Haifa in Israel remains its symbolic centre. The current Baha'i leadership is also drawn largely from these areas. Yet the demographic strength of the religion is elsewhere, in poorer regions of global society, above all in India. Followers there make up a large if not exactly the majority of Baha'is worldwide. In consequence, there are quite a few Baha'is spread widely around the world. Their religion is highly organized and programmatically convergent to the point of sometimes showing a rather authoritarian face (Cole 1998). Yet Baha'i does not have the sort of incontrovertible recognition by outsiders that, for instance, Sikhism has. Symptomatically, while Western universities can count Bahai's in probably disproportionate numbers among their staff and students, courses on Baha'i are comparatively rare and separate treatment in world religions textbooks equally inconsistent. Such lack of visibility and overt recognition does not amount to rejection, however, except in countries like Iran. Baha'i is mostly accepted. Where it has thus far failed to reach a critical threshold level is not as religion or even as a religion, but as a 'world' religion, as one of those religions that significantly informs the globalized model of a religion. This likely has to do with its low number of adherents worldwide, especially among the more powerful.

African Traditional Religion in Africa

In terms of clearly formed and recognized religions, the African continent is evidently a place where Christianity and Islam dominate. Yet in terms of the practices and beliefs, the communications that exhibit the elemental structure of religion, what usually is called African Traditional Religion is, if not dominant, than at least very broadly present in the sub-Saharan region. Its status as religion, however, is ambiguous and inconsistent. The number of religious movements and religious organizations that have incorporated various features of this African Traditional Religion (ATR) is almost too numerous to count. Their history is long and they have arisen in various places from Ghana to Zambia, from Kenya to South Africa. A great many of these movements and organizations present creative combinations of features from the established world religions like Islam or Christianity, ATR and new prophecies and revelations (see Bennetta 1997; Geschiere 1999; Hackett 1991; Olupana and Nyang 1993; Onwurah 1987). Perhaps the most widespread of these are the African Instituted churches. These movements have in most cases, as we have seen, been accepted as part of Christianity; but in their earlier history they had difficulty being accepted as such, in some measure because they incorporated too many ATR features and styles for the dominant Western Christians. What is comparatively rare among such movements, however, are those which seek deliberately to lend the form of a modern religion to ATR, which is to say to re-imagine and reconstruct ATR explicitly as one or more recognized religions of the global religious system, distinct from others and especially from Christianity and Islam. As we saw in the East Asian case, the reasons for this relative absence may have to do in part with the refusal on the part of its elite potential carriers to engage in such reconstruction, and this for any number of reasons. In the African case it undoubtedly also has a great deal to do with the fact that colonialists, colonizers and their indigenous converts to Christianity or Islam have in the past dismissed ATR as so much superstition, evil religion or simply evidence of barbarism (see Chidester 1996; Peterson 2002); or more positively, as culture, not religion. Since most of the modernizing African intelligentsia of the past century have themselves been adherents of one of the world religions or the hybrid religions, or socialist atheists, movements to reconstruct ATR as independent religion or religions have also lacked a natural group of elite carriers, in particular those also involved in nationalist movements. What would be involved in such a re-imagination and therefore the current status of ATR in the global religious system can in exemplary fashion be read from recent post-apartheid South African efforts to move precisely in this direction.

A prominent proponent of this South African endeavour is University of Cape Town professor Nokuzola Mndende. Aside from public lobbying efforts, in two published articles (Mndende 1998, 1999) she outlines quite clearly what is at issue: the alternative between classifying ATR as religion or culture; the distinction of ATR from other religions, especially Christianity and Islam; the incorporation of ATR as religion in other function systems, in particular the state, law and education; and, less clearly, the internal reconstruction of ATR as a religion. Together her arguments nicely illustrate several of the key dynamics of new religion construction.

Mndende puts forth ATR as the real and actual indigenous religion of black African peoples. The recognized world religions are for her all imports and a product of colonial imposition. Yet far from denigrating these religions as such, she insists rather that ATR be placed on a par with them. Her claim is that most black South Africans practise and adhere to this religion; and that their majority Christian identification is largely strategic, a holdover from colonial and apartheid days when everyone was obliged to appear as an adherent of one of the world religions for practical reasons. In addition, she rejects two alternatives to such recognition: ATR as culture, which she considers a lesser status; and ATR as authentically embodied in the African Indigenous churches (AICs), which she regards as a de-naturing of ATR to make it look like Christianity or another world religion. Mndende and her supporters also insist that recognition include equal status as one of the religions in various inter-faith events, incorporation in the curricula of South African schools, and the elevation of ATR leaders to the same level of public presence and authority as is accorded the leaders of other religions, including the AICs. Where Mndende's argument is less clear is in the matter of the internal structure of ATR. Already the name, African Traditional Religion, points to a problem here. It is singular only in this name and in the idea which it signifies. Corresponding names in African languages are multiple, corresponding to the different linguistic and cultural groups that practise it. The implicit question is then, what exactly belongs to ATR and what does not? What is ATR and what is accretion from another, imported religion? Who speaks for ATR? These abstract questions in other religions receive institutionally concrete, if usually contested, answers. These forms are largely missing in ATR which is one reason why post-liberation black South African leaders have difficulty seeing it on the same plane as other religions or are tempted to classify it elsewhere, such as an undifferentiated aspect of African culture or as something that forms as religion through the AICs.

Seen in this light, Mndende's argument gives us a good example of how the global religious system works, how communication that is from an analytic standpoint obviously religion does not become solidly incorporated into that system unless it is explicitly formed as one of the religions, recognized by outsiders and constructed as such by insiders. Until and unless that happens, like ATR, such religiosity will appear marginal or marginalized, sort of as religion but in critical respects not quite. In the case of ATR, both outside observation as a single religion and internal formation as a single religion has been weak. ATR therefore seems to lack precisely 'systemicity',[2] but what is really missing are the social movements, the organizations and the observation of such convergent form. Mndende is correct in seeing the lack of recognition as a core issue. Yet the deliberate formation, orthodoxification, selection by the ostensible adherents of this religion is also what is largely still missing.

New religions of the twentieth century

The study of new religions in much of the scholarly world has over the last 40 years tended to focus heavily on New Religious Movements (NRMs) that first came to prominence in Western countries, movements like the Unification church, ISKCON (International Society for Krishna Consciousness), or the Church of Scientology. These and many others (for example, Rajneesh Puram/Osho, the Children of God/Family or Soka Gakkai) have their origins in various parts of the world, have spread more or less around the world, and been the subject of much controversy. As such, any one of them could illustrate the sorts of difficulty that are involved in becoming a legitimate 'new' religion in the global religious system. In the following, I select the Church of Scientology, in part because it illustrates certain aspects of the question with particular clarity, in part because it bears no strong relation to one of the already recognized religions.

Although the literature on these NRMs does not ignore their relations to these religions, neither is this question usually seen as particularly important. The focus has rather been on whether these movements are 'religions' and, in that context, on why people join them. The religion/non-religion distinction has been far more central than the religion/religion one. A different set of new religions are in fact better suited to illustrate the latter, namely Japanese New Religions of the same post-war period. Some of these have also been surrounded by controversy, including Soka Gakkai in the 1960s (Brannen 1968; White 1970) and especially Aum Shinrikyo in the 1990s (Kisala and Mullins 2001). Much of the literature has therefore also centred on their legitimacy as religions. Yet what is indicative about this literature is not just this focus, but the fact that a disproportionately large part of all literature on religion in post-war Japan is on these new religions (Inoue 2005; Shimazono 2004). In the context of the global religious system, the reasons for this imbalance are not difficult to discern: the new religions are the greater part of that system as it has particularized itself in Japan. The relation of these religions to the main globally recognized ones therefore tells us much about this peculiarity, and by extension, about the construction of 'new' religions in the global religious system. It is for this reason that I turn first to the Japanese New Religions and only then to Scientology.

Japanese New Religions

One of the more outstanding differences in the observation of Japanese New Religions when compared to the NRMs is that, whereas most of the latter have been conceived as either more or less entirely new or of 'foreign' origin,[3] the former were understood primarily as selective recombinations or developments from religious traditions with a long history in Japan, notably Buddhism and Shinto. Only Christian movements seem to be the exception in this regard (Earhart 1982; Inoue 2000, 2005; Shimazono 2004). Moreover, where the historical narrative of the NRMs usually begins only after World War II with the experiences and activities of founders like Sun Myung Moon and L. Ron Hubbard, the corresponding Japanese story covers the period of Japanese 'modernization' beginning in the mid-nineteenth century, for example with Miki Nakayama's Tenrikyo in the late 1830s. These differences are significant in the present context.

Religious movements like Tenrikyo, Konkokyo and Reiyukai predate the promulgation of the new category of *shukyo*, but they gain their relevance in the narrative from their successful claim to be precisely that once the concept becomes formalized and institutionalized in the late nineteenth century. They and an increasing number thereafter, such as Omotokyo, Soka Gakkai, Seicho no Ie and Rissho Koseikai, to name only some of the more prominent, become the concrete manifestations of the new category in Japan. They, more clearly than long-standing Buddhist orders and temples, not to mention Shinto priesthoods and shrines, manifest *shukyo*; but they are also historically new, *shin*, hence 'new religions' or *shin shukyo*. In the West, by contrast, the new religious movements have not had nearly such a significant role in concretizing the category of religion. That had already been accomplished by the various Christian movements dating back to the Reformation. Instead, the NRMs merely raised the question of additional organized religious forms beside the church, sect and denomination; and helped undermine prevailing understandings of the place of religion in a modern society.

A particular aspect of how the Japanese New Religions accomplished this institutionalization of modern religion deserves special attention, namely the critical role of organization as a dominant social form. As noted in Chapter 5, organized religion is actually quite strong in Japan; the majority belongs to religious organizations and participates at least occasionally in the rituals offered by them. Yet it is precisely the 'religious' character of much of this belonging and participation that is questionable because so many people neither impart nor understand the communication associated with it as religious. In part, that lack of religiousness reflects itself in the possibility and reality of multiple belonging. The new religions offer a sharp contrast in these respects. Their members belong, in most cases exclusively, they engage in explicitly religious practice, and are often highly involved. Such incorporation is usually on a mass scale, meaning among other things that the new religions typically measure their strength in terms of their (lay) membership and participation. Moreover, quite a few of the new religions have carried organization to quite high levels, creating different ones for different categories of members (e.g. youth, women's, men's), horizontal/geographical and vertical/hierarchical ones, and ones for different functions such a businesses and schools, even universities (see e.g. Métraux 1994). Normally one associates such a 'pillarization' strategy with large Western Christian organizations like the Roman Catholic church. This way of giving religion clear and differentiated form is, however, also a hallmark of the Japanese New Religions and shows again how important organization can be and usually is for giving form to religion and here creating new religions in the global religious system.

Two examples can serve as illustration, but will also introduce the question of how these new religions relate to the 'old' ones, above all the 'world religions' as manifested in Japan. Soka Gakkai and Shinnyo-en are both sizeable Buddhist new religions dating from the pre-war era. The former is an expression of Nichiren and the latter of Shingon Buddhism. Until the 1990s, Soka Gakkai still was related formally to the monastic organization, Nichiren Shoshu, but conflicts over authority led to their separation (Métraux 1994). Shinnyo-en maintains its affiliation with the Daigoji monastery of Shingon Buddhism (Shinnyo-en Buddhist Order

2005). Both put stress on lay participation, a feature notably absent from older, more strictly monastic Buddhist orders/organizations. Soka Gakkai is by far the larger and has an elaborate organizational network, including a university. Shinnyo-en is more modest in this respect. Both are actively involved in social issues, and both have an international presence, indicating a claim to universal relevance in terms of the range of people they seek as adherents and the domains of life upon which they claim to have a bearing.

Although not all the Japanese New Religions are thus such clear expressions of one of the globally recognized and constructed religions, Shinnyo-en and Soka Gakkai demonstrate very well how the status of new religion in Japan does not require problematizing the religion/religion boundary: these two new religions are typical in that they are both 'new religions' and Buddhism. To the extent that Buddhism – and, even more clearly, Shinto – as such, as *a* religion, has not been appreciably reconstructed in Japan as a differentiated religion beyond its core monastic expressions, these new religions accomplish precisely that and do so using the social forms typical for other religions in other parts of the world. Their newness is in this form and in the differentiation to which it gives expression. While it would be tempting to declare this feature as something that distinguishes the Japanese way of doing religion as unique, it is probably closer to the mark to say that Japanese New Religions demonstrate with particular clarity a more general feature of how religions are mutually constructed in the global system. In effect, any new religious movement *could become* a new religion. Whether it does so or not is not a matter of its particular characteristics, whether its programmatic content is different enough from others according to a set of abstract criteria. It is rather a question of how both those involved in it and those who observe it from the outside understand that movement. The fluidity and even arbitrariness that this statement suggests is perfectly demonstrated in the Japanese New Religions: they are most often both new and old religions. What does not seem to be a question, however, is whether or not they are religions. The religion/non-religion boundary is the one that they most clearly express and establish. For the contrasting situation as concerns new religions in the global system, I turn again to a Western NRM, Scientology.

Scientology

The Church of Scientology has from its foundation in the 1950s attracted controversy and opposition often to the point of vilification. In recent decades, it has received a fair amount of recognition as a religion in some regions, notably North America; but in other countries like France and Germany, it remains virtually synonymous with 'evil cult' in politics, law, the mass media and among the representatives of the dominant religion

(Kent 1999b; Wilson and Cresswell 1999). This problem of legitimacy endures in spite of consistent efforts by Scientology to defend itself as a religion, and to appear for all the world as a religion (Kent 1999a). The reasons for the rejection or acceptance undoubtedly have much to do with peculiarities of the regions and countries involved, in particular the different ways they have managed religious plurality in general and, correspondingly, the prevailing expectations in each as to the proper place of religions. In other respects, however, the situation of Scientology illustrates some typical features of the global religious system, both in terms of what this church does and does not have or do. Three issues are especially revealing. They have to do with Scientology's deliberate appropriation of the typical mechanisms of other function systems and therefore its perceived 'encroachment' on these systems, with its visible and short history as a religious movement and organization, and with its perceived methods of enforcing its own convergence (see Kent 1999a, 1999b). My contention is that the first of these factors is by far the most important. It demonstrates the degree to which religion as a function system depends significantly on the simultaneous existence of the other function systems against which it appears in profile.

Even a cursory examination of its programmatic self-description shows that Scientology exhibits the typical core features of most of the other recognized religions. In tune with much of what is generally called New Age spirituality, it centres on a transcendentalized concept of the self as the locus of foundational reality and power. Thetans are what in other religions are superempirical or spiritual beings. Scientology's religious practice is centred on a clear variation on the core religious binary code, one that could be styled as liberation/ensnarement. The aim of its core elements, its religious communication, is to attain realization of one's existence as a thetan and thereby gain liberation from the limiting bonds of normal human existence. The process of arriving at this goal is long and arduous, requiring an indeterminate number of stages along the way and thereby constant devotion or engagement in its programmatic practices. The meaning of the practice, like the practice itself, is contained within the Scientological programme. It is self-referential, justified entirely within the terms of the programme itself. Not only does Scientological theology and practice thus resemble that of other religions, notably monastic Buddhism and forms of Hinduism centred on meditative techniques, church representatives positively encourage such comparisons (Kent 1996). They thereby demonstrate not only their requisite religious tolerance and acceptance of religious pluralism, but also their awareness that religious legitimacy in our world depends at least in part on an implicit modelling of new religions on those already established and accepted. If one adds that Scientology deliberately presents itself as a church complete with a professional clergy, and thus as a 'normal' religious organization; that it is in fact highly and visibly organized; and that it actively seeks to demonstrate its normality, one might wonder what all the fuss is about.

Certainly one factor in the difficulty Scientology has in finding legitimation is its recent origins. Dating only from the early 1950s, and with its controversial founder, L. Ron Hubbard, having died only in the 1980s, Scientology is a visibly constructed religion without the deep historical roots that are such a critical aspect of other religions' claim to authenticity. Indeed, a living charismatic founder in contemporary society is probably at least as much of a disadvantage as an advantage. Beside its brief history, one might also locate some of the difficulty in the closed nature of Scientology's upper echelons. Those members who have attained the higher levels of religious status typically live in isolation from outside scrutiny, for example on a ship where only those qualified are permitted. For observers already inclined towards suspicion, such elite secrecy reinforces the idea that Scientology 'has something to hide'. These two factors alone, however, hardly offer a satisfactory picture, especially when one takes into consideration the vehemence of some of the opposition.

Another perhaps more satisfactory way of approaching the issue is to begin by asking under what circumstances already clearly recognized religions also suffer from denial or withdrawal of legitimacy. What is the equivalent for established religions of being accused of being a 'cult'? One such dubious category is without question that of 'fundamentalism', a pejorative label whose laudable opposite is not always that clear. For most outside observers, fundamentalism is a term reserved for religion that is somehow excessive and thereby problematic. It is also a rubric reserved for movements identified with one of the major 'world' religions. Searching for features that all so-called fundamentalisms have in common is not easy, yet one characteristic stands out, namely the express political ambitions of these movements, their goal of having their programmatic religious norms transformed into state regulation and law. Fundamentalism became a globally generalized term for the first time in the context of the rise of the New Christian Right in the United States and the Islamic revolution in Iran, both expressly religio-*political* movements. Since then it has been applied to a wide variety of movements, but most consistently to other religio-political movements of this stripe. Fundamentalisms are from that perspective branded as illegitimate because they are deemed to threaten the structural logic of functional differentiation.

Transposing this analysis to the case of Scientology, the salient system boundaries are not those between religion and the state or the legal system. Scientology is actually a largely apolitical religion. It is rather in relation to a combination of three other systems that the problem lies. These are the economic, the health and, to a lesser extent, the scientific and educational systems. As regards the first, the fact that Scientology has from early on marketed its religious practices in the form of 'fee for service' courses has the effect of commodifying or appearing to commodify communication that is supposed to be religious. It introduces economic criteria into the recursive structures of the religious system. The involvement of money in religion is not the issue; it is rather the apparent use of one set of systemic criteria to structure the core communication of another system. The situation is analogous to the selling of political influence or of indulgences. In the context of functional differentiation, these both appear as 'corruption'. Very much related to this boundary problem, however, is another. In two other systems one finds 'fee for service' arrangements, in the educational system and in the health system. Scientology structures its religious practice a bit like either of these, but the main systemic cross-over is into the health system. Among the best-known stances of the Church of Scientology is its long-standing and concerted opposition to the psychiatric profession which it accuses of being the 'real cult'. Quite aside from the question of which techniques are more effective, presenting one's practices as 'better medicine', if done more than metaphorically, invites the application of the medical code to those practices or, what is the same, the incorporation of Scientological practice into the recursive structures of the medicalized health system (see Kent 1999a). In terms of elements, religious practice becomes diagnosis and treatment, subject to the basic medical code of ill/healthy. Quite aside from the matter of 'medical qualification', this translation is problematic if everyone is by (religious) definition 'ill', and no amount of treatment will result in the status of healthy. While psychiatric technique might sometimes appear to be vulnerable to the second criticism, it generally is not to the first. Accordingly, Scientology, rather than presenting as religion using the code of liberation/ensnarement, appears as medical charlatanism, a fate, by the way, suffered by a great deal in the realm of 'alternative medicine', which itself is therefore not infrequently subject to observation as religion. In this context, it is perhaps indicative that Scientology, virtually from its foundation, has eschewed the sorts of scientific testing of its results, especially its status of 'clear', that is typically applied to medical procedures. Religion in today's world cannot easily be medicine, at least not without inviting delegitimation as religion. Finally, but less severely, Scientology as a religious organization has been among those that do not take kindly to scientific scrutiny, or at any rate scientific research that results in published conclusions contradictory of its religious programme and self-description. Scientology is by no means alone in this regard, as the perils of scientifically scrutinizing the programmatic cores of almost any religion sometimes attest. Yet Scientology has been particularly intolerant in this regard, perhaps the surest symptom of which is that comparatively little research on Scientology is undertaken.

This analysis, of course, in no way undermines Scientology's actual structure as a religion. What it does show is that in the context of a society in which function systems constitute the dominant social divisions, a subsystem of one of them is subject to a variety of what to the carriers of that system may seem to be unjustified and arbitrary 'interferences'. In a nutshell, it appears that at least part of the problem Scientology has with legitimacy and recognition as a religion is that it appears to violate important systemic boundaries, not those between one religion and another, but rather that between religion and non-religion. It is not alone in this respect, sharing its fate with a number of other religious movements both old and new. Hence, in the prevailing classifications for things that appear religious but are not quite recognized as such, Scientology is often slotted, not under fundamentalism, but under cult.

Spirituality as religion(s)

To this point, I have been concentrating on the issue of constructing and recognizing additional, and in that sense new, religions as subsystems of the global religious system. The illustrations provided all deal with cases in which the carriers of the new religions actively pursue these goals. Yet, just as the case of Confucianism (and to a lesser extent Shinto) among the so-called 'world religions' demonstrates how it is possible to refuse such construction and recognition on that scale, so are there cases of potentially 'new' religions for which the carriers eschew or otherwise ignore this direction. Moreover, if categories such as 'cult' or 'heresy' signal the refusal of outsiders to accept a particular religion as legitimate, then the corresponding terms for designating what insiders wish not to fall under that category include above all 'spirituality' and, as in the case of Confucianism, 'culture'. If there are advantages to being recognized as one of the religions, that categorization also carries with it certain restrictions attendant upon differentiation. It is these restrictions, having above all to do with compartmentalization and authority, that are almost always at the source of this kind of refusal. To illustrate what is involved, I deal with two instances of refusal, North American Aboriginal spirituality and New Age spirituality, followed by the more ambiguous cases of New World African religions.

Religious ways of Aboriginal peoples in North America

The case of African Traditional Religion (ATR) gave an example in which representatives of what have sometimes been called 'tribal religions' actively construct these as a religion among the others. The North American case is historically in many ways quite similar to the African: colonizers first denigrated and dismissed local religious cultures, sought to convert the 'heathens' to Christianity, then engaged in a prolonged period of active suppression; but since the middle of the twentieth century there have been concerted movements of revival among Aboriginal peoples including revival of Native religious traditions. Important aspects of this religious revival are different when compared to Africa. On this continent there has been an almost constant stream of religious movements based in or incorporating aspects of ATR. In North America, there has been a similar incidence of 'prophetic' movements since the late eighteenth century (Grant 1984), but very few of them have been large or long lasting; two exceptions have been the Longhouse Religion with its origins in the early nineteenth century (Wallace 1970) and the twentieth-century Native American church (Stewart 1987), both of which borrow heavily from Christianity and are therefore more analogous to the African Instituted churches in Africa. They are both constructed as religions, in particular the Native American church which is both organized and has received legal recognition as a religion (Smith and Snake 1996). The reasons for this difference are of course multidimensional. It is worth speculating, however, whether it is not related to the fact that North American Native peoples have not had at their disposal state-based movements for asserting their identities and thereby their claims to inclusion. 'Nationalism', in other words, has not been able to root itself very well in the assertion of political control over a specific territory. In that context, it becomes more important to maintain ownership of as many cultural particularities as possible, including religious traditions.

However one interprets the difference of context, the result thus far has been that North American Native peoples have for the most part eschewed the reconstruction of their 'spiritual' traditions as religion or religions. This does not mean that observers have failed to identify and analyze Aboriginal traditions as religions (see e.g. Gill 1982; Hultkrantz 1987). Yet, as I have argued for a number of other cases, construction as one of the religions requires more than outside observation of clusters of seemingly religious elements as a religion. Such recognition, while essential, has to be combined with active efforts and formation in this direction by the carriers of the supposed religion itself. The refusal also does not mean that there has not been a revitalization of these traditions and even a certain pan-Indian convergence around key elements of belief and practice. What makes the North American Aboriginal case significant in the current context is that there has been such a revival and at least some convergence without those developments leading to the actual formation of a religion or religions. Comparing it to other cases already discussed, the situation is a bit similar to the promulgation of State Shinto in Japan after the Meiji Restoration or the vision of some Hindu nationalists, except here without the critical implication of the state and the parallel construction of Hinduism and Shinto precisely as religions.

Beside the preservation and reassertion of many particular and varied religious beliefs and practices of the various Aboriginal subgroups in North America, certain elements appear to have become more widespread across different Nations, thereby assuming the status of pan-Indian religious symbols. These include, for example, on the cognitive side, a kind of Native North American monotheism with frequent reference to the Creator; a stress on the four cardinal directions and on the sacred status of the land or the earth (often, 'Mother Earth'; cf. Gill 1987); and an emphasis on how the 'Native' view of the world is fundamentally different from that of the 'white man'. In terms of practices, examples are the prominent role of ritual use of sacred pipes and the burning/smudging of plants like tobacco, sage and sweetgrass; drumming; and purification practices such as the sweat lodge.[4] These commonalities are, however, rarely recursively joined in theological reflections and they stand beside or are even overshadowed by the assertion and acute awareness of the differences among Native religious traditions. This simultaneity points to what is really important here: the revitalization of spiritual or religious traditions is an aspect of cultural, and in that sense national, assertion. To the extent that all Native peoples in North America have experienced a common history of colonization and marginalization vis-à-vis the dominant Euro-North Americans and the power systems that these have carried, their cultural and hence religious identity is similar. It receives common symbolic expression in movements of reassertion. But the stronger identities in this respect are the 'tribal' or 'national' ones and therefore their particular, including religious, expression takes priority.

What is therefore at most ambiguously present in North American Aboriginal spiritual revival is the sort of universalism that is typical of almost all the religions. Symptomatically, even more than in perhaps similar cases such as the Hindu, the Shinto and perhaps most significantly the Jewish, the possibility of outsiders converting to 'Native religion' is more or less non-existent. Indeed, North American Aboriginal people are generally rather dismissive and suspicious of outside pretenders to 'Native spirituality' (Porterfield 1990). While it is definitely possible to convert to Judaism, to Hinduism, or to Shinto in new religions like Omotokyo or Konkokyo, such a purely religious transition happens rarely, if ever, in the Aboriginal case. It is as difficult as 'converting' to being Russian, Chinese or other ethno-cultural identities. North American Aboriginal spirituality has not universalized so as to be subject to various particularizations – except among the Aboriginal peoples themselves.

If one can accept this interpretation, what then is the status of Aboriginal spirituality in the global religious system? Does it reproduce this system? As with this case as a whole, the answer is ambiguous. Based on outsider observation and on the visible homology between revitalized Aboriginal religious traditions and the elements of the more clearly constructed religions, the answer would be yes. If, however, one considers that the construction of the global religious system has depended on and even consists in the (re)construction of religions, then the answer would be no. To understand this equivocal outcome better, one can turn to two further examples, African religions of the New World and the New Age phenomenon.

African religions of the New World

To a large degree, the topic of African religions in the New World is continuous with that of African Traditional Religions in Africa itself. There is much continuity of programmatic material and, of course, the majority of practitioners of the New World varieties are themselves of African descent. Moreover, within the New World movements, continuity with religious traditions of Africa is usually quite important and part of their self-image. That said, New World African religions like Candomblé, Santería, Umbanda, Voudon and Rastafarianism are also quite different, not always in content as is the case with Rastafarianism, but more critically in terms of form.

Like the religio-cultural traditions of various Aboriginal – including, of course, African – peoples around the world, those of New World Africans have in the past been the subject of much denigration by outside observers as 'primitive', as 'barbarism', as magic, as superstition, and similar epithets. A critical additional factor in this case, however, has been that those who brought these traditions to the Americas originally arrived as slaves, and as such were forbidden by their masters from practising their ancestral cults lest these be the basis of solidarity and resistance. The imposition of Christianity, whether Protestant or Catholic, was in many respects the obverse of that prohibition. One widespread result in the Catholic regions was that the Africans and their descendants for the longest time even after the official end of slavery in the nineteenth century established a kind of parallelism between elements of the Catholic programme and their African traditions. Beside some borrowing from Christian ritual, this tendency expressed itself mainly in the matching of particular Christian saints with corresponding African deities. Under the repressive conditions of slavery, the latter could be worshipped as these saints without the knowledge of the overseers. The carrying on of African traditions thus received a clandestine face, such that it seemed to many observers that two religious traditions were being artificially juxtaposed, with the Catholic presenting the public face of what was secretly African. The notion of syncretism expresses this idea: the artificial melding of not only different but supposedly incommensurate religious traditions. While much ink has been spilled over whether this term is appropriate or derogatory, the most intriguing aspect in the current context is the way the term assumes the existence of the entities that are ostensibly contradictory. Not only is Catholicism assumed to be an internally consistent and self-referential religion, so are by implication the African religious systems. The label 'syncretism', in other words, signals the passage in the eye of the observer of the African traditions from the category of amorphous and benighted superstition to at least the implicit status of a religion. Unsurprisingly, therefore, the criticism of the word as an accurate description of what the practitioners had been doing gains credence at exactly the same time as both inside and outside observers begin to re-imagine the African material as one or more religions beside the others.

The increasingly solidified theologization, orthodoxification and organization of Brazilian Candomblé offers an instructive example. As Roberto Motta (1998) puts it, over the past few decades Candomblé has been undergoing a process of 'churchifying' and even 'canon formation', by which he means both the repudiation of previous 'syncretic dependence' (45) on Catholicism and the development of an independent African, more especially Yoruba, theology. Of particular note in this process is that it has involved the collaboration of outside observers, notably anthropologists, and internal leaders of individual Candomblé organized centres or *terreiros*. These leaders and their allies claim to speak for and defend an authentic and long-standing African religion which is both separate from other religions and equal in authenticity to them. By all reports, they are increasingly successful in having these claims accepted by others, including more and more of the Candomblé practitioners and the Brazilian state. Should this development continue, we may be witnessing elements of a much broader re-imagination, namely that several religious movements of New World African origin, such as Cuban Santería, Haitian Vodoun, Brazilian Umbanda and others, will come to see themselves and even go so far as to organize themselves as variations of a single African religion. This process has already been happening among academic observers (see e.g. the contributions in Clarke 1998); it remains for it to become the undertaking of the carriers of these religious directions.

Whatever the future holds for these other traditions, developments in Candomblé can be seen as symptomatic of the increasing incorporation of New World African religious forms into the global religious system. In spite of the lesser degree of deliberate, recursive construction, the other New World African traditions are for the most part understood and imparted by their practitioners as religion, or at least these do not reject that observation on the part of outsiders, which accordingly is much more positive than in the past: Rastafarianism, Voudon and the others are increasingly seen as religion – indeed as religions – and not as one of the negative 'other' categories like superstition or, in the older suspect sense, syncretism. While these religions often lack representative organization, they are solidly institutionalized in various areas as social networks of interaction and as social movements; and, by that token, increasingly as distinct religions. The recent developments in Candomblé merely demonstrate what steps may yet be taken (or deliberately eschewed) in this direction.

New Age spirituality

New Age is to a large extent an outside observer's term. Depending on the author, it encompasses a wider or narrower range of phenomena, many of the carriers of which would certainly refuse the label of religion for their activity, some of whom would even reject the word 'spirituality'. Overall, however, spirituality is a very frequently occurring self-description (see e.g. Batstone 2001) and certainly the characteristics of the most typical communications deemed to be New Age indicate that we are dealing with religious communication. Whether it be styled as the 'inner self', ancient or extraterrestrial 'masters', the universe or the spirits of dead people, core communication involves non-empirical actors who are the source of ultimate power and knowledge (Hammer 2001; Hanegraaff 2002; Heelas 1996). The widespread scholarly and mass media tendency to regard it as religion is therefore understandable, even if this by itself does not accomplish the incorporation of New Age into the religious system. The structure and systemic form of New Age communication, however, go some distance to accomplishing exactly that.

The primary observational access point to the New Age phenomenon is a vast array of publications and the authors of these works who serve as the equivalent of the movement's professionals or virtuosi. Much of the scientific literature on the New Age uses these as their data sources. Through them one discovers a fairly convergent programmatic vision which, like any of the institutionalized religions, is nonetheless variable in its details. In a nutshell, what many call New Age is a religious complex rooted in Western esoteric traditions such as exemplified, for instance, in hermeticism, spiritualism, Swedenborgian currents, Theosophy, New Thought and Transcendentalism, but strategically combined with religio-cultural material drawn from Chinese, Indian and North American Aboriginal resources (Hanegraaff 2002; Heelas 1996; Rothstein 2001). The programmatic unity of New Age consists in the belief that this imaginative combination reflects an underlying unity of 'all religions'; that the various religious currents thus synthesized are different strands and versions of the same eternal truth and structure of reality. New Age theology from this perspective is therefore quite similar to the neo-Vedantic vision of Hinduism as espoused, for instance, by Vivekananda. New Age, however, has thus far many fewer movements and organizations which include in their aims the fostering of unity among New Age currents so that the participants will conceive of their communication and structure their communication as a self-referential manifestation of the same thing. It is the self-identification and its effect on New Age communication that is relatively weak when compared to the more clearly institutionalized and formed religions.

The comparatively unformed nature of New Age as religion reflects itself in both the programmatic and social system aspects of the phenomenon. A fairly consistent characteristic of New Age visions is their emphasis on the individual self as the locus of spiritual or religious authenticity and authority. New Age is what Poewe and Hexham have styled as 'shumanistic', centred on the idea that individual humans are the locus of divinity and thus transcending ultimacy; and that the difficulty is that most of us are ignorant of this fact (Hexham and Poewe 1997). The religious code takes the form roughly of spiritual empowerment/obstruction, one similar to religions such as Hinduism, Buddhism and Daoism (to the degree that this is formed as a religion), but also somewhat different in its emphasis on empowerment as primarily this-worldly capability. Diverse and eclectic as New Age manifestations are, they almost all tilt towards offering a this-worldly gnosis or capability to be more powerful in 'this life'. It is probably for this reason that neo-Paganism tends to get associated with the New Age in spite of the protests of so many of its adherents that it is something different. Both religious movements stress this personal empowerment, whether this is conceptualized as 'magick' or some other variation on religious empowerment.

The emphasis on the individual as locus of religious authority and authenticity reflects itself in the relative formlessness of New Age, that characteristic which casts some doubt as to whether or not it operates as religion or as one or more religions in today's world. To a large extent, New Age is what Stark and Bainbridge have called an 'audience cult' (Stark and Bainbridge 1985), essentially an unorganized communicative network in which people rarely if ever meet face to face or belong to an organization or networked community. It also has many 'client cult' manifestations in which practitioners avail themselves on an occasional basis of the service of a New Age provider such as the authors of books, organizers of workshops, mediums, therapists and the like. In the social system terms that I am using here, this characteristic is symptomatic of the prevailing form of New Age as a convergent social form, and that is as a social movement. It is the combination of a programmatic and convergent ideology (theology) and irregular but also reasonably frequent events that lend New Age its identity. And like most social movements, this means a fair degree of amorphousness since there are no sufficiently powerful social systems which can claim to represent the unity within all the variation. New Age makes itself manifest in the publications, as mass media stories/programmes, in the periodic events such as exhibitions, workshops, fairs, public events, and through countless publications. To an extent it also has associated with it a whole array of organized forms, mainly those instances in which New Age providers have founded organizations like centres, institutes, shops and clinics which, like temples in other religions, are places where New Age communication can be concentrated and offered on a regular basis. As concerns the incorporation or embodiment of New Age in non-religious function systems, the main ones that come into view are the systems for mass media, for art and entertainment, and for economy. From theosophically oriented painting such as that of Mondrian and Kandinsky earlier in the twentieth century, to magazines, films and television shows that portray New Age themes, to what one might call the 'spirituality industry' of books, therapies, services, workshops and a wide range of religious products, the movement has a serious presence in these systems. Where it is still more or less absent is in the critical systems for politics, law and education, institutions in which all the more clearly formed religions are explicitly present or actively seek recognition. This is one of the ways in which, socio-structurally speaking, New Age distinguishes itself from its close cousin among Western religious movements, namely the neo-Pagans or Wiccans. Various versions of this movement, while trying to avoid organization and the institutionalization of convergent authority, nonetheless seek the official recognition for their religion that one typically finds through the legal and political systems.

Different observers include a great diversity of phenomena under the heading of New Age; and, as noted, its practitioners frequently reject the category of religion for what it is that they do. In that light, both the singularity of New Age and whether it contributes to the effective reproduction of the religious function system of global society are questions that need some further scrutiny. Is it religion and is it a religion?

As noted briefly above, if we regard all the things that count as New Age from the perspective of the character of its most typical communications, then it is at least religious. Its carriers' deliberate and recurring use of spirituality to designate their concern points in the same direction because, as I have argued, this sort of distinguishing concept – like cult, sect, magic, superstition, heresy, apostasy and the like – is actually better seen as a symptom of contestation over the range of religious influence and over religious programmes than it is the demarcation of non-religion. Spirituality is a term which seeks escape from the perceived limitations of religion constructed as one of the function systems. It tries to steer between the social form of religion with its peculiar restrictions and the social form of other function systems, notably capitalist economy, art, empirical science, and especially medicalized healing. These are all the realms of the 'material' as opposed to the 'spiritual'. Understandably, New Age communication therefore sees itself as an alternative or at least as a necessary addition to these modalities, as is typical for religion in today's society. In the face of the power and the difference of the other systems, religion asserts its importance as addressing indispensable concerns that the others ignore in their materiality, and as oriented towards that which is the foundation of all these other domains. It makes for 'real' healing, 'real' knowledge, 'real' art and, for some, 'real' economic success. The 'this-worldly' orientation of New Age makes these almost oppositional and even anti-systemic stands that much more evident (cf. Beyer 1998b). As long as we do not insist that all religion has to look like those religions which stress other-worldliness, the character of New Age as religion can appear as only too evident.

Arguing for the social reality of New Age as religion is not, however, the same as claiming that it is a singular religion, self- and other-identified as such, featuring the programmatic convergence and recursiveness of its communications. As regards this question, it should first be admitted that scientific and mass media observation as exactly that does have some effect. Observing it as singular from the perspective of other function systems can go some way to constructing that singularity. Yet, without the corresponding reflexive efforts on the part of its carriers, those typically engaged in its communication, it is unlikely that socially operative convergence as a single religion with variations will occur. Whether such self-identification is occurring in anything like sufficiently effective ways can remain an open question. It may happen and it may not. Perhaps more likely is the continued hiving off of self-identified religions from what one might call the New Age core, religions like Wicca and Scientology. Just as 'new' religions like Baha'i and Sikhism have formed out of the core of other religions, or at least as other religions were also forming, so a plurality of religions which owe more or less to what we call New Age may be the future result. Irrespective of which is the eventual outcome, the social movement that we observe as New Age does contribute to the reproduction of the global religious system in this way, as a social movement which prominently features religious communication. The question is not whether it does, but rather in what precise social form it does.

The question of de-institutionalized religion

These various examples of 'religious complexes' that are somewhat formed as religion(s), but in most cases not as clearly as the more solidly constructed and recognized religions of the previous sections and chapters, point logically to a related but more general question regarding the thesis of a global religious system: what about the possibility and, according to not a few observers, the increasing social presence of more or less entirely de-institutionalized religiosity? If the examples discussed in the previous section are illustrations of religions that are ambiguously constructed as such and that sometimes avail themselves deliberately of terms like 'spirituality' or 'culture' to resist incorporation as religions, how is it with religious phenomena in our world that appear to be not even partially included in formed or even ambiguously formed religions? In keeping with the basic orientation I have adopted in this book, this is not a question about social forms that are not formed as religion but can be seen to 'function' like religion, things like Marxism, nationalism, ice hockey or golf.

Rather, it is about communication that has the characteristics of elements of the substantive religious system, but is not meaningfully included in that system.

From the theoretical perspective that informs my efforts here, an answer to this question has two sides. One looks at the type of system involved, the other at the degree to which communications are or are not elements of a religious system. The two sides are related: if a communication is not an element in a religious system, then of what system is it an element?

The literature on this subject is actually quite old, dating back at least to Ernst Troeltsch's category of mysticism (1931) and theologically at least to Friedrich Schleiermacher (cf. Firsching and Schlegel 1998). More recent contributions include above all Thomas Luckmann's invisible religion thesis and his concept of *bricolage* (1967), Robert Bellah *et al.* and their notion of 'Sheilaism' (1985), the suggestion of the increasing dominance of a 'spiritual marketplace' (Roof 1999) and even the thesis that we are witnessing a 'spiritual revolution' (Heelas *et al.* 2005). What all these conceptualizations have in common is the 'subjectivization' of religion, the idea that religiosity is less and less located in authoritative and 'outside' religious institutions and more and more within the 'internal' control and consciousness of individuals. To the degree that such religiosity or spirituality involves the sort of religious communication that is the focus of the present analysis, it would be highly personal communication, perhaps involving only imparting and understanding attributed by the human individuals to themselves and some postulated transcendent partner, however conceived. Such communication would be marginally social, let alone marginally religion. Its status as either of these would therefore depend on how this communication is incorporated into actual social systems of whatever sort. All communication, after all, assumes the consciousness of individual human beings. It cannot occur without them. But consciousness and communication are not the same. The former is reproductive of psychological systems; only the latter reproduces social systems. The question that must be asked with respect to this subjectivization of the religious, then, is: what are the implications for social systems that reproduce religion?

To answer this question, I take the examples from the literature just mentioned. It may be that mysticism, *bricolage* or Sheilaism are highly individualized, that the perceived locus of authority, authenticity and convergence of religious communications is the individual. That, however, is just another way of asserting that this locus is not somewhere else, namely in a social system, usually of a very specific sort like a religious organization. Yet one must be careful not to confuse the set of communications in which an individual participates and social systems. 'Sheila' (or 'Bruce') may well engage in a *bricolage* of religious beliefs and practices that is unique to her, but that involvement may actually also help reproduce several religious systems. Exclusive religious involvement by individuals is not necessary to constitute religious systems, no more than an economic enterprise like a business corporation requires that its customers purchase exclusively from them or even that a person be the citizen or resident of only one state. The requirement of religious exclusivity is a feature of certain religious programmes, not a characteristic of religious systems as such. If 'Sheila' engages in Episcopalian ritual in the morning, participates in a Wiccan coven in the afternoon, and buys a New Age publication in the evening, then she is helping to reproduce the religious systems that each of these represents: the Episcopalian church, the Wiccan movement or the New Age organization/movement. Alternatively, however, 'Sheila' may invent her own religious (or spiritual) practice and belief of which only she is aware and in which only she participates. As noted, such (marginal) communication cannot be said to reproduce any actual religious system, any more than growing vegetables in one's garden and eating them reproduces the economic system. A third possibility is more interesting in the present context and hovers between the other two. 'Sheila' may participate in a unique, in Troeltsch's terms, 'mystical' group that she perhaps helped found and that, like an informal book club that meets once a month, may only last a few years before its members move on to other things. Such activity reproduces interaction systems that clearly have a religious character, but their contribution to the reproduction of any larger religious system is marginal, if only because of their minimal scope.

This sort of 'house church' spirituality poses the question of de-institutionalized religiosity most sharply because it represents the endless multiplication of increasingly small and often evanescent religious interaction networks, none of which achieves much more than very local scope and few of which are in sufficient contact with one another to eventuate in anything larger and more permanent. If the religious system in global society or even in a region of global society came to be dominated by this sort of religiosity, then that would effectively spell the end of that system. It would not have sufficient convergence on a broad enough scale to constitute anything more than local interaction networks, even if the 'locality' were on the Internet. Put another way, the religious system cannot stand the endless production of religious subsystems: if there are too many 'religions', then the religious system dissipates to the point of non-existence as a system. Just as there cannot be too many states, the number of business enterprises that can survive is limited; academic disciplines, sports and even schools cannot multiply endlessly if there are to be global political, economic, scientific, sports and educational systems; and so is it with religion. The question then becomes: what prevents such endless religious multiplication from happening; or is it in fact happening? It is to a partial answer to that question that I now turn.

Freedom and control of religion: an obverse/reverse relationship

One of the ways that religion and religions gain form in global society is through thematization and thereby selective incorporation in the processes of other function systems beside the religious. Several systems help shape religion in this fashion, as I have noted. Each of these is worthy of separate attention, not least because each is a periodic and persistent area of contention between the carriers of these systems and those of religion. Religious representatives attempt to have religion introduced into curricula and indeed to exercise control over schools, seek to create and control religious programming, and worry about how artists treat religious themes and symbols. What is at issue in all these cases is control over the image of religion, the range of its influence, and over resources for generating religious communication. Put briefly, these are matters of different systemic interests; they are a key aspect of how the formation of all the function systems depends on mutual differentiation and on a corresponding mutual identification.

Of all such inter-systemic relations, the two that are the most salient as concerns the boundaries and range of religion are those with the political and legal systems. As loci of regulation and law, it is here that questions such as what counts as religion and what are the limits of religious power become the subject of authoritative and collectively binding communication beyond the range of voluntary adherents. Above and in previous chapters, I have paid attention to the ways that religion seeks to avail itself of these systems (see also Beyer 1994). Here it is important to examine the reverse direction, namely the control of religion in and through these other systems. Somewhat ironically, the most frequent way of discussing this topic is under the heading of 'freedom of religion'. The irony lies in the fact that, while almost all countries in the world today officially declare that their citizens enjoy freedom of religion and write this freedom into their laws (especially constitutions), *none* of them actually allows the unfettered exercise of that freedom. In fact, all of them seek overtly to control and to restrict that freedom (Boyle and Sheen 1997). They thereby reinforce, whether overtly or not, the local hegemony of one religion, a small set of religions, or even a formally atheistic or other national ideology; but more critically they contribute to circumscribing the religious field as such.

The question of freedom of religion has two dimensions which correspond to the two main lines of contestation, the religion/religion distinction and that between religion and non-religion. Accordingly, one can speak of two kinds of religious freedom. *Freedom of religion* concerns the range of religious power and influence as such, and thus its ability to determine the lives of its adherents and to affect the processes of non-religious systems. *Freedom of religions* pertains to what is allowed to count as one of the legitimate religions whose adherents can then effectively claim to exercise their religion freely. All states and legal systems set limits in both regards. Far from singling religion out for special treatment, however, such restriction applies to all systems: modern states have a penchant for regulating everything whether that is law, education, sport, art, science, families, individual life or whatever else. Religion is simply not an exception. To be sure, religions do typically claim a very broad relevance to all aspects of human and social life and therefore both the actual reach of its influence and the religions that can effectively put this range into operation have to be limited. If the foundational orientations of religion determine everything, then that will undermine the other systems; if what counts as such a foundational orientation has no limits, then either the range of influence of any of them will have to be limited severely or the structure of the religious systems itself will be undermined. Both directions are distinct possibilities, but one should not be surprised if states and legal systems apply their typical modes of communication to prevent them. In any case, a similar analysis applies to all other systems, perhaps the classic case being that of the political and legal frameworks without which the modern capitalist economy has difficulty operating, and the corresponding tendency of states and laws to prevent the effective commodification of everything.

Any number of examples can serve to illustrate the nature of this political and legal control of religion/religions and its varying circumstances. The examples of China and Japan have already been the topic of analysis in Chapter 5. The South African case arose above in the context of examining the contemporary construction of African Traditional Religions. Here I expand those considerations with a look at the cases of Indonesia, India, Egypt, Russia, France and Canada. The comparison thus produced shows a remarkable consistency in the logic of religious regulation and legislation, but also a revealing variation.

Indonesia

The situation with regard to the idea of religion in Indonesia is remarkably similar to that of China. Yet it is also a kind of mirror image of that East Asian country. Even more than in China, Indonesian governments since the 1960s have sought to define and control both what counts as religion, as well as which religions count. Basing itself on the *pancasila* ('five points') doctrine promulgated in the state's 1945 Constitution, the New Order (Sukarno and Suharto) government after 1966 enforced a policy which is still largely in effect. In it eventually only five religions qualified as *agama* (religion), namely Islam, Protestantism, Roman Catholicism, Buddhism and Hinduism.[5] Three aspects of this policy stand out in the current context: the compulsory belonging by all citizens to one of the official religions, the degree to which the implicit model for what a religion is and looks like is in this case at least as much Islam as it is Christianity, and the official contrast of religion (*agama*) and culture (*adat*).

Citizens of Indonesia gain distinct benefits and in certain senses only full citizenship rights if they belong officially to one of the five sanctioned religions. Thus, even though the practice of various other religions like Judaism, Daoism, more recently Confucianism, and a wide range of mystical traditions is not banned, such religions are also not (or no longer) accorded the status of religion, namely *agama*. At best they receive an intermediate and inferior recognition as 'faiths' or *kepercayaan* (the mystical groups), a category notably under the jurisdiction, not of the Department of Religion, but of the Department of Culture and Tourism (Howell forthcoming-b). From that perspective, they are rather treated as culture, *adat*. In this context, one's official identity card must designate a religion, almost always one of the five; without the card employment is difficult to find and one cannot vote (United States Department of State 2004). The reasons for this more or less compulsory adherence are undoubtedly multidimensional, but they include the conviction that religion is at the foundation of sound social order, that religion should be 'modern', meaning that it should take certain forms, the wish to deflect demands for an expressly Islamic state in a country where over 80 per cent of the population is officially counted as Muslim, and a corresponding virulent anti-communism.[6] The plurality of sanctioned religions is thus a way of claiming the supposed suitability of religion for fostering modern progress and social control, while at the same time not subordinating the state to the dictates of one particular religion: that is, maintaining a differentiation of religion and state as functional domains while simultaneously asserting the foundational character of the former. In this context, some observers have regarded *pancasila* itself as a kind of state or civil religion which one could profitably compare to the already discussed 'religions that are not religions' in China and Japan (cf. Spyer 1996).

A number of indicators show that Islam serves at least as a key part of the main model for a religion. These include that the Ministry of Religious Affairs, while subdivided according to the five religions, is dominated by Muslim clerics at the top and especially in the ministerial government portfolio. As well, the proper marks of a religion are said to be a prophet, a scripture and a belief in one God, the last of these in fact being the first of the five 'points' (*sila*). Moreover, when movements to formalize local traditions do so by becoming part of one of the official ones, they express this transformation by outfitting their *agama* with typical accoutrements, including holy books, religious scholars, regular daily prayer rituals and the like (see e.g. Hefner 1985; Schiller 1997). The fact that such movements have happened also points to the Islamic way that official Indonesia uses to circumscribe what may look like religion but is not, namely the conceptualization of *adat*, significantly an Arabic term.

Adat is usually translated as 'custom', 'usage' or 'practice' (see Geertz 1983). Culture might be a better translation if we mean something like received knowledge or tradition that is more or less beyond question. In the official Indonesian context, *adat* contrasts with *agama* along mutually reinforcing lines: *adat* is human usage whereas *agama* rests on divine precept; *adat* can change but *agama* reflects the absolute. The importance of *adat* in the official Indonesian context is that it is the term used to reflect the 'local' cultural and, in an analytic sense, religious practices of the wide variety of peoples inhabiting the country. The religious ways of local and Aboriginal people, including the various versions of what is deemed to be pre-Islamic Indonesian religious ways, to the degree that they are acceptable, they are *adat* and not *agama*. Adherence to the former is not sufficient as the mark of good citizenship. For the former to be accepted fully as the latter, it must re-imagine, restructure and affiliate itself with one of the five established religions. And these transformations have happened on more than one occasion.[7]

Current Indonesian government control over religion is therefore in the direction of controlling both the range of religious influence and the variety of religions that count fully as such. Such restrictive policies do affect the ways that religions form and present themselves in Indonesia, although they do not simply determine them. They undoubtedly have an effect on the number of people who publicly adhere to each religion. The control does not, however, prevent religiously based conflict, nor does it preclude religious militancy. In terms of such outcomes, Indonesia is somewhat similar to India, even though the latter seems to have more liberal state and legal policies with respect to both the control dimensions.

India

If Indonesia presents us with an example that is in some sense a mirror image of China, then the Indian case may be viewed as a mirror image of the Indonesian example, without, however, thereby being all that similar to China. The Indian circumstance, in fact, goes some way to demonstrating that the institutionalization of the modern category of religion with regard to the state and the law can happen in various ways. It is far from being a simple matter of acceptance or rejection; one can do both at the same time, and this in different ways.

Like Japan, the official Indian position is to guarantee the freedom of religion without at the same time trying to limit and officially declare which religions count and are therefore afforded this freedom. Nonetheless, like Indonesia, there is a parallel Indian tendency to subsume religious diversity under a limited number of headings and a *de facto* (but not *de jure*) privileging of the putatively and numerically majority religion, in this case Hinduism. Yet because the concept of a singular religion called Hinduism is itself a relatively recent neologism, it cannot serve as this kind of implicit model for a religion that Islam (and Christianity) does in Indonesia. Accordingly, much of the contestation around the notion of religion in India centres on the nature, role and composition of Hinduism itself.

Exemplifying the fault lines in this debate is a reference to four religions in the Indian constitution. In a clause entitled 'right to freedom of religion', one reads 'reference to Hindus shall be construed as including a reference to persons professing the Sikh, Jaina or Buddhist religion' (National Informatics Centre 2001: Article 25, Explanation II). While one cannot make too much of a small secondary clause like this, it does point to the fact that, in effect, 'Hindu' in India can operate both as an inclusive and as a particular term. It is probably no coincidence that contemporary Hindu nationalists also consider Hindu religion to include these same three other religions (see e.g. Vishva Hindu Parishad 2001). Hindu is in India in some senses a 'default' religious *and cultural* category. Even though the Supreme Court of India has recognized a positive definition of Hinduism (Hinduism Today 1999), there is also a strong sense in which the term operates in India to mean 'not-Muslim-or-Christian' (and less critically 'not-Jewish-or-Parsi'). Again following the perhaps extreme version of the Hindu nationalists, Hindu designates both a religious and a national-cultural identity. It can mean a particular religion, but it can also play the same role that *pancasila* does in Indonesia or State Shinto did in Japan, namely a worldview that is more of a national(ist) ideology than it is a religion and yet has many of the trappings of a religion.

Hindu nationalists are of course only one force in India. And their penchant for using the indigenous word for religion, (variations on) *dharma*, as both what Hinduism is and what is at the foundation of society (see Vishva Hindu Parishad 2001: http://www.vhp.org/englishsite/a-origin_&_growth/origin.html#basis) is clearly not shared by all and cannot even be said to be an official identification. Nonetheless, the neo-Vedantic vision of Hinduism that is shared by many of the Hindu middle class and elite styles this religion, echoing especially such leading lights as Swami Vivekananda, as above all tolerant, as being capable of subsuming within itself an infinite variety of religious expressions.[8] And one of the main reasons for the partition of British India in 1947 to create Pakistan was that Muslims did not trust an independent united India *not* to be Hindu dominated (see e.g. Pandey 1992). Accordingly, it is quite clear that the major 'world religions' are recognized in Indian official practice (especially in the constitution and legal system) as being Christianity, Islam, Judaism, Zoroastrianism on the one hand; and then Hinduism, Sikhism, Jainism and Buddhism on the other. Hinduism is both just another religion and yet also the overarching moniker for at least this and also the last four. This ambiguity reflects a situation in which Hindus have since the nineteenth century reconstructed Hinduism as one of the religions, and yet there exists at the same time a kind of unease with this re-imagination and with the modern category of religion itself, a unease reflected in what happened in Japan and China.

Egypt

Egypt is an overwhelmingly Sunni Muslim country, a key region in the Muslim heartland that stretches from Morocco to Pakistan. Unlike Indonesia, however, Islam is much more explicitly established in law and constitution rather than only serving as an implicit model for religion. Yet Egypt also guarantees freedom from discrimination on the basis of religion and freedom of religious belief and observance. The balance between Islamic 'establishment' and this freedom is what makes the Egyptian case revealing and, even though not an extreme case like Iran, representative of a broad range of Muslim countries.

Egypt, like other Muslim countries of the region, has inherited the older, Islamic way of structuring a limited religious pluralism through the Ottoman *millet* system by which select non-Islamic, religiously identified communities (that is, groups of people) are accorded the right to regulate many of their own internal affairs according to their own religious norms and by their own religious authorities. The limitations on this independence are principally of two sorts: the groups so designated are defined in Islamic terms, namely people considered 'people of the book', above all Christians and Jews; and such *dhimmi* status is also a subordinate one. Only Muslims and Islam, in practice if not in official policy and law, have full rights and protection under law and the state, such that, for example, Coptic Christians find it more difficult to establish churches and frequently are subject to Islamic laws in various areas. Conversion to Christianity as opposed to Islam is discouraged in fact if not in principle, and Islamic education receives express and full state support, extending to private Islamic schools but not to those of Christians and other religious groups. The restriction of such relative tolerance to Abrahamic, revealed and text-based religions means that other groups are not even recognized as religions. Hindus, for instance, should any find themselves in Egypt wishing to erect a temple, would simply be denied the right to publicly visible religious observance. Moreover, and of more practical import, Baha'is, while meeting the restricted criteria of what counts in almost all respects, find themselves the subject of overt discrimination because their faith is also defined in Islamic terms, in this case a proscribed heresy. Overall, the practical state policies of Egypt, if not actually the laws, but especially the practical attitudes and behaviour of the majority Muslim population, limit religious tolerance to what the dominant form of Islam will allow. The more Muslim one is, the more rights one has; the less Muslim one is, the greater become the restrictions.

Both in Egypt's constitution and in actual social practice, Islam has the *de facto* if not entirely the *de jure* status of being seen, not just as the religion of the majority, but as foundational of proper social order as such. In Egypt today, along with and in competition with a more secular nationalism, it structures the equivalent of that country's 'civil religion', the religion that is binding but thereby considered to be more than a 'mere religion' or simply as ultimately the only proper religion. Analogous to what the RSS and VHP envisage for Hinduism in their vision of India, Egypt limits all other religions by granting this exceptional status to Islam. Where Indonesia has *pancasila* or China has its socialism, both of which provide corresponding justifications for limiting religious freedom, Egypt puts Islam in this position, not just implicitly and by dint of the overwhelming Muslim majority, but in various ways explicitly and officially in law and state regulation (Boyle and Sheen 1997: 26ff.; United States Department of State 2004: 13994pf.htm).

Russia

During the Soviet era, much as in other socialist states, religion in Russia was subject to severe control and suppression. The state sought to enforce the then reigning Marxist-Leninist socialist 'civil religion', and part of that ideology was that all forms of religion represented repressive 'false consciousness' antithetical to the progress of socialism towards the communist utopia. After the collapse of the Soviet Union in 1989, Russia emerged as the main successor state. Like the other former Soviet republics, it had to re-imagine itself while undergoing a prolonged and difficult period of restructuring. To no one's surprise, the emerging new self-conception centres on Russian nationalism, but two aspects of this revived cultural identity remain somewhat indeterminate and have a significant effect on the issues of freedom of religion, freedom of religions and therefore on how religion works in Russia. For one, the loss of status as one of the two superpowers has left in its wake a strong sense of vulnerability and uncertainty, especially given the turmoil that has been a constant feature of Russian life ever since 1989. In that context, a positive and well-defined national identity takes on a symbolic importance that it might not have in more stable and prosperous times. For another, a clearly dominant version of the new self-image has not yet established itself. Post-Soviet Russian state policies with regard to religion reflect both the uncertainty and the fluidity.

After the collapse, a wide variety of religious organizations and movements from both within and outside the former USSR sought to take advantage of the transitional period to establish and re-establish themselves. These include above all the Russian Orthodox church, perhaps the main victim and target of Soviet anti-religion policy. In addition, however, the Roman Catholic church, a large number of Protestant churches ranging from Lutheran, Baptists and Salvation Army to Pentecostal groups and Jehovah's Witnesses sought to replenish the religious field. Beside these one must also count numerous new religious movements like Scientology, neo-Paganism and ISKCON, and movements representing non-Christian religions, especially Islam, Buddhism and Judaism, all three with a long history in certain parts of the republic. In terms of the simple presence of different religions and different religious groups, Russia has become in a short time a religiously very pluralistic country, not just in the main metropolises of Moscow and St Petersburg, but also in the far reaches of Siberian Russia in centres like Vladivostok and Novosibirsk (Barchunova 2002). While the vast majority of those who actually identify with a religion count themselves as Russian Orthodox, and all the other religions combined do not include a large portion of the overall population, the relatively sudden appearance of this plethora of religions is one important indicator of a country in uncertain transition. Not everyone is involved in these religious groups, but everyone is undergoing the passage of which they are the harbingers.

The new Russian constitution, like so many others, guarantees freedom of religion. Various pieces of legislation, however, in particular a 1997 law, favour certain religions over others, above all those that have been present in Russia for a longer time; implicitly and in effect especially the Russian Orthodox church which most Russians evidently regard as a self-evident element in their national identity, even if the vast majority does not actively practise this religion in any consistent and regular fashion. Orthodoxy is important as a cultural symbol and therefore conversion to another religion appears suspect to many as a kind of *depaysage*, as the indicator of a foreign invasion which threatens to de-Russify the population. It is for this reason that Roman Catholicism is among the more controversial religions along with the usual suspects like Scientology and Jehovah's Witnesses. It is not a 'cult' so much as simply a potentially menacing foreign power. The problem is comparable to the situation in other countries such as India. There as well, Hindu nationalists regard conversion to Christianity or Islam as equivalent to robbing the nation of its citizens, of threatening the health and existence of the nation. To be sure, Orthodoxy is not the core of a *de facto* replacement 'civil religion' in Russia any more than Hinduism now occupies that role in India; but there are influential movements in both countries that would wish this to become the case. And although this championing of Orthodoxy may have little to do with actual religious practice, its legislative, legal and popular favouring does aid the Russian Orthodox in funnelling resources for its reconstruction far beyond what the low level of involvement (or incidence of religious communication) might otherwise warrant (Boyle and Sheen 1997: 372ff.).

Beside these cultural reasons for the controversial nature of religion and thus the felt need for the state to control it, Russia also evidences sources of restriction common to so many other countries ranging from Japan and China to France and Argentina. In particular, the Russian state is also concerned to control 'suspect religions', those entities labelled 'cults' because of their supposed danger to vulnerable citizens, and to limit or suppress overly militant religious movements, above all Islamic ones – significantly, under the pejorative label of 'Wahabism' – in Chechnya and other predominantly Muslim parts of the republic (United States Department of State 2004: 13958pf.htm).

In comparison with other countries, therefore, the image, category and place of religion and the religions is much as it is in the other states examined in this section. Religion is a domain of 'freedom', one separate from others and clearly recognizable in the form of a delimited, if controverted, set of religions. These religions should, on the one hand, not overstep their bounds, which is to say respect their differentiated position; but on the other hand, religion also appears as an undifferentiated dimension of national cultural identity, in this case sometimes explicitly, sometimes implicitly. The situation, in other words, is quite similar to that in Indonesia and India especially.

France

As one of the Western countries most associated with the development of the idea of human rights, it is perhaps a little surprising that France, as a state, places such clear limits on religious freedom as it does. This has much to do with the reigning French ideology of *laïcité*, the notion that state and society should have as its governing public principle a version of Western Enlightenment rationality, one which excludes expressly religious legitimation and opposes the influence and even the visibility of religion in national public life. Thus, although freedom of religion is constitutionally guaranteed, the range of visible religious influence as well as of the sorts of things that count as religion are subject to various forms of government control. A seemingly minor but nonetheless significant example is how tax-exempt status is apportioned to religious organizations. Only those which can demonstrate that their activity is limited to 'worship' (*associations cultuelles*) receive this status; otherwise religious organizations, say for education, for publishing, or for representing the interests of a religious group, do not have this status and are considered cultural organizations (*associations culturelles*). One notes again the use of the idea of culture to delimit religion. As such, however, the latter organizations are eligible for government subsidies (United States Department of State 2004: 13938pf.htm); they are treated like any other organized body of 'civil society'. Although this distinction may seem rather bureaucratic, it translates into public policy what is in effect a strict limitation on what counts as religion and is therefore guaranteed freedom: the cultural organizations cannot as easily assert themselves on the basis of this freedom because, strictly speaking, they are not religious organizations. Implied is that religion as such is limited to the performance of ritual. Obviously this policy has serious implications for *most* religion, whose representatives will almost invariably claim a far broader range for their typical communication, from the moral signification of human action to the idea that religions are worldviews and ways of life. The way of life favoured in such policies is that conceived as *laïcité*. It is, if one wishes, the officially established 'civil religion' of France: except that it is precisely not constructed or generally understood as religion.

The wish to restrict religion strictly to the 'private sphere' has recently received further demonstration in *l'affaire des foulards*, the controversy over whether Muslim girls should be allowed to wear *hijab* in public schools. Various schools and schools boards had sought to forbid this practice, and French courts often upheld their right to do so (Boyle and Sheen 1997: 298f.). Now, with the recent passage of a law proscribing the wearing of 'ostentatious' religious symbols in public institutions, that policy has been formalized. Official policy, like French public opinion, wants religion to be publicly invisible, restricted to the private performance of its most typical communication.

France is also one of the states that has gone furthest in seeking to control and even suppress what it considers 'bad' religion, above all in its anti-cult legislation. The About–Picard law passed in 2001, while not defining what a 'cult' is, allows the French government to take criminal action against any association, including specifically religious ones (*associations cultuelles*), whose actions are deemed fraudulent (read: make claims to 'this-worldly' efficacy for their practices), take advantage of individual 'weakness', or are damaging to the dignity of individuals. The wording would allow almost any religious organization to be taken to task, but it is indicative that those targeted under this and other legislation are the 'usual suspects', including Jehovah's Witnesses, Scientologists and other, for the French, unfamiliar and new groups. Although, as *l'affaire des foulards* demonstrates, French governments and public opinion are concerned about Muslim refusal to restrict religion to the individual and invisibly private sphere, the anti-cult legislation does not seem to be directed against the 'standard' world religions. They are too well institutionalized as religion to allow easy classification as 'false' religions. There is, however, little doubt that the specifically French variant on the need for religious control, as expressed in the ideology of *laïcité*, operates in the background of both issues. The new religions, like the Islam of some French Muslims, challenge the hegemony of *laïcité*.

Taken as a whole, the French situation bears some resemblance to the situation in otherwise quite different countries. China's insistence on controlling religion very precisely and limiting its range of influence, as well as its fear of 'cults' or *xiejiao*, serves the interests of a different publicly binding ideology, namely Chinese socialism; but the logic is quite similar. Religion in both countries is legitimate but suspect. As long as it 'stays in its place', freedom of religion can be permitted. As soon as religions show signs of extending their systemic logic, of wishing to 'colonize' the broader life-world and other systems, the state in both cases sees itself obliged to interfere and control, even suppress. Moreover, unlike the Indonesian, Indian or even American situation, where the 'civil' ideology is far more visibly resonant with a particular religion (i.e. Islam, Hinduism and Protestant Christianity respectively), the public ideologies of China and France construct themselves more or less explicitly, if not or no longer anti-religiously then certainly in opposition to the typical modality of modern religion. The latter, as in most other countries, they conceive in very similar fashion.

Canada

Officially, Canada prides itself on being an inclusive and tolerant country, in which multiculturalism and freedom of religion are enshrined in law and in the country's constitution. It goes almost without saying that the idea of religion that reigns here is very much the modern one that has been the object of discussion. Perhaps precisely because this almost goes without saying, the kind of clarity or at least public visibility of the category that one finds in the other countries is lacking. In Canada, too, what counts as the religions is the standard set of 'world religions' for which the implicit model is Christianity. And religions that are not on the list or do not look sufficiently like the model have more trouble being recognized and enjoying the privileges accorded those that do. This implied limitation and modelling is, for instance, evident in how the courts tend to have doubts about the status of religions that do not so fit (see e.g. Beaman 2002). Thus, although Canadians and Canadian governments and law courts may believe that 'freedom of religion' is thoroughly enshrined in the county's ideals and practice, as in the other countries examined above, that freedom is effectively granted much more easily if the religious expression at issue fits the model. That model dictates that the list of religions can be enumerated and that those so listed will have certain characteristics. Official conceptions in countries like Indonesia and China do this rather more narrowly and explicitly, but the Canadian situation is really not all that much different.

Where Canada differs from the other examples is in the way it combines the possible characteristics of religion and attitudes towards the category. Like post-war Japan, it does not have an official ideology (or, if one wishes, official 'civil religion') that looks like a religion but is not considered to be one. Unlike Japan (and China), however, the prevailing attitude towards the category is more or less positive. In this respect it resembles India and Indonesia, but unlike the latter of these, religion is deemed to be optional. One indicator of this similarity but difference can actually be found in the results of the decennial Canadian census, which asks a religious identification question. Referring to the 2001 results, one discovers that the majority population of European extraction tends to identify with a religion (usually Christianity), although about 16 per cent declare that they have 'no religion'. By contrast, people of South Asian and Southeast Asian origin overwhelmingly identify with a religion, with only about 3 per cent declaring 'no religion'. Finally, people from East Asia, who are mostly Chinese, sometimes identify with a religion, but around 60 per cent in fact declare that they have none (Beyer 2003b). The multicultural Canadian population thus to a certain extent reproduces the differences in how people around the world perceive the idea of religion. The 'Europeans' treat it as clear but optional; the 'South(east) Asians' largely consider it clear and obligatory; the 'East Asians' know what it means, but are very often suspicious of it.

Summary and conclusion

Three kinds of religious marginality have been the subject of this chapter. The first concerns new religions that have actively sought recognition as one of the religions, whether they are actually historically all that new or not. Then there are those phenomena that very often receive recognition as religion, but which seek to refuse that categorization or pursue it only in some of their manifestations. A third variety includes religious communication that neither seeks recognition nor generally receives it. Both the difficulty of forming new religions of the religious system and the seeming ease with which new religions can be formed in global society then provided the context for examining how two other function systems, the political and the legal, incorporated, thematized and thereby sought to control what religions could effectively be recognized and the range of what those recognized religions could claim and do. A main reason for introducing this last section into such questions of marginal religions/religiousness is to demonstrate that what is at issue is more than an academic or a theological question; it concerns more than science and religion, but rather by implication all the major function systems that structurally dominate global society. Evidence of the reality of the 'reified' religions is that they are in fact matters of concern for the scholar, for the person of faith, and for a great many others (Smith 1991: 12).

An important conclusion that thereby follows from these examinations of marginality is that the most important structural issue with respect to the religious system of global society concerns not just religiousness or religious communication as such, but more centrally the formation or non-formation, including the recognition or non-recognition, of religions as religions. This development for the religious system is analogous to state formation/recognition for the political system, academic discipline formation/recognition for the science system, sport formation/recognition for the sports system, or disease recognition for the medical system. And just as contention, change and marginality are regular questions as concerns these structures in those systems, so is it for religions in the religious system. The existence and even increase of phenomena like the New Age, the proliferation of new religions (together with their occasional disappearance), and personal or informal group religious *bricolage* are prime symptoms of the dynamism and social importance of this religious system, not just occurrences that highlight the contingency, historicity, selectivity and out-and-out ambiguity of the entire affair. And yet there is no doubt that contingency, as non-necessity, does bring us back to the central hypothesis that informs my efforts here: to what extent is there a single, global religious system?

Notes

1 My presentation in this section relies substantially on Smith 1987.
2 As a revealing example, Irving Hexham criticizes Western scholars for paying insufficient attention to African religions in their writings and textbooks, focusing especially on Ninian Smart's more recent world religions text (Smart 1989). He cites Smart who writes that, in contrast with, for instance, Hinduism, African religion 'has never been a single system'. See Hexham 2002. See the contrasting discussion of Candomblé below.
3 For example, Stark and Bainbridge's influential classification distinguished between a 'sect', a movement that separates from an already locally familiar or established religion, and a 'cult', a movement that is new or new to a region. The latter includes most NRMs. See Stark and Bainbridge 1985.
4 I thank Marie-Françoise Guédon for insight into these and other aspects of the current religious situation among North American Native peoples.
5 Originally, Sukarno also recognized Confucianism as one of the *agama*, but that status was subsequently revoked. See Howell forthcoming-a.
6 Which has had the curious result that a good portion of the ethnically Chinese population in Indonesia has converted officially to one of the two Christianities, even though Indonesia was one of the few places where expressly Confucian churches have existed since the 1920s. See Coppel 1981. Evidently the Chinese have had to demonstrate their 'non-communism' in this way. See Spyer 1996: 176. Recently, however, in the wake of the overthrow of the old regime, the Indonesian government lifted the ban on the practice of Confucianism along with that on a few other hitherto outlawed religions and

religious groups like the Jehovah's Witnesses, the Baha'is and the Rosicrucians. See United States Department of State 2004.

7   See Hefner 1985; Schiller 1997, for two examples of *adat* which reinvented themselves as forms of Hinduism. Perhaps a bit ironically, 'Hinduism' seems to operate practically as the religion to which one belongs if one doesn't belong to one of the others, a position analogous to Hinduism's status in India itself. See the section on India immediately below.

8   Reminiscent of this attitude is this quote from a well-known Indian Muslim, Salman Rushdie: 'The selfhood of India is so capacious, so elastic, that it accommodates 1 billion kinds of differences. It agrees with its billion selves to call all of them "Indian"' (Rushdie 1997).

Conclusion

At the outset of this book, I made the claim that much could be gained by observing religion in our contemporary world as a modern function system, in particular that many of the long-standing and inconclusive debates in the sociology of religion could be clarified or at least moved forward through this theoretical strategy. The basic argument is as follows: religion is not just a social institution that exists more or less in all societies and all periods of human history, but only takes on different forms in different circumstances. Form and content are not so easily separable. Instead it is the modern form that religion has taken, its social differentiation precisely as religion, that makes it seem almost self-evident to us as observers that it has always and everywhere been there *in some form*. From that perspective, and given that social reality is always continuous as well as discontinuous with what went before, such abstract religion has not been difficult to find. Yet without taking sufficient cognizance of the context from which we observe – of the eye with which we see – it is all too easy to arrive at seemingly paradoxical observations and their prime symptoms, interminable debate. Is today's society secularized/secularizing or are we witnessing a resacralization? How and why is it that religion that has become more differentiated and therefore more clearly institutionalized ('reified') weakens on that account, whereas it appears that undifferentiated religiousness is by that token stronger or more effective religion? In that connection, why does it seem that strong religion must somehow be oppositional (e.g. 'strict')? None of these questions is of course new in sociological history. Classic thinkers like Durkheim, Weber and Simmel were each in their own way already very much occupied with them, as have been a whole host of more recent ones like Wilson, Parsons, Luckmann, Berger, Luhmann, Martin and Stark, to name only a few. That concerns particularly the whole debate about differentiation and secularization.

To summarize what I have argued in the foregoing chapters, observing religion as a globalized function system makes a potentially significant contribution in this context, and by the following logical route. First, the most consequential difference of modern society is not differentiation as such, but rather giving structural primacy to functionally differentiated societal systems such as capitalist economy or empirical science. That shift has had tremendous power consequences, both qualitative and quantitative. Second, historically this shift has globalization as we have seen it develop over the last centuries as one of its principal outcomes. These two points are in one version or another effectively standards of the sociological literature since the early nineteenth century. Third, however, religion, far from remaining more or less constant during these transformations and thereby suffering or at the least being challenged to *re*assert itself, has actually been a critical carrier and example of the entire process. Religion, like capitalism, the nation-state or modern science, has been a carrier of modernization and globalization, not a barrier or victim. Modern religions such as I have been presenting them are to 'traditional religion' (the religious dimension of previous societies) as modern capitalism is to 'traditional economies' or the modern state is to 'traditional empires'. There is both continuity and discontinuity in each case, but the differences have made the difference. Fourth, the idea of social systems generally and function system in particular provides the conceptual wherewithal for being able to see that parallelism. Through the notion of system, we can see at the same time how religion is like capitalist economy but also unlike it, how it is like the sovereign state but also unlike it, how it is like empirical science but also unlike it, and so forth. What forms religion takes, how it has taken those forms, whether it is strong or weak, 'real' or 'illusory', thereby becomes a question of comparison, not in the first order with 'times past', but principally with the other systems in 'times present'. The peculiarity and arbitrary selectiveness of modern religion, the fact that certain 'modern inventions' like the 'world religions' seem to count more than others, its 'complicity' in imperialism and other dimensions of power asymmetry, the fact that it seems to be both present and not present in different parts of the world, its orthogonality with other modes of social power, and indeed the persistent contestations that it engenders, these and much else can be seen in terms of and as consequences of the structuring of religion as function system. And all this without having somehow to locate 'real' religion more in the past; without having to rely on religious self-descriptions (theologies) as the basis for scientific and sociological understanding.

The last point should be stressed. Observing contemporary religion as a function system does not privilege an 'insider's' perspective. Rather, it seeks to incorporate the understandings that prevail in religious communication within a social scientific explanation, as scientific and not as religious observation. That distinction, of course, assumes the systemic differentiation between science and religion that the theory seeks to encompass. My observation, the sociological theory presented here, reappears in the observation itself. It does not pretend to be anything but a selective narrative operating within and helping to reproduce a social system analogous to the one that is its prime object of observation. That is why the advantages I claim for it envisage in the first instance the sociology of religion, sociology more broadly, but also very directly the discipline of religious studies. Application of the understandings that the theory offers is of course possible in other domains, first of all in other disciplines such as history, anthropology or political science, but then also outside of science, for example in the theological, the educational or the political spheres. Those possibilities, however, are not my business here.

Even if all these claims are acceptable, there remains the question of the several ambiguities and insufficiencies that the systems perspective also introduces. It is in the nature of modern scientific observation that it construct itself as provisional, as inevitably to be superseded. For the most part, of course, I leave that to others. To be criticized is, after all, the hoped for outcome of publication. As the presentations in all the chapters, but especially Chapters 5 and 6, made clear, observing religion as a function system seems to leave a great deal of 'religiousness' out or on the ambiguous margins. Even by its own definition of core religious elements as those involving the attribution of communicative partnership to non-human realities, this is the case. That may be the chief problem towards the outside. To it must be added an internal ambiguity, and this is the question of just how coherent this 'religious system' is *as a single social system*. The problem is especially evident, again within the terms of the theory itself, when discussing the singularity of the binary code that is at the core of this system. Even if one were to accept my suggestion that this code is at root blessed/cursed and not, for instance, transcendent/immanent or sacred/profane, the problem would remain that few if any of the constructed religions rely expressly or dominantly on any of them. Compared to other systems, there does not seem to be a clear religious equivalent to economic 'property' or political 'government'. Whether that is a problem of the system or with the theory is not entirely clear. Something similar can be said about the vagueness with which several of 'the religions' themselves appear to be formed, the seeming proliferation in all of them of almost endless subunits to the point that virtually only the internal and external observation of these subunits as part of the same religion is what constitutes its unity. That may or may not be enough, but it does pose the question with some seriousness as to whether this is better understood as a feature of the religious system or as a difficulty with the theory. My contention, of course, is that it is more the former than the latter. Only subsequent and different efforts which better illuminate these and other aspects of the situation of what we call religion in our world will determine the provisional answer.

Bibliography

Abu-Lughod, J. (1989) *Before European Hegemony: The World System A.D. 1250–1350*, New York and Oxford: Oxford University Press.

Adams, C. J. (1983) 'Mawdudi and the Islamic State', in J. L. Esposito (ed.) *Voices of Resurgent Islam*, Oxford: Oxford University Press, pp. 99–133.

Adogame, A. (2000) 'The Quest for Space in the Global Spiritual Marketplace: African Religions in Europe', *International Review of Mission*, 89, 409.

Agadjanian, A. and Roudometof, V. (eds) (2005) *Eastern Orthodoxy in a Global Age*, Walnut Creek, CA: Altamira.

Ahlemeyer, H. W. (1995) *Soziale Bewegungen als Kommunikationssystem: Einheit, Umweltverhältnis und Funktion eines sozialen Phänomens*, Leverkusen: Leske and Budrich.

Albrow, M. (1990) 'Globalization, Knowledge and Society', in M. Albrow and E. King (eds) *Globalization, Knowledge and Society: Readings from International Sociology*, London: Sage, pp. 3–18.

Alitto, G. S. (1979) *The Last Confucian: Liang Shu-ming and the Chinese Dilemma of Modernity*, Berkeley, CA: University of California Press.

Almond, P. C. (1988) *The British Discovery of Buddhism*, Cambridge: Cambridge University Press.

Andersen, W. K. and Damle, S. D. (1987) *The Brotherhood in Saffron: The Rashtriya Swayamsevak Sangh and Hindu Revivalism*, Boulder, CO: Westview.

Appadurai, A. (1983) *Worship and Conflict under Colonial Rule: A South Indian Case*, Hyderabad: Orient Longman.

——(1996) *Modernity at Large: Cultural Dimensions of Globalization*, Minneapolis, MN: University of Minnesota Press.

Arjomand, S. A. (1984) *The Shadow of God and the Hidden Imam: Religion, Political Order, and Societal Change in Shi'ite Iran from the Beginning to 1890*, Chicago: University of Chicago Press.

Asad, T. (1993) *Genealogies of Religion: Discipline and Reasons of Power in Christianity and Islam*, Baltimore, MD: Johns Hopkins University Press.

Axford, B. (1995) *The Global System: Economics, Politics, Culture*, New York: St Martin's Press.

Axtell, J. (2001) *Natives and Newcomers: The Cultural Origins of North America*, New York: Oxford University Press.

Babb, L. (1986) *Redemptive Encounters: Three Modern Styles in the Hindu Tradition*, Berkeley, CA: University of California Press.

Babb, L. and Wadley, S. S. (eds) (1995) *Media and the Transformation of Religion in South Asia*, Philadelphia: University of Pennsylvania Press.

Baird, R. B. (ed.) (2001) *Religion in Modern India*, New Delhi: Manohar.

Balagangadhara, S. N. (1994) *'The Heathen in His Blindness . . . ': Asia, the West, and the Dynamic of Religion*, Leiden: E. J. Brill.

Bamyeh, M. A. (1993) 'Transnationalism', *Current Sociology*, 41, 3, 1–95.

Barchunova, T. V. (2002) 'Faith-Based Communities of Practice in Novosibirsk', paper delivered to conference on Local Forms of Religious Organization as Structural Modernisation: Effects on Community-Building and Globalisation, Marburg, Germany.

Barrier, N. G. (ed.) (1983) *The Census in British India*, New Delhi: Manohar.

Batstone, D. (2001) 'Dancing to a Different Beat: Emerging Spiritualities in the Network Society', in D. N. Hopkins, L. A. Lorentzen, E. Mendieta and D. Batstone (eds) *Religions/Globalizations: Theories and Cases*, Durham, NC: Duke University Press, pp. 226–42.

Baumann, M. (2000) *Migration – Religion – Integration: Buddhistische Vietnamesen und hinduistische Tamilen in Deutschland*, Marburg: Diagonal Verlag.

Bayly, C. A. (1988) *Indian Society and the Making of the British Empire*, Cambridge: Cambridge University Press.

Beaman, L. (2002) 'Aboriginal Spirituality and the Legal Construction of Freedom of Religion', *Journal of Church and State*, 44 (Winter), 135–49.

Beckford, J. A. (1989) *Religion and Advanced Industrial Society*, London: Unwin Hyman.

Bellah, R. N., Madsen, R., Sullivan, W. M., Swidler, A. and Tipton, S. M. (1985) *Habits of the Heart: Individualism and Commitment in American Life*, San Francisco: Harper and Row.

Bennetta, J.-R. (1997) 'At the Threshold of the Millennium: Prophetic Movements and Independent Churches in Central and Southern Africa', *Archives de sciences sociales des religions*, 99, 153–67.

Berger, P. (1967) *The Sacred Canopy: Elements of a Sociological Theory of Religion*, New York: Doubleday Anchor.

Berman, H. J. (1983) *Law and Revolution: The Formation of the Western Legal Traditions*, Cambridge, MA: Harvard University Press.

Berryman, P. (1987) *Liberation Theology: The Essential Facts about the Revolutionary Movement in Latin America and Beyond*, New York: Pantheon.

Beyer, P. (1992) 'The Global Environment as a Religious Issue: A Sociological Analysis', *Religion*, 22, 1–21.

——(1994) *Religion and Globalization*, London: Sage.

——(1997) 'Religion, Residual Problems, and Functional Differentiation: An Ambiguous Relationship', *Soziale Systeme*, 3, 219–35.

——(1998a) 'Globalized Systems, Global Cultural Models, and Religion(s)', *International Sociology*, 13, 79–94.

——(1998b) 'Nature Religion in a Global Society: Critique, Alternative, and Paradox', in J. Pearson, R. H. Roberts and G. Samuel (eds) *Nature Religion Today: The Pagan Alternative in the Modern World*, Edinburgh: Edinburgh University Press, pp. 11–21.

——(1998c) 'Sociological Theory of Religion between Description and Prediction: A Weberian Question Revisited', in B. Wilson, R. Laermans and J. Billiet (eds)

Secularization and Social Integration: Papers in Honor of Karel Dobbelaere, Leuven: Leuven University Press, pp. 83–105.

——(2001) 'Religion as Communication in Niklas Luhmann's *Die Religion der Gesellschaft*', *Soziale Systeme*, 7, 46–55.

——(2002) 'Religions and Religiosity in Global Society: Secularization, De-Institutionalization and Exceptionalism?' *Suomen Antropologi*, 27, 3, 2–18.

——(2003a) 'Conceptions of Religion: On Distinguishing Scientific, Theological, and "Official" Meanings', *Social Compass*, 50, 141–60.

——(2003b) 'Religion in Canada as Viewed from Canadian Census Data, 1981–2001: Transformation and Pluralism', unpublished manuscript.

Bilimoria, P. (1996) *The Hindus and Sikhs in Australia: Religious Community Profile*, Canberra: Bureau of Immigration, Multicultural and Population Research.

Boyle, K. and Sheen, J. (1997) *Freedom of Religion and Belief: A World Report*, London: Routledge.

Brannen, N. S. (1968) *Soka Gakkai: Japan's Militant Buddhists*, Richmond, VA: John Knox Press.

Brekke, T. (2002) *Makers of Modern Indian Religion*, Oxford: Oxford University Press.

Brook, T. (1993) 'Rethinking Syncretism: The Unity of the Three Teachings and Their Joint Worship in Late-Imperial China', *Journal of Chinese Religions*, 21 (Fall), 13–44.

Burghart, R. (ed.) (1987) *Hinduism in Great Britain: The Perpetuation of Religion in an Alien Cultural Milieu*, London: Tavistock.

Casanova, J. (1994) *Public Religions in the Modern World*, Chicago: University of Chicago.

Chan, S. (1985) *Buddhism in Late Ch'ing Political Thought*, Hong Kong and Boulder, CO: Chinese University Press and Westview.

Chan, W. (1978) *Religious Trends in Modern China*, New York: Octagon.

Chandra, S. (1995) 'Whose Laws? – Notes on a Nineteenth Century Hindu Case of Conjugal Rights', in V. Dalmia and H. von Stietencron (eds) *Representing Hinduism*, New Delhi: Sage, pp. 154–75.

Chang, H. (1971) *Liang Ch'i-ch'ao and Intellectual Transition in China, 1890–1907*, Cambridge, MA: Harvard University Press.

Channa, V. C. (1984) *Hinduism*, New Delhi: National Publishing House.

Chatterjee, P. (1995) 'History and the Nationalization of Hinduism', in V. Dalmia and H. von Stietencron (eds) *Representing Hinduism*, New Delhi: Sage, pp. 103–28.

Chesneaux, J., Bastid, M. and Bergère, M.-C. (1976) *China from the Opium Wars to the 1911 Revolution*, New York: Pantheon.

Chidester, D. (1996) *Savage Systems: Colonialism and Comparative Religion in Southern Africa*, Charlottesville, VA: University Press of Virginia.

Clarke, P. B. (1986) *West Africa and Christianity*, London: Edward Arnold.

——(ed.) (1998) *New Trends and Developments in African Religions*, Westport, CT: Greenwood.

Clarke, P. B. and Byrne, P. (1993) *Religion Defined and Explained*, London: St Martin's Press.

Clémentin-Ojha, C. (1994) 'La Suddhi de l'Aria samaj ou l'invention d'un rituel de (re)conversion à l'hindouisme', *Archives de sciences sociales des religions*, 87, 99–114.

—(2001) 'A Mid-Nineteenth Century Controversy over Religious Authority', in V. Dalmia, A. Molinar and M. Christoff (eds) *Charisma and Canon*, New Delhi: Oxford University Press, pp. 183–201.

Cole, J. R. (1998) 'The Baha'i Faith in America as Pantopticon, 1963–97', *Journal for the Scientific Study of Religion*, 37, 234–48.

Coleman, S. (2000) *The Globalisation of Charismatic Christianity: Spreading the Gospel of Prosperity*, Cambridge: Cambridge University Press.

Collins, R. (1975) *Conflict Sociology: Toward an Explanatory Science*, New York: Academic Press.

Conlon, F. F. (1992) 'The Polemic Process in Nineteenth-Century Maharashtra: Vishnubawa Brahmachari and Hindu Revival', in K. W. Jones (ed.) *Religious Controversy in British India: Dialogues in South Asian Languages*, Albany, NY: State University of New York Press, pp. 5–26.

Conrad, D. (1995) 'The Personal Law Question and Hindu Nationalism', in V. Dalmia and H. von Stietencron (eds) *Representing Hinduism*, New Delhi: Sage, pp. 306–37.

Coppel, C. A. (1981) 'The Origins of Confucianism as an Organized Religion in Java, 1900–1923', *Journal of Southeast Asian Studies*, 12, 179–96.

Cox, H. (1965) *The Secular City: Secularization and Urbanization in Theological Perspective*, New York: Macmillan.

——(1995) *Fire from Heaven: The Rise of Pentecostal Spirituality and the Reshaping of Religion in the Twenty-First Century*, Reading, MA: Perseus Books.

Dalmia, V. (1995) '"The Only Real Religion of the Hindus": Vaisnava Self-Representation in the Late Nineteenth Century', in V. Dalmia and H. von Stietencron (eds) *Representing Hinduism*, New Delhi: Sage, pp. 176–210.

——(1998) 'The Modernity of Tradition: Hariscandra of Banaras and the Defence of Hindu Dharma', in W. Radice (ed.) *Swami Vivekananda and the Modernization of Hinduism*, New Delhi: Oxford University Press, pp. 77–92.

Dalmia, V. and von Stietencron, H. (eds) (1995) *Representing Hinduism: The Construction of Religious Traditions and National Identity*, New Delhi: Sage.

Davie, G. (2000) *Religion in Modern Europe: A Memory Mutates*, Oxford: Oxford University Press.

de Bary, T., Chan, W. and Tan, C. (eds) (1964) *Sources of Chinese Tradition. vol. 2*, New York: Columbia University Press.

Defarges, P. M. (2002) *La mondialisation*, Paris: Presses universitaires de France.

Délumeau, J. (1983) *Le péche et la peur: La culpibilisation en Occident, XIIIe – XVIIIe siècles*, Paris: Fayard.

Dempster, M. W., Klaus, B. D. and Petersen, D. (eds) (1999) *The Globalization of Pentecostalism: A Religion Made to Travel*, Oxford: Regnum Books International.

Despland, M. (1979) *La religion en occident: Evolution des idées et du vécu*, Montreal: Fides.

Dessai, E. (1993) *Hindus in Deutschland*, Moers: Aragon.

Dobbelaere, K. (1981) 'Secularization: A Multi-Dimensional Model', *Current Sociology*, 29, 2, 1–216.

Donohue, J. J. and Esposito, J. L. (eds) (1982) *Islam in Transition: Muslim Perspectives*, New York: Oxford University Press.

Douglas, M. (1966) *Purity and Danger: An Analysis of the Concepts of Pollution and Taboo*, New York: Praeger.

——(1970) *Natural Symbols: Explorations in Cosmology*, New York: Vintage.

——(1975) 'Self-Evidence', *Implicit Meanings: Essays in Anthropology*, London: Routledge and Kegan Paul, pp. 276–318.

Dumoulin, H. and Maraldo, J. C. (eds) (1976) *Buddhism in the Modern World*, London and New York: Macmillan.

Durant, W. (1935) *The Story of Civilization. Volume 4: The Age of Faith*, New York: Simon and Schuster.

Durkheim, É. (1965) *The Elementary Forms of the Religious Life*, New York: Free Press.

Earhart, H. B. (1982) *Japanese Religion: Unity and Diversity*, Belmont, CA: Wadsworth.

Ebaugh, H. R. and Chafetz, J. S. (eds) (2000) *Religion and the New Immigrants: Continuities and Adaptations in Immigrant Congregations*, Walnut Creek, CA: AltaMira.

Eisenstadt, S. N. (2001) 'The Vision of the Modern and Contemporary Society', in E. Ben-Rafael and Yitzhak Sternberg (eds) *Identity, Culture and Globalization*, Leiden: Brill, pp. 25–47.

Eliade, M. (1963) *Patterns in Comparative Religion*, Cleveland, OH: World Publishers.

Embree, A. (1990) *Utopias in Conflict: Religion and Nationalism in Modern India*, Berkeley, CA: University of California Press.

Esposito, J. L. (ed.) (1983) *Voices of Resurgent Islam*, New York: Oxford University Press.

——(ed.) (1999) *The Oxford History of Islam*, Oxford: Oxford University Press.

Esposito, J. L. and Voll, J. O. (eds) (2001) *Makers of Contemporary Islam*, Oxford: Oxford University Press.

Fairbank, J. K. and Liu, K. (eds) (1980) *The Cambridge History of China: Late Ch'ing, 1800–1911*, Cambridge: Cambridge University Press.

Featherstone, M. (1990) *Global Culture: Nationalism, Globalization, and Modernity*, London: Sage.

——(1995) *Undoing Culture: Globalization, Postmodernism and Identity*, London: Sage.

Featherstone, M., Lash, S. and Robertson, R. (eds) (1995) *Global Modernities*, London: Sage.

Feil, E. (1986) *Religio: Die Geschichte eines neuzeitlichen Grundbegriffs vom Frühchristentum bis zur Reformation*, Göttingen: Vandenhoeck and Ruprecht.

——(1992) 'From the Classical Religio to the Modern Religion: Elements of a Transformation between 1550 and 1650', in M. Despland and G. Vallée (eds) *Religion in History: The Word, the Idea, the Reality*, Waterloo, ON: Wilfrid Laurier University Press, pp. 31–43.

——(1997) *Religio: Die Geschichte eines neuzeitlichen Grundbegriffs zwischen Reformation und Rationalismus (ca. 1540–1620)*, Göttingen: Vandenhoeck and Ruprecht.

——(2001) *Religio: Die Geschichte eines neuzeitlichen Grundbegriffs im 17. un 18. Jahrhundert*, Göttingen: Vandenhoeck and Ruprecht.

Ferm, D. W. (ed.) (1986) *Third World Liberation Theologies: A Reader*, Maryknoll, NY: Orbis.

Finke, R. and Stark, R. (1992) *The Churching of America, 1776–1990: Winners and Losers in Our Religious Economy*, New Brunswick, NJ: Rutgers University Press.

Firsching, H. and Schlegel, M. (1998) 'Religiöse Innerlichkeit und Geselligkeit. Zum Verhältnis von Erfahrung, Kommunikabilität und Sozialität – unter besonderer Brücksichtigung des Religionsverständnisses Friedrich Schleiermachers', in H. Tyrell, V. Krech and H. Knoblauch (eds) *Religion als Kommunikation*, Würzburg: Ergon Verlag, pp. 31–82.

Fitzgerald, T. (1990) 'Hinduism and the World Religion Fallacy', *Religion*, 20, 101–18.

——(1997) 'A Critique of "Religion" as a Cross-Cultural Category', *Method & Theory in the Study of Religion*, 9, 91–110.

Franke, W. (1968) *The Reform and Abolition of the Traditional Chinese Examination System*, Cambridge, MA: East Asian Research Center, Harvard University.

Freud, S. (1985) 'The Future of an Illusion', in A. Dickson (ed.) *Civilization, Society, and Religion*, Vol. 12, Harmondsworth: Penguin, pp. 181–241.

Frykenberg, R. E. (1976) 'The Impact of Conversion and Social Reform upon Society in South India during the Late Company Period: Questions Concerning Hindu-Christian Encounters with Special Reference to Tinnevelly', in C. H. Philips and M. D. Wainwright (eds) *Indian Society and the Beginnings of Modernization c. 1830–1850*, London: SOAS, pp. 187–243.

——(1989) 'The Emergence of Modern "Hinduism" as a Concept and as an Institution: A Reappraisal with Special Reference to South India', in G. D. Sontheimer and H. Kulke (eds) *Hinduism Reconsidered*, Delhi: Manohar, pp. 29–49.

Gardet, L. (1960 [1980]) 'Din', in H. R. Gibb and others (eds) *Encyclopedia of Islam*, Vol. 2, Leiden: Brill, pp. 293–6.

Geertz, C. (1966) 'Religion as a Cultural System', in M. Bainton (ed.) *Anthropological Approaches to the Study of Religion*, London: Tavistock, pp. 1–46.

——(1983) *Local Knowledge: Further Essays in Interpretive Anthropology*, n.p. [New York]: Basic Books.

Gellner, E. (1969) 'A Pendulum Swing Theory of Islam', in R. Robertson (ed.) *Sociology of Religion*, Harmondsworth: Penguin, pp. 127–38.

——(1983) *Nations and Nationalism*, Oxford: Basil Blackwell.

Geschiere, P. (1999) 'Globalization and the Power of Indeterminate Meaning: Witchcraft and Spirit Cults in Africa and East Asia', in B. Meyer and P. Geschiere (eds) *Globalization and Identity: Dialectics of Flow and Closure*, Oxford: Blackwell, pp. 211–37.

Giddens, A. (1990) *The Consequences of Modernity*, Stanford, CA: Stanford University Press.

——(1991) *Modernity and Self-Identity: Self and Society in the Late Modern Age*, Stanford, CA: Stanford University Press.

Gifford, P. (1998) *African Christianity: Its Public Role*, London: Hurst.

Gill, R. (2003) *The 'Empty' Church Revisited*, Aldershot, UK: Ashgate Publishing.

Gill, S. (1982) *Native American Religions: An Introduction*, Belmont, CA: Wadsworth.

——(1987) *Mother Earth: An American Story*, Chicago: University of Chicago Press.

Gold, D. (1991) 'Organized Hinduisms: From Vedic Tradition to Hindu Nation', in M. E. Marty and R. S. Appleby (eds) *Fundamentalisms Observed*, Chicago: University of Chicago Press, pp. 531–93.

Gössman, E. (1971) *Glaube und Gotteserkenntnis im Mittelalter*, Freiburg, Basel, Vienna: Herder Verlag.

Grant, J. W. (1984) *Moon of Wintertime: Missionaries and Indians of Canada in Encounter since 1534*, Toronto: University of Toronto Press.

Grieder, J. (1981) *Intellectuals and the State in Modern China: A Narrative History*, New York: Free Press.

Hackett, R. (1991) 'Revitalization in African Traditional Religion', in J. K. Olupana (ed.) *African Traditional Religions in Contemporary Society*, New York: Paragon House, pp. 139–48.

Haddad, Y. Y. (1983) 'Sayyid Qutb: Ideologue of the Islamic Revival', in J. L. Esposito (ed.) *Voices of Resurgent Islam*, New York: Oxford University Press, pp. 67–98.

Hammer, O. (2001) 'Same Message from Everywhere: The Sources of Modern Revelation', in M. Rothstein (ed.) *New Age Religion and Globalization*, Aarhus: Aarhus University Press, pp. 42–57.

Hanegraaff, W. J. (2002) 'New Age Religion', in L. Woodhead, P. Fletcher, H. Kawanami and D. Smith (eds) *Religions in the Modern World: Traditions and Transformations*, London: Routledge, pp. 249–63.

Hannerz, U. (1996) *Transnational Connections: Culture, People, Places*, London: Routledge.

Hardacre, H. (1989) *Shinto and the State, 1868–1988*, Princeton, NJ: Princeton University Press.

Hardy, F. (2001) 'The Formation of Srivaisnavism', in V. Dalmia, A. Malinar and M. Christof (eds) *Charisma and Canon: Essays on the Religious History of the Indian Subcontinent*, New Delhi: Oxford University Press, pp. 41–61.

Harrison, P. (1990) *'Religion' and the Religions in the English Enlightenment*, Cambridge: Cambridge University Press.

Hastings, A. (1996) *The Church in Africa: 1450–1950*, Oxford and New York: Clarendon Press and Oxford University Press.

Haussig, H.-M. (1999) *Der Religionsbegriff in den Religionen: Studien zum Selbst- und Religionsverständnis in Hinduismus, Buddhismus, Judentum und Islam*, Berlin: Philo-Verlag.

Heelas, P. (1996) *The New Age Movement: The Celebration of Self and the Sacralization of Modernity*, Oxford: Blackwell.

Heelas, P., Woodhead, L., Seel, B., Szerszyinski, B. and Tusting, K. (2005) *The Spiritual Revolution: Why Religion is Giving Way to Spirituality*, Oxford: Blackwell.

Hefner, R. W. (1985) *Hindu Javanese: Tengger Tradition and Islam*, Princeton, NJ: Princeton University Press.

Hexham, I. (2002) *Recognizing Academic Bias*. Website, at http://www.ucalgary.ca/~hexham/study/T-1.html (21 November 2002).

Hexham, I. and Poewe, K. (1997) *New Religions as Global Cultures: Making the Human Sacred*, Boulder, CO: Westview.

Himalayan Academy (2002) *Hinduism Online*. Website, at http://www.saivasiddhanta.com (18 March 2003).

Hindu Students Council (2003) *The Hindu Universe*. Website, at http://www.hindunet.org/ (14 March 2003).

Hinduism Today (1995) *Supreme Court to RK Mission: 'You're Hindus'*. Website, at http://www.hinduismtoday.com/1995/9/1995-9-04.html (14 March 2003).

——(1999) *Who is a Hindu?* Website, at http://www.hinduismtoday.com/1999/11/1999-11-02.html (14 March 2003).

Hines, C. (2000) *Localization: A Global Manifesto*, London: Earthscan.

Hollenweger, W. J. (1972) *The Pentecostals*, London: SCM Press.

Horstmann, M. (2000) 'The Flow of Grace: Food and Feast in the Hagiography and History of the Dadupanth', *Zeitschrift der deutschen morgenländischen Gesellschaft*, 150, 513–80.

Howard, R. C. (1967) *'Japan's Role in the Reform Program'*, in J.-P. Lo (ed.) *K'ang Yu-wei: A Biography and a Symposium*, Tucson, AZ: University of Arizona Press, pp. 280–312.

Howell, J. D. (forthcoming-a) 'Modernity and the Borderlands of Islamic Spirituality in Indonesia's New Sufi Networks', in M. van Bruinessen and J. D. Howell (eds) *Sufism and the 'Modern' in Indonesian Islam*, London: I. B. Tauris.

——(forthcoming-b) 'Muslims, the New Age and Marginal Religions in Indonesia: Changing Meanings of Religious Pluralism', *Social Compass*.

Hsiao, K. (1975) *A Modern China in a New World: K'ang Yu-wei, Reformer and Utopian, 1958–1927*, Seattle: University of Washington Press.

Hsu, I. C. Y. (1995) *The Rise of Modern China*, Oxford: Oxford University.

Huang, P. C. (1972) *Liang Ch'i-ch'ao and Modern Chinese Liberalism*, Seattle: University of Washington Press.

Hudson, D. D. (1992) 'Arumuga Navalar and the Hindu Renaissance among the Tamils', in K. W. Jones (ed.) *Religious Controversy in British India: Dialogues in South Asian Languages*, Albany, NY: State University of New York Press, pp. 27–51.

Huff, T. E. (2003) *The Rise of Early Modern Science: Islam, China, and the West*, Cambridge: Cambridge University Press.

Hultkrantz, A. (1987) *Native Religions of North America: The Power of Visions and Fertility*, San Francisco: Harper and Row.

Hunter, A. (1991) 'Two Mountains in China', *The Middle Way*, 66, 85–9.

——(1992) 'A Survey of Buddhism in the People's Republic of China', *The Middle Way*, 67, 91–8.

Inoue, N. (2000) *Contemporary Japanese Religion*, Tokyo: Foreign Press Center/Japan.

——(2005) 'How Are the Concepts of "New Religion" and "NRM" Related', paper delivered to International Association for the History of Religions, Tokyo, Japan.

Isichei, E. A. (1995) *A History of Christianity in Africa: From Antiquity to the Present*, Grand Rapids, MI and Lawrenceville, NJ: W. B. Eerdmans and Africa World Press.

Jaffrelot, C. (1994) 'Les (Re)conversions à l'hindouisme (1885–1990): politisation et diffusion d'une "invention" de la tradition', *Archives de sciences sociales des religions*, 87, 73–98.

——(1996) *The Hindu Nationalist Movement in India*, New York: Columbia University Press.

Jensen, L. M. (1997) *Manufacturing Confucianism: Chinese Traditions and Universal Civilization*, Durham, NC: Duke University Press.

Jones, K. W. (1976) *Arya Dharm: Hindu Consciousness in 19th Century Punjab*, Berkeley, CA: University of California Press.

——(1989) *Socio-Religious Reform Movements in British India*, Cambridge: Cambridge University Press.

——(1998) 'Two Sanatan Dharma Leaders and Swami Vivekananda: A Comparison', in W. Radice (ed.) *Swami Vivekananda and the Modernization of Hinduism*, Delhi: Oxford University Press, pp. 224–43.

——(2001) 'Politicized Hinduism: The Ideology and Program of the Hindu Mahasabha', in R. D. Baird (ed.) *Religion in Modern India*, Delhi: Manohar, pp. 241–73.

Juergensmeyer, M. (1991) *Radhasoami Reality: The Logic of a Modern Faith*, Princeton, NJ: Princeton University Press.

Kapur, R. (1986) *Sikh Separatism: The Politics of Faith*, London: Allen and Unwin.

Kedourie, E. (1960) *Nationalism*, New York: Praeger.

Kelley, D. M. (1972) *Why Conservative Churches Are Growing: A Study in Sociology of Religion*, New York: Harper and Row.

Kent, S. A. (1996) 'Scientology's Relation with Eastern Religious Traditions', *Journal of Contemporary Religion*, 11, 21–36.

——(1999a) 'The Creation of "Religious" Scientology', *Religious Studies and Theology*, 18, 97–126.

——(1999b) 'The Globalization of Scientology: Influence, Control, and Opposition in Transnational Markets', *Religion*, 29, 147–69.

Khosrokhavar, F. and Roy, O. (1999) *Iran: Comment sortir d'une révolution religieuse*, Paris: Seuil.

King, R. (1999) 'Orientalism and the Modern Myth of "Hinduism"', *Numen*, 46, 147–85.

King, U. (1989) 'Some Reflections on Sociological Approaches to the Study of Modern Hinduism', *Numen*, 36, 72–97.

Kisala, R. J. and Mullins, M. R. (eds) (2001) *Religion and Social Crisis in Japan: Understanding Japanese Society through the Aum Affair*, New York: Palgrave.

Klandermans, B., Kriesi, H. and Tarrow, S. (eds) (1988) *From Structure to Action: Comparing Social Movement Research Across Cultures*, Greenwich, CT: JAI Press.

Kopf, D. (1969) *British Orientalism and the Bengal Renaissance: The Dynamics of Indian Modernization, 1773–1835*, Berkeley, CA: University of California Press.

——(1979) *The Brahmo Samaj and the Shaping of the Modern Indian Mind*, Princeton: Princeton University Press.

Kourvetaris, G. A. (2005) 'The Greek Orthodox Church in the United States: (Private) Crisis of Transition?' in A. Agadjanian and V. Roudometof (eds) *Eastern Orthodoxy in a Global Age*, Walnut Creek, CA: Altamira, pp. 245–74.

Kumar, P. (2000) *Hindus in South Africa: Their Traditions and Beliefs*, Durban, SA: University of Durban-Westville.

Kurzman, C. (ed.) (1998) *Liberal Islam: A Sourcebook*, New York and Oxford: Oxford University Press.

——(ed.) (2002) *Modernist Islam, 1840–1940*, Oxford: Oxford University Press.

Lanternari, V. (1998) 'From Africa to Italy: The Exorcistic-Therapeutic Cult of Emmanuel Milingo', in P. B. Clarke (ed.) *New Trends and Developments in African Religions*, Westport, CT: Greenwood, pp. 263–83.

Lapidus, I. M. (1988) *A History of Islamic Societies*, Cambridge: Cambridge University Press.

Larson, G. J. (1995) *India's Agony over Religion*, Albany, NY: State University of New York Press.

Lawson, E. T. and McCauley, R. N. (1990) *Rethinking Religion: Connecting Cognition and Culture*, Cambridge: Cambridge University Press.

Lawson, R. (1990) 'Geopolitics within Seventh-day Adventism', *Christian Century*, 107, 1197–9, 1203–4.

——(1999) 'When Immigrants Take Over: The Impact of Immigrant Growth on American Seventh-day Adventism's Trajectory from Sect to Denomination', *Journal for the Scientific Study of Religion*, 38, 83–102.

Leach, E. (1976) *Culture and Communication*, Cambridge: Cambridge University Press.

Lefever, E. W. (1987) *Nairobi to Vancouver: The World Council of Churches and the World, 1975–1987*, Washington, DC: Ethics and Public Policy Center.

Levenson, J. R. (1970) *Liang Ch'i-ch'ao and the Mind of Modern China*, Berkeley, CA: University of California Press.

Levitt, T. (1983) 'The Globalization of Markets', *Harvard Business Review*, 61, 92–102.

Liang, C. (1959) *Intellectual Trends in the Ch'ing Period*, Cambridge, MA: Harvard University Press.

Luard, E. (1990) *The Globalization of Politics: The Changed Focus of Political Action in the Modern World*, New York: New York University Press.

Luckmann, T. (1967) *The Invisible Religion: The Problem of Religion in Modern Societies*, New York: Macmillan.

Luhmann, N. (1971) 'Die Weltgesellschaft', *Archiv für Rechts- und Sozialphilosophie*, 57, 1–35.

——(1977) *Funktion der Religion*, Frankfurt/M: Suhrkamp.

——(1984) *Soziale Systeme: Grundriß einer allgemeinen Theorie*, Frankfurt/M: Suhrkamp.

——(1989a) 'Die Ausdifferenzierung der Religion', *Gesellschaftsstruktur und Semantik: Studien zur Wissenssoziologie der modernen Gesellschaft, Vol. 3*, Frankfurt/M: Suhrkamp, pp. 259–357.

——(1989b) *Die Wirtschaft der Gesellschaft*, Frankfurt/M: Suhrkamp.

——(1990) *Die Wissenschaft der Gesellschaft*, Frankfurt/M: Suhrkamp.

——(1993) *Das Recht der Gesellschaft*, Frankfurt/M: Suhrkamp.

——(1995) *Die Kunst der Gesellschaft*, Frankfurt/M: Suhrkamp.

——(1997) *Die Gesellschaft der Gesellschaft*, Frankfurt/M: Suhrkamp.

——(2000a) *Die Politik der Gesellschaft*, Frankfurt/M: Suhrkamp.

——(2000b) *Die Religion der Gesellschaft*, Frankfurt/M: Suhrkamp.

——(2002) *Das Erziehungssystem der Gesellschaft*, Frankfurt/M: Suhrkamp.

Luo, Z. (ed.) (1991) *Religion under Socialism in China*, trans D. E. MacInnis and X. Zheng, Armonk, NY and London: M. E. Sharpe.

Lütt, J. (1995) 'From Krishnalila to Ramarajya: A Court Case and Its Consequences for the Reformulation of Hinduism', in V. Dalmia and H. von
Stietencron (eds) *Representing Hinduism*, New Delhi: Sage, pp. 142–53.

Maboia, S. I. (1994) 'Causes for the Proliferation of the African Independent
Churches', in G. C. Oosthuizen, M. C. Kitshoff and S. W. D. Dube (eds) *Afro-
Christianity at the Grass-Roots: Its Dynamics and Strategies*, Leiden: E. J. Brill,
pp. 122–36.

McCutcheon, R. T. (1997) *Manufacturing Religion: The Discourse on Sui Generis
Religion and the Politics of Nostalgia*, Oxford: Oxford University Press.

——(ed.) (1999) *The Insider/Outsider Problem in the Study of Religion: A Reader*,
London and New York: Cassell.

McFarland, H. N. (1967) *The Rush Hour of the Gods: A Study of New Religious
Movements in Japan*, New York: Macmillan.

McGovern, A. F. (1989) *Liberation Theology and Its Critics: Toward an Assessment*, Maryknoll, NY: Orbis.

McGrew, A. and Lewis, P., *et al.* (1992) *Global Politics: Globalization and the
Nation-State*, Cambridge: Polity Press.

McGuire, M. (2002) *Religion: The Social Context*, 5th edn, Belmont, CA:
Wadsworth.

MacInnis, D. E. (1989) *Religion in China Today: Policy and Practice*, Maryknoll,
NY: Orbis.

McLeod, H. and Ustorf, W. (eds) (2003) *The Decline of Christendom in Western
Europe, 1750–2000*, Cambridge: Cambridge University Press.

McLeod, W. H. (1989a) *The Sikhs: History, Religion, and Society*, New York:
Columbia University Press.

——(1989b) *Who is a Sikh? The Problem of Sikh Identity*, Oxford: Clarendon.

McMichael, P. (2000) 'Globalization: Myths and Realities', in J. T. Roberts and A.
Hite (eds) *From Modernization to Globalization: Perspectives on Development
and Social Change*, Oxford: Blackwell, pp. 274–91.

MacMillan, M. (2003) *Paris 1919: Six Months that Changed the World*, New
York: Random House.

McMullen, M. (2000) *The Baha'i: The Religious Construction of a Global
Identity*, New Brunswick, NJ: Rutgers University Press.

Malinar, A. (1995) 'The *Bhagavadgita* in the *Mahabharata* TV Serial: Domestic
Drama and Dharmic Solutions', in V. Dalmia and H. von Stietencron (eds)
*Representing Hinduism: The Construction of Religious Traditions and National
Identity*, New Delhi: Sage, pp. 442–67.

Marshall, P. J. (ed.) (1970) *The British Discovery of Hinduism in the Eighteenth
Century*, Cambridge: Cambridge University Press.

——(1987) *Bengal: The British Bridgehead: Eastern India 1740–1828*, Cambridge:
Cambridge University Press.

Martin, D. (1978) *A General Theory of Secularization*, Oxford: Blackwell.

——(1990) *Tongues of Fire: The Explosion of Protestantism in Latin America*,
Oxford: Blackwell.

——(2000) 'Canada in Comparative Perspective', in D. Lyon and M. Van Die (eds)
Rethinking Church, State, and Modernity, Toronto: University of Toronto Press,
pp. 23–33.

——(2002) *Pentecostalism: The World Their Parish*, Oxford: Blackwell.

Marx, K. and Engels, F. (n.d.) *On Religion*, Moscow: Foreign Languages Publishing House.

Melucci, A. (1985) 'The Symbolic Challenge of Contemporary Movements', *Social Research*, 52, 789–816.

Metcalf, B. D. (1982) *Islamic Revival in British India: Deoband, 1860–1900*, New Delhi: Oxford University Press.

Métraux, D. (1994) *The Soka Gakkai Revolution*, Lanham, MD: University Press of America.

Meyer, B. (1999) 'Commodities and the Power of Prayer: Pentecostalist Attitudes towards Consumption in Contemporary Ghana', in B. Meyer and Peter Geschiere (eds) *Globalization and Identity: Dialectics of Flow and Closure*, Oxford: Blackwell, pp. 151–76.

Meyer, J. (1987) 'The Image of Religion in Taiwan Textbooks', *Journal of Chinese Religions*, 15, 44–50.

Meyer, J. W., Boli, J., Thomas, G. M. and Ramirez, F. O. (1997) 'World Society and the Nation-State', *American Journal of Sociology*, 103, 1, 144–81.

Mignolo, W. D. (1998) 'Globalization, Civilization Processes, and the Relocation of Languages and Cultures', in F. Jameson, and M. Miyoshi (eds) *The Cultures of Globalization*, Durham, NC: Duke University Press, pp. 32–53.

Mndende, N. (1998) 'From Underground Praxis to Recognized Religion: Challenges facing African Religions', *Journal for the Study of Religion*, 11, 115–24.

——(1999) 'From Racial Oppression to Religious Oppression: African Religion in the New South Africa', in T. G. Walsh and F. Kaufmann (eds) *Religion and Social Transformation in Southern Africa*, St Paul, MN: Paragon House.

Moore, W. E. (1966) 'Global Sociology: The World as a Singular System', *American Journal of Sociology*, 71, 475–82.

Motta, R. (1998) 'The Churchifying of Candomblé: Priests, Anthropologists, and the Canonization of the African Religious Memory in Brazil', in P. B. Clarke (ed.) *New Trends and Developments in African Religions*, Westport, CT: Greenwood, pp. 45–57.

Murakami, S. (1980) *Japanese Religion in the Modern Century*, Tokyo: University of Tokyo Press.

National Informatics Centre (2001) *Parliament of India, Constitution of India*. Website, at http://alpha.nic.in (30 May 2001).

Nederveen Pieterse, J. (1995) 'Globalization as Hybridization', in M. Featherstone, S. Lash and R. Robertson (eds) *Global Modernities*, London: Sage, pp. 45–68.

Neill, S. (1986) *A History of Christian Missions*, Harmondsworth: Penguin.

Nettl, J. P. and Robertson, R. (1968) *International Systems and the Modernization of Societies: The Formation of National Goals and Attitudes*, New York: Basic Books.

Niebuhr, H. R. (1929) *The Social Sources of Denominationalism*, New York: Meridian.

Noll, M. A. (1992) *A History of Christianity in the United States and Canada*, Grand Rapids, MI: Eerdmans.

Nosco, P. (1996) 'Keeping the Faith: Bakuhan Policy towards Religions in Seventeenth-Century Japan', in P. F. Kornicki and I. J. McMullen (eds) *Religion in Japan: Arrows to Heaven and Earth*, Cambridge: Cambridge University Press, pp. 136–55.

Oberoi, H. (1994) *The Construction of Religious Boundaries: Culture, Identity, and Diversity in the Sikh Tradition*, Chicago: University of Chicago Press.

O'Dea, T. (1966) *The Sociology of Religion*, Englewood Cliffs, NJ: Prentice Hall.

Olupana, J. K. and Nyang, S. S. (eds) (1993) *Religious Plurality in Africa: Essays in Honour of John S. Mbiti*, Berlin: Mouton de Gruyter.

Onwurah, E. (1987) 'The Remaking of African Traditional Religions under the Influence of Modernity', *Journal of Dharma*, 12, 180–91.

Ositelu, R. (2002) *African Instituted Churches: Diversities, Growth, Spirituality, and Ecumenical Understanding of African Instituted Churches*, Münster: Lit.

O'Toole, R. (1984) *Religion: Classical Sociological Approaches*, Toronto: McGraw-Hill Ryerson.

Paden, W. E. (1992) *Interpreting the Sacred: Ways of Viewing Religion*, Boston: Beacon Press.

Pailin, D. A. (1984) *Attitudes to Other Religions: Comparative Religion in Seventeenth- and Eighteenth-Century Britain*, Manchester: Manchester University Press.

Pandey, G. (1992) *The Construction of Communalism in Colonial North India*, Delhi: Oxford University Press.

Paper, J. (1995) *The Spirits are Drunk: Comparative Approaches to Chinese Religion*, Albany, NY: State University of New York Press.

Parsons, T. (1966) *Societies: Evolutionary and Comparative Perspectives*, Englewood Cliffs, NJ: Prentice-Hall.

——(1971) *The System of Modern Societies*, Englewood Cliffs, NJ: Prentice-Hall.

Pas, J. (ed.) (1989) *The Turning of the Tide: Religion in China*, Oxford: Oxford University Press.

Penner, H. H. (1989) *Impasse and Resolution: A Critique of the Study of Religion*, New York: Peter Lang.

Peterson, D. (2002) 'Gambling with God: Rethinking Religion in Colonial Central Kenya', in D. Peterson and D. Walhof (eds) *The Invention of Religion: Rethinking Belief and Politics in History*, New Brunswick, NJ: Rutgers University Press, pp. 37–58.

Pinch, W. R. (1998) 'Historicity, Hagiography, and Hierarch in Gangetic India, 1918–36', in W. Radice (ed.) *Swami Vivekananda and the Modernization of Hinduism*, Delhi: Oxford University Press, pp. 244–63.

Pirenne, H. (1957) *Mohammed and Charlemagne*, Cleveland and New York: Meridien.

Pobee, J. S. (2002) *World Council of Churches*. Website, at http://www.wcc-coe.org/wcc/what/ecumenical/aic-e.html, Geneva.

Poewe, K. (ed.) (1994) *Charismatic Christianity as a Global Culture*, Columbia, SC: University of South Carolina Press.

Porterfield, A. (1990) 'American Indian Spirituality as a Countercultural Movement', in C. Vecsey (ed.) *Religion in Native North America*, Moscow, ID: University of Idaho Press, pp. 152–64.

Prebish, C. S. and Baumann, M. (eds) (2002) *Westward Dharma: Buddhism beyond Asia*, Berkeley, CA: University of California Press.

Preuss, J. S. (1996) *Explaining Religion: Criticism and Theory from Bodin to Freud*, Atlanta, GA: Scholars Press.

Qutb, S. (n.d.) *Milestones*, Cedar Rapids, IA: Unity Publishing.

Radhakrishnan, S. (1980 [1927]) *The Hindu View of Life*, London: Unwin Paperbacks.

Radice, W. (ed.) (1998) *Swami Vivekananda and the Modernization of Hinduism*, Delhi: Oxford University Press.

Rahman, F. (1982) *Islam and Modernity: Transformation of an Intellectual Tradition*, Chicago: University of Chicago Press.

Rajagopalachari, C. (1970 [1959]) *Hinduism: Doctrine and Way of Life*, Bombay: Bharatiya Vidya Ghavan.

Ramadan, T. (2004) *Western Muslims and the Future of Islam*, Oxford: Oxford University Press.

Ramirez, F. O. and Boli, J. (1987) 'The Political Construction of Mass Schooling: European Origins and Worldwide Institutionalization', *Sociology of Education*, 60, 2–17.

Rashid, A. (2000) *Taliban: Militant Islam, Oil and Fundamentalism in Central Asia*, New Haven, CT: Yale University Press.

Reader, I. (1991) *Religion in Contemporary Japan*, Honolulu: University of Hawaii Press.

Reid, D. (1991) *New Wine: The Cultural Shaping of Japanese Christianity*, Berkeley, CA: Asian Humanities Press.

The Republic of China Yearbook (2002) Taipei: Government Information Office.

Riesebrodt, M. (1993) *Pious Passion: The Emergence of Modern Fundamentalism in the United States and Iran*, Berkeley: University of California Press.

Roberts, J. T. and Hite, A. (eds) (2000) *From Modernization to Globalization: Perspectives on Development and Social Change*, Oxford: Blackwell.

Robertson, R. (1992) *Globalization: Social Theory and Global Culture*, London: Sage.

——(1995) 'Glocalization: Time-Space and Homogeneity-Heterogeneity', in M. Featherstone, S. Lash and R. Robertson (eds) *Global Modernities*, London: Sage, pp. 25–44.

Robertson, R. and Chirico, J. (1985) 'Humanity, Globalization, Worldwide Religious Resurgence: A Theoretical Exploration', *Sociological Analysis*, 46, 219–42.

Robertson, R. and Lechner, F. (1985) 'Modernization, Globalization, and the Problem of Culture in World-System Theory', *Theory, Culture & Society*, 2, 3, 103–17.

Roof, W. C. (1999) *Spiritual Marketplace: Baby Boomers and the Remaking of American Religion*, Princeton, NJ: Princeton University Press.

Rothstein, M. (ed.) (2001) *New Age Religion and Globalization*, Aarhus: Aarhus University Press.

Roudometof, V. (2001) *Nationalism, Globalization, and Orthodoxy: The Social Origins of Ethnic Conflict in the Balkans*, Westport, CT: Greenwood Press.

Roy, O. (1992) *L'échec de l'Islam politique*, Paris: Éditions du Seuil.

Rukmani, T. S. (ed.) (1999) *Hindu Diaspora: Global Perspectives*, Montreal: Chair in Hindu Studies, Concordia University.

Rushdie, S. (1997) 'Children of Midnight', *Time Magazine*, 23 August: 28.

Saha, S. (2004) 'Creating a Community of Grace: A History of the Pusti Marga in Northern and Western India (1470–1905)', unpublished thesis, University of Ottawa.

Schiller, A. (1997) *Small Sacrifices: Religious Change and Cultural Identity among the Ngaju of Indonesia*, Oxford: Oxford University Press.

Schreiner, P. (2001) 'Institutionalization of Charisma: The Case of Sahajananda', in V. Dalmia, A. Molinar and M. Christoff (eds) *Charisma and Canon: Essays on the Religious History of the Indian Subcontinent*, New Delhi: Oxford University Press, pp. 155–70.

Segal, R. A. (1992) *Explaining and Interpreting Religion: Essays on the Issue*, New York: Peter Lang.

Sekar, R. (2001) 'Global Reconstruction of Hinduism: A Case Study of Sri Lankan Tamils in Canada', unpublished thesis, University of Ottawa.

Sen, K. M. (1961) *Hinduism*, Harmondsworth: Penguin.

Shimazono, S. (2004) *From Salvation to Spirituality: Popular Religious Movements in Modern Japan*, Melbourne: Trans Pacific Press.

Shinnyo-en Buddhist Order (2005) *Shinnyo-en*. Website, at http://www.shinnyo-en.org (23 August 2005).

Shryrock, J. K. (1966) *The Origin and Development of the State Cult of Confucius: An Introductory Study*, New York: Paragon.

Sigmund, P. E. (1990) *Liberation Theology at the Crossroads: Democracy or Revolution?* New York: Oxford University Press.

Simmel, G. (1959) *Sociology of Religion*, New York: Philosophical Library.

——(1971) 'How is Social Order Possible?' in D. N. Levine (ed.) *On Individuality and Social Forms: Selected Writings*, Chicago: University of Chicago Press, pp. 6–22.

Simpson, J. H. (1988) 'Religion and the Churches', in J. C. A. L. Tepperman (ed.) *Understanding Canadian Society*, Toronto: McGraw-Hill Ryerson, pp. 345–69.

Smart, N. (1989) *The World's Religions: Old Traditions and Modern Transformations*, Cambridge: Cambridge University Press.

Smith, A. D. (1986) *The Ethnic Origins of Nations*, Oxford: Basil Blackwell.

Smith, C. (1991) *The Emergence of Liberation Theology: Radical Religion and Social Movement Theory*, Chicago: University of Chicago.

Smith, H. and Snake, R. (eds) (1996) *One Nation Under God: The Triumph of the Native American Church*, Santa Fe, NM: Clear Light Publishers.

Smith, J. Z. (1982) *Imagining Religion: From Babylon to Jonestown*, Chicago: University of Chicago Press.

Smith, P. (1987) *The Babi and Baha'i Religions: From Messianic Shi'ism to a World Religion*, Cambridge: Cambridge University Press.

Smith, R. J. (1983) *China's Cultural Heritage: The Ch'ing Dynasty, 1644–1912*, Boulder, CO: Westview.

Smith, W. C. (1991) *The Meaning and End of Religion*, Minneapolis, MN: Fortress Press.

Sontheimer, G. D. and Kulke, H. (eds) (1989) *Hinduism Reconsidered*, New Delhi: Manohar.

Southern, R. W. (1970) *Western Society and the Church in the Middle Ages*, Harmondsworth: Penguin.

——(1995) *Scholastic Humanism and the Unification of Europe*, Oxford: Blackwell.

Spence, J. D. (1991) *The Search for Modern China*, New York: Norton.

Spickard, J. V. (2002) 'Human Rights through a Religious Lens: A Programmatic Argument', *Social Compass*, 49, 227–38.

Spiro, M. E. (1987) *Culture and Human Nature: Theoretical Papers of Melford E. Spiro*, Chicago: University of Chicago Press.

Spybey, T. (1996) *Globalization and World Society*, Cambridge: Polity Press.

Spyer, P. (1996) 'Serial Conversion/Conversion to Seriality: Religion, State, and Number in Aru, Eastern Indonesia', in P. Van der Veer (ed.) *Conversion to Modernities: The Globalization of Christianity*, New York and London: Routledge, pp. 171–98.

Stark, R. (1999) 'Micro Foundations of Religion: A Revised Theory', *Sociological Theory*, 17, 264–89.

Stark, R. and Bainbridge, W. S. (1985) *The Future of Religion: Secularization, Revival, and Cult Formation*, Berkeley, CA: University of California Press.

——(1987) *A Theory of Religion*, New York: Peter Lang.

Stark, R. and Iannaccone, L. (1994) 'A Supply-Side Reinterpretation of the "Secularization" of Europe', *Journal for the Scientific Study of Religion*, 33, 230–52.

Stewart, O. C. (1987) *Peyote Religion: A History*, Norman, OK: University of Oklahoma Press.

Stichweh, R. (1996) 'Science in the System of World Society', *Social Science Information*, 35, 327–40.

——(2000) *Die Weltgesellschaft: Soziologische Analysen*, Frankfurt/M: Suhrkamp.

Tambiah, S. J. (1986) *Sri Lanka: Ethnic Fratricide and the Dismantling of Democracy*, Chicago: University of Chicago Press.

Tamney, J. B. (1995) *The Struggle over Singapore's Soul: Western Modernization and Asian Culture*, Berlin and New York: Walter de Gruyter.

Ter Haar, G. (1995) 'Ritual as Communication: A Study of African Christian Communities in the Bijlmer District of Amsterdam', in J. Platvoet and K. van der Toorn (eds) *Pluralism and Identity: Studies in Ritual Behaviour*, Leiden: E. J. Brill, pp. 115–42.

——(1998) 'The African Diaspora in the Netherlands', in P. B. Clarke (ed.) *New Trends and Developments in African Religions*, Westport, CT: Greenwood, pp. 245–62.

Thal, S. (2002) 'A Religion that was Not a Religion: The Creation of a Modern Shinto in Nineteenth-Century Japan', in D. Peterson and D. Walhof (eds) *The Invention of Religion: Rethinking Belief in Politics and History*, New Brunswick, NJ: Rutgers University Press, pp. 100–14.

Thapar, R. (1989) 'Imagined Religious Communities? Ancient History and the Modern Search for a Hindu Identity', *Modern Asian Studies*, 23, 209–31.

Thiel-Horstmann, M. (1989) 'Bhakti and Monasticism', in G. D. Sontheimer and H. Kulke (eds) *Hinduism Reconsidered*, New Delhi: Manohar, pp. 127–40.

Thomas, G. M., Meyer, J. W., Ramirez, F. O. and Boli, J. (1987) *Institutional Structure: Constituting State, Society and the Individual*, London: Sage.

Tomka, M. (forthcoming) 'Is Conventional Sociology of Religion Apt to Deal with Differences between Eastern and Western European Developments?' *Social Compass*.

Troeltsch, E. (1931) *The Social Teachings of the Christian Churches*, New York: Macmillan.

Turner, J. H. (1986) *The Structure of Sociological Theory*, Chicago: Dorsey Press.

Tyrell, H. (2002) 'Religiöse Kommunikation', in K. Schreiner (ed.) *Frömmigkeit im Mittelalter: Politisch-soziale Kontexte, visuelle Praxis, körperliche Ausdrucksformen*, Munich: Wilhelm Fink Verlag, pp. 41–93.

Tyrell, H., Krech, V. and Knoblauch, H. (eds) (1998) *Religion als Kommunikation*, Würzburg: Ergon Verlag.

United States Department of State – Bureau of Democracy Human Rights and Labor (2004) *International Religious Freedom Report 2004*. Website, at http://www.state.gov/g/drl/rls/irf/2002 (20 March 2005).

Ursinus, M. O. H. (1960 [1980]) 'Millet', in H. A. R. Gibb and others (eds) *The Encyclopedia of Islam*, Leiden: Brill, pp. 61–64.

Van den Hoonaard, W. C. (1996) *The Origins of the Baha'i Community in Canada, 1898–1948*, Waterloo, ON: Wilfrid Laurier University Press.

Van der Veer, P. (1994a) 'Hindu Nationalism and the Discourse of Modernity: The Vishva Hindu Parishad', in M. E. Marty and R. S. Appleby (eds) *Accounting for Fundamentalisms: The Dynamic Character of Movements*, Chicago: University of Chicago Press, pp. 653–68.

——(1994b) *Religious Nationalism: Hindus and Muslims in India*, Berkeley, CA: University of California Press.

VanElderen, M. and Conway, M. (2001) *Introducing the World Council of Churches*, Geneva: World Council of Churches.

Vásquez, M. A. and Marquardt, M. F. (2003) *Globalizing the Sacred: Religion across the Americas*, New Brunswick, NJ: Rutgers University Press.

Vertovec, S. (1992) *Hindu Trinidad: Religion, Ethnicity and Socio-Economic Change*, London: Macmillan Caribbean.

Vishva Hindu Parishad (2001) *Vishva Hindu Parishad*. Website, at http://www.vhp.org (30 May 2001).

Volkov, D. (2005) 'Living Eastern Orthodox Religion in the United States', in A. Agadjanian and V. Roudometof (eds) *Eastern Orthodoxy in a Global Age*, Walnut Creek, CA: Altamira, pp. 224–44.

Voll, J. O. (1982) *Islam: Continuity and Change in the Modern World*, Boulder, CO: Westview.

——(1999) 'Foundations for Renewal and Reform: Islamic Movements in the Eighteenth and Nineteenth Centuries', in J. L. Esposito (ed.) *The Oxford History of Islam*, Oxford: Oxford University Press, pp. 509–47.

Wallace, A. F. C. (1970) *The Death and Rebirth of the Seneca*, New York: Knopf.

Wallerstein, I. (1974–80) *The Modern World System*, New York: Academic Press.

——(1979) *The Capitalist World-Economy*, Cambridge: Cambridge University Press.

Ware, T. (1964) *The Orthodox Church*, Harmondsworth: Penguin.

Waters, M. (1995) *Globalization*, London and New York: Routledge.

Weber, M. (1946) 'Religious Rejections of the World and Their Directions', in H. H. Gerth and C. W. Mills (eds) *From Max Weber: Essays in Sociology*, New York: Oxford University Press, pp. 323–59.

——(1968) 'Die "Objektivität" sozialwissenschaftlicher und sozialpolitischer Erkenntnis', in J. Winckelmann (ed.) *Methodologische Schriften: Studien Ausgabe*, Frankfurt/M: S. Fischer Verlag, pp. 1–64.

——(1978) *Economy and Society*, Berkeley, CA: University of California Press.

——(1992 [1930]) *The Protestant Ethic and the Spirit of Capitalism*, London and New York: Routledge.

Welch, H. (1968) *The Buddhism Revival in China*, Cambridge, MA: Harvard University Press.

Weller, R. (1996) 'Horizontal Ties and Civil Institutions in Chinese Societies', unpublished manuscript.

White, J. W. (1970) *The Soka Gakkai and Mass Society*, Stanford, CA: Stanford University Press.

Wilkinson, M. (1999) 'Global Migration and Transformation among Canadian Pentecostals', unpublished dissertation, University of Ottawa.

Williams, R. (1983) *Culture and Society, 1780–1950*, New York: Columbia University Press.

Williams, R. B. (1984) *A New Face of Hinduism: The Swaminarayan Religion*, Cambridge: Cambridge University Press.

——(1988) *Religions of Immigrants from India and Pakistan: New Threads in the American Tapestry*, New York: Cambridge University Press.

Wilson, B. (1966) *Religion in Secular Society: A Sociological Comment*, London: C.A. Watts.

——(1979) 'The Return of the Sacred', *Journal for the Scientific Study of Religion*, 18, 268–80.

Wilson, B. and Cresswell, J. (eds.) (1999) *New Religious Movements: Challenges and Response*, London: Routledge.

Wolff, P. (1968) *The Awakening of Europe*, trans. A. Carter, Harmondsworth: Penguin.

Woodward, W. P. (1972) *The Allied Occupation of Japan 1945–1952 and Japanese Religions*, Leiden: E. J. Brill.

Yang, C. K. (1967) *Religion in Chinese Society*, Berkeley, CA: University of California Press.

Zald, M. N. and McCarthy, J. D. (eds) (1987) *Social Movements in an Organizational Society: Collected Essays*, New Brunswick, NJ: Transaction.

Zydenbos, R. J. (2001) 'Madhva and the Reform of Vaisnavism in Karnataka', in V. Dalmia, A. Molinar and M. Christoff (eds) *Charisma and Canon: Essays on the Religious History of the Indian Subcontinent*, New Delhi: Oxford University Press, pp. 113–28.

Index

Related titles from Routledge

New Religious Movements in Global Perspective
Peter B. Clarke

New Religious Movements in Global Perspective is a fresh in-depth account of new religious movements, and of new forms of spirituality from a global vantage point. Ranging from North America and Europe to Japan, Latin America, South Asia, Africa and the Carribean, this book provides students with a complete introduction to NRMs such as Falun Gong, Aum Shirikyo, the Brahma Kumaris, the Ikhwan or Muslim Brotherhood, Sufism, the Engaged Buddhist and Engaged Hindi movements, Messianic Judaism, and Rastafarianism.

Peter B. Clarke explores the innovative character of new religious movements, charting their cultural significance and global impact, and how various religious traditions are shaping, rather than displacing, each other's understanding of notions such as transcendence and faith, good and evil, of the meaning, purpose and function of religion, and of religious belonging. In addition to exploring the responses of governments, churches, the media and general public to new religious movements, Clarke examines the reactions to older, increasingly influential religions, such as Buddhism and Islam, in new geographical and cultural contexts. Taking into account the degree of continuity between old and new religions, each chapter contains not only an account of the rise of the NRMs and new forms of spirituality in a particular region, but also an overview of change in the regions' mainstream religions.

Peter B. Clarke is Professor Emeritus of the History and Sociology of Religion at King's College, University of London, and a professorial member of Faculty of Theology, University of Oxford. Among his publications are (with Peter Byrne) *Religion Defined and Explained* (1993) and *Japanese New Religions: In Global Perspective* (ed) (2000). He is the founding editor of the *Journal of Contemporary Religion*.

Hb: 0–415–25747–6
Pb: 0–415–25748–4

Available at all good bookshops
For ordering and further information please visit:
www.routledge.com

Related titles from Routledge

Religion and Cyberspace
Edited by Morten T. Højsgaard and Margit Warburg

In the twenty-first century, religious life is increasingly moving from churches, mosques and temples onto the Internet. Today, anyone can go online and seek a new form of religious expression without ever encountering a physical place of worship, or an ordained teacher or priest. The digital age offers virtual worship, cyber-prayers and talk-boards for all of the major world faiths, as well as for pagan organisations and new religious movements. It also abounds with misinformation, religious bigotry and information terrorism. Scholars of religion need to understand the emerging forum that the web offers to religion, and the kinds of religious and social interaction that it enables.

Religion and Cyberspace explores how religious individuals and groups are responding to the opportunities and challenges that cyberspace brings. It asks how religious experience is generated and enacted online, and how faith is shaped by factors such as limitless choice, lack of religious authority, and the conflict between recognised and non-recognised forms of worship. Combining case studies with the latest theory, its twelve chapters examine topics including the history of online worship, virtuality versus reality in cyberspace, religious conflict in digital contexts, and the construction of religious identity online. Focusing on key themes in this groundbreaking area, it is an ideal introduction to the fascinating questions that religion on the Internet presents.

Contributors: Eileen Barker, Lorne L. Dawson, Debbie Herring, Morten T. Højsgaard, Massimo Introvigne, Mun-Cho Kim, Michael J. Laney, Alf G. Linderman, Mia Lövheim, Mark MacWilliams, Stephen D. O'Leary, David Piff and Margit Warburg.

Hb: 0–415–35767–5
Pb: 0–415–35763–2

Available at all good bookshops
For ordering and further information please visit:
www.routledge.com